MARKETING INSIGHTS FOR THE
ASIA PACIFIC

MARKETING INSIGHTS FOR THE ASIA PACIFIC

by

Siew Meng Leong, Swee Hoon Ang, and Chin Tiong Tan

Asia Pacific Marketing Federation

Published by

ASIA PACIFIC MARKETING FEDERATION
51 Anson Road #03-53
Anson Centre
Singapore 079904

and

HEINEMANN SOUTHEAST ASIA,
a member of the Reed Elsevier plc group
1 Temasek Avenue #17-01
Millenia Tower
Singapore 039192

OXFORD   LONDON   EDINBURGH   MELBOURNE   SYDNEY
AUCKLAND   MADRID   ATHENS   IBADAN   NAIROBI
GABORONE   HARARE   KINGSTON   PORTSMOUTH (NH)

ISBN 9971-64-532-7

© Siew Meng Leong, Swee Hoon Ang, and Chin Tiong Tan 1996
First published 1996

Cover by Sam & Matt Design
Typeset by Linographic Services Ptd Ltd (11/13pt Janson Text)
Printed in Singapore by Chong Moh Offset Printing Pte Ltd

Contents

Preface

Marketing in general continues to be a fascinating profession. Marketing in Asia and Asian marketing management in particular are no exception. These observations were brought home to us when we attempted to assemble a useful collection of current and timely articles that would appeal to students and practitioners of Asian marketing strategy and management.

In positioning this book, our primary target market was defined as advanced business undergraduates and MBA students enrolled in the marketing management course. Secondary segments include participants in executive development programs in marketing management, candidates registered for advanced diploma programs on Asian marketing, and students in international business and international marketing electives focusing on the Asia-Pacific region.

Four principles were employed in our selection of 25 readings for this book. First, we included readings that are of vital interest to those in marketing management in Asia rather than to specialists or technicians in marketing research, advertising, or sales management. Second, we incorporated articles spanning a wide range of marketing situations — consumer, industrial, and services. Third, we picked papers which yielded a good coverage of the countries in the Asia Pacific region. Fourth, we selected some important articles which were cited in *Marketing Management: An Asian Perspective*, by Philip Kotler, Swee Hoon Ang, Siew Meng Leong, and Chin Tiong Tan. This will enable users of that text to obtain information and insights on key marketing concepts and applications directly from some of the key source articles cited there.

Reflecting the fourth principle, the structure of this reader is similar to that of *Marketing Management: An Asian Perspective*. Specifically, this reader is organized into six parts, starting with understanding marketing management and proceeding to analyzing marketing opportunities, researching and selecting target markets, developing marketing strategies, planning marketing programs, and organizing, implementing, and controlling the marketing effort.

We wish users of this book happy reading and hope they will be able to derive actionable Asian marketing management insights from it.

Siew Meng Leong
Swee Hoon Ang
Chin Tiong Tan

National University of Singapore

Acknowledgements

Many individuals and institutions made *Marketing Insights for the Asia-Pacific* possible. First and foremost, we thank the authors of the articles included in this book. Their research has shed light on marketing management and strategy in the Asia-Pacific region. They are:

Masaru Ariga
David L. Blenkhorn
Bruce Cheesman
Min Chen
Howard Davies
Vanaga Dhanan
Al Dizon
Louise do Rosario
Kin Gatbonton
Kyung-Il Ghymn
Ibarra C. Gutierrez
Laurence W. Jacobs
Stephanie Jones
Warren Keegan
Charles F. Keown
Kam-Hon Lee
Thomas K. P. Leung
Sherriff T. K. Luk
Ken Matejka

Neal McGrath
Lee Miller
Marieke K. de Mooij
A. Hamid Noori
Yigang Pan
Carl R. Ruthstrom
Bernd H. Schmitt
Don Shapiro
Hideo Sugiura
Norihiko Suzuki
David K. Tse
Ilan Vertinsky
Barry Wain
Frederick E. Webster, Jr.
Donald A. Wehrung
Roy Westbrook
Peter Williamson
Yiu-hing Wong
Pam Woodall
Charles Y. Yang

We are also grateful to the publishers of the following journals, periodicals and books from which our articles were sourced:

Advances in International Marketing
Advertising Worldwide

Asian Business
Asian Journal of Marketing
Business Horizons
California Management Review
European Management Journal
Industrial Marketing Management
Japan 1991 Marketing and Advertising Yearbook
Journal of International Business Studies
Journal of Marketing
Marketing Intelligence & Planning
Research in Marketing
Sloan Management Review
The Asian Manager
The Economist
The Singapore Marketer
World Executive's Digest

Our appreciation to the Asia Pacific Marketing Federation which furnished the catalyst for our editorial efforts. The vision of its founding honorary president, Michio Torii, is especially acknowledged. We also record our thanks to the Marketing Institute of Singapore and the National University of Singapore for their facilitating the publication process. We are grateful to the staff of Heinemann Southeast Asia, notably Vivian Tan and Andrew Yeo, who were instrumental in creating the physical product before you.

Last but not least, we are indebted to our respective families, whose love and support we will always cherish. Fittingly, it is to them that we dedicate this book.

Siew Meng Leong
Swee Hoon Ang
Chin Tiong Tan

National University of Singapore

About the Authors

Siew Meng Leong is a Senior Lecturer at the Faculty of Business Administration, National University of Singapore. He received his MBA and Ph.D. in business administration at the University of Wisconsin, Madison. He is a co-author of *Marketing Management: An Asian Perspective* and *Cases in Marketing Management and Strategy: An Asia-Pacific Perspective*. Dr. Leong has published in *Journal of Marketing*, *Journal of Marketing Research*, *Journal of Consumer Research*, *Journal of International Business Studies*, *Decision Sciences*, and other international journals and conference proceedings. His research focuses on consumer behavior, sales management, and marketing research.

Dr. Leong is editor of the *Asian Journal of Marketing* and serves on the editorial boards of the *Journal of Marketing Communications* and *Marketing Education Review*. He has consulted for such clients as Coopers & Lybrand, Economic Development Board of Singapore, Hagemeyer Electronics, Johnson & Johnson Medical, Malayan Bank, Motorola Electronics, Singapore Pools, Singapore Telecoms, and Wisma Atria. Dr. Leong also serves on the council for the Marketing Institute of Singapore.

Swee Hoon Ang is a Lecturer at the Faculty of Business Administration, National University of Singapore. She received her Ph.D. degree in marketing at the University of British Columbia. She is a co-author of *Marketing Management: An Asian Perspective* and *Cases in Marketing Management and Strategy: An Asia-Pacific Perspective*. In addition, she has written several articles for journals and conferences, including *Journal of Advertising*, *Psychology and Marketing*, *Journal of Contemporary Issues in Business and Government*, *Journal of Marketing Communications*, and *Journal of Retailing and Consumer Services*. She also received a Best Paper Award at the 1988 Services Marketing Conference organized by the American Marketing Association. Her research and teaching interests are in advertising, consumer behavior, and services marketing.

Dr. Ang serves as a council member for the Marketing Institute of Singapore and chairs its National Business Strategy Competition. She has also consulted for several Singaporean and multinational companies including Cold Storage Supermarket, Glaxo Pharmaceuticals, Johnson & Johnson Medical, Port of Singapore Authority, Singapore Bus Services, Tiger Balm, and United Overseas Bank.

Chin Tiong Tan is an Associate Professor and Head of the Department of Marketing at the Faculty of Business Administration, National University of Singapore. He received his Ph.D. degree in marketing at Pennsylvania State University. He was a Visiting Professor at the Helsinki School of Economic and Business and University of Witwatersrand (South Africa), and a Visiting Scholar at the Stanford Business School, Stanford University. He is a co-author of *Marketing Management: An Asian Perspective* and *Cases in Marketing Management and Strategy: An Asia-Pacific Perspective*. Dr. Tan has published in *Journal of Consumer Research*, *Journal of International Business Studies*, *International Marketing Review*, *European Journal of Marketing*, *Psychology and Marketing*, and other international journals and conference proceedings.

Dr. Tan sits on the editorial boards of several international journals. He is also on the boards of several companies and committees of government agencies. He is currently the president of the Marketing Institute of Singapore and a board director of the Asia-Pacific Marketing Federation. He is also the Academic Advisor to the Singapore Airlines' Management Development Center and has consulted internationally for companies like Acer Computer, Altron Group, Inchcape, Singapore Telecoms, Standard Chartered Bank, and Swiss Bank Corporation.

I   Understanding Marketing Management

The nature of marketing management in the Asia Pacific varies from a more traditional personalized to a more modern orientation. Irrespective of these approaches, a strategic approach appears necessary for companies operating in the region. The readings in this first part thus set the tone for a strategic overview of marketing management as it evolves in the region.

After reading the three papers in this part, you should have a better grasp of the following aspects of marketing management in the Asia Pacific:

1   The role of marketing in a professionally managed modern corporation.
2   The direction of marketing management as it heads towards the next century.
3   Asian dimensions which provide texture to marketing practices in the region.

1 The Changing Role of Marketing in the Corporation

Frederick E. Webster, Jr.

New organization forms, including strategic partnerships and networks, are replacing simple market-based transactions and traditional bureaucratic hierarchical organizations. The historical marketing management function, based on the microeconomic maximization paradigm, must be critically examined for its relevance to marketing theory and practice in the 1990s. A new conception of marketing will focus on managing strategic partnerships and positioning the firm between vendors and customers in the value chain with the aim of delivering superior value to customers. Customer relationships will be seen as the key strategic resource of the business.

For the past two decades, some subtle changes in the concept and practice of marketing have been fundamentally reshaping the field. Many of these changes have been initiated by industry, in the form of new organizational types, without explicit concern for their underlying theoretical explanation or justification. On the academic side, prophetic voices have been speaking (Arndt 1979, 1981, 1983; Thorelli 1986; Van de Ven 1976; Williamson 1975) but seldom heard because, representing several different disciplines, they did not sing as a chorus. More basically, perhaps, few listeners were ready to hear the message or to do the intellectual work necessary to pull the several themes together. Like the Peruvian Indians who thought the sails of the Spanish invaders on the horizon were some phenomenon of the weather and did nothing to prepare themselves for attack (Handy 1990), marketers may ignore some important information in their environment simply because it is not consistent with their past experience.

The purpose of this article is to outline both the intellectual and the pragmatic roots of changes that are occurring in marketing, especially marketing

Reproduced with permission from *Journal of Marketing*, 56 (October 1992), pp. 1–17.

management, as a body of knowledge, theory, and practice and to suggest the need for a new paradigm of the marketing function within the firm. First, the origins of the marketing management framework, the generally accepted paradigm of the marketing discipline for the past three decades, are considered. Then shifting managerial practice is examined, especially the dissolution of hierarchical bureaucratic structures in favor of networks of buyer-seller relationships and strategic alliances. Within those new forms of organization, the changing role of marketing is discussed and a reconceptualization of marketing as a field of study and practice is outlined.

Marketing as a social and economic process

It is sobering to recall that the study of marketing did not always have a managerial focus. The early roots of marketing as an area of academic study can be found, beginning around 1910, in midwestern American land-grant universities, where a strong involvement with the farm sector created a concern for agricultural markets and the processes by which products were brought to market and prices determined. The analysis was centered around commodities and the institutions involved in moving them from farm, forest, sea, mine, and factory to industrial processors, users, and consumers. Within this tradition, three separate schools evolved that focused on the *commodities* themselves, on the marketing *institutions* through which products were brought to market, especially brokers, wholesalers, and retailers in their many forms and variations (Breyer 1934; Duddy and Revzan 1953), and finally on the *functions* performed by these institutions (McGarry 1950; Weld 1917). All of these approaches tended to be descriptive rather than normative, with the functional being the most analytical and leading to the development of a conceptual framework for the marketing discipline (Bartels 1962; Rathmell 1965).

These early approaches to the study of marketing are interesting because of the relative absence of a *managerial* orientation. Marketing was seen as a set of social and economic processes rather than as a set of managerial activities and responsibilities. The institutional and functional emphasis began to change in 1948, when the American Marketing Association (1948, p. 210) defined marketing as:

> The performance of business activities directed toward, and incident to, the flow of goods and services from producer to consumer or user.

This definition, modified only very slightly in 1960, represented an important shift of emphasis. Though it grew out of the functional view, it defined marketing functions as business activities rather than as social or economic processes. The managerial approach brought relevance and realism to the study of marketing, with an emphasis on problem-solving, planning, implementation, and control in a competitive marketplace.

Marketing management

The *managerial* approach to the study of marketing evolved in the 1950s and 1960s. Several textbooks using a marketing management perspective appeared during this period (Alderson 1957; Davis 1961; Howard 1957; Kotler 1967; McCarthy 1960). These early managerial authors defined marketing management as a decision-making or problem-solving process and relied on analytical frameworks from economics, psychology, sociology, and statistics. The first marketing casebook, incorporating a managerial framework by definition, had emerged from the Harvard Business School very early (Copeland 1920), but without any descriptive material or analytical framework to accompany the cases. Marketing management became a widely accepted business function, growing out of a more traditional sales management approach, with an emphasis on product planning and development, pricing, promotion, and distribution. Marketing research gained prominence in management practice as a vehicle for aligning the firm's productive capabilities with the needs of the marketplace. The articulation of the marketing concept in the mid to late 1950s posited that marketing was the principal function of the firm (along with innovation) because the main purpose of any business was to create a satisfied customer (Drucker 1954; Levitt 1960; McKitterick 1957). Profit was not the objective; it was the reward for creating a satisfied customer.

The managerial focus was *not* readily accepted by everyone in academic circles, nor was the marketing concept completely adopted by industry (McNamara 1972; McGee and Spiro 1988; Webster 1988). In academia, the functionalists and institutionalists held their ground well into the 1960s, stressing the value of understanding marketing institutions and functions and viewing marketing from a broader economic and societal perspective. Over the previous 50 years, a substantial body of theory and empirical knowledge had been developed and mature marketing scholars felt compelled to defend and protect it. The argument *against* the managerial point of view centered on its inability to consider the broader social and economic functions and issues associated with marketing, beyond the level of the firm. For example, the Beckman and Davidson (1962) text, built around a functionalist perspective, and the most widely used text in the field at the time, was promoted as follows: "Balanced treatment of the development and the present status of our marketing system; Conveys a broad understanding of the complete marketing process, its essential economic functions, and the institutions performing them; Strengthens the social and economic coverage of marketing in all its significant implications; Proper emphasis accorded to the managerial viewpoint" (advertisement, *Journal of Marketing*, April 1962, p. 130). It is the last phrase, "proper emphasis," that implies the criticism that the managerial approach, by itself, is incomplete.

The analytical frameworks of the new managerial approach were drawn from economics, behavioral science, and quantitative methods. The incorporation of the behavioral and quantitative sciences gave important legitimacy to marketing as a separate academic discipline. Such frameworks were consistent with the very strong thrust of the 1960s toward more rigorous approaches in management education, encouraged by two very influential foundation studies (Gordon and Howell 1959; Pierson 1959). These studies advocated education based on a rigorous, analytical approach to decision making as opposed to a descriptive, institutional approach which, it was argued, should be held to "an irreducible minimum" (Gordon and Howell 1959, p. 187). The managerial perspective became the dominant point of view in marketing texts and journals, supported by management science and the behavioral sciences.

Marketing as an optimization problem

Scholars on the leading edge of marketing responded with enthusiasm to the call for greater analytical rigor. At the root of most of the new managerial texts and the evolving research literature of marketing science was the basic microeconomic paradigm, with its emphasis on profit maximization (Anderson 1982). The basic units of analysis were transactions in a competitive market and fully integrated firms controlling virtually all of the factors of production (Arndt 1979; Thorelli 1986). Market transactions connected the firm with its customers and with other firms (Johnston and Lawrence 1988).

Analysis for marketing management focused on demand (revenues), costs, and profitability and the use of traditional economic analysis to find the point at which marginal costs equals marginal revenue and profit is maximized. Behavioral science models were used primarily to structure problem definition, helping the market researcher to define the questions that are worth asking and to identify important variables and the relationships among them (Massy and Webster 1964). Statistical analysis was used to manipulate the data to test the strength of the hypothesized relationships or to look for relationships in the data that had not been hypothesized directly.

The application of formal, rigorous analytical techniques to marketing problems required specialists of various kinds. Marketing departments typically included functional specialists in sales, advertising and promotion, distribution, and marketing research, and perhaps managers of customer service, marketing personnel, and pricing. Early organizational pioneers of professional marketing departments included the consumer packaged goods companies with brand management systems, such as Procter & Gamble, Colgate-Palmolive, General

Foods, General Mills, and Gillette. In other companies, the marketing professionals were concentrated at the corporate staff level in departments of market research and operations research or management science. Examples of the latter include General Electric, IBM, and RCA. Large, full-service advertising agencies built strong research departments to support their national advertiser account relationships. Other large firms, such as Anheuser-Busch and General Electric, also entered into research partnerships with university-based consulting organizations.

Such specialized and sophisticated professional marketing expertise fit well into the strategy, structure, and culture of large, divisionalized, hierarchical organizations.

The large, bureaucratic, hierarchical organization

When we think of marketing management, we think of large, divisionalized, functional organizations — the kind depicted by the boxes and lines of an organization chart. The large, bureaucratic, hierarchical organization, almost always a corporation in legal terms, was the engine of economic activity in this country for more than a century (Miles and Snow 1984). It was characterized by multiple layers of management, functional specialization, integrated operations, and clear distinctions between line and staff responsibilities. It had a pyramid shape with increasingly fewer and more highly paid people from the bottom to the top.

The larger the firm, the more activities it could undertake by itself and the fewer it needed to obtain by contracting with firms and individuals outside the organization. The logic of economies of scale equated efficiency with size. The epitome of the fully integrated firm was the Ford Motor Company, and most notably its River Rouge plant, which produced a single, standardized product, the Model A. Ford-owned lake steamships docked at one end of the plant with coal and iron ore (from Ford's own mines) and complete automobiles and tractors came out at the other end. Molten iron from the blast furnaces was carried by ladles directly to molds for parts, bypassing the costly pig iron step. Waste gases from the blast furnaces became fuel for the power plant boilers, as did the sawdust and shavings from the body plant. Gases from the cooking ovens provided process heat for heat-treatment and paint ovens (Ford 1922, p. 151–153). Elsewhere, Ford owned sheep farms for producing wool, a rubber plantation in Brazil, and its own railroad to connect its facilities in the Detroit region (Womack, Jones, and Roos 1991, p. 39). Integration required large size. Large size beget low cost.

Large, hierarchical, integrated corporate structures were the dominant organization form as the managerial approach to marketing developed in the 1950s and 1960s, and firms created marketing departments, often as extensions of the old sales department. Such large organizations moved deliberately, which is to say slowly, and only after careful analysis of all available data and options for action. The standard microeconomic profit maximization paradigm of marketing management fit well in this analytical culture. Responsible marketing management called for careful problem definition, followed by the development and evaluation of multiple decision alternatives, from which a course of action would ultimately be chosen that had the highest probability, based on the analysis, of maximizing profitability.

When the world was changing more slowly than it is today, such caution was wise in terms of preserving valuable assets that had been committed to clearly defined tasks, especially when those assets were huge production facilities designed for maximum economies of scale in the manufacture of highly standardized products. The task of the marketing function was first to develop a thorough understanding of the marketplace to ensure that the firm was producing goods and services required and desired by the consumer. With an optimal product mix in place, the marketing function (through its sales, advertising, promotion, and distribution subfunctions) was responsible for generating demand for these standardized products, for creating consumer preference through mass and personal communications, and for managing the channel of distribution through which products flowed to the consumer. Sound marketing research and analysis provided support for conducting these activities most efficiently and effectively, for testing alternative courses of action in each and every area.

Marketing as a management function tended to be centralized at the corporate level well into the 1970s. Marketing organizations were often multitiered, with more experienced senior managers reviewing and coordinating the work of junior staff and relating marketing to other functions of the business, especially through the budgeting and financial reporting process. Corporate centralization allowed the development of specialized expertise and afforded economies of scale in the purchase of marketing services such as market research, advertising, and sales promotion. It also permitted tighter control of marketing efforts for individual brands and of sales efforts across the entire national market. This arrangement began to change in the late 1970s and into the 1980s as the concept of the strategic business unit (SBU) gained widespread favor and corporate managements pushed operating decisions, and profit and loss responsibility, out to the operating business units. Though marketing became a more decentralized function in many large companies, it is not clear that the result was always heightened marketing effectiveness.

The larger the organization, the larger the number of managers, analysts, and planners who were not directly involved in making or selling products. The burden of administrative costs, mostly in the form of salaries for these middle layers of management, became an increasing handicap in the competitive races that shaped up in the global marketplace of the 1970s and 1980s. More and more organizations found it necessary to downsize and delayer, some through their own initiative and many more through threatened or actual acquisition and restructuring by new owners whose vision was not clouded by the continuity of experience. Global competition resulted in increasingly better product performance at lower cost to the customer. Rapid advances in telecommunications, transportation, and information processing broadened the choice set of both industrial buyers and consumers to the point that a product's country of origin was relatively unimportant and geographic distance was seldom a barrier, especially in areas where non-American producers had superior reputations for quality, service, and value. In most American industries, companies had little choice but to reduce costs through reorganization and restructuring of assets, as well as through technological improvements in products and manufacturing processes.

The organizational response

During the 1980s, new forms of business organization became prominent features of the economic landscape. Even before the forces of global competition became clearly visible, there was a trend toward more flexible organization forms, forms that are difficult to capture with a traditional organization chart (Miles and Snow 1984, 1986; Powell 1990; Thorelli 1986). The new organizations emphasized partnerships between firms; multiple types of ownership and partnering within the organization (divisions, wholly owned subsidiaries, licensees, franchisees, joint ventures, etc.); teamwork among members of the organization, often with team members from two or more cooperating firms; sharing of responsibility for developing converging and overlapping technologies; and often less emphasis on formal contracting and managerial reporting, evaluation, and control systems. The best visual image of these organizations may be a wheel instead of a pyramid, where the spokes are "knowledge links" between a core organization at the hub and strategic partners around the rim (Badaracco 1991). These forms were pioneered in such industries as heavy construction, fashion, weapon systems contracting, and computers, where markets often span geographic boundaries, technology is complex, products change quickly, and doing everything yourself is impossible. Such organizations today are found in businesses as diverse as glass, chemicals, hospital supplies, book publishing, and tourism.

These confederations of specialists are called by many names including "networks" (Miles and Snow 1986; Thorelli 1986), "value-adding partnerships" (Johnston and Lawrence 1988), "alliances" (Ohmae 1989), and "shamrocks" (Handy 1990). All are characterized by flexibility, specialization, and an emphasis on relationship management instead of market transactions. They depend on administrative processes but they are not hierarchies (Thorelli 1986); they engage in transactions within ongoing relationships and they depend on negotiation, rather than market-based processes, as a principal basis for conducting business and determining prices, though market forces almost always influence and shape negotiation. The purpose of these new organization forms is to respond quickly and flexibly to accelerating change in technology, competition, and customer preferences.

Types of relationships and alliances

There is no strong consensus at the present time about the terminology and typology for describing the new organization forms. However, some important distinctions among types of relationships and alliances are necessary before we can consider the role of marketing within them. We can think of a continuum from pure transactions at one end to fully integrated hierarchical firms at the other end (Figure 1). As we move along this continuum, we see that firms use more administrative and bureaucratic control and less market control in the pursuit of economic efficiency. One step away from pure transactions is repeated transactions between buyer and seller. The next step is a long-term relationship that is still adversarial and depends heavily on market control. Then comes a real partnership, in which each partner approaches total dependence on the other in a particular area of activity and mutual trust replaces the adversarial assumptions. Prices are now determined by negotiation, subject to some market pressures, rather than by the market itself. The next step is strategic alliances, which are defined by the formation of a new entity such as a product development team, a research project, or a manufacturing facility, to which both parties commit resources and which serves clear strategic purposes for both. Joint ventures, resulting in the formation of a new firm, are the epitome of strategic alliances. Like their parents, joint ventures are fully integrated firms

Figure 1 The range of marketing relationships

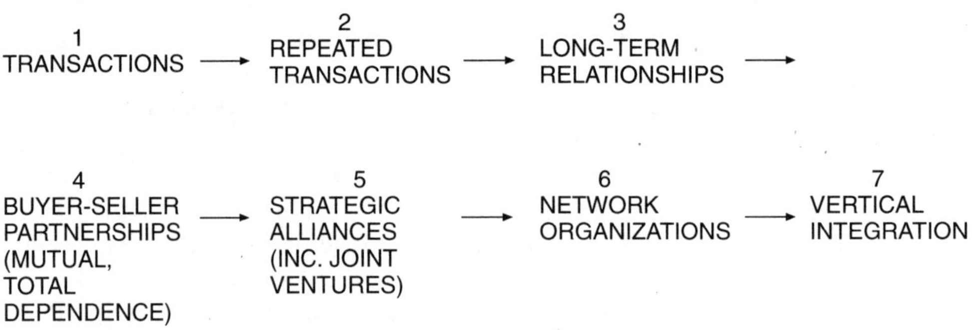

1 TRANSACTIONS	→	2 REPEATED TRANSACTIONS	→	3 LONG-TERM RELATIONSHIPS	→
4 BUYER-SELLER PARTNERSHIPS (MUTUAL, TOTAL DEPENDENCE)	→	5 STRATEGIC ALLIANCES (INC. JOINT VENTURES)	→	6 NETWORK ORGANIZATIONS	→ 7 VERTICAL INTEGRATION

with their own capital structures, something that other forms of strategic alliance lack. Network organizations are the corporate structures that result from multiple relationships, partnerships, and strategic alliances.

We can now consider how the role of the marketing function changes in the focal firm as we move along the continuum from transactions to network organizations.

Markets and transactions

The starting point of this analysis is a *transaction* between two economic actors in the competitive marketplace. In a pure *market* form of economic organization, all activity is conducted as a set of discrete, market-based transactions and virtually all necessary information is contained in the price of the product that is exchanged. The marketing job is simply to find buyers.

In the traditional microeconomic profit-maximization paradigm, the firm engages in market transactions as necessary to secure the resources (labor, capital, raw materials, etc.) it requires for the production of the goods and services it sells in the competitive marketplace. Each transaction is essentially independent of all other transactions, guided solely by the price mechanism of the free, competitive market as the firm seeks to buy at the lowest available price.

In addition to the costs associated with the price paid, however, there are costs associated with the transaction itself, what Coase (1937, p. 390) called the "cost of using the price mechanism." These costs include the costs of discovering what the relevant prices are, of negotiating and contracting, and of monitoring supplier performance, including quality and quantity of goods delivered. For Coase, the problem was to explain why, given these "marketing costs" (as he called them, p. 394, *not* "transactions costs", the phrase we use today), the firm did not internalize virtually all exchanges of value rather than depending on the competitive market. Coase proposed that the reason is that costs are also associated with internal performance of value-creation activities, including decreasing returns to the entrepreneurial function and misallocation of resources to activities in which the firm is incapable of creating value to the same extent as a specialist. It is worth noting that this suggestion, stated in an article published in 1937, is very similar to the notion of "distinctive competency" that appeared in the strategy literature more than 50 years later (Prahalad and Hamel 1990).

Pure transactions are rare, though they mark the beginning of the continuum for thinking about types of relationships and alliances and provide a useful starting point for theoretical analysis. In fact, throughout the 1970s, the marketing literature emphasized transactions as a central construct and the basic unit of analysis for the marketing discipline (Bagozzi 1975). Some authors even advocated a definition of a transaction that included *any* exchange of value between two parties, thus broadening the concept of marketing to include virtually all human interaction (Kotler and Levy 1969). A pure transaction is a one-time exchange of value between two parties with no prior or subsequent interaction. Price, established in the competitive marketplace, contains all of the information necessary for both parties to conclude the exchange. In a pure transaction, there is no brand name, no recognition of the customer by the seller, no credit extension, no preference, no loyalty, and no differentiation of one producer's output from that of another.

Most transactions in fact take place in the context of ongoing relationships between marketers and customers. Nonetheless, there has been a long-standing and clear tendency for marketing practice and theory to focus on the sale, the single event of a transaction, as the objective of marketing activity and the dependent variable for analysis. This emphasis on single transactions fits well with the profit-maximization paradigm and the related analytical techniques of optimization. There is no need to consider people or social processes when the units of analysis are products, prices, costs, firms, and transactions.

Repeated transactions — the precursors of a relationship

One step along the continuum from a pure transaction is the repeated, frequent purchase of branded consumer packaged goods and some industrial components, maintenance, and operating supplies. In the marketing of such products, advertising and sales promotion are key activities and each brand spends aggressively to try to win the customer's preference, loyalty, and repeat purchase. Marketing's role is to guide product differentiation and to create preference and loyalty that will earn higher prices and profits. Direct contact between customers and the marketer is unlikely. The sale is the end result of the marketing process and, though repeat purchases are important to the economics of advertising and sales promotion activity, there is no meaningful, ongoing relationship between company and customer. Even here, however, the presence of brand loyalty and repeat purchase means we have moved beyond a pure transaction. The rudiments of trust and credibility are present, which can be the foundations of a relationship. Consumers simply find it easier and more convenient to shop in the same store and to buy a familiar brand, thus minimizing the time and effort needed to obtain and process information about different alternatives. Consumers can negotiate more favorable terms of sale from a vendor who is attracted to the possibility of future transactions with them. Relationships make transactions more cost efficient.

The importance of *relationships* in marketing is more clearly seen in industrial markets, though it is now also better understood in consumer markets as resellers have gained increased power and as information technology has put individual consumers in more direct contact with resellers and manufacturers. Interactive databases are making relational marketing a reality for consumer goods. For products such as consumer durable goods, whose benefits are derived over a long period of time rather than being consumed in a single use and for which after-sale service is often required, there is an ongoing relationship with the customer, though responsibility for the relationship is often an issue and a source of conflict between customer, reseller, and manufacturer.

As an historical footnote, Henry Ford never had any doubt on this question. He wrote, "When one of my cars breaks down I know I am to blame" (Ford 1922, p. 67) and "A manufacturer is not through with this customer when a sale is completed. He has then only started with this customer. In the case of an automobile the sale of the machine is only something in the nature of an introduction" (p. 41). Likewise, L. L. Bean's original promise to his customers 80 years ago, what he called his Golden Rule, is now held up as a standard for others to follow:

> Everything we sell is backed by a 100% guarantee. We do not want you to have anything from L. L. Bean that is not completely satisfactory. Return anything you buy from us at any time for any reason if it proves otherwise.

These quotations help to underscore the fact that relationship marketing is not new in management thinking. However, there appears to have been a fairly long period of time when it was not a top priority for most companies, and it was not part of the basic conceptual structure of the field as an academic discipline.

Long-term relationships

In industrial markets, buyer-seller relationships have typically involved relatively long-term contractual commitments, but even here the relationship was often arm's-length and adversarial, pitting the customer against the vendor in a battle focused on low price. It was common practice for a buyer to maintain a list of qualified vendors who would be invited to submit bids for a particular procurement on a product with specifications drawn in a way to attract maximum competition (Corey 1978; Spekman 1988).

The importance of managing these buyer-seller relationships as strategic assets began to be recognized in the marketing literature of the 1980s (Jackson 1985; Webster 1984). Jackson proposed that industrial marketers characterize firms as either transaction or relationship customers and scale the commitment of resources accordingly. In these longer term buyer-seller relationships, prices are an outcome of a negotiation process based on mutual dependence, not determined solely by market forces, and quality, delivery, and technical support become more important. Competitive forces in the global marketplace of the 1980s forced many firms to move significantly along the continuum from arm's-length relationships with vendors and customers to much stronger partnerships characterized by much greater interdependence. In traditional manufacturing businesses such as those in the automobile industry, the world was changing so fast that the standard ways of doing business were passé.

In the 1980s, the automobile industry became the bellwether for new forms of relationship with industrial suppliers (Womack, Jones, and Roos 1991), and it is instructive to look briefly at the auto business specifically. Ford's River Rouge plant was an exception to the way the industry organized production. Ford got into trouble soon after the plant was opened as Alfred Sloan's General Motors began to offer consumers a much wider range of models, colors, and features, and the Model A fell from favor with customers. GM depended heavily on other vendors, including its own wholly owned but independent subsidiaries such as Harrison Radiator, AC Spark Plug, and Saginaw Steering (Womack, Jones, and Roos 1991, p. 138–139), for almost 70% of the value of production. The automobile manufacturers for decades had depended on thousands of vendors, with many vendors for each item, in a system that was fundamentally and intentionally adversarial. Relationships were short-term. Suppliers were adversaries for their customers, competing for an "unfair" share of the economic value created by the use of their products in the customer's manufacturing process. They fought over price. Competition among vendors, through systems of competitive bidding around extremely tight product specifications, was the method by which vendor greed and opportunism were controlled. The largest share of the business usually went to the vendor with the lowest price, though several others were given smaller shares to keep them involved, to keep pressure on the low price supplier, and to provide alternative sources of supply in the event of delivery or quality problems. Incoming inspection was the key step in quality control and reject rates tended to be high.

Mutual, total-dependence buyer-seller partnerships

Global competitors saw an opportunity in all of this. The Japanese manufacturers, in particular, striving to compete in the North American market thousands of miles from home, had learned a valuable lesson: quality does not just sell better, *it also costs less*. Designing products for manufacturability as well as performance and doing it right the first time costs less than detecting and removing defects later. Quality and low cost depend heavily on a system of strategic partnerships with a small number of vendors that are incorporated in the early stages of product development, a pattern of cooperation virtually unknown in the adversarial sourcing systems of the U.S. manufacturers

(Womack, Jones, and Roos 1991). Japanese *kanban* or *just-in-time* systems provided a new model for American manufacturers: reliance on one or a few vendors for a particular part who promise to deliver 100% usable product, usually in quantities just sufficient for one eight-hour production shift, on an incredibly tight schedule whereby trucks must arrive within a very few minutes of the programmed time. Higher quality and lower inventory costs and other related costs resulted from total reliance on a network of sole-source vendors in a system of total interdependence (Frazier, Spekman, and O'Neal 1988).

Firms in the American automobile industry studied their Japanese competitors and attempted to incorporate the lessons learned in their management of procurement and relationships with vendors. The rest of America began to learn from what was happening in the automobile industry, as well as in telecommunications, computers, office equipment, and other fields. American marketers began to see the necessity of moving away from a focus on the individual sale, the transaction as a conquest, and toward an understanding of the need to develop long-term, mutually supportive relationships with their customers. Many of America's premier industrial firms such as GE, IBM, DuPont, Monsanto, and Honeywell restructured themselves around the fundamental concept of strategic customer partnerships with customers such as American Airlines, Ford, Milliken, Procter & Gamble, and the federal government.

Another Japanese institution, the *keiretsu*, provides yet another model that is shaping the new American organizational landscape (Gerlach 1987). *Kanban* systems depend on the close relationship of suppliers and subcontractors with the *keiretsu*. In many respects, the *keiretsu* are the predecessors of the networks and alliances now emerging in the Western world (not to mention the obvious fact that many alliance partners are, in fact, Japanese firms). The *keiretsu* are complex groupings of firms with interlinked ownership and trading relationships. They are neither formal organizations with clearly defined hierarchical structures nor impersonal, decentralized markets. They are bound together in long-term relationships based on reciprocity. The trading partners may hold small ownership positions in one another, but primarily to symbolize the long-term commitment of the relationship rather than strictly for financial gain. A key outcome of this arrangement is great stability in these long-term relationships. Such stability contributes to a sharing of information among the companies and promotes aggressive, long-term growth policies (Gerlach 1987). The experience of Japanese managers with keiretsu and similar forms of interfirm cooperation is a major reason for their greater skill and comfort level in the management of strategic alliances in comparison with American managers (Montgomery and Weiss 1991).

Strategic alliances

In some cases, the partnership between a supplier and its customer stakes the form of an entirely new venture, a true strategic alliance. One of the essential features of a true strategic alliance is that it is intended to move each of the partners toward the achievement of some long-term, *strategic*, goal. This strategic objective is one distinguishing feature that separates strategic alliances from previous forms of interfirm cooperation. According to Devlin and Bleakley (1988, p. 18), "Strategic alliances take place in the context of a company's long-term strategic plan and seek to improve or dramatically change a company's competitive position." This definition of strategic alliances, with its emphasis on improving a firm's competitive position, supports the notion that they are an important *marketing* phenomenon. Another important characteristic of strategic alliances is shared objectives and a commitment of resources by both parties.

There are multiple types of strategic alliances; virtually all are within the theoretical domain of marketing as they involve partnerships with customers or resellers or with real or potential competitors for the development of new technology, new products, and new markets. Some are new ventures formed between vendors and customers to ensure a smooth flow of raw materials, components, or services into the customers' manufacturing operations. Others are formed between potential competitors in order to cooperate in the development of related or convergent technologies, in the development of a new product or class of products, or in the development of a new market. Some alliances are formed between manufacturers and resellers. All strategic alliances are collaborations among partners involving the commitment of capital and management resources with the objective of enhancing the partners' competitive positions. Strategic alliances are much closer to the *hierarchy* end of the transactions (market) — hierarchy continuum, but they stop short of internalizing the functions with the firm itself. Instead, they create a separate entity to be managed by bureaucratic and administrative controls.

Joint ventures

Joint ventures, as the term is used here, are only one kind of strategic alliance, though the terms are often used interchangeably. The unique feature of a joint venture is that a new firm is created, with its own capital structure, as well as the sharing of other resources. Joint ventures are typically established to exist in perpetuity, though the founding partners may subsequently change their ownership participation. Other types of strategic alliances, such as a product development project, have a finite life by definition. In fact, this finiteness with its inherent flexibility is one of the advantages of strategic alliances in comparison with more traditional organization forms. Interestingly, the joint venture soon faces all of the problems of its parent firms in terms of creating multiple partnerships and alliances and determining its core competence and its unique positioning in the value chain between vendors and customers.

Networks

Networks are the complex, multifaceted organization structures that result from multiple strategic alliances, usually combined with other forms of organization including divisions, subsidiaries, and value-added resellers. (Some authors have mistakenly used the terms "strategic alliances" and "networks" interchangeably.) The alliances are the individual agreements and collaborations between partners, such as Ford and Mazda in the creation of the new Escort and Explorer automobiles or General Motors and Toyota in the formation of the NUMMI joint venture. General Motors, though still a classic example of a traditional, hierarchical, bureaucratic, multidivisional organization and currently in the throes of a major downsizing (Taylor 1992), is evolving toward a network organization with multiple joint-venture partners including global competitors Toyota, Daewoo, Volvo, Suzuki, and Isuzu, as well as a host of strategic partnerships with vendors. Ford likewise has a large number of partnerships and alliances and is evolving into a network organization.

The basic characteristic of a network organization is *confederation*, a loose and flexible coalition guided from a hub where the key functions include development and management of the alliances themselves, coordination of financial resources and technology, definition and management of core competence strategy, developing relationships with customers, and managing information resources that bind the network. In the context of the network organization, marketing is the function responsible for keeping all of the partners focused on the customer and informed about competitor product offerings and changing customer needs and expectations.

James Houghton, Chairman of Corning, Incorporated, for example, describes his company as a network with alliances as a key part of its structure (Houghton 1989). At the hub of the wheel (Figure 2) is a set of functional specialities such as contract negotiation, legal services, and financial coordination that provide the linkages that bind together technology, shared values, and shared resources. The center is also responsible for establishing priorities and managing the linkages that define the network; information management is a central strategic function and information technology has been a key facilitator of these new organizational forms. Another key responsibility of the center is to define, develop, and maintain the core competencies that are at the heart of the firm's ability to compete successfully in the global marketplace (Prahalad and Hamel 1990). In fact, one of the key core competencies of a network organization may be the ability to design, manage, and control strategic partnerships with customers, vendors, distributors, and others.

Figure 2 Network organizations

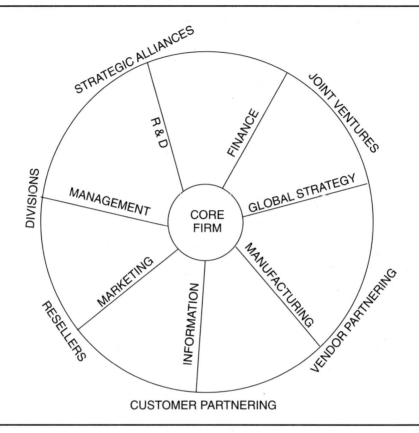

There is an interesting paradox here: in the move toward strategic alliances, even the largest firms become more focused and specialized in their core activities. They realize that there is an increasingly smaller set of activities that represent true distinctive competence on their part. The trick is to avoid trying to do everything, especially the things they cannot do well, and to find other firms that also need a partner that *can* do the things the large firm does best. Strategic alliances become a primary tool in developing the firm's core competence and competitive advantage.

Instead of vertical integration being the preferred model, the network paradigm is built around the assumption that small is better, that each part or process or function should be the responsibility of a specialized, independent entity, efficiently organized and managed, that has world class competence. Across the board — for all factors of production including parts and subassemblies, services such as transportation and maintenance, and professional marketing services such as marketing research, some selling functions, and most distribution functions — the bias has shifted from "make" to "buy," from ownership to partnership, from fixed cost to variable cost, but in the context of stable, long-term relationships. A firm must define ever more narrowly those core competencies to which it will devote scarce resources in order to develop new knowledge and skills. For all other areas, it must depend on strategic partners who have placed their own focused bets in the game of becoming world class competitors.

IBM is another example of a firm that is reinventing itself as a network organization. As one of the first steps in this direction, the personal computer was designed over a long weekend by an IBM management taskforce gathered informally at a Florida retreat. Actual manufacturing relied on a network of hardware and software suppliers for all components. Besides the design work, IBM's own contribution to the manufacturing process was an assembly plant and several minutes of assembly and testing time per machine. Gradually, some of the vendor partnerships and alliances were terminated as IBM brought some manufacturing activities back into the firm. Subsequently, IBM committed itself to "open architecture," making IBM's technology widely available to all software writers who wanted to develop applications programs, in recognition of the fact that not even IBM had the resources necessary to do the job of writing software for thousands of distinct applications segments. (Some observers have argued that open architecture and reliance on outside vendors meant that IBM itself no longer had any distinctive competitive advantage of its own.) Most recently, IBM has announced a major strategic alliance with Apple Computer and a substantial downsizing and restructuring into a set of more autonomous, independent businesses (Carey and Coy 1991). A key strategic issue for IBM management is to define the set of skills and resources that represent the distinctive competencies of IBM *per se* and a set of technical and strategic challenges and opportunities that require the scope and scale of an IBM.

To sum up, there is a clear evolution away from arm's-length transactions and traditional hierarchical, bureaucratic forms of organization toward more flexible types of partnerships, alliances, and networks. Within these new types of organizations, traditional ways of organizing the marketing function and of thinking about the purpose of marketing activity must be reexamined, with focus on long-term customer relationships, partnerships, and strategic alliances.

Redefining marketing's role

From an academic or theoretical perspective, the relatively narrow conceptualization of marketing as a profit-maximization problem, focused on market transactions or a series of transactions, seems increasingly out of touch with an emphasis on long-term customer relationships and the formation and management of strategic alliances. The intellectual core of marketing management needs to be expanded beyond the conceptual framework of microeconomics in order to address more fully the set of organizational and strategic issues inherent in relationships and alliances. In focusing on relationships — though we are still talking about buying and selling, the fundamental activities of interest to marketing — we are now considering phenomena that have traditionally been the subject of study by psychologists, organizational behaviorist, political economists, and sociologists. The focus shifts from products and firms as units of analysis to people, organizations, and the social processes that bind actors together in ongoing relationships.

In the following sections, the changing role of marketing within the organization is examined more closely. Then suggestions are made for how the conceptual base of marketing must be expanded. Finally, some implications for management action are discussed and suggestions are made for the research areas that should be given highest priority if marketing's knowledge and theory base is to address the most important issues facing managers and organizations.

In the new organization environment, the marketing function as we know it is undergoing radical transformation and, in some cases, has disappeared altogether as a distinct management function at the corporate level. Just as the distinction between the firm and its market environment (both suppliers and customers) becomes blurred in network organizations built around long-term strategic partnerships, so do traditional functional boundaries within the firm become less distinct.

To consider the new role of marketing within the evolving corporation, we must recognize that marketing really operates at three distinct levels, reflecting three levels of strategy. These can be defined as the corporate, business or SBU, and functional or operating levels (Boyd and Walker 1990: Hofer and Schendel 1978). Much of the confusion over the years about a definition of marketing and an understanding of the marketing concept can be traced to a failure to make these distinctions (Houston 1986; McGee and Spiro 1988; McNamara 1972; Shapiro 1988). One of the results of the movement toward new organizational forms will be to make these distinct roles more explicit.

In addition to the three levels strategy, we can identify three distinct dimensions of marketing — marketing as *culture*, marketing as *strategy*, and marketing as *tactics*. Though each marketing dimension is found at each level of strategy, the emphasis accorded the separate dimensions of marketing varies with the level of strategy and the level within the hierarchy of the organization.

Marketing as culture, a basic set of values and beliefs about the central importance of the customer that guide the organization (as articulated by the marketing concept), is primarily the responsibility of the corporate and SBU level managers. Marketing as strategy is the emphasis at the SBU level, where the focus is on market segmentation, targeting, and positioning in defining how the firm is to compete in its chosen businesses. Atthe operating level, marketing managers must focus on marketing tactics, the "4Ps" of product, price, promotion, and place/distribution, the elements of the marketing mix. Each level of strategy, and each dimension of marketing, must be developed in the context of the preceding level. As we move down the levels of strategy, we move from strategy formulation to strategy implementation.

At the corporate level: market structure analysis, customer orientation and advocacy, and positioning the firm in the value chain

At the corporate level, the strategic problem is to define what business the company is in and to determine the mission, scope, shape, and structure of the firm. Increasingly, firms are paying specific attention to the question of firm scope and shape, as seen in the decision to enter into strategic alliances. In other words, the question of whether to depend on markets, long-term relationships, strategic alliances, or integrated multifunctional hierarchy is seen to require specific management analysis and judgment. The first order of business in the strategic puzzle, then, is to determine the firm's position in the value chain: What will it buy? What will it make? What will it sell? These decisions require careful assessment of the firm's distinctive competencies (Prahalad and Hamel 1990) and a decision to focus on the things the firm does best. As mentioned previously, this is the question raised theoretically in 1937 by Ronald Coase, whose work received the Nobel Prize in Economics in 1991: When should the firm depend on outside suppliers and when should it perform activities and functions internally? Today's analysis permits consideration of a much more flexible set of organization forms — relationships and alliances of various kinds.

At this level of strategy, the role of marketing is threefold: (1) to assess market attractiveness by analyzing customer needs and requirements and competitive offerings in the markets potentially available to the firm, and to assess its potential competitive effectiveness, (2) to promote customer orientation by being a strong advocate for the customer's point of view versus that of other constituencies in management decision making, as called for by the marketing concept (Anderson 1982), and (3) to develop the firm's overall value proposition (as a reflection of its distinctive competence, in terms reflecting customer needs and wants) and to articulate it to the marketplace and throughout the organization. A major function of the statement of mission, distinctive competence, and overall value proposition is to make clear what the firm will *not* do, as well as what it will do as stated by corporate objectives and goals. At the corporate level, marketing managers have a critical role to play as advocates, for the customer and for a set of values and beliefs that put the customer first in the firm's decision making, and to communicate the value proposition as part of that culture throughout the organization both internally and in its multiple relationships and alliances.

In network organizations, the marketing function has a unique role that is different from its role in traditional hierarchical structures — to help design and negotiate the strategic partnerships with vendors and technology partners through which the firm deploys its distinctive competence to serve particular market opportunities. Thus, marketing may be involved in relationships with vendors at least as much as, if not more than, relationships with customers as part of the process of delivering superior value to customers. Negotiating skills traditionally associated with managing major customer accounts may be equally valuable in managing vendor relationships. Some firms are already moving managers between sales/marketing and procurement responsibilities, recognizing the transferability of these skills.

At the business (SBU) level: market segmentation and targeting, positioning the product, and deciding when and how to partner

At the business unit or SBU level, the key strategy question is *how* to compete in the firm's chosen businesses. This level of competitive strategy is developed by managers in the individual business units. Business strategy is based on a more detailed and careful analysis of customers and competitors and of the firm's resources and skills for competing in specific market segments (Day and Wensley 1988). The key outcomes of this planning process are market segmentation, market targeting, and positioning in the target segments. A trend of the last decade was to delegate more of the strategic planning process from corporate headquarters out to the individual business units, helping to clarify the distinction between corporate and business-level strategy. These planning activities were historically associated with marketing strategy at the corporate level in hierarchical organizations. Clearly, in network organizations, these responsibilities devolve to the business unit level. In fact, at the SBU level, the distinction between marketing and strategic planning can become blurred; in some firms these functions are likely to be performed by the same people.

In network organizations, marketing managers at the business unit level also have a new responsibility for deciding which marketing functions and activities are to be purchased in the market, which are to be performed by strategic partners, and which are to be performed internally. This responsibility applies to the whole range of professional services (marketing research, telemarketing, advertising, sales promotion, package design, etc.) as well as to suppliers of raw materials, components, and subassemblies and to resellers. When is a vendor merely a vendor and when is it a strategic partner committed to a mutually dependent long-term relationship in delivering solutions to customer problems? Similar questions must be asked about channel members. In a customer-oriented company, committed to the marketing concept at the corporate level, marketing management at the business unit level has a critical role in guiding the analysis that leads to answers to these questions. In all cases, the answer will be that which enables the business to deliver superior value to customers in comparison with its competitors. It is the unique characteristic of network organisations that these questions are asked and that the organization form — transaction versus relationships versus hierarchy — remains flexible, depending on what the market requires. In this sense, network organizations are by definition "market-driven" and represent a maturation of the marketing concept.

At the operating level: the marketing mix and managing customer and reseller relationships

At the operating or tactical level, we are back on the more familiar ground of the marketing mix — decisions about products, pricing, promotion, and distribution that implement the business strategy. This is the level of strategy normally called "functional strategy," and in our case "*marketing* strategy," as distinct from corporate and business strategies. It, too, is the responsibility of business-level managers, but at the operating level it is delegated to functional specialists, the marketing managers. This is where the tools of management science and the optimization paradigm apply, as the business attempts to allocate its financial, human, and production resources to markets, customers, and products in the most productive fashion. But even here, marketing is taking on a new form, in both consumer goods and industrial products and services companies, as market forces compel companies to do a more thorough job of responding to customer needs and developing long-term customer relationships.

Regis KcKenna, a popular marketing consultant and writer, has described well the new requirements for the marketing function (at both the SBU and operating levels) in a recent *Harvard Business Review* article (McKenna 1991, p. 148):

> The marketer must be the integrator, both internally — synthesizing technological capability with market needs — and externally — bringing the customer into the company as a participant in the development and adaptation of goods and services. It is a fundamental shift in the role and purpose of marketing: from manipulation of the customer to genuine customer involvement; from telling and selling to communicating and sharing knowledge; from last-in-line function to corporate-credibility champion. . . .

> The relationships are the key, the basis of customer choice and company adaptation. After all, what is a successful brand but a special relationship? And who better than a company's marketing people to create, sustain, and interpret the relationship between the company, its suppliers, and its customers?

For firms like Corning and IBM that are redefining themselves as networks of strategic alliances, the key activities in the core organization have to do with strategy, coordination, and relationship management. These activities are essentially knowledge-based and involve the management of information. CEOs manage "the central cores of worldwide webs of product and knowledge links" (Badaracco 1991, p. 148).

To summarize, there is a clear evolution toward entirely new forms of organization for conducting business affairs in the global marketplace and it requires reconceptualization of the role of the marketing function within the organization. In the traditional view, the firm was a distinct entity whose borders were defined by an organization chart, which clearly delineated the boundary between the firm and the external environment. The external environment consisted of markets, in which firms engaged in transactions with vendors for the resources needed to conduct their affairs and with customers who purchased their products and services. The fundamental difference in the new economic order is that *this clear distinction between firms and markets, between the company and its external environment, has disappeared* (Badaracco 1991). It is highly significant, for example, that the management of General Electric Company, the sixth largest American firm in terms of sales and assets, and the country's leading exporter after Boeing, has articulated a vision of GE as "a boundary-less company" for the 1990s. According to the 1990 GE Annual Report:

> In a boundary-less company, suppliers aren't "outsiders." They are drawn closer and become trusted partners in the total business process. Customers are seen for what they are — the lifeblood of a company. Customers' vision of their needs and the company's view become identical, and every effort of every man and woman in the company is focused on satisfying those needs.

> In a boundary-less company, internal functions begin to blur. Engineering doesn't design a product and then "hand it off" to manufacturing. They form a team, along with marketing and sales, finance, and the rest. Customer service? It's not somebody's job. It's everybody's job.

Clearly, evolving organization forms, emphasizing flexibility in responding to changing customer needs, create new definitions of marketing's role and responsibilities. We have examined how these new responsibilities differ at the corporate, business, and operating levels. In each instance, the new emphasis on long-term relationships and ongoing assessment of which functions and activities to purchase, to perform internally, or to engage in with a strategic partner creates new dimensions to the marketing task. These new responsibilities and tasks cannot be well understood by using only the traditional profit-maximizing optimization framework that has been the core of marketing theory for the past four decades.

The need for an expanded conceptual framework

The marketer must manage three sets of relationships — with customers, with suppliers, and with resellers. In both industrial buyer-seller relationships and in manufacturer-reseller relationships, we are talking about *interorganizational* relationships. In the microeconomic paradigm, the units of analysis are products, prices, firms, and transactions. In the new world of marketing management, we must also look at people, processes, and organizations.

Marketing scholars face two mandates for the 1990s. The first is to develop an expanded view of the marketing function within the firm, one that specifically addresses the role of marketing in firms that go to market through multiple partnerships and that is sensitive to the multiple levels of strategy within the organization. The second is to develop a base of empirical research that broadens our understanding of the forces leading to the development of long-term customer relationships, strategic partnerships with vendors, alliances for the codevelopment of technologies, and the issues involved in creating, managing, and dissolving these partnerships over time. Whereas the historical marketing management model has depended most heavily on economics, statistics, mathematics, psychology, and social psychology, the broadened view of the marketing function calls for work that spans the disciplines of political economy, organizational psychology, legal analysis, political science (government), and cultural anthropology.

In contrast to the microeconomic paradigm and its emphasis on prices, the political economy paradigm is better suited to understanding these firm-to-firm relationships. This is the argument first presented by Johan Arndt in articles published in 1979, 1981, and 1983. The political economy paradigm looks at marketing organizations as social systems — "dynamic, adapting, and internally differentiated. Important dimensions of marketing behavior are authority and control patterns, distributions of power, conflict and conflict management, and external and internal determinants of institutional change" (Arndt 1983, p. 52). Political economy has obvious potential to help us understand the role of marketing in managing relationships with other organizations and in developing support within the firm for activities necessary to respond to the changing marketplace. The political economy model has recently been applied most aggressively in the study of channel conflict (Dwyer, Schurr, and Oh 1987; Frazier 1983), but it offers solid potential for better understanding of all types of relationships and alliances in marketing (Day and Klein 1987). It is cited here as evidence of the availability of alternative conceptualizations of the functions of marketing to move the field beyond its historically narrow focus on transactions and prices based on the traditional microeconomic paradigm.

The field of organizational behavior also offers many opportunities for productive partnerships for marketing scholars who want to address such areas as negotiation, coalitions, team-building, conflict resolution, and group processes related to such activities as new product development that are part of managing marketing partnerships. At the intersection of the organizational behavior, economics, and strategic management disciplines, there is an effort to develop a resource-based theory of the firm, one that moves beyond traditional emphases of the microeconomic paradigm. This integrative approach has potential to address the issues of developing distinctive competence and defining the firm's position in the value chain, finding those sources of competitive advantage that are knowledge-based and "costly to copy" and therefore the *raison d'être* of the firm (Conner 1991; Grant 1991). Customer knowledge and a culture of customer orientation are two important examples of such resources.

The focus of the political economy and organizational behavior models seems to be more appropriate for a *strategic* view of the marketing function as distinct from the *sales* or demand stimulation function, for which the microeconomic paradigm is still more fitting. Whereas the microeconomic model centers on consumers and transactions, the political economy and organizational behavior models are more useful in analyzing relationships with industrial customers, suppliers, joint venture partners, resellers, and other stakeholders (Anderson 1982). It should help us to understand better the changing role of marketing in the corporation. The conceptual foundations of marketing must be enriched, blending economics, political science, and organizational behavior as well as appropriate frameworks from legal analysis, sociology, anthropology, and social psychology to enhance our understanding of the processes of negotiation, coordination, and cooperation that define marketing relationships. Just as we know that most marketing transactions take place in the context of longer term relationships, so we need models that focus on the relationships themselves, not just on the market exchanges that are the subject of the microeconomic paradigm.

Theory development must be accompanied by aggressive programs of empirical research for understanding strategic marketing relationships more completely. Programs of clinical and survey research should be guided by strong theoretical frameworks from allied social science disciplines. Top priority should be given to analysis of the forces and factors that cause firms to move along the continuum from transactions to long-term relationships to strategic alliances and, perhaps, back again.

Some studies have shown modest success rates for strategic alliances, especially those that involve partners of different nationalities and cultures (Bleeke and Ernst 1991; Harrigan 1986). Marketers in collaboration with scholars in the field of cultural anthropology could productively turn their attention to analyzing the differences in values, beliefs, decision making, information processing, and teamwork, among other variables, that must be managed to achieve success in transnational partnerships (Montgomery 1991; Montgomery and Weiss 1991; Webster and Deshpandé 1990).

More careful analysis is needed of the forces reshaping the marketing function at both the corporate and the SBU levels. In collaboration with organizational behavior researchers, marketers need to get into companies and examine the multiple new forms marketing is taking. What is the relationship between marketing and purchasing work together in designing and managing strategic vendor partnerships? What issues arise in blending these functions?

In consumer goods marketing, research is needed to understand the factors that lead consumers to seek out and value ongoing relationships with brands, manufacturers, and resellers of various kinds. What are the factors that consumers find attractive in dealing with direct marketers? How can marketers develop and manage these long-term relationships, given the power of databases and interactive marketing? What is the marketing potential inherent in such new developments as the Prodigy network and other extensions of information technology into the household? How will customer expectations about their relationships with marketers be shaped by these new capabilities?

A successful program of research will develop and refine models of the marketing function, incorporating concepts and propositions from multiple behavioral and organizational science disciplines. The net result will be a much richer understanding of those activities we call marketing and have defined as a distinct field of inquiry. Marketing is more than an economic optimization problem; it is a central component of the guidance system of the firm and we need to understand its functioning in much richer detail, especially within the complicated structures of network organizations.

Conclusions

Marketing is responsible for more than the sale, and its responsibilities differ depending on the level of organization and strategy. It is the management function responsible for making sure that every aspect of the business is focused on delivering superior value to customers in the competitive marketplace. The business is increasingly likely to be a network of strategic partnerships among designers, technology providers, manufacturers, distributors, and information specialists. The business will be defined by its customers, not its products or factories or offices. This is a critical point: in network organizations, it is the ongoing relationship with a set of customers that represents the most important business asset. Marketing as a distinct management function will be responsible for being expert on the customer and keeping the rest of the network organization informed about the customer. At the corporate and business unit levels, marketing may merge with strategic planning or, more generally, the strategy development function, with shared responsibility for information management, environmental scanning, and coordination of the network activities.

There has been a shift from a transaction to a relationship focus. Customers become partners and the firm must make long-term commitments to maintaining those relationships with quality, service, and innovation (Anderson and Narus 1991). Given the increased importance of long-term, strategic relationships with both customers and vendors, organizations must place increased emphasis on relationship management skills. As these skills reside in people, rather than organization structures or roles or tasks, key marketing personnel who have these skills will become increasingly valuable as business assets (Thorelli 1986). These skills may define the core competence of some organizations as links between their vendors and customers in the value chain. This common focus on customer value and relationship management may result in much stronger coordination of the procurement, sales, and marketing functions in a manner analogous to the merchandising function in retailing firms. Such coordination would be consistent with the two major trends of elimination of boundaries between management functions within organizations and a blurring of the boundaries between the firm and its market environment. In a world of strategic partnerships, it is not uncommon for a partner to be simultaneously customer, competitor, and vendor, as well as partner. Consequently, it is difficult to keep the traditional management functions distinct in dealing with strategic partners.

Marketing can no longer be the sole responsibility of a few specialists. Rather, everyone in the firm must be charged with responsibility for understanding customers and contributing to developing and delivering value for them (Webster 1988). It must be part of everyone's job description and part of the organization culture. Organization culture, focused on the customer, will be increasingly seen as a key strategic resource defining the network organization's uniqueness and coordinating its several parts toward common mission and objectives (Conner 1991; Fiol 1991).

Firms that are unable to achieve this focus on the customer will either disappear or become highly specialized players, taking strategic direction from others, in a network organization. Customer focus may require increasingly large investments in information and information technology, giving some advantage to firms large enough to make pre-emptive investments in these areas.

Impersonal, mass communications, especially media advertising, are becoming less effective, whereas personal, targeted, special purpose communications have become more important. This change is reflected in the decline of the traditional advertising business — independent advertising agencies developing ads and placing them in broadcast and print media. In their place have emerged global communication companies, international networks of specialists and integrated marketing communications mega-agencies working with their multinational clients on specific projects.

Distributors must be treated as strategic partners (Anderson and Nurs 1990), linked to the manufacturing firm with sophisticated telecommunications and data-processing systems that afford seamless integration of manufacturing, distribution, and marketing activities throughout the network. Consumer marketers continue to shift resources toward the trade and away from the consumer *per se*, and traditional selling functions for the field sales organization are evolving toward a broader definition of responsibilities for relationship management, assisted by interactive information management capability.

The implementation of market-driven strategy will require skills in designing, developing, managing, and controlling strategic alliances with partners of all kinds, and keeping them all focused on the ever-changing customer in the global marketplace. The core firm will be defined by its end-use markets and its knowledge base, as well as its technical competence, not by its factories and its office building. Customer focus, market segmentation, targeting, and positioning, assisted by information technology, will be the flexible bonds that hold the whole thing together.

REFERENCES

Alderson, W. (1957), *Marketing Behavior and Executive Action*. Homewood, IL: Richard D. Irwin, Inc.

American Marketing Association (1948), "Report of the Definitions Committee," R.S. Alexander, Chairman, *Journal of Marketing*, 13 (October), 202–10.

Anderson, James C. and James A. Narus (1990), "A Model of Distributor Firm and Manufacturer Firm Working Partnerships," *Journal of Marketing*, 54 (January), 42–58.

_____ and _____ (1991), "Partnering as a Focused Market Strategy," *California Management Review*, 33 (Spring), 95–113.

Anderson, Paul F. (1982), "Marketing, Strategic Planning and the Theory of the Firm," *Journal of Marketing*, 46 (Spring), 15–26.

Arndt, Johan (1979), "Toward a Concept of Domesticated Markets," *Journal of Marketing*, 43 (Fall), 69–75.

_____ (1981), "The Political Economy of Marketing Systems: Reviving the Institutional Approach," *Journal of Macromarketing*, 1 (Fall), 36–47.

_____ (1983), "The Political Economy Paradigm: Foundation for Theory Building in Marketing," *Journal of Marketing*, 47 (Fall), 44–54.

Badaracco, Joseph L. (1991), *The Knowledge Link: How Firms Compete Through Strategic Alliances*. Boston: Harvard Business School Press.

Bagozzi, Richard (1975), "Marketing as Exchange," *Journal of Marketing*, 39 (October), 32–9.

Bartels, Robert (1962), *The Development of Marketing Thought*. Homewood, IL: Richard D. Irwin, Inc.

Beckman, Theodore N. and William R. Davidson (1962), *Marketing*, 7th ed. New York: The Ronald Press Co. (The original edition of this book was published in 1927 as *Principles of Marketing*, by Maynard, Wielder, and Davidson.)

Bleeke, Joel and David Ernst (1991), "The Way to Win in Cross Border Alliances," *Harvard Business Review*, 69 (November–December), 127–35.

Boyd, Harper W., Jr. and Orville C. Walker, Jr (1990), *Marketing Management: A Strategic Approach*. Homewood, IL: Richard D. Irwin, Inc.

Breyer, Ralph (1934), *The Marketing Institution*. New York: McGraw-Hill Book Company, Inc.

Carey, John and Peter Coy (1991), "The New IBM," *Business Week*, 3244 (December 16), 112–18.

Coase, Ronald H. (1937), "The Nature of the Firm," *Economica*, 4, 386–405.

Conner, Kathleen R. (1991), "A Historical Comparison of Resource-Based Theory and Five Schools of Thought Within Industrial Organization Economics: Do We Have a New Theory of the Firm?" *Journal of Management*, 17 (1), 121–54.

Copeland, M. T. (1920), *Marketing Problems*. New York: A. W. Shaw.

Corey, E. Raymond (1978), *Procurement Management: Strategy, Organization, and Decision-Making*. Boston: CBI Publishing Co., Inc.

Davis, K. R. (1961), *Marketing Management*. New York: The Ronald Press Co.

Day, George S. and Saul Klein (1987), "Cooperative Behavior in Vertical Markets: The Influence of Transaction Costs and Competitive Strategies," in *Review of Marketing*, Michael J. Houston, ed. Chicago: American Marketing Association, 39–66.

_____ and Robin Wensley (1988), "Assessing Advantage: A Framework for Diagnosing Competitive Superiority," *Journal of Marketing*, 52 (April), 1–20.

Devlin, Geoffrey and Mark Bleakley (1988), "Strategic Alliances — Guidelines for Success," *Long-Range Planning*, 21 (5), 18–23.

Drucker, Peter F. (1954), *The Practice of Management*, New York: Harper & Row Publishers, Inc.

Duddy, E. A. and Revzan, D. A. (1953), *Marketing: An Institutional Approach*, 2nd ed. New York: McGraw-Hill Book Company.

Dwyer, F. Robert, Paul H. Schurr, and Sejo Oh (1987), "Developing Buyer-Seller Relationships," *Journal of Marketing*, 51 (April), 11–27.

Fiol, C. Marlene (1991), "Managing Culture as a Competitive Resource: An Identity-Based View of Sustainable Competitive Advantage," *Journal of Management*, 17 (1), 191–211.

Ford, Henry (1922), *My Life and Work*. New York: Double-day, Page & Company. (Reprinted by Ayer Company, Publishers, Salem, NH, 1987.)

Frazier, Gary L. (1983), "Interorganizational Exchange Behavior in Marketing Channels: A Broadened Perspective," *Journal of Marketing*, 47 (Fall), 68–78.

_____, Robert E. Spekman, and Charles R. O'Neal (1988), "Just-in-Time Exchange Relationships in Industrial Markets," *Journal of Marketing*, 52 (October) 52–67.

General Electric Company (1991), *1990 Annual Report* (March). Gerlach, Michael (1987), "Business Alliances and the Strategy of the Japanese Firm," *California Management Review*, 30 (Fall) 126–42.

Gordon, R. A. and J. E. Howell (1959), *Higher Education for Business*. New York: Columbia University Press. (This study was sponsored by the Ford Foundation.)

Grant, Robert M. (1991), "The Resource-Based Theory of Competitive Advantage: Implications for Strategy Formulation," *California Management Review*, 33 (Spring), 114–35.

Handy, Charles (1990), *The Age of Unreason*. Boston: Harvard Business School Press.

Harrigan, Kathryn R. (1986), *Managing for Joint Venture Success*. Lexington, MA: Lexington Books.

Hofer, Charles W. and Dan Schendel (1978), ·*Strategy Formulation: Analytical Concepts*. St. Paul: West Publishing Company.

Houghton, James R. (1989), "The Age of the Hierarchy Is Over," *The New York Times* (Sunday, September 24), Sec. 3, 3.

Houston, Franklin S. (1986), "That Marketing Concept: What It Is and What It Is Not," *Journal of Marketing*, 50 (April), 81–7.

Howard, J. A. (1957), *Marketing Management: Analysis and Planning*. Homewood, IL: Richard D. Irwin, Inc.

Jackson, Barbara B. (1985), "Build Customer Relationships That Last," *Harvard Business Review*, 63 (November–December), 120–8.

Johnston, Russell, and Paul R. Lawrence (1988), "Beyond Vertical Integration — The Rise of the Value-Adding Partnership," *Harvard Business Review*, 66 (July–August), 94–101.

Kotler, Philip (1967), *Marketing Management: Analysis, Planning, and Control*. Englewood Cliffs, NJ: Prentice-Hall, Inc.

_____ and Sidney J. Levy (1969), "Broadening the Concept of Marketing," *Journal of Marketing*, 33 (January), 10–15.

Levitt, Theodore (1960), "Marketing Myopia," *Harvard Business Review*, 38 (July–August), 24–47.

Massy, William F. and Frederick E. Webster, Jr. (1964), "Model-Building in Marketing Research," *Journal of Marketing Research*, 1 (May), 9–13.

McCarthy, E. J. (1960), *Basic Marketing: A Managerial Approach*. Homewood, IL: Richard D. Irwin, Inc.

McGarry, Edmund D. (1950), "Some Functions of Marketing Reconsidered," in *Theory in Marketing*, Reavis Cox and Wroe Alderson, eds. Homewood, IL: Richard D. Irwin, Inc., 268.

McGee, Lynn W. and Rosann Spiro (1988), "The Marketing Concept in Perspective," *Business Horizons*, 31 (May–June), 40–5.

McKenna, Regis (1991), "Marketing Is Everything," *Harvard Business Review*, 69 (January–February), 65–79.

McKitterick, J. B. (1957), "What Is the Marketing Management Concept?" in *The Frontiers of Marketing Thought*, Frank M. Bass, ed. Chicago: American Marketing Association, 71–82.

McNamara, Carlton P. (1972), "The Present Status of the Marketing Concept," *Journal of Marketing*, 36 (January), 50–7.

Miles, Raymond and Charles Snow (1984), "Fit, Failure, and the Hall of Fame," *California Management Review*, 26 (Spring), 10–28.

_____ and _____ (1986), "Network Organizations: New Concepts for New Forms," *California Management Review*, 28 (Sprint), 62–73.

Montgomery, David B. (1991), "Understanding the Japanese as Customers, Competitors, and Collaborators," *Japan and the World Economy*, 3 (1), 61–91.

_____ and Allan M. Weiss (1991), "Managerial Preferences for Strategic Alliance Attributes," Research paper #1134 (August), Graduate School of Business, Stanford University.

Ohmae, Kenichi (1989), "The Global Logic of Strategic Alliances," *Harvard Business Review*, 67 (March–April), 143–54.

Pfeffer, Jeffrey, and Gerald R. Salancik (1978), *The External Control of Organizations*. New York: Harper & Row Publishers, Inc.

Pierson, F. C. (1959), *The Education of American Businessmen*. New York: McGraw-Hill Book Company. (This study was sponsored by the Carnegie Foundation.)

Powell, Walter W. (1990), "Neither Market Nor Hierarchy: Network Forms of Organization," *Research in Organizational Behavior*, 12, 295–336.

Prahalad, C. K. and Gary Hamel (1990), "The Core Competence of the Corporation," *Harvard Business Review*, 68 (May–June) 79–91.

Rathmell, John M. (1965). "The Marketing Function." Chapter 1 in *Marketing Handbook*, 2nd ed., Albert Wesley Frey, ed. New York: The Ronald Press Co. 1–33.

Shapiro, Benson P. (1988), "What the Hell Is Market Oriented?" *Harvard Business Review*, 65 (November–December), 119–25.

Spekman, Robert E. (1988), "Strategic Supplier Selection: Understanding Long-Term Buyer Relationships," *Business Horizons*, 31 (July–August), 75–81.

Taylor, Alex, III (1992), "Can GM Remodel Itself?" *Fortune*, 124 (January 13), 26–34.

Thorelli, Hans (1986), "Networks: Between Markets and Hierarchies," *Strategic Management Journal*, 7 (1986), 37–51.

Vaile, R. S., E. T. Grether, and R. Cox (1952), *Marketing in the American Economy*. New York: The Ronald Press Co.

Van de Ven, Andrew (1976), "On the Nature, Formation, and Maintenance of Relations Among Organizations," *Academy of Management Review*, 1 (October), 24–36.

Webster, Frederick E., Jr. (1984), *Industrial Marketing Strategy*, 2nd ed. New York: John Wiley & Sons, Inc.

_____ (1988), "The Rediscovery of the Marketing Concept," *Business Horizons*, 31 (May–June), 29–39.

_____ and Rohit Deshpandé (1990), *Analyzing Corporate Cultures in Approaching the Global Marketplace*, Report No. 90–111 (June). Cambridge, MA: Marketing Science Institute.

Weld, L. D. H. (1917), "Marketing Functions and Mercantile Organization," *American Economic Review* (June), 306–18.

Williamson, Oliver (1975), *Markets and Hierarchies*. Glencoe, IL: The Free Press.

Womack, James P., Daniel T. Jones, and Daniel Roos (1991), *The Machine That Changed the World*, Harper Perennial Edition. New York: Harper Collins Publishers.

FREDERICK E. WEBSTER, JR., is the E. B. Osborn Professor of Marketing and Faculty Director for Executive Education, Amos Tuck School of Business Administration, Dartmouth College. The author thanks his Tuck School colleagues Rohit Deshpandé, Scott Neslin, and Brian Wansink, as well as three anonymous *JM* reviewers, for helpful comments on drafts of this article.

2 Marketing in the Year 2000: An International Perspective

Siew Meng Leong and Chin Tiong Tan

This paper reports the result of a survey of 170 corporate-level executives from the United States, Europe, and Japan regarding the business environment and marketing strategies in the year 2000. Findings indicate a strong consensus concerning the globalization of business activities although market fragmentation may provide opportunities for more customized marketing programs. Marketing's pivotal status in the organization is affirmed and the most important marketing mix elements were found to be product and price. Several cross-regional differences in expectations were also obtained. Implications of the findings are discussed.

I Introduction

Profiling the future of marketing has been a recent focal point of inquiry in the discipline. This interest extends beyond the conventional anticipation of the future environment which has always been a part of the process of strategic marketing planning. The challenge is to seek views of expert, high-level executives and respected scholars to predict future trends and developments in the discipline (Laczniak and Lusch 1986; Laczniak, Lusch, and Udell 1977; Lazer et al. 1989; Lusch, Udell, and Laczniak 1976; Udell, Laczniak, and Lusch 1976).

Clearly, these efforts will assist marketers to develop ideas about the future — the objective of the American Marketing Association's Commission on Marketing in the year 2000. However, one possible shortcoming of these studies is their exclusive focus on the views of American executives and academics to the neglect of foreign marketers. As several authors have commented (Bartels 1983; Garda 1988), the emergence of global markets and international competition demands a 'de-domestication' of research and perspective. The broadening of

Reproduced with permission from *Research in Marketing*, 11 (1992), pp. 195–220.

marketing's horizons to encompass international, comparative, and cross-cultural dimensions is therefore essential.

To this end, the research reported in this paper provides an international perspective to the prediction of trends in the business environment and marketing strategy. Specifically, the views of American, Japanese, and European senior executives are incorporated and comparisons made of expectations regarding marketing in the year 2000. According to Ohmae's (1987) concept of the triad market, North America, Japan, and Europe are the most important and largest markets of today and the future. Moreover, most major multinational corporations are headquartered in these regions.

The organization of the remainder of this paper is as follows. The next section provides the methodology employed in the study and its rationale. Next, the survey results are presented. In particular, executives' perceptions of the business environment in the year 2000 are first depicted. Subsequently, trends in the orientation and status of marketing and its management are delineated. Implications of the research findings are then discussed.

II   Method

A   Sample

A major consideration of research in future trends is that respondents be willing and able to provide the necessary information (cf. Campbell 1995). Past attempts have involved leaders in the futures literature(e.g. Naisbitt 1982; Toffler 1971, 1980). Noted experts within the field including senior advertising and marketing managers (Bogart 1985: Laczniak and Lusch 1986), leading academics (Laczniak, Lusch, and Udell 1977), and chief executive officers (Lazer et al. 1989) have also been approached.

Clearly, respondents in this study should be executives of sufficiently high corporate standing to possess the likely expertise and bird's eye view necessary to provide an informed, integrated perspective of marketing in the year 2000. To ensure sample comparability across countries, such executives are likely to hod job titles of at least manager, vice-president, or their equivalent. Moreover, they should represent multinational corporations with worldwide interests. Finally, they should provide input almost simultaneously so that enhanced comparability is possible within a given time frame (Sekaran 1983).

One opportunity presented itself that enabled these criteria to be satisfied. A global strategies conference was organized in October 1988 by the Singapore Economic Development Board. Top officers of MNCs around the world were invited to Singapore to participate in the three-day seminar. Some 170 executives — 85 from the United States, 47 from Japan, and 38 from 9 European countries (Denmark [3 respondents], Finland [1], France [3], Holland [1], Norway [1], Sweden [4], Switzerland [8], the United Kingdom [8], and West

Germany [9]) participated at the meeting and formed the sample for this study. Table 1 contains the sample profile characteristics.

As Table 1 indicates, the respondents held senior management positions within the 135 organizations they represented. Indeed, the modal organization title held was managing director or general manager. In nearly 96 per cent of

Table 1 Sample characteristics

Characteristic	Percentage
Industry Category	
Electrical/Electronics	25.7
Computers	12.5
Metals/Metal Products	10.6
Chemicals	9.2
Transportation Equipment	4.7
Rubber/Plastics	3.3
Petroleum Refining	2.6
Food/Beverage	2.6
Scientific/Photographic Equipment	2.0
Printing/Publishing	2.0
Pharmaceuticals	1.3
Other Manufacturing	7.9
Services (Financial, Medical, Telecommunication, etc.)	15.9
Size of Organization (Number of Employees)	
Less than 1,000	13.4
1,000 – 9,999	40.1
10,000 – 49,999	24.8
50,000 – 99,999	12.1
100,000 and above	9.6
Sales ($million)	
Less than $100	9.7
$100 – 999	36.6
$1,000 – 4,999	27.6
$5,000 – 9,999	8.9
$10,000 and above	17.2
Organization Title/Rank	
CEO/President/Chairman/Partner	10.1
Managing Director/General Manager	53.2
Director/Deputy Managing Director	11.9
Vice-President	16.0
Manager/Senior Manager	4.8
Other (Financial Controller, Consultant, etc.)	4.0

the cases, respondents were involved in overseeing or were responsible for the corporate planning function of their organization. Executives also hailed from a cross-section of industries out of which 16 per cent were service-oriented and the remainder manufacturing-based. All organizations were large concerns as indicated by average annual sales in 1987 of about $6,000 million with the number of employees averaging approximately 36,000. Sales of American firms represented in the survey averaged $4,452 million compared to $9,375 million and $5,408 million for Japanese and European organizations respectively. More than 90 per cent were well-known companies on the Fortune Industrial, International, and Service 500 lists. All had corporate interests in at least three continents — North America, Europe, and Asia. The number of employees average about 34,200, 20,200, and 64,200 for American, Japanese, and European corporations respectively.

B   Measurement

A survey questionnaire was designed to collect responses from participants regarding their perceptions of marketing in the year 2000. A set of 24 statements was generated based on prior research in the futures and functional literature cited previously. The items related to evaluation of the business situation in the year 2000 followed by perceptions of marketing in general and then each of the components of the marketing mix. This is similar to the approach employed in the Laczniak and Lusch (1986; Laczniak, Lusch, and Udell 1977; Lusch, Udell, and Laczniak 1976; Udell, Laczniak, and Lusch 1976) studies as well as the schema used by Lazer et al. (1989) to categorize the information from interviews of chief executives. Respondents indicated their extent of agreement to statements on five-point Likert-type scales. Following this, respondents provided rankings of various marketing and corporate activities in the year 2000. Sample profile data was also collected.

The survey was administered prior to the start of the conference. The questionnaire was contained in the registration package and participants were requested to complete it before the first session. Only one version of the survey — in English — was prepared. Professional interpreters thoroughly briefed on the contents of the instrument were on hand to render translation assistance if needed. None was found necessary. The questionnaire took about 15 to 20 minutes to complete.

III   Results

Tables 2 through 8 contain the results of the survey.[1] Where ratings are concerned, higher scores reflect stronger agreement. The tables also contain information on the overall per centage of respondents indicating either agreement or strong agreement for all statements. In terms of rankings, lower scores reflect higher rankings. All pairwise comparisons across respondent subsamples were conducted at the .05 level of significance based on mean ratings and rankings. Only statistically significant differences are displayed.

A   Business environment in the year 2000

Two general aspects of the business environment in the year 2000 were explored. First, respondents indicated their extent of agreement to nine statements pertaining to environmental conditions facing marketers in the year 2000 (see Table 2). Next, respondents provided rankings in respect of the importance of six geographical regions for corporate activities in the year 2000 (Table 3).

ENVIRONMENTAL TRENDS

Several significant findings emerge from Table 2. First and foremost, there was almost univocal agreement that companies will become more global in orientation (99 per cent) and consider the world as one large market (82 per cent). Indeed, only about 36 per cent of respondents felt that the world's markets would become more protectionist by that time. Interestingly, American executives agreed more strongly than their Japanese counterparts that increased globalization in production, distribution, and marketing would occur.

Second, there was a somewhat lower consensus regarding government and legal influences in the year 2000. Most respondents (68 per cent) believed that there was a trend towards increased regulation of consumer/marketing practices. In particular, European executives felt more strongly on this point than Japanese respondents. One reason for this may be that the state of business and professional ethics would have become an international issue of debate. Approximately 77 per cent of all respondents concurred with this statement. However, there would not be universal erection of increased legal restrictions. Specifically, almost 63 per cent of respondents thought that several regulated industries would be more deregulated as greater reliance would be placed on competitive forces to protect the public interest. Executives were nearly divided on the corporate cultures of excellent companies of the future vis-à-vis those at present. Nearly 49 per cent held the position that differences in corporate cultures would arise, 17 per cent were neutral and 35 per cent thought excellent companies in the year 2000 would not have different corporate cultures from those of today.

Finally, the potential impact of technology was explored. Only a small minority (9 per cent) anticipated that the pace of technology would slow down and lead to a decrease in corporate research and development budgets. Nearly 79 per cent expected otherwise. Japanese executives, in particular, disagreed more strongly on this issue than their European counterparts. Despite

Table 2   Business environment in the year 2000

Statement	Total % Agree/ Strongly Agree	Overall Mean	U.S. Mean	Japan Mean	Europe Mean	Significant Differences
1. Companies will become more global in their production, distribution, and marketing systems as domestic markets become more saturated.	98.8	4.65	4.69	4.51	4.70	US > J
2. Companies must learn to operate as if the world were one large market — ignoring superficial regional and national differences.	81.8	4.14	4.24	4.00	4.11	NS
3. The state of business and professional ethics will have become an international issue of debate.	76.5	3.88	3.81	3.87	4.05	NS
4. Government legislation regulating consumer/marketing practices will have increased.	67.6	3.60	3.62	3.43	3.76	E > J
5. Several regulated industries will become less regulated as more reliance is placed on competitive forces to protect the public interest.	62.7	3.61	3.60	3.57	3.68	NS
6. Corporate cultures of excellent companies will be very different from those of excellent companies today.	48.8	3.19	3.18	3.15	3.26	NS
7. Natural resources will become less important with technological developments in agriculture, materials science, etc.	47.6	2.88	2.91	2.74	3.00	NS
8. The world's markets will have become more protectionist.	35.9	3.02	3.07	2.94	3.03	NS
9. Corporate research and development budgets will decrease as the pace of technological change slows down.	8.9	2.11	2.12	2.26	1.89	J > E

Table 3 Importance of geographic regions for corporate activities in the year 2000

Region	Mean Importance Ranking				Significant Differences
	Overall	U.S.	Japan	Europe	
North America	1.92	1.81	1.81	2.27	US > E
Asia	1.95	2.01	1.62	2.22	J > US; J > E
Europe	2.42	2.48	2.83	1.78	US > J; E > US; E > J
Latin America	4.51	4.44	4.64	4.49	NS
Middle East	4.66	4.67	4.64	4.65	NS
Africa	5.55	5.53	5.55	5.59	NS

technological advancements, only about 48 per cent of executives believed that natural resources will become less important in the year 2000.

REGIONAL IMPORTANCE

From Table 3, the results showed that North America will be the most important region for corporate activity in the year 2000. However, Asia emerged as a close runner-up with a mean ranking of 1.95 versus 1.92 for North America. Europe was a clear third (2.42). Fourth was Latin America (4.51), with the Middle East fifth (4.66), and Africa (5.55).

Rankings were consistent for the last three regions across the three respondent subsamples. However, the ordering was slightly different in respect of the three most important ones. In particular, only American executives believed North America to be the most important region for corporate activity in the year 2000 followed by Asia and Europe. Indeed, it was the heavy weightage of the American subsample that boosted North America to first place. For Japanese executives, Asia ranked first ahead of North America and Europe. European respondents placed Europe in front of Asia with North America in third place.

Given these differences, it can be expected that several subsample variations in importance rankings be found. Thus, American executives ranked North America higher than their European counterparts while Japanese executives believed Asia as being more important than both American and European executives. Finally, both American and European executives considered Europe as being more important than their Japanese counterparts, with European executives furnishing a statistically significant higher ranking than the Americans as well.

B   Marketing in the year 2000

MARKETING ORIENTATION

Table 4 contains the reactions of executives to six statements pertaining to marketing in general in the year 2000. The highest level of agreement (94 per cent) was reached for the statement regarding companies paying greater attention to consumer needs. Executives also widely anticipated that marketers will work more closely with other functional departments (91 per cent) and that the societal marketing concept will be more widely practiced (88 per cent). However, the Japanese executives felt more strongly that the role of marketing will focus increasingly on enhancing the quality of life in society compared to American executives.

Table 4   Marketing orientation in the year 2000

Statement	Total % Agree/ Strongly Agree	Overall Mean	U.S. Mean	Japan Mean	Europe Mean	Signi- ficant Differ- ences
1. Companies will pay greater attention to consumer needs.	94.1	4.43	4.33	4.49	4.58	NS
2. Marketers will work together more with other functional departments in the firm to achieve total company objectives.	90.6	4.17	4.08	4.23	4.29	NS
3. The role of marketing will increasingly focus on enhancing the quality of life in society.	88.2	4.18	4.01	4.40	4.26	J > US
4. There will be increased fragmentation in the marketplace thus requiring more sophisticated ways of segmenting the market.	77.6	3.91	3.81	3.87	4.16	E > US
5. Marketers will concentrate their efforts more on profits than on sales volume.	59.4	3.61	3.36	3.89	3.80	J > US; E > US

Most interestingly, while executives had pointed to increased globalization, most (78 per cent) also thought that there will be increased market fragmentation requiring more sophisticated segmentation techniques to be employed. Executives were more equivocal on the remaining two issues. Nearly 60 per cent expected sales volume. On this statement, both Japanese and European executives were in firmer agreement than American respondents.

MARKETING'S STATUS

Respondents also furnished their rankings of the importance of various functions in the year 2000 (Table 5, Panel A) , the likelihood of chief executives coming from a particular background (Table 5, Panel B), the importance of the individual marketing mix elements (Table 6), and the importance of eight types of marketing research (Table 7).

Table 5 clearly suggests that marketing will be the key functional area of an enterprise in the year 2000. Its mean ranking of 1.75 heads that of production (2.36) and personnel (2.71). Surprisingly, finance (3.18) was rated least importance despite the current focus on mergers and acquisitions. Both American and European executives attached greater importance to marketing activities than the Japanese. In contrast, American and Japanese executives perceived production as being more important than Europeans. Finally, Japanese and European executives gave personnel greater weight than the Americans.

Table 5 Marketing's status in the year 2000

A. Importance of corporate activities in the year 2000

Activity	Mean Importance Ranking				Significant Differences
	Overall	U.S.	Japan	Europe	
Marketing	1.75	1.56	2.13	1.68	US > J; E > J
Production	2.36	2.30	2.12	2.74	US > E; J > E
Personnel	2.71	2.99	2.36	2.53	J > US; E > US
Finance	3.18	3.16	3.30	3.06	NS

B. CEO background in the year 2000

Background	Mean Likelihood Ranking				Significant Differences
	Overall	U.S.	Japan	Europe	
Marketing	1.82	1.67	2.13	1.78	US > J
Finance	3.18	3.11	3.78	2.58	US > J; E > J
Engineering	3.31	3.27	3.00	3.81	J > E
Production	3.81	3.68	3.91	3.97	NS
Computer Science	5.32	5.12	5.32	5.75	NS
Personnel	6.04	6.71	4.89	6.03	J > US; E > US; J > E
Accounting/Taxation	6.19	6.21	6.34	5.97	NS
Legal	6.24	6.17	6.53	6.03	NS

Table 6   Importance of marketing mix elements in the year 2000

Element	Mean Ranking				Significant Differences
	Overall	U.S.	Japan	Europe	
Product	1.37	1.38	1.32	1.42	NS
Price	2.72	2.74	2.70	2.68	NS
Distribution	2.93	2.90	3.06	2.84	NS
Promotion	3.01	3.05	2.91	3.05	NS

Table 7   Importance of types of marketing research in the year 2000

Element	Mean Ranking				Significant Differences
	Overall	U.S.	Japan	Europe	
Product	2.70	2.38	2.67	3.37	US > E
Consumer Behavior	2.80	3.26	2.43	2.29	J > US; E > US
Market Intelligence	3.38	3.26	3.48	3.50	NS
Competitive Behavior	4.30	4.25	4.50	4.18	NS
Pricing	4.98	4.95	4.77	5.29	NS
Segmentation	5.55	5.62	5.67	5.26	NS
Channels	6.08	6.15	6.17	5.82	NS
Advertising	6.19	6.05	6.07	6.61	NS

Confirmatory evidence of marketing's status as the prime function of a commercial enterprise is that chief executive officers in the year 2000 are ranked as being most likely to have a marketing background (mean ranking 1.82). Significantly, while several differences in rank ordering across nationalities appeared, none concerned marketing, which American, Japanese, and European respondents all considered as the background CEOs in the year 2000 were most likely to have.

However, American executives accorded a higher mean ranking to marketing than Japanese respondents. Overall, marketing was followed by finance, engineering, and production. Computer science, personnel, accounting/ taxation, and law occupied the lower half of the rankings.

STATUS OF THE 4PS

Respondents' ranking of the relative status of the marketing mix components (see Table 6) indicates that product was overall most important followed by price, distribution, and promotion. No statistically significant differences in mean rankings were obtained across the three sub-samples. Indeed, except for the

Japanese executives who perceived promotion to be slightly more important than distribution, the rank ordering was consistent across respondents.

IMPORTANCE OF TYPES OF MARKETING RESEARCH

Of the eight types of marketing research covered in the survey, product research ranked as overall most important. This was followed by consumer research, market intelligence gathering, competitive behavior, pricing, segmentation, channels, and advertising research (see Table 7). American respondents furnished a higher ranking for product research than Europeans, while both Japanese and European respondents considered consumer research as being more important than American executives. No statistically significant differences in mean importance rankings were found for the other six types of marketing research.

C Marketing mix in the year 2000

Table 8 (Panels A through D) contain respondents' evaluation of product, pricing, promotion, and distribution management respectively in the year 2000.

PRODUCT

Consistent with earlier results reported, 93 per cent of the respondents agreed that new product development will assume even greater importance in the firm. Most (82 per cent) also felt that global brands will become more prominent in the market place. In this connection, both American and European executives agreed more strongly than their Japanese counterparts. There was also general consensus (75 per cent agreement) that post-purchase services would become the new bases for competition. However, only 57 per cent of respondents thought that basic product quality will become more important than styling, packaging, and other secondary product features, albeit Japanese executives expressed stronger agreement than European respondents on this issue. Finally, only 17 per cent of respondents believed that there will be an increased emphasis on the marketing of manufactured goods rather than services. Japanese executives felt more strongly about this trend than either American or European respondents.

PRICING

No statistically significant differences in perception were found across the three respondents subsamples with regard to pricing practices in the year 2000. The highest level of agreement (81 per cent) was found in respect of the need for more creative pricing policies and a shift from traditional cost-based practices. An almost equivalent level of concurrence (80 per cent) was found for the use

Table 8 Marketing mix in the year 2000

Statement	Total % Agree/ Strongly Agree	Overall Mean	U.S. Mean	Japan Mean	Europe Mean	Significant Differences
A. Product management in the year 2000						
1. New product development will assume even greater importance in the firm.	93.0	4.23	4.16	4.34	4.24	NS
2. Global brands will become more prominent in the marketplace.	82.3	3.98	4.06	3.74	4.08	US > J; E > J
3. Post-purchase services (e.g., maintenance, warranties, etc.) will become the new bases for product competition.	74.7	3.88	3.80	3.91	4.03	NS
4. Basic product quality will become more important than styling, packaging, and other secondary features.	57.0	3.51	3.49	3.70	3.32	J > E
5. There will be increased emphasis on the marketing of manufactured goods rather than on services.	17.1	2.71	2.62	3.02	2.53	J > US; J > E
B. Pricing in the year 2000						
1. Companies will have to become more creative in their pricing policies, shifting from traditional cost-based pricing.	80.6	3.90	3.91	3.83	3.97	NS
2. Pricing strategies to achieve long-term corporate objectives rather than short-term gains will be widely used.	79.4	3.83	3.78	3.96	3.79	NS
3. Differential cost structures of companies in different countries producing similar products will cause greater problems in price setting.	5.12	3.35	3.40	3.43	3.16	NS
4. Dumping and other predatory pricing practices will become more common.	23.0	2.84	2.85	2.68	3.00	NS
5. There will be increased governmental rules and regulations on pricing practices.	17.7	2.64	2.72	2.51	2.61	NS

Table 8 (cont'd)

Statement	Total % Agree/ Strongly Agree	Overall Mean	U.S. Mean	Japan Mean	Europe Mean	Significant Differences
C. Promotional strategies in the year 2000						
1. Global promotional activities (e.g., international trade shows and exhibitions) will be more widely used.	78.1	3.85	3.75	4.11	3.74	J > US; J > E
2. Sales management and personal selling will increase in importance.	72.2	3.70	3.58	3.89	3.71	J > US
3. The trend towards giant global advertising agencies will continue.	70.0	3.69	3.71	3.77	3.55	NS
4. Broadcast media advertising (e.g., TV and radio) will be more important than print media advertising (e.g., newspapers and magazines).	63.9	3.60	3.55	3.68	3.61	NS
5. Advertising themes will become more standardized around the world.	47.4	3.25	3.27	3.34	3.11	NS
D. Distribution channels in the year 2000						
1. Companies will increasingly employ different distribution methods to reach different markets.	87.0	3.98	3.96	3.91	4.08	NS
2. The length of marketing channels will be shortened as less reliance is placed on traditional intermediaries (e.g., wholesalers, retailers and brokers).	74.0	3.76	3.74	3.81	3.74	NS
3. There will be an increased reliance on global rather than domestic distribution systems.	72.2	3.77	3.89	3.79	3.47	US > E
4. Direct marketing and telemarketing will increasingly replace traditional distribution and promotional methods.	68.7	3.69	3.68	3.68	3.71	NS
5. There will be continued growth in the use of vertical integrated marketing systems (e.g., franchising, single ownership of channels).	53.9	3.56	3.62	3.51	3.47	NS

of pricing strategies to focus on achieving long-term rather than short-term corporate goals. Respondents were more equivocal with regard to the effects of differential cost structures. About 51 per cent agreed that such structures of companies operating in different countries producing similar products will aggravate problems in price setting, while 22 per cent either disagreed or strongly disagreed. Significantly, only 23 per cent of respondents thought that dumping and other predatory pricing practices would be more prevalent in the year 2000. This sentiment tallies with the earlier finding indicating protectionist tendencies would not be prevalent. Finally, only about 18 per cent of respondents believed that there will be increased governmental control on pricing practices.

PROMOTION

The trend toward globalization received qualified support in the case of promotion strategies in the year 2000. Some 78 per cent of respondents agreed with the statement that global promotional activities (e.g., international trade shows and exhibitions) will be more widely employed. Japanese executives tended to concur more strongly than American and European executives on this point. The present trend towards giant global advertising agencies is also likely to continue (70 per cent agreement). However, only 47 per cent of respondents felt that there would be more use of standardized advertising themes worldwide. In terms of advertising media, nearly 64 per cent of respondents felt that broadcast media (e.g., TV and radio) would be more important than print media (e.g., newspapers and magazines). No subsamples differences were found on these three items. Last, some 72 per cent of respondents agreed that sales management and personal selling will increase in importance in the year 2000. Japanese executives believed this more strongly than their American counterparts.

DISTRIBUTION

The use of multiple channels for different target markets was strongly affirmed given an 87 per cent overall agreement rate. The use of more direct channels is also evident given that 69 per cent of respondents who thought that direct and telemarketing will increasingly replace traditional methods of distribution and promotion. Moreover, 74 per cent of respondents felt that the length of marketing channels will be shorter as less reliance is placed on traditional intermediaries. Less univocal support (54 per cent) was obtained for the statement that there will be continued growth of vertical marketing systems in the year 2000. However, most (72 per cent) respondents believed that more emphasis would be placed on global rather than domestic distribution systems. American executives felt more strongly on this issue than European respondents.

IV Discussion

Several implications for the future of marketing and marketing strategy will now be discussed. They center on the major findings of the study that (1) there will be greater globalization of business activity, (2) companies will become more socially responsible and marketing oriented, (3) product and price will become more important to successful marketing management although promotion and distribution practices will also witness change, and (4) differences across American, European, and Japanese executives exist in predicting particular trends in the business environment and in marketing strategy. These subsample differences will be incorporated in the discussion of the other implications.

A Globalization implications

Ever since the publication of Levitt's (1983) provocative thesis, many scholars have debated the nature of global marketing and its associated connotation of offering globally standardized products (see, e.g., Chakravarthy and Perlmutter 1985; Daniels 1987; Martenson 1978; Rau and Preble 1987; Simmonds 1985). The findings of our survey provide qualified support for Levitt's position. Executives from the three regions appear to endorse his position that companies must operate "as if the world were one large market — ignoring superficial regional and national differences" (1983, p. 92). In addition, they anticipated that global brands will become more prominent in the market place, that international trade shows and exhibitions will be more widely used, that more giant global advertising agencies will be established, and that greater reliance would be placed on global rather than domestic distribution systems.

Further integration of the world's economy also appears to contribute towards global marketing practices. Counter to the present tendency against free trade (Ohmae 1987), executives did not believe that the world's market would become more protectionist (cf. Lazer et al. 1989). Deregulation of certain industries, the saturation of domestic markets, and the international concern over the state of business and professional ethics will help create a more globalized competitive environment. They will compel companies to become more global in their operations and philosophy.

Finally, technological developments do not appear to be slowing down. Such advances are likely to affect global communication patterns. The pervasive effects of broadcast media advertising will be accentuated and the use of direct and telemarketing will receive added impetus from advances in information technology and telecommunications. The notion of a "global village" seems very plausible by the year 2000. Already, interactive television with home shopping facilities is being test marketed (*Advertising Age* 1989).

Levitt (1983, p. 94) argues that "technology has homogenized the globe. Even small local segments have their global equivalents everywhere and become subject to global competition." However, Ohmae (1987) asserts that as information access becomes important in modern societies, it fragments markets into individualized segments while the overall needs of the world population become increasingly homogeneous. Executives surveyed in this study believed that such market fragmentation would necessitate the development of more sophisticated bases of segmentation. This is in accord with the view that traditional methods of international segmentation founded on nationality and ethnicity are outmoded (Cunningham and Green 1984; Levitt 1983). An example of the new generation of segmentation approaches may be Kale and Sudharshan's (1987) method of strategically equivalent segmentation which recognizes and aggregates consumers who may cross national boundaries but nevertheless would respond similarly to a firm's marketing mix.

Despite these expectations, globalization may not equally affect all aspects of marketing. In particular, less than half of executives surveyed were of the opinion that advertising themes would become more standardized worldwide in the year 2000. Ironically, it was in the area of advertising which initially spawned the customization-standardization debate in marketing practices (Ryans 1969). Clearly, executives were cognizant of differences in language, media, and government regulations (cf. *The New York Times* November 13, 1985). Nonetheless, the continued amalgamation of advertising agencies worldwide points to the creation of holding companies for groups of merged agencies. These promise greater efficiency, more specialization, enhanced coordination of international campaigns, and increased global service (Terpstra 1987; Wells, Burnett, and Moriarty 1989).

Last, certain regional differences in expectations also emerged in respect of specific aspects of the globalization trend. Most noteworthy was the finding that American executives expressed stronger agreement that globalization of production, distribution, and marketing would occur than their Japanese counterparts. American executives also expected more global distribution systems to emerge than their European counterparts. However, Japanese more than American and European executives anticipated increased global promotional activities such as trade shows and exhibitions. Overall, the findings indicate that American enterprise is losing its alleged insularity and becoming more international in marketing orientation.

On importance of geographical regions for corporate activities, the results generally support the notion of a World Triad advanced by Ohmae (1987). The most important regions anticipated by executives in the year 2000 were North America, Europe, and Asia. The other three areas surveyed lagged far behind these regions in corporate importance. Clearly, our findings suggest that economic progress would continue to come from these three regions in the future.

Interestingly, however, differences emerged when the sample was decomposed for analysis. A regional bias seemed evident to the extent that executives from each region rated their own as being the most important for their corporate activities in the year 2000. Hence, it may be implied that while companies will become more global in outlook, their principal focus would still be within their own regions. One plausible reason for this may be that executives believed their corporations' primary operating base and major sphere of strategic influence resides within their region.

The findings also show that executives were most divergent in respect of their evaluation of Europe's importance for their corporations in the year 2000. Statistically significant differences in rankings emerged between European and American respondents as well as between American and Japanese respondents. It seems that the establishment of a unified market in 1992 provides most opportunities for European corporations although American firms will also be focusing their efforts in this continent (Tulley 1988). It would appear that the Japanese would prefer to accord Asia a higher priority in the year 2000. European, and particularly American, executives apparently perceived fewer opportunities in Asia-Pacific nations despite their current economic ascendency (Kraar 1988).

B Implications for corporate outlook

Executives surveyed were divided over the nature of corporate cultures that will be effective in the year 2000. Some anticipated changes whereas others did not. This may be attributed to the diverse industry backgrounds of respondents. However, two aspects appear to meet with more univocal acceptance. First, companies will appear to be more societally conscious, and second, there will be greater emphasis placed on marketing in the year 2000. Two expected environmental trends — one legislative and the other ethical — seem to contribute to greater corporate social responsibility in the year 2000. In particular, executives believed that there will be increased regulation over consumer and marketing practices. Curiously, European more than Japanese respondents thought this would be the case — a finding contrary to the expectations of free trade with the opening up of a unified European market in 1992. Second, consistent with other results (Lazer et al. 1989), ethical issues will assume greater proportions internationally. This may encourage companies to embrace the societal marketing concept more readily.

Executives fully endorsed marketing's greater role in the corporation in the year 2000. This is congruent with the results of previous surveys using strictly American samples (Laczniak and Lusch 1986; Yeskey and Burnett 1986). Marketing ranked highest both in terms of corporate importance and likelihood of chief executive officer background. While executives of all three regions considered marketing to have first priority, American executives accorded it higher status than their Japanese counterparts. This may not be too surprising given that "Japanese companies operate almost entirely without marketing departments or market research of the kind so prevalent in the West" (Levitt 1983, p. 99). Indeed, for Japanese executives to opine their CEOs of the future are most likely to come from a marketing (rather than technical) background represents a fundamental shift in philosophy.

Further evidence of this direction is the increased attention to be paid to consumer needs and the high ranking of consumer research — second only to product research — found in the survey. The latter result contrasts with the little attention CEOs in the Lazer et al. (1989) study paid to consumer behavior. It appears that consumers of the future will become even more sophisticated, demanding, and conscious of their rights (McKenna 1988) and thus will have to be studied closely.

Moreover, executives believed that close coordination will be needed between marketing and other organizational functions. This suggests that a greater corporate market orientation will be achieved in the year 2000. Such inter-functional interaction should bring about a total customer focus and sharing of information on important buying influences across departments (Shapiro 1988). As such, respondents did not appear to share Kotler's (1986) view that the responsibilities of nonmarketing executives may be impinged upon by marketers exercising their power to accomplish corporate objectives. Instead, there was a strong preference for cooperation and working together between marketing and other functional areas in the year 2000.

One possible outcome of this more intimate interfacing may be the shift from the goal of market share dominance to one of maximizing total corporate profitability. Nearly 60 per cent of respondents believed that efforts will be concentrated towards profits rather than sales. Surprisingly, it was the Japanese who felt most strongly about this — a finding not intuitively obvious given their well-known approach of market penetration. European executives also agreed more firmly than their American counterparts on this issue, perhaps reflecting the latter's emphasis on short-run results.

C Marketing management implications

Executives considered product and price to be the more important components of marketing strategy. This is consistent with Levitt's (1983) view that effective world competitors must offer high-quality products at low cost. In particular, they felt that new product development will be vital and accorded product research first priority among the eight research areas surveyed. This finding is similar to those of Lazer et al. (1989) and Lusch and Laczniak (1986). This may be attributable to the escalation of global competition and acceleration in technological advancements in the year 2000. It is consistent with expectations of a growing internationalization of product development and further shortening of product life cycles (Terpstra 1987).

Executives provided mixed views on the issue of intrinsic improvements in product quality over secondary features such as styling and packaging. Japanese respondents expressed stronger agreement on this issue than European executives which may reflect their firmer belief that technology will have a greater impact on businesses in the year 2000. Only a handful of executives surveyed felt that manufactured goods would be more important than services. This suggests that the growth in the service sector will continue globally. Canton (1984) has argued that manufacturers explore opportunities in the service economy by capitalizing on their existing assets, resources, and knowledge. To the extent that 84 per cent of executives surveyed were manufacturing-based, the possibility that the new competition will be offering enhanced post-purchase services appears to be acknowledged, particularly among the Europeans and Americans (cf. Laczniak and Lusch 1986).

Pricing would need to be more creative as global production may complicate traditional cost-based approaches. Executives felt that pricing would be used to achieve more strategic long-run corporate objectives rather than as a short-term tactical weapon. These findings are in accord with those of Lazer et al. (1989) who argue that longer time frames and different bases may be used to establish cost/price relationships for many products. To the extent that Japanese more than American executives in this survey believed that efforts be focused on profit rather than sales goals, it appears that they have a longer pricing horizon than their American counterparts.

Executives surveyed were optimistic that there would be no increases in government controls over pricing and that dumping and other predatory pricing practices would not increase. This is in line with their expectations of there being no increased pressure on protectionist policies. Perhaps executives realize that in the long run, low-cost producers can overcome such policies regardless of where their manufacturing bases are located (Levitt 1983).

Beyond the impact of global advertising and sales promotion activities discussed earlier, executives believed that personal selling and sales force management will be more important in the year 2000. This may be because of their intelligence gathering capability as well as problem solving role given the need to get closer to customers and provide a total package of services to them (cf. Lazer et al. 1989). Complex product innovations also need to be effectively communicated to customers — a task well suited to the sales force of tomorrow. Technological developments (e.g., international 800 telephone numbers and video sales presentations) may enhance sales force effectiveness by enabling closer customer contact and allowing for uniformly high quality of presentations in different markets (Terpstra 1987). Interestingly, it may be the Japanese who lead the way in this direction. The Japanese executives surveyed concurred more strongly than their American counterparts regarding the importance of the sales function.

Finally, distribution will also appear to be going through a metamorphosis in the year 2000. Reliance will be placed on multiple channels to more precisely match the requirements and characteristics of different market segments. There will also be increased emphasis on improving productivity via direct and shorter marketing channels. Once again, developments in telecommunication and transportation technology may facilitate this trend. Customer preference for quick delivery (e.g., fresh food) may also impel the establishment of shorter channels of distribution (Lazer et al. 1989).

However, respondents were more equivocal regarding the growth of vertical marketing systems. Clearly, VMSs afford greater manufacturer control in distribution. Yet, they also bring responsibilities, commitment, and attendant risks (Ahmed 1977). These internalized channel configurations were favored in the 1970s for reaching foreign markets as firms largely preferred to act alone rather than rely on joint ventures and licensing arrangements (Terpstra 1987). With the recent successes of strategic alliances involving companies of different nationalities (Kotler 1986), managers are likely to be more confident of employing alternative distribution arrangements in the year 2000. The belief that a wider variety of channels will become evident as global distribution systems evolve implies a probable increase in using international cooperative ventures, licensing agreements, management contracts, and consortia for market entry and service arrangements. That European executives agree somewhat less strongly than their American counterparts regarding the globalization of the distribution function may be due to the planned establishment of a free market in Europe in 1992. As such, their focus may be slightly more regional given the abundant opportunities afforded by a truly European Common Market.

V   Conclusion

Long-range forecasting is generally a hazardous task. Respondents are prone to employ current trends as overweighted anchors to predict future developments. The executives surveyed in our study do envisage several contemporary environmental and marketing directions to prevail in the year 2000. Most notable among these is the continued globalization of the world's economy as well as many aspects of the marketing mix. Yet, they also foresee that certain future developments (e.g., less protectionism, fewer charges of predatory pricing practices) that run counter to present tendencies. The strong consensus on many issues by executives of such diverse national and industrial backgrounds also engenders confidence in the predictions rendered.

To conclude on an optimistic note, marketers have been known to be highly critical of themselves and the profession to which they belong. The enhanced role of marketing as predicted by this international sample of senior-level executives augurs well for the discipline and its practitioners. Perhaps this is the time to discard self-flagellation tendencies and work towards achieving marketing's status as the window to the world.

Acknowledgements

Siew Meng Leong and Chin Tiong Tan are Senior Lecturer and Associate Professor respectively in the Department of Marketing, National University of Singapore. The authors thank Jeannie Teoh for her research assistance, William Stoever and Joseph Cote for their helpful comments, and the Singapore Economic Development Board for their cooperation in data collection. This research was funded by a grant from the National University of Singapore to the second author.

NOTE

1. The possible problem of multiple responses from the same organization over-representing a particular corporate point of view was investigated by re-running the analysis based on the responses of the most senior-level respondent from each organization. The results yielded no statistically significant differences in mean ratings and rankings for the statements studied.

REFERENCES

Advertising Age. (1989). "Ten Categories to Watch in 1989." 60 (January 2), 14.

Ahmed, A.A. (1977). "Channel Control in International Markets." *European Journal of Marketing*, 11 (4), 327–336.

Bartels, R. (1983). "Is Marketing Defaulting Its Responsibilities?" *Journal of Marketing*, 49 (Fall), 32–35.

Bogart, L. (1985). "War of the Words: Advertising in the Year 2010." *Across the Board*, 22 (January), 21–28.

Campbell, D.T. (1955). "The Informant in Quantitative Research." *American Journal of Sociology*, 60, 339–342.

Canton, I.D. (1984). "Learning to Love the Service Economy." *Harvard Business Review*, 62 (May–June), 89–97.

Chakravarthy, B.S. and H.V. Perlmutter. (1985). "Strategic Planning for a Global Business." *Columbia Journal of World Business*, 18 (Summer), 3–10.

Cunningham, W. and R. Green. (1984). "From the Editor." *Journal of Marketing*, 48 (Winter), 9–10.

Daniels, J.D. (1987). "Bridging National and Global Marketing Strategies through Regional Operations." *International Marketing Review*, 4 (Autumn), 29–44.

Garda, R.A. (1988). "Comment." *Journal of Marketing*, 52 (October), 32–41.

Kale, S.H. and S. Sudharshan. (1987). "A Strategic Approach to International Segmentation," *International Marketing Review*, 4 (Summer), 60–70.

Kotler, P. (1986). "Megamarketing." *Harvard Business Review*, 64 (March–April), 117–124.

Kraar, L. (1988). "The New Powers of Asia." *Fortune*, International Edition, 117 (March 28) 40–46.

Laczniak, G.R. and R.F. Lusch. (1986). "Environment and Strategy in 1995: A Survey of High-Level Executives." *Journal of Consumer Marketing*, 3 (Spring), 27–45.

———, R.F. Lusch, and J.G. Udell. (1977). "Marketing in 1985: A View From the Ivory Tower." *Journal of Marketing*, 41 (October), 47–56.

Lazer, W., P.A. LaBarbera, J. MacLachlan, and A.E. Smith. (1989). "Moving Marketing Plans Toward The Year 2000." working paper, College of Business, Florida Atlantic University.

Levitt, T. (1983). "The Globalization of Markets." *Harvard Business Review*, 61 (May–June), 92–102.

Lusch, R.F., J.G. Udell, and G.R. Laczniak. (1976). "The Future of Marketing Strategy." *Business Horizons*, 19 (December), 65–64.

Martenson, R. (1987). "Is Standardization of Marketing Feasible in Culture-Bound Industries? A European Case Study." *International Marketing Review*, 4 (Autumn), 7–17.

McKenna, R. (1988). "Marketing in an Age of Diversity." *Harvard Business Review*, 66 (September–October), 88–95.

Naisbitt, J. (1982). *Megatrends: Ten New Directions Transforming Our Lives*, New York: Warner Books.

The New York Times. (1985). "Global Marketing Debated." *Advertising Column*, (November 13).

Ohmae, K. (1987). "The Triad World View." *Journal of Business Strategy*, 7 (Spring), 8–19.

Rau, P. and J.F. Preble. (1987). "Standardization of Marketing Strategy by Multinationals." *International Marketing Review*, 4 (Autumn), 18–28.

Ryans, J.K., Jr. (1969). "Is It Too Soon To Put A Tiger in Every Tank?" *Columbia Journal of World Business*, 4 (March–April), 69–75.

Sekaran, U. (1983). "Methodological and Theoretical Issues and Advancements in Cross-Cultural Research." *Journal of International Business Studies*, 14 (Fall), 61–74.

Shapiro, B.P. (1988). "What the Hell is 'Market Oriented'?" *Harvard Business Review*, 66 (November–December), 119–125.

Simmonds, K. (1985). "Global Strategy: Achieving the Geocentric Ideal." *International Marketing Review*, 2 (Spring), 8–17.

Terpstra, V. (1987). "The Evolution of International Marketing." *International Marketing Review*, 4 (Summer), 47–59.

Toffler, A. (1971). *Future Shock*, NY: Bantam Books.

———, (1980). *The Third Wave*, NY: William Morrow and Co.

Tulley, S. (1988). "Europe Gets Ready for 1992." *Fortune*, International Edition, 117 (February), 64–68.

Udell, J.G., G.R. Laczniak, and R.F. Lusch. (1976). "The Business Environment of 1985." *Business Horizons*, 19 (June), 45–54.

Wells, W., J. Burnett, and S. Moriarty. (1989). *Advertising : Principles and Practice*, Englewood Cliffs, New Jersey: Prentice-Hall.

Yesky, D.P. and C.D. Burnett. (1986). "A Marketing Outlook for U.S. Businesses." *Journal of Business Strategy*, 7 (Fall), 5–12.

3 The Benefits of "Guanxi" The Value of Relationships in Developing the Chinese Market (B) relevance

Howard Davies, Thomas K. P. Leung,
Sherriff T. K. Luk, and Yiu-hing Wong

The early 1990s have seen a radical change in China's position as a market, giving a new urgency to the need to address that market effectively. It has long been recognized that doing business in China is particularly difficult and that a key difference between Chinese and Western business practices lies in the relative importance of personal relationships ("guanxi") in the former, as opposed to the specification and enforcement of contracts in the latter. However, previous studies of this issue have tended to focus on the perceptions of Western executives, and they have not identified in any detail the nature of the benefits that accrue to the establishment of guanxi or their relative importance. This study uses data gathered from Hongkong Chinese executives experienced in Chinese business practices in order to identify their perceptions of the nature of the benefits that arise from guanxi and their relative importance. The results provide a ranking of benefits and suggest that there is an underlying structure of four factors, which may be characterized as procurement, information, bureaucracy, and transaction-smoothing.

Introduction

It is now a commonplace to note that the People's Republic of China (PRC) is becoming a major economic power, that its population makes up approximately one-fifth of the world's consumers, and that its GNP might overtake that of the United States within a decade or so [15].

Nevertheless, relatively little attention has been paid to China as a market, or to the requirements for effective market entry and exploitation, perhaps because the country has been seen largely as a source of low-cost labor and land from which to source production destined for elsewhere. It is now clear that the situation changed significantly in the course of 1992 and 1993 for a number of

Reproduced with permission from *Industrial Marketing Management*, 24 (1992), pp. 207–214.

reasons. First, paramount leader Deng Xiaoping made a highly publicized tour of rapidly growing areas in South China, giving his explicit support to the pace and direction of change in those areas and encouraging other parts of the country to emulate their success. Secondly, the Fourteenth Party Congress, held in October 1992, confirmed that the commitment to market-based reform would be maintained, thereby increasing confidence that rapid growth rates could be continued. Thirdly, it became clear that the reported figures for national income, and hence the size of the Chinese market, are almost certainly quite substantial underestimates. Fourthly, it has been shown in the course of 1993 and 1994 that the program of austerity measures put in place to curb "overheating" has not had the effect of reducing growth and may even have been abandoned.

Finally, there have been some spectacular demonstrations of the existence of a large consumer market. When McKinsey estimates that the number of relatively "affluent" Chinese consumers is presently 60 million and will rise to more than 200 million by 2000 [19], when the Beijing branch of McDonald's is reported to be one of the largest and most profitable in the world, and when Avon has 15,000 salesladies in Guangdong province alone, the time has come to take China very seriously.

1992 to 1994, therefore, has been a watershed in which it was realized that the Chinese domestic market is already much larger than has been appreciated, and it was confirmed that its recent growth would not be reversed by major changes in policy.

At the same time, the government of the PRC has made further moves to reduce controls on the economy and to open the vast domestic market to foreign competition. Price controls have been relaxed for many kinds of raw material and commodities, customs duties have been reduced for more than 200 types of consumer and industrial goods, and the administrative organs of the state have been restructured in an attempt to expedite the process of business negotiation. Sino-foreign joint ventures and wholly owned foreign enterprises have been actively promoted, and the attempt to accommodate the GATT requirements for membership have led to the liberalization of imports and the removal of further structural constraints. Just as the Chinese market has become larger, so have the formal barriers to business been lowered.

The difficulty of doing business in China

Despite the abundant opportunities now presented by the China market, the evidence suggests that doing business in China can be more difficult than is anticipated by many foreign businessmen. Studies report that foreign companies commonly experience apprehension and discouragement while conducting business with their Chinese counterparts [12]. Many frontline practitioners have complained that creating joint ventures in China is more complex and timeconsuming than is necessary [4]. Foreign companies are often dismayed by the lengthy negotiation process and, in particular, by bureaucratic delays, the difficulty of identifying the real decision-maker in Chinese business dealings [8], and by the number of prenegotiation contacts that are required [14]. Philip Stevenson, Business Development Manager of the Australian firm Bundy Tubing, for example, has estimated that completing the paperwork alone for their joint venture took 18 months of effort [20].

Western management scholars have interpreted this experience in two different ways. One approach has been to characterize the negotiation process in China as slow and inefficient and to attribute that inefficiency to structural constraints, poor administration, management incompetence, ideological rigidities, and policy factors [7, 8, 10]. An alternative approach [2] is to recognize that the establishment of personalized trust through networks is particularly crucial to the conduct of business in China. The daunting outcomes experienced by Western businesspeople arise from the need for investment in network-building, after which the transacting process may be quite efficient. As Thorelli [17] puts it:

> in Oriental cultures, trust is a vital supplement to contractual arrangements; it may even take their place. In precontractual contexts the establishment of trust frequently takes more time than Western executives are used to investing.

Networks and the phenomenon of guanxi

A network may be described [6] as:

> a model, or a metaphor which describes a number, usually a large number, of entities that are connected. In the case of industrial . . . networks the entities are actors involved in the economic processes that convert resources to finished goods and services for consumption by end users whether they be individuals or organizations.

Western marketing literature has increasingly seen the management of networks as an important aspect of strategic behavior and the networking paradigm as a "means of understanding the totality of relationships amongst firms engaged in production, distribution, and the use of goods and services" [1]. There is a belief that networking can enhance a company's competitive position and also bridge the gap between businesspeople of different nations and cultures, stimulating trade that might not otherwise take place at all [16]. Networks enhance competitive advantage by providing access to the resources of other network members, and are particularly important in respect of market entry, where their strategic role has been well-documented.

Most of the networking literature is relatively recent and has been largely concerned with the Western business context. However, that is somewhat ironic because history suggests that networks, translated as guanxi, have been the dominant form of transactional governance in China since long before the concept was taken up by Western theorists.

How-to guides to doing business in China [11] commonly refer to the importance of guanxi (best briefly translated as "personal connections/ relationships") in Chinese business. An experienced American General Manager of a joint venture packaging company in Nanjing [13] observes that the most common contrast between Western and Chinese management practice lies in the emphasis placed on written contracts and procedures in the former, compared with personal relationships in the latter. Whereas that statement is adequate as a brief description of the differences between the two systems, contracts of language and culture mean that it is a poor means to convey the full meaning and ubiquity of the concept of guanxi.

The same American executive provides perhaps the best description [for Westerners] to date of the phenomenon, in the following passage [13]:

To Chinese managers, guanxi is laden with powerful implications. To "la guanxi" (literally to "pull" guanxi) means to get on the good side of someone, to store political capital with them, and carries no negative overtones. To "gua guanxi" (literally to "work on" guanxi) means roughly the same but with a more general, less intensive feeling and usually carries negative overtones. "Meiyou guanxi" ("without" guanxi) has become an idiom meaning "it doesn't matter." "Guanxi gao jiang" (guanxi made ruined) means the relationship has gone bad, usually because of a lack of flexibility of those involved. "Lisun guanxi" ("straighten out" guanxi) means to put a guanxi back into proper or normal order, often after a period of difficulty or awkwardness. "You guanxi" ("to have" guanxi) [which is utterly unlike the American idiom "to have a relationship"], means to have access to needed influence. "Youde shi guanxi" ("what one does have" or "the one thing one does have" is guanxi), is sometimes negative, meaning that one has all the guanxi one needs, but something else essential is lacking. "Guanxi wang" ("guanxi net") means the whole network of guanxi through which influence is brokered. "Guanxi hu" ("guanxi family") means a person, organization, even government department, occupying a focal point in one's guanxi network.

Guanxi seems to be the lifeblood of the Chinese business community, extending into politics and society. Without guanxi one simply cannot get anything done. Or, what Western managers soon find, things can be done without guanxi if one invests enormous personal energy, is willing to offend even close friends and trusted associates, and is prepared to see such Pyrrhic victories melt away like snow on a hot day while one is off on a business trip or home leave. On the other hand, with guanxi anything seems possible.

From an analytical point of view, the concept of networking is well-suited to capture some of the key features of guanxi as described here. In particular, it emphasizes that networks are not discrete events in time, concerning self-liquidating transactions, but are continuous relationships ("relational contracting" in economic analysis [18]). That continuity requires that "activities undertaken by the parties in a relationship cannot be completed without the active and reciprocal involvement of both parties" [9]. The Western concept of networking, therefore, also included the notion of continuing reciprocal obligation that is so firmly inherent in the Chinese concept of guanxi. At the same time it should be appreciated that guanxi relates to personal, not corporate, relations and that the exchanges which take place amongst members of the guanxi network are not solely commercial, but also social, involving the exchange of favors ("renqing") and the giving of face ("mianzi") or social status. Such exchanges need to be handled with sensitivity as Western businessmen are in danger of overemphasizing the gift-giving and winning-and-dining components of a guanxi relationship, thereby coming dangerously close to crass bribery or to being perceived as "meat and wine friends," which is a Chinese metaphor for mistrust.

Identifying the benefits of guanxi

Whereas the importance of guanxi is well-established, the research to date has tended to focus on establishing its perceived importance, describing it, analyzing its origins and ethics, and commenting on its implications for the efficiency of the Chinese economic system [5]. The existing literature has also tended to draw on the perception of Western executives [3], as opposed to the Chinese. None of the previous research has attempted to identify the specific benefits that arise from the development of guanxi, as seen by those on the inside or the areas of activity in which it is most important. This article extends our knowledge in this area by examining the perceptions of Hongkong Chinese executives with respect to the benefits that may be secured from the development and utilization of networks.

Empirical work

The empirical work for this study is based upon a survey carried out in 1992 as part of an International Marketing course run by two of the authors. As part of the classwork, the students (who were all practising managers) were required to develop an appropriate survey instrument, under the supervision of the authors, and then to administer a mail survey to a population consisting of Hongkong Chinese executives having experience in Chinese business practices.

The survey took the form of a questionnaire (in English and Chinese), which was mailed to 1,000 Hongkong Chinese executives. The response rate was 15%, providing 150 usable questionnaires on which to base the empirical analysis.

As a starting point for the survey form, each executive was asked to give an importance rating, on a scale of 1 to 6, to a series of activities, including the development of guanxi. They almost unanimously (98%) confirmed that "personal connections with local Chinese organizations" were a highly rated (5 to 6) factor in their business life.

The survey form then went on to list a series of benefits hypothesized to arise from the establishment of guanxi and asked the executives to give an importance rating to each of them. The list was arrived at through a priori theorizing, examination of the earlier literature, and focus group discussions.

Those discussions provided numerous examples of the use made of personal connections, which suggested a series of general headings under which the more specific benefits of guanxi might be identified. The first concerned sources of information. Published sources of market intelligence are very limited in China, so that members of a guanxi network can be an important source of information on market trends and business opportunities. Networks are also a useful means of gathering information on government policies, especially import regulations and restrictions, which change rapidly, are rarely well codified, and can be interpreted differently in different local jurisdictions. When the "rule of man" is more important than the "rule of law," access to the person becomes an important substitute for access to the law. Many of the Hongkong Chinese managers taking part in the study were able to point to examples of apparently rigid regulations that proved to be malleable for those with the appropriate guanxi.

The second general category of benefit identified concerns sources of resources. Under the traditional central planning system in China all means of production were under the control of central or local governments and the bureaucratic maze of permission-seeking is still extremely complicated and important. For instance, production materials are classified into three categories, each of which is controlled by different authorities at different administrative levels. Materials decreed to be most important to the national economy and people's lives are under unified state control, that is to say that they are managed by the State Bureau of Materials at both central and local levels. Materials that are deemed comparatively important to the national economy and specialized materials produced or used by individual sectors are controlled by the industrial ministries concerned and, finally, production materials not included in the other categories, including bricks, plaster, power equipment are controlled by local governments. With the overlapping involvement of bureaus, ministries, departments, provinces, regions, and municipalities, it can be imagined how difficult it can be to locate sources of resources. Recent years have seen very substantial change as the economy is gradually marketized, but in the medium term that has simply made life more complicated as many resources are available through a variety of administrative, legitimate market, and black market channels. As networks can facilitate sorting, mapping, and locating facilities, the focus group discussions with managers suggested that guanxi also yields benefits in respect of securing access to tangible resources in the form of land, labor, raw materials, and electricity, as well as resources in the form of rights, such as import licenses, local government approvals, and central government approvals.

Three additional benefits that were suggested by the focus groups were smoothing transport arrangements, smoothing collection of payments, and building up the company reputation and image. As these did not fit easily into any of the other categories of benefit they were simply described as other areas.

For each of the areas the specific benefits hypothesized were listed, and the respondents were asked to give them a rating on a 6-point scale ranging from "least important" (1) to "most important" (6). Table 1 shows the results. The first column sets out the mean score for each hypothesized benefit, and the ranking of that mean score. As the means differ only slightly and there is a tendency for the responses to bunch around the center of the scale, the table also shows the number and proportion of respondents who rated each benefit "least important" (1) and "most important" (6).

As Table 1 shows, smooth collection of payment was seen as the most highly rated benefit accruing to the establishment of guanxi, followed by information on import regulations and restrictions, and on government policies. The benefits rated least important concerned the approval of advertisements, recruitment of labor, and the securing of raw materials. In general, benefits concerning the smooth running of routine and frequent transactions (payment and transport) received the highest ratings, followed by benefits concerning information, with benefits concerning access to resources being perceived as less important.

The categories of benefit used in Table 1 were arrived at a priori through the focus group discussions, and they seem to have some merit in describing the general nature of the benefits that arise. A more sophisticated approach to identifying categories of benefit is to use factor analysis to empirically determine the existence of factors underlying the structure of the responses to the 15 variables identified. That analysis identified four factors having eigenvalues greater than 1, accounting cumulatively for 62.5% of the total variance, with the factor loadings as shown in Table 2.

Examination of Table 2 suggests that the four factors identified empirically relate reasonably closely to the three categories that were used in the questionnaire. However, it also suggests a slightly different set of interpretable underlying factors that could represent the data more parsimoniously. Factor 1 relates very directly to "procurement" and variation in that factor accounts for the largest proportion of the total variance in the data. Factor 2 appears to be well-

Table 1 Perceived benefits of guanxi

	Mean	Score Rank	% Rating 6	% Rating 1
Sources of information				
Market trends	4.14	10	16.0	3.3
Government policies	4.53	3=	24.7	2.0
Import regulations	4.56	2	27.3	4.7
Business opportunities	4.51	5	28.7	2.7
Sources of resources				
Import license applications	4.38	8	30.0	8.7
Approval of advertisement	3.07	15	2.0	18.0
Approval of applications to provincial government	4.47	6	30.0	4.0
Approval of applications to central government	4.39	7	28.7	6.7
Recruitment of labor	3.25	14	2.7	14.7
Securing land for joint ventures	3.60	12	12.0	14.0
Securing electricity for joint ventures	3.81	11	20.7	14.0
Securing raw materials for joint ventures	3.45	13	11.3	20.0
Other areas				
Building up the company's reputation/image	4.30	9	22.0	4.0
Smooth transportation arrangements	4.53	3=	24.7	2.0
Smooth collection of payment	4.70	1	39.3	4.7

Table 2 Factor loadings on variables (for loadings $\geqslant 4$)

	Factor 1	Factor 2	Factor 3	Factor 4
Sources of information				
Market trends			.6692	
Government policies		.4401	.4424	
Import regulations		.4854	.4528	
Business opportunities			.5877	
Sources of resources				
Import license applications		.5883		
Approval of advertisements				
Approval of applications to provincial government		.8922		
Approval of applications to cental government		.6957		
Recruitment of labor	.5281			
Securing land for joint ventures	.9048			
Securing electricity for joint ventures	.7591			
Securing raw materials for joint ventures	.6426			
Other areas				
Build up the company's reputation/image				.5002
Smooth transportation arrangment				.4922
Smooth collection of payment			.4311	

Good summary below

characterized as a "bureaucracy" variable, being highly loaded on the variables concerning information about regulations and securing administrative approvals. Factor 3 relates well to the original category of "information." Factor 4 is more difficult, being heavily loaded on to two variables representing the efficiency of frequent transactions and another (company reputation and image) that would appear to have little in common, except insofar as reputation and image may be built on reliability with respect to payments and transport.

Managerial implications and conclusions

It is clear from the experience of both Western and Hongkong Chinese executives that the China market cannot be tackled effectively without paying due attention to the construction and maintenance of good guanxi. Business transactions with Chinese individuals and organizations need to be approached in the knowledge that the Chinese will place them in the context of their own guanxi networks, which may require meeting obligations to individuals who have no direct involvement in the matter on hand. Hence the common Western complaint that the "real" decision-maker cannot be identified. In China's collectivist culture, the "real" decision-maker may be the network as a whole, not some mysterious and unseen individual. At the same time, Western businessmen should appreciate that they themselves need to establish guanxi of their own, which requires looking beyond the transaction at hand to its implications for the development of personal relationships.

By bestowing favor and face through considerate and sensitive giving of minor gifts, hosting appropriate dinners, and (most importantly) giving personal attention, a businessperson can demonstrate the good faith that forms the basis for a gradual transition from outside to insider.

Once good guanxi has been established, a number of benefits will accrue. According to the Hongkong Chinese insiders surveyed in this study, the most important benefits arise in respect of the smooth running of routine business operations, in securing information about government policies, and in securing administrative approvals. These results need to be qualified in a number of ways. The managers questioned may not have had a full view of their company's use of guanxi. Different respondents, having different business functions and experiences, may have answered the questions with completely different contexts in mind, some being concerned with marketing, some with production, some with finance, some with the maintenance of existing activities, some with new developments such as market entry or negotiations over joint venture establishment. Further work needs to be done in order to control the context in which guanxi is investigated. Nevertheless, the study has helped to develop a vocabulary with which to describe the benefits arising from guanxi, and has taken a step toward a fuller understanding of the ways in which the management of guanxi can contribute to the enhancement of competitive advantage.

REFERENCES

1. Andersson, Pan, Analyzing Distribution Channel Dynamics: Loose and Tight Coupling in Distribution Networks, *European Journal of Marketing* 26, 47–68 (1992).
2. Brunner, James, Chen, Jiwei, Chao, Sun, and Zhao, Nanping, The Role of "Guanxi" in Negotiations in the Pacific Basin, *Journal of Global Marketing* 3, 7–23 (1989).
3. Brunner, James A., and Taoka, George M., Marketing and Negotiating in the People's Republic of China: Perceptions of American Businessmen Who Attended the 1975 Canton Fair, *Journal of International Business Studies* Fall/Winter, 69–82 (1977).
4. Davidson, William H., Creating and Managing Joint Ventures in China, *California Management Review* Summer, 77–94 (1987).
5. Davies, Howard A., Interpreting "Guanxi": The Role of Personal Connections in a High Context Transitional Economy, in *China Business: Context and Issues*, H. Davies, ed., Longman Asia, Hongkong (in press).
6. Easton, Geoffrey, Introduction, in *Industrial Networks: A New View of Reality*, Bjorn Axelsson and Geoffrey Easton, eds., Routledge, London and New York, 1992.
7. Eiteman, David K., American Executives' Perceptions of Negotiating Joint Ventures with the People's Republic of China: Lessons Learned, *Columbia Journal of World Business* Winter, 59–67 (1990).
8. Frankenstein, John, Trends in Chinese Business Practice: Changes in the Beijing Wind, *California Management Review* Fall, 148–160 (1986).
9. Hakansson, H., and Snehota, I., No Business Is an Island: The Network Concept of Business Strategy, In *Industrial Networks: A New View of Reality*, Axelsson and Easton, eds., Academic Press, 1990, pp. 526–540.
10. Hendryx, Steven R., Implementation of a Technology Transfer Joint Venture in the People's Republic of China: A Management Perspective, *Columbia Journal of World Business*, Spring, 57–66 (1986).
11. de Keijzer, Arne, *China: Business Strategies for the 90s*. Pacific View Press, Berkeley, CA 1992.
12. Lindsay, Cindy P., and Dempsey, Bobby L., Ten Painfully Learned Lessons about Working in China: The Insights of Two American Behavioral Scientists, *Journal of Applied Behavioral Science* 19, 265–276 (1983).
13. McInnes, Peter, Guanxi or Contract: A Way to Understand and Predict Conflict Between Chinese and Western Senior Managers in China-based Joint Ventures, *Paper given at the Symposium on Multinational Business Management*, sponsored by Nanjing University and Florida Atlantic University, Nanjing, December 10–12, 1992.
14. Stewart, Sally, and Keown, Charles F., Talking with the Dragon: Negotiating in the People's Republic of China, *Columbia Journal of World Business* Fall, 68–72 (1989).
15. Summers, Lawrence, The Rise of China, *International Economic Insights* May/June, 17 (1992).
16. Thorelli, Hans B., Networks: Between Markets and Hierarchies, *Strategic Management Journal* 7, 37–51 (1986).
17. Thorelli, Hans B., Networks: The Gay Nineties in International Marketing, in *International Marketing Strategy*, Hans B. Thorelli and S. Tamer Cavusgil, eds., Pergamon, Oxford and New York, 1990.

18. Williamson, Oliver, Transaction-Cost Economics: The Governance of Contractual Relations, *Journal of Law and Economics* 22, 233–261 (1979).
19. Yip, Leslie, The Emergence of Modern Retailing, in *China Business: Context and Issues*, H. Davies, ed., Longman Asia, Hongkong (in press).
20. Zhang, Jingzhi, Managing Sino-Foreign Joint Ventures: Lessons Learned from Experience, in *China Business: Context and Issues*, H. Davies, ed., Longman Asia, Hongkong (in press).

Address correspondence to Howard Davies, Department of Business Studies, Hong Kong Polytechnic University, Hung Hom, Kowloon, Hong Kong.

HOWARD DAVIES is Associate Dean of the Faculty of Business and Information Systems at Hong Kong Polytechnic University.

THOMAS KIM-PING LEUNG is Lecturer in Marketing in the Department of Business Studies at Hong Kong Polytechnic University.

SHERRIFF TIN-KWONG LUK is Lecturer in Marketing in the Department of Business Studies at Hong Kong Polytechnic University.

YIU-HING WONG is Lecturer in Marketing in the Department of Business Studies at Hong Kong Polytechnic University.

II Analyzing Marketing Opportunities

One implication of the marketing concept is that Asian marketing managers must continually look for opportunities in the marketplace. An ongoing evaluation of environmental opportunities and threats to the organization is thus critical to the survival and growth of Asian companies. Important environmental dimensions include economic, legal, political, social, cultural, and technological forces. Marketing managers in the Asia Pacific must understand consumer and industrial buyer behavior.

After reading the four papers in this part, you should have a deeper appreciation for the following aspects of marketing in the region:

1   The use of consumer attitudes and behavior to develop marketing strategies and assign managerial priorities and resources.
2   How market intelligence is gathered by some of Asia's most aggressive companies to obtain information to stay ahead of their competitors.
3   Social and cultural aspects of consumer values and lifestyles in the Asia Pacific.

4 Assessing National Competitive Superiority: An Importance-Performance Matrix Approach

Siew Meng Leong and Chin Tiong Tan

A well established strategic marketing technique assesses Singapore's strengths and weaknesses in attracting foreign investments.

It is well accepted that effective strategy is founded on continuous and diagnostic monitoring of one's competitive position. Evidence revealing the skills and resources affording the greatest leverage on future cost and differentiation advantages is particularly critical. Businesses that succeed are those which develop distinctive competences and manage for lowest delivered cost or differentiation through superior customer value (Day and Wensley, 1988).

Increasingly, the same dictum appears applicable on a more macro level. Competition for capital and human resources has intensified between nations with the globalization of markets and business operations. Both capitalist and socialist Governments are now turning towards some form of international strategic marketing planning (Nielsen, 1983) in an effort to solve problems of high unemployment, sluggish growth and low foreign exchange earnings (Weigand, 1985).

Germane to this process is a thorough and balanced assessment of the reasons for the competitive position of a country in attracting foreign investments. Ideally, such assessments of national competitive superiority should be both competitor-centred and customer-focused. The former necessitates a comparison of the relative skills, resources and cost position of the country with target competitors. The latter requires such an evaluation to be conducted with key consumers rather than be based on internal, managerial sources. It is therefore consistent with the marketing concept which seeks to satisfy the needs and wants of target customers more effectively and efficiently than the

Reproduced with permission from *Marketing Intelligence & Planning*, 10 (no. 1, 1992), pp. 42–48.

competition. Gathering insights from the marketplace thus provides a more intimate understanding of customer needs and wants.

One technique which permits such simultaneous assessment is the Importance-Performance Matrix approach (Martilla and James, 1977). This method uses customer judgements of the importance of various attributes and the relative performance of a company on the attributes in assessing comparative advantage. It has a long history of successful use by consumer goods companies and has recently been adapted to equally good effect by industrial and service-oriented firms (Root, 1986). Du Pont, for example, has found that the overall ratings of competitive standing correlate well with market share.

The Importance-Performance Matrix approach appears ideally suited to assessing national competitive superiority in attracting foreign investments. By obtaining customer evaluations of relative country performance based on customer judgements of attribute importance, insights may be gathered regarding: (1) the particular consideration set of nations used in relative performance evaluation; and (2) the strengths and weaknesses of a particular country on the attributes studied. Diagnostic information regarding the priority and extent of resource allocation in rectifying weaknesses may also be obtained.

This article thus employs the Importance-Performance Matrix approach in assessing the competitive standing of one nation — Singapore — with its key foreign investors. Singapore is a particularly appropriate context for this application because it relies heavily on foreign investments in achieving its economic mission of evolving into a "global city with a total business orientation" (Economic Development Board, 1987/88).

The remainder of this article is organized as follows. The next section discusses in greater detail the rationale and nature of the Importance-Performance Matrix approach. This is followed by a description of the research method used in data collection and analysis. The results of the study are then presented. Finally, implications of the research findings are discussed.

The Importance-Performance Matrix

The fundamental assumption of the Importance-Performance Matrix is that not all attributes contribute equally to corporate success. To the extent that an enterprise performs well in attributes considered important to consumers, its likelihood of success is enhanced. On the other hand, poor performance on important attributes may have detrimental consequences for the firm.

Essentially, a four-cell matrix is obtained via a dichotomization of two dimensions of the approach. Attributes are divided into those of low or moderate importance versus those of high importance to the firm. Similarly, an enterprise's performance on these attributes can also be divided into excellent versus adequate or poor levels. Based on the locations of attributes in the matrix, enhanced understanding of the enterprise's strengths and weaknesses can be obtained. Remedial action can be undertaken to correct the weaknesses of the enterprise.

In extending this framework to analyze a nation's strategic position, the resultant matrix may have the following dimensions: (1) the target country's competitiveness on attributes used by investors; and (2) the importance of the attributes. Both may be dichotomized into high and moderate levels, thus yielding the matrix depicted in Figure 1.

Figure 1 Importance-Performance Matrix

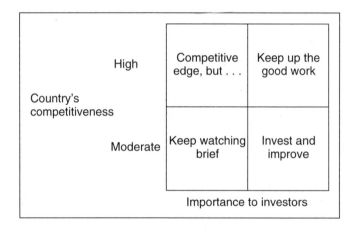

Figure 1 illustrates the implications based on a particular attribute's location on the matrix. Specially, four categories of attributes may be delineated and actions implemented based thereon. Where a country is highly competitive on a highly important attribute, the strategy is one of maintenance — of keeping up the good work. In contrast, where a country is only moderately competitive on an important attribute, it needs to invest and improve on that attribute. High competitiveness on moderately important attributes provides a competitive edge but may be a sign of over-investment. Finally, moderate competitiveness on moderately important attributes suggests keeping a watching brief — improvements need to be made but are of a lower priority.

The Importance-Performance Matrix is sufficiently flexible to be generalized. Thus the cost competitiveness of a country in respect of various factor inputs may be analyzed relative to the importance of the various factor inputs. In all cases, the approach requires the identification of key customers (investors), and seeking their inputs in respect of the importance of various attributes (or factor inputs), and the target country's performance (or cost competitiveness) on those attributes.

Method

Respondents

Respondents were international companies based in Singapore of world-class standing. The Singapore Economic Development Board (EDB) identified 50 such companies out of which 37 (74 per cent) participated. Table 1 provides the background data for the survey respondents.

Attributes

It is essential to generate a representative and preferably exhaustive list of attributes for respondents to evaluate to ensure an adequate operationalization of the Importance-Performance Matrix approach. To this end, a pre-test was used to elicit the relevant attributes for inclusion in the survey. The pre-test was conducted at the Global Strategies Conference, a three-day seminar at which senior-level executives from major corporations from around the world participated.

Based on the open-ended responses of 211 of the executives, and with input from the EDB's Planning Division, a list of 28 attributes was employed in the survey. These fell into five major categories: (1) physical infrastructure (five attributes, e.g. seaport); (2) industrial infrastructure (three attributes, e.g. training centres); (3) services (five attributes, e.g. financial services); (4) quality of human resource skills (five attributes, e.g. technical); and (5) living environment (ten attributes, e.g. health care facilities).

Table 1 General data on respondents

	Percentage
Sector	
Manufacturing	83
Services	17
Country	
US	33
Europe	28
Japan/Asia	39
Global sales	
More than US$10B	13
US$1B to US$10B	50
Less than US$1B	37

Measurement

Respondents evaluated the importance of each attribute on five-point scales with end-points of 5 = very important and 1 = not important. Respondents then named the country they were next most likely to consider for the location of new activities besides Singapore. They evaluated Singapore's performance on the same attributes on five-point scale (5 = Singapore is much better and 1 = Singapore is much worse) *vis-à-vis* the competing nation mentioned.

Respondents then furnished their impressions of the importance of various factor inputs in production. The inputs selected were a subset of ten of the attributes previously elicited. Five-point rating scales (5 = very important and 1 = not important) were employed for this purpose. They then evaluated Singapore's cost competitiveness relative to the next alternative investment option using five-point scales (5 = Singapore is much better and 1 = Singapore is much worse).

Finally, respondents provided background data and responded to some open-ended questions regarding general suggestions for improvement and plans for upgrading.

Results

Major competitors

Companies generally consider a subset of available alternatives in choosing between locations for future investments. The evoked set of Singapore's key customers is depicted in Table 2.

Table 2 Next most likely country of investment

Country	Percentage of mentions
Developed countries and NIEs	
UK	10
Hong Kong	10
Australia	5
South Korea	5
ASEAN countries	
Malaysia	50'
Thailand	5
Philippines	5
Other countries	
People's Republic of China	5
India	5
Total	100

Clearly, most (50 per cent) international key customers consider Malaysia to be the alternative location for investments. No other country received more than 10 per cent of such mentions. ASEAN countries received 60 per cent of mentions in total, while the developed countries and Newly Industrialized Economies (NIEs) received 30 per cent. Singapore thus faces dynamic competition from other countries in terms of business location, from developed countries to newly industrializing countries to even the more advanced developing countries like Malaysia. The latter, for example, are developing the capability to produce some of the products manufactured by the more established industries in Singapore.

Importance-Performance Matrix analysis

Following identification of its major competitors, it is now appropriate to conduct an analysis of Singapore's competitiveness, using the Importance-Performance Matrix. Table 3 documents the mean ratings of the importance of the attributes selected for study and how well Singapore performs on them relative to her closest competitors.

Examination of Singapore's performance scores reveal her strong competitiveness on all the attributes studied. In no case did an average performance rating fall below the scale mid-point. Thus Singapore was perceived to be generally more competitive than her closest rivals on all the attributes studied. However, added insights may be obtained using the Importance-Performance Matrix. To obtain this, the two sets of scores in Table 3 were dichotomized, using median splits into highly and moderately important attributes and high and moderate levels of competitive superiority of Singapore. This produced Figure 2.

Figure 2 clearly indicates that Singapore must keep up the good work on its hardware support. The airport, seaport, telecommunications, health care facilities, public utilities and road transport network were important attributes in the eyes of key customers, where Singapore enjoyed a distinct advantage *vis-à-vis* competitors. Physical safety and financial services were seen in the same way.

Singapore also performed well on the attributes of Government skills-training centres, training centres, Government technical/R&D centres, pollution level, professional support services and information network.

However, these attributes were considered somewhat less important to key customers. While Singapore's competitive superiority in these attributes needs to be preserved, care must be taken not to over-invest in these attributes nor to over-emphasize them in promotional programmes targeted at investors.

Singapore needs to improve performance in five critical areas — schooling facilities, supporting industries, and executive/managerial, professional and

Table 3 Infrastructural and environment ratings

Item	Mean ratings	
	Importance	*Competitiveness*
Technical human resources	4.89	3.88
Telecommunications	4.86	4.51
Executive/managerial human resources	4.67	3.96
Professional human resources	4.62	3.96
Airport	4.59	4.62
Public utilities	4.54	4.44
Physical safety	4.50	4.55
School facilities	4.45	4.18
Health care facilities	4.43	4.48
Seaport	4.37	4.84
Financial services	4.37	4.30
Supporting industries	4.22	3.96
Road transport network	4.08	4.55
Information network	4.08	4.30
Industrial land/factories	4.02	3.69
Clerical/support human resources	3.97	3.76
Training centres	3.94	4.40
Government skills-training centres	3.94	4.41
Pollution level	3.94	4.25
Direct (shopfloor) human resources	3.80	3.41
Professional support services	3.78	4.23
Publication/freedom of press	3.73	3.11
Religious freedom	3.55	3.85
Recreational amenities	3.43	3.55
Entertainment facilities	3.43	3.48
Censorship policies	3.33	3.26
Shopping amenities	3.27	4.22
Government technical centres	3.22	4.40

Figure 2   Importance-Quality Competitiveness Matrix: infrastructure and environment (with respect to next most likely country of investment)

		Moderate	High
Competitiveness of Singapore	**High**	Government skills training centres Government technical/ R&D centres Pollution level Professional support services Information network Training centres	Seaport Airport Physical safety Road transport network Telecommunications Health care facilities Public utilities Financial services
	Moderate	Shopping amenities Religious freedom Clerical/Support human resources Industrial land/factories Recreational amenities Entertainment amenities Direct (shopfloor) human resources Censorship policies Publication/freedom of press	School facilities Executive/Managerial human resources Professional human resources Supporting industries Technical human resources
		Moderate	High
		Importance to investors	

technical human resource quality. These are attributes which are highly important to investors but on which Singapore does not enjoy a clear-cut competitive advantage over her nearest rivals. Significantly, three of these five attributes concerned her "liveware" — her human resources.

Attention also needs to be directed towards enhancing Singapore's competitiveness in shopping amenities, religious freedom, clerical/support and direct (shopfloor) human resource quality, industrial land/factories, recreational amenities, entertainment amenities, censorship policies and publication/freedom of press. However, these attributes merit less immediate and/or less extensive attention — given that they are considered moderately important to investors.

Cost competitiveness

Table 4 contains the mean importance and competitiveness ratings of ten attributes by investors that will be used in assessing Singapore's cost superiority relative to her closest rivals. These scores were used to construct Figure 3, which illustrates a Factor Price Importance-Competitiveness Matrix of Singapore *vis-à-vis* her competitors. Scale mid-points of three were used as cut-off points to categorize factors into moderately/very important/competitive.

Table 4 Factor pricing ratings

| | Mean ratings | |
Item	Pricing importance	Price competitiveness
Telecommunications	4.48	4.14
Skilled labour costs	4.49	2.85
Public utilities	4.45	3.76
Financial services	4.32	3.50
Overall labour costs	4.28	2.30
Land costs	4.13	2.34
Office/factory rental	4.13	3.50
Unskilled labour costs	4.08	1.73
Infrastructural costs	3.89	3.48
Semi-skilled labour costs	3.83	2.29

Figure 3 Factor Price Importance-Competitiveness Matrix

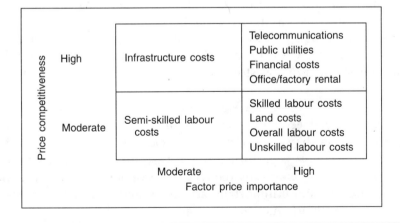

Figure 3 suggests that Singapore should maintain her highly competitive offerings of four key cost factors — telecommunications, public utilities, financial services and office/factory rental. These were highly important price factors on which Singapore enjoyed a much superior competitive pricing advantage. Singapore's infrastructural costs were also competitive, although these were of moderate price importance to investors.

However, Singapore must concentrate efforts on enhancing price competitiveness on such highly important pricing considerations as skilled, overall and unskilled labour costs, as well as land costs. On these factors prices, Singapore was less competitive than her nearest rivals (all mean scores of price competitiveness were less than the scale mid-point). Some attention towards enhancing price competitiveness on semi-skilled labour costs also warrants consideration, albeit of a less crucial nature, given its moderate importance to investors.

Discussion

The relationship between marketing and economic development has long been recognized. Early research sought to determine this relationship via the comparative analysis of the marketing systems of different nations (Cundiff, 1965; Douglas, 1971; Goldman, 1972; Hilger, 1978; Moyer, 1964). More recently, various macromarketing approaches have been employed towards optimizing national economic development (Cundiff, 1982; Darian, 1985; Dominguez and Vanmarcke, 1987; Hosley and Wee, 1988).

This article continues the latter line of inquiry by drawing the parallel between the formulation of corporate marketing strategy and national economic policy (see Figure 4). Both must be predicated on an intimate understanding of the strategic position of the company (country) and its products (infrastructural and environmental attributes) in the marketplace. The success or failure of a business or nation may well hinge on how well it competes against other businesses or nations, as well as on the ability to capitalize on its strengths and rectify its weaknesses. Clearly, such an understanding is most valuable if the views of its customers or investors are sought and competitive considerations incorporated.

The Importance-Performance Matrix approach is a simple, sound and flexible method that national economic planners may consider employing. It forces planners to focus on the views of investors regarding the importance of various attributes and the country's performance on these attributes relative to its closest competitors. This counteracts the tendency of economic planners presuming to know what are the most important attributes and how well or poorly the country fares on them. Astute judgements from economic planners are, however, required in implementing the approach. The dichotomization of

Figure 4 Parallels between Corporate Strategic Formulation and National Economic Planning

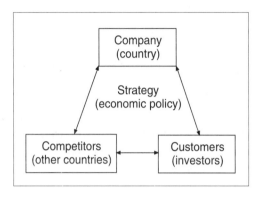

attributes into high versus moderate importance and performance is one area which calls for considerable attention. In the illustration presented, median splits were used in obtaining the Importance-Quality Competitiveness Matrix, while scale mid-points were employed to construct the Factor Price Importance-Competitiveness Matrix. The choice of one approach over the other was a function of the range of scores obtained. In the former case, all mean scores exceeded the scale mid-point. Using scale mid-points would thus provide little, if any, diagnostic insights regarding which attributes merit attention in resource allocation decisions.

The Importance-Performance Matrix approach requires advanced, precise, and detailed specification of the attributes to be studied. Such specificity comes at a cost, as the attributes selected may be highly correlated, but the diagnostic insights obtained are certainly superior (Day and Wensley, 1988). Use of the approach also reduces the temptation of economic planners to develop every aspect of a country's resources simultaneously and with equal attention. It directs a rational and systematic review of which attributes require higher priorities for resource allocation at different stages of the country's development.

In the case of Singapore, human resources appear to be the principal strategic area for improvement quality and cost competitiveness. The future success of Singapore is very dependent on its ability to provide access to an adequate supply of human resources at all levels and elevate their skills to world-class standing. Moreover, Singapore's focus must be to attract companies which intensively utilize those factors on which Singapore enjoys a clear-cut cost and quality competitive advantage — telecommunication, public utilities and financial services. Typically, these include higher value-added industries and service firms which may benefit from Singapore's superior infrastructure and excellent total business capability.

In addition, it is imperative that Singapore does not allow factor costs to become out of line with those of her competitors. Increments in costs can be justified only by commensurate, if not greater, increases in value offered to customers *vis-à-vis* Singapore's competitors. Such value enhancements may take the form of improvement in productivity, quality, time-savings, worker attitude and work ethic.

Finally, the Importance-Performance Matrix approach suggests that an entity's competitiveness is measured with respect to a particular consideration set. In Singapore's case, investors viewed Malaysia as the major alternative location for their investments. If Singapore is unable to overcome land and labour shortages (e.g. through reclamation projects and more relaxed immigration policies, respectively), it makes strategic sense: (1) to avoid attracting low-labour cost manufacturing and companies with extensive land requirements; and (2) to develop linkages or networking arrangements with her neighbour. The latter is analogous to corporations forming strategic alliances (Kotler, 1986) with each other. Singapore may, in fact, be positioned as a conduit through which international investors may channel, oversee and monitor their investments in the Asia-Pacific region.

Conclusion

The Importance-Performance Matrix approach has been introduced and applied to analysis of a nation's competitive superiority in attracting foreign investments. Obtaining the views of key customers and acting on them will enhance national competitiveness and lead to a more market-driven philosophy in economic planning. The application presented is illustrative. Future research may consider a wider array of countries and attributes. Direct comparisons with specific nations (e.g. Malaysia in the case of Singapore) may be envisaged. Other key attributes (e.g. nature of regulatory framework, existence of incentives or subsidies, trade bloc membership, market size, geographic location, and costs of using various infrastructural facilities such as seaports) may likewise be included for more comprehensive analyses. Longitudinal studies may also be useful to track investor changes in preferences and perceptions. Additional insights may also be garnered through segmentation of investors by industry and country of origin to more finely tuned plans targeted at particular sets of investors.

To conclude, Porter (1990) has argued that nations succeed in particular industries because their home environment is the most dynamic and challenging. This stimulates them to upgrade and widen their competitive advantage over time. By attracting globally-oriented, successful corporations, countries like Singapore may provide an environment that catalyses domestic entrepreneurship. Such a development may be facilitated by technology transfer, the nurturing of local supporting industries,. and increased domestic competition. Investor firms, on the other hand, may also be challenged to improve and upgrade, based on insights and assistance from host nations which themselves possess competitive advantage as suppliers (Porter, 1990). Clearly, a mutually beneficial relationship can be fostered between host nations and foreign investor firms.

REFERENCES

Cundiff, E.W. (1965), "Concepts in Comparative Retailing", *Journal of Marketing*, Vol. 29, January, pp. 59–63.

Cundiff, E.W. (1982), "A Macromarketing Approach to Economic Development", *Journal of Macromarketing*, Vol. 2, Spring, pp. 14–19.

Darian, J.C. (1985), "Marketing and Economic Development: A Case Study from Classical India", *Journal of Macromarketing*, Vol. 5, Spring, pp. 14–26.

Day, G.S. and Wensley, R. (1988), "Assessing Advantage: A Framework for Diagnosing Competitive Superiority", *Journal of Marketing*, Vol. 52, April, pp. 1–20.

Dominguez, L.V. and Vanmarcke, C. (1987), "Market Structure and Marketing Behavior in LDCs: The Case of Venezuela", *Journal of Macromarketing*, Vol. 7, Fall, pp. 4–16.

Douglas, S.P. (1971), "Patterns and Parallels of Marketing Structures in Several Countries", *MSU Business Topics*, Vol. 19, Spring, pp. 38–48.

Economic Development Board (1987/88), *Annual Report*, Singapore.

Goldman, A. (1972), "Outreach of Consumers and the Modernization of Urban Food Retailing in Developing Countries", *Journal of Marketing*, Vol. 38, October, pp. 8–16.

Hilger, M.T. (1978), "Theories of the Relationship between Marketing and Economic Development: Public Policy Implications", in White, P.D. and Slater, C.C. (Eds), *Macromarketing: Distributive Processes from a Societal Perspective: An Elaboration of Issues*, Graduate School of Business Administration, University of Colorado, Boulder, CO.

Hosley, S. and Wee, C.H. (1988), "Marketing and Economic Development: Focusing on the Less Developed Countries", *Journal of Macromarketing*, Vol. 8, Spring, pp. 43–53.

Kotler, P. (1986), "Megamarketing", *Harvard Business Review*, Vol. 64, March–April, pp. 117–24.

Martilla, J.A. and James, J.C. (1977), "Importance-Performance Analysis", *Journal of Marketing*, Vol. 51, January, pp. 77–9.

Moyer, R. (1964), "The Structure of Markets in Developing Economies", *MSU Business Topics*, Vol. 12, Fall, pp. 43–60.

Nielsen, R.P. (1983), "Should a Country Move toward International Strategic Market Planning?", *California Management Review*, Vol. 25, January, pp. 34–44.

Porter, M.E. (1990), *The Competitive Advantage of Nations*, The Free Press, New York.

Root, H.P. (1986), "Industrial Market Intelligence Systems: A Source of Competitive Advantage", paper presented at the Business-to-Business Marketing Conference, American Marketing Association, New Orleans, April.

Weigand, R.E. (1985), "Searching for Investments: The Race Is On; The Runners Should be Wary", *Business Horizons*, Vol. 28, March/April, pp. 46–52.

5   Competing through Intelligence

Lee Miller, Stephanie Jones, Vanaga Dhanan,
Al Dizon, and Don Shapiro

How some of Asia's most aggressive competitors get the information they need to stay ahead.

Most Singaporeans have heard from the Wywy Group at one time or another. More than 9,000 people receive sales calls from Wywy every working day. The marketer, distributor, and retailer of high-tech office equipment makes more than two million sales calls each year.

Wywy's 600 direct sales people also regularly call on 3,000 dealers — partly to pump them for information about the competition. "Through the data we get from customers and dealers, we are able to identify where to position products," says Wywy chairman Wong Yin Yan. "We thrive on information. It's key to identifying opportunities before they become obvious, and to implementing strategies ahead of competitors."

Valuable information

Philips Taiwan product division heads call on customers at least twice a year. Declares executive vice president L. P. Hsu, "Your customers may provide valuable competitive information." A subsidiary of the Dutch electronics giant, the firm cannot pay close attention to every competitor. There are simply too many of them. So it concentrates only on its top rivals. The firm's benchmarking program constantly monitors these competitors' strengths and weaknesses.

Twelve clerks employed by chartered surveyors and property consultants Brooke Hillier Parker spend every working day combing the "Day Book" of Hongkong's Land Registry for records of property sales agreements. "We make

Reproduced with permission from *World Executive's Digest*, 14 (April 1993), pp. 12–14.

8,000 entries in our database every week," says senior partner Nicholas Brooke.

The firm claims to know the name of every tenant in every office building in Hongkong, and when their leases will end. "We do it by cold-calling every office," adds Brooke. "And we watch our competitors all the time. We couldn't have grown so dramatically — from six people two years ago to more than 100 now — without concentrating on competitor and market intelligence."

Aggressively competitive firms like Brooke Hillier Parker, Wywy, and Philips Taiwan have a lesson for all marketing and sales managers: To stay ahead of the competition, you must do more than just adopt a marketing orientation. You need a competitor focus. To achieve that, you need information on your competitors. Then you need to turn that information into intelligence — competitive intelligence.

In Asia, where information may not be generally available, obtaining and analyzing data is a critical competitive advantage. The region's most imaginative and aggressive competitors know how to get the competitive intelligence they need, and how to use it to beat their rivals.

There is nothing fancy about Wywy's information-gathering system. The people behind the success of Wywy (annual turnover : $187 million) are its direct sales force. The firm has 600 people in the field as sales persons, logistics personnel, and field engineers. Under the company's WHAM (Wywy High Activity Management) system, sales people fill out call reports in the field. The information is fed into a central Siemens computer and analyzed using custom-designed software.

"Each person in the field makes 15 to 20 sales calls every working day," says Wong. "Our system opens up multiple channels for customer feedback. We determine customers' and potential customers' needs. We keep our customers this way. The best customer is the existing customer."

Weekly sales report are produced and analyzed. Then strategies are formulated. "It is critical that we understand potential customers, who they are, how they are changing, and how best to reach them," says Wong.

Wong calls Wywy's information gatherers a "hybrid marketing network" of direct sales people, dealers, and retailers. The network was established 17 years ago and the company's original customer list was founded on cold calls. Wywy adds to the list through face-to-face visits.

Spectacular success

The system has had spectacular success in Singapore and Malaysia. The initial success of the Singapore shops (25 were set up within a year with an investment of $40 million) was repeated in West Malaysia, Sabah, and Sarawak, where 22 Wywy shops have been established. Another 33 retail outlets are being developed throughout Malaysia.

And the information that the system generates makes Wywy hard to beat. Its rivals say there is no tougher competitor. A consultant to one of the leading ones confides, "Every time we think up of a new marketing strategy and target specific customers, we find out that Wywy has already called on them. They've got their ear to the ground, and they move fast."

Taiwan can be a convenient or challenging place from which to gather market intelligence. It depends on the industry. Information on the electronics industry is easy to gather, mainly because the Taiwan government supports the development of high-tech industries. "The information available here is as good as anywhere in the world," says Philips Taiwan's Hsu.

Philips Taiwan makes full use of a number of information sources offered by government and semi-official organizations. These include reports on the computer products industry by the semi-official Institute for Information Industry. A newsletter that tracks developments in the Japanese electronics industry is published by the government-backed Industrial Technology Research Institute. A computerized information service operated by the government's National Science Council provides data from throughout the world on technical and management subjects.

Smart executives have learned to rely on a multitude of information channels to ensure they are well-informed, says Hsu. "Keeping abreast of published information provides a good understanding of general industrial trends. But you also need specific intelligence about the market, customer needs, and competitors' activities," he adds. "Communication with the customer gets the highest priority at Philips."

For consumer products, especially those aimed at the local market, information-gathering can be far more troublesome in Taiwan. "The Taiwan market is relatively undifferentiated," says Brian Spengler, director of Investec Coopers & Lybrand, a joint-venture company specializing in market and industrial research. "You don't have large differences in income within the population, which can make it hard to segment the market and find an attractive niche of your own to exploit."

Production statistics gathered by government agencies or industrial associations are not always reliable. Some manufacturers under-report their figures for tax reasons, while others over-report to gain "face." In addition, the dominance of small producers makes collection of data more complicated than in many other countries.

In Taiwan's service sector, real-estate executive Yang Ching-Ping, president of R+R International Inc., depends on multiple channels for business intelligence. Published information — mainly newspaper clippings about the property market or general economic trends — is collected by her staff and placed on her desk each morning.

Yang believes her most valuable information comes from questionnaires filled out by prospective buyers and sellers. The forms serve as sales leads. But when data is tabulated and entered into personal computers on a weekly basis, Yang also has a clear picture of the shape and movement of the market by geographical district and type, size, and cost of property.

"From responses, we could see recently that Taiwan's real-estate slump has bottomed out and that price resistance has just about disappeared," says Yang. "As a result, we are prepared to make a major sales drive in 1993."

Yang maintains a wide circle of personal contacts. "My friends know there is nothing I like more than talking about housing. They are always coming to me with questions, or passing along things they've heard. Their comments often help me feel the pulse of the market," she says.

"Competitive intelligence is of key importance to us," says Nicholas Brooke of Brooke Hillier Parker. "We are in the information-gathering business. Our clients want to know who's bought what property and who's sold what property, and for how much.

"To outscore our competitors, it's not enough just to collect material. We analyze information to produce summaries of rates per square foot, and the extent to which prices are moving up or down. We produce user-friendly rental contour maps. We provide a subscriber service. A client can buy a floppy disk with all the sales figures and analysis on it. But we keep our client subscriber list small because information can be devalued if it is spread around too many people."

Brooke says his firm has to be careful about the security of its data. "The bigger the system and the more people using it, the greater the danger that someone will sell your data. It's happened to us, and I'm sure to many others too. Much confidential information comes our way, but we turn it down because it's probably been stolen."

Demand for competitive intelligence is also growing in Malaysia, and more companies are providing research services, says Adam Hodgson, media development director of Survey Research Malaysia. "Demand for business-to-business and industrial research is growing," he adds.

There has been a change in the attitude of smaller Malaysian business houses, mainly in the consumer sector, says Eugene Wong, deputy managing director of SRM. "Operating on gut feel is no longer a viable way of doing business," he adds.

It certainly isn't at Sime UEP Properties. An in-house research unit scans newspaper and trade publication articles and advertisements. interviews developers, and visits competitor's sales offices. "You need to be systematic in getting first-hand information," says a marketing executive at the firm. "Information issued publicly by a competitor is not reliable."

All information on competitors and the market is then channeled to the sales and marketing department, where a special planning unit analyzes the data, using a custom-made computer program. The analysis focuses on areas like pricing, product type, product size, designs, and special features of houses. Its intelligence-gathering and analyzing capabilities have enabled Sime UEP to establish a reputation as the leading innovator in the industry.

Competitive intelligence should supplement market research, not replace it. Land and Houses executives in Thailand do not spend too much of their time worrying about the competition. Their philosophy is to compete with each other, according to executive vice-president Adisorn Thananannarapool.

"Certainly we study the other companies, but in this business it's essential to be demand oriented; to study the customer's needs rather than who is building what," he says. "We achieved this by organizing the company into seven groups, each run as a profit center."

Each unit focuses on one area of Bangkok and its suburbs. The groups gather demographic data through independent surveys, joint projects with universities, and by utilizing government census information. They also conduct group interviews and call door-to-door on people to find out what they require in a home. All this information is fed into computers and then analyzed by the company's electronic data control department.

The result is intra-company entrepreneurship and friendly competition among executives, Adisorn says. More importantly, these methods enable Land and Houses to understand the residential property market from buyers' perspectives. "Designing and building houses is relatively easy if you know what people want," Adisorn says.

In 1992, the company's after-tax profit was $50 million, an increase of 78% over 1991 despite a real-estate glut and political tensions in Thailand. The company controls about 12% of the detached housing market and is making significant inroads into the townhouse segment. Land and Houses focuses on medium- to upper-income clients.

"Land and Houses does business differently from other real-estate companies," says Teerawat Chongtaweephol, a senior analyst for Capital Securities. "It is the only developer that has fully computerized its operations. It has an excellent research department and the best credit of any firm in the property industry in Thailand."

Says Adisorn, "Because we have the database and standard designs at our disposal, each new project we undertake is like franchising. Like McDonald's, all we have to do is to maintain our high standards, provide the products our customers want, and give them good value."

Its emphasis on market research has enabled the company to stay ahead of the competition in Thailand by building a substantial land bank. "Most of the 2,000 acres in our land bank won't be used for another five to six years," Adisorn says.

"We are not buying land simply for price appreciation. We want to make sure that each location will be marketable for a future project. That's why we put so much effort into knowing what is going to happen in our business, and why it's going to happen."

6   Lifestyle Research in Asia

Marieke K. de Mooij and Warren Keegan

Consumer research has traditionally examined the effects of demographic characteristics on buying behavior. More recently, however, considerable attention has been directed towards consumer values and lifestyles and how they might affect consumption patterns. Known as psychographic research, such studies have shed greater light on the activities, interests, and opinions of consumers. Given its applied orientation, marketing managers have responded readily to incorporate psychographic findings in designing their marketing programs.

As has generally been the case, lifestyle research originated from the United States. Since then, the usefulness of such research to marketing management has led to its being diffused to other parts of the world. Asia is no exception. The following reports on the results of various lifestyle research conducted in such Asian countries as Japan, Malaysia, Singapore, Taiwan, and Thailand.*

CORE, Japan

Kazuaki Ushikubo, president of Research and Development, Inc., Tokyo, describes[1] how CORE, his company's research system, studies people's wants in Japan. He believes that people's wants can be properly described in terms of a structure consisting of a variety of elements which change over time as people enter different life phases and situations. Wants or desires are considered to be a force which motivates specific behaviour. In contrast to Maslow's theory of a hierarchy of needs, Ushikubo describes an individual's wants as structured in a group with components which vary in importance according to the environment. These components can be categorized by the following process:

Reproduced with permission from *Advertising Worldwide*, New York: Prentice-Hall, 1991, pp. 119–132.

*   Summary of this article by Siew Meng Leong.

1. Two major social factors appear to be particularly relevant to human wants. One is "chaos and order". It is in the state of chaos that creation and innovation occur. The other is "outer and inner direction", the interface between an individual and society. These two social factors are used as axes.
2. The most important personal factors are those of mobility and communication. Mobility is the degree of personal attachment to, or detachment from, the environment. Communication refers to the strength of the relationship with other human beings.
3. These axes provide a framework for positioning the four basic wants of change, participation, freedom and stability.

Figure 1 shows a model for structuring wants.

Figure 1   Structuring of wants

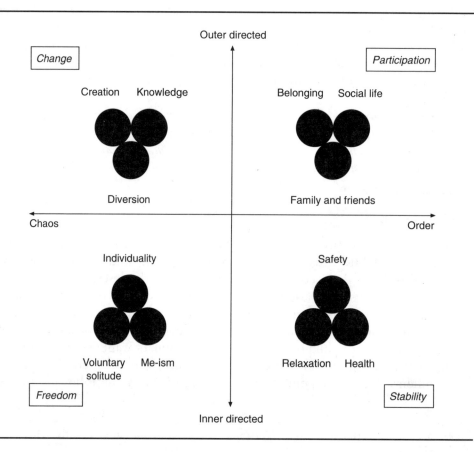

Source: Kazuaki Ushikubo, 1986: "A method of structure analysis for developing product concepts and its applications", *European Research*.

In Figure 1 twelve factors from Murray's list of human wants have been integrated into the four quadrants.[2] These basic wants and wants factors have implications for the general life-style, as described in Table 1.

Table 1 Basic wants and wants factors

Basic wants	Wants factors	Meaning
Change	Diversion	I want to change my lifestyle occasionally
	Knowledge	I want to know more
	Creation	I want to do something to enhance myself
Participation	Family and friends (*Danran*)	I want to have a pleasant time with my family and friends
	Belonging	I want to be like others
	Social life	I want to keep company with many different people
Freedom	Me-ism	I want to live as I like regardless of others
	Individuality	I want to be distinctive from others
	Voluntary solitude	I want to have my own world, apart from others
Stability	Relaxation	I want to relax and take a rest
	Safety	I want to keep myself safe
	Health	I want to be healthy in mind and body

Source: Kazuaki Ushikubo, *European Research,* 1986.

Similar explanations of lifestyles are given for specific areas such as food and beverages, clothing, housing and leisure. The desire for safety, *danran* (having a happy time, enjoying communications with your family and the company of good friends), knowledge and creation seem to be crucial in the domain of food and beverages. For different domains of life, the expression of wants varies considerably.

The CORE system has been used mainly to study innovative products and services. Benefits and targets have been analyzed for the launch of such diverse products as word processors, fashion goods, the Tokyo Disneyland and a new type of shopping centre, called MARION, in the Ginza.

The INFOPLAN study — Japan

Japanese lifestyles, attitudes to products and consumer behaviour have changed considerably during the last decade. Attitudes towards work and leisure time have changed, and personal wealth has grown. INFOPLAN[3] has conducted studies of changing lifestyles within specific Japanese groups, such as "the new teenager", "the new singles", "the new *jitsunen*" (those in their 50s and 60s) and most recently "the new rich". This emerged from a study undertaken in 1989 among 1,000 Japanese males and females with a yearly income of over 10 million yen (US $80,000) — an interesting group as far as luxury products and services are concerned. The following sub-categories were found:

1. *The Quiet Rich*: 28 per cent of the total. This group is largely female, consisting of wives in traditional roles, who are becoming increasingly resentful of their roles and of the expectations forced on them.
2. *The Classic Rich*: 22 per cent of the total. This group represents the social and leadership elite of Japan. They are rather more flexible than the typical conservative Japanese, somewhat more male-oriented, and very well-educated; 53 per cent are university graduates. They tend to come from old, established families.
3. *The Conservative Rich*: 19 per cent of the total. These people are conservative; they are not sociable, nor are they interested in the pleasures of consumption. They are older and largely male.
4. *The Modern Rich*: one of the two New Rich types, and 15 per cent of the total. This is a new, younger, more independent, individualistic type, which is rather revolutionary in Japan. These Modern Rich are the youngest of all the types and the best educated; over 60 per cent are university graduates.
5. *The Overt Rich*: 16 per cent of the total, and the second New Rich type. The Overt Rich are into heavy consumption. They will buy and try anything. With the highest income of the five groups, these people are an important new category in Japan, and they also have the most fun.

INFOPLAN also found changes in attitudes towards tradition, marriage and relationships. One general observation is that the rich do not want to spend their money on "things" but on "experiences". Table 2 shows the major changes among Japanese consumers which are of importance to marketers.

Four life models

Like other large advertising agencies, Dentsu[4] has also researched values and lifestyles. The Dentsu Consumer Value Survey was used for this purpose from 1976 to 1988, with the aim of developing creative concepts for advertising. Four life models were found — "Achievers", "Intelligent", "Group Merit" and "Membership-dependent". The attitudes and values attached to the four life models are as follows:

1. *Achiever*: enterprising; attaches importance to individuality and to human relationships.
2. *Intelligent:* attaches importance to individuality in the area of intelligence,

Table 2 Major trends in Japan

Homogeneity	⟶	Variety
Traditional expectations	⟶	Personal preferences

"Large"
  (TV)
  (Superstores)
	⟶	"Small"
		  (Magazines)
		  (Boutiques)

"The company"	⟶	"The works"
"Work-driven"	⟶	Balanced life
Things	⟶	Experiences

Source: INFOPLAN/Robert Wilk, "The new rich: a psychographic approach to marketing to the wealthy
Japanese consumer", ESCOMAR conference, June 1990.

culture and arts; attaches importance to nature and communion with nature;
lacking in collective heritage.

3. *Group Merit*: makes full use of the organization to own best advantage;
   attaches importance to human relationships; has a great interest in arts and
   culture.

4. *Membership-dependent*: highly loyal to the organization; family centred; has a
   deep interest in nature.

Figure 2 shows the four life models and the attitudes towards life change
implicit in them.

Research in Malaysia, Singapore, Taiwan and Thailand

The Survey Research Group (SRG), which has offices in many Asian countries
including Singapore, Malaysia, Taiwan, Thailand, Hongkong and Indonesia, has
conducted lifestyle surveys in Malaysia, Singapore, Thailand and Taiwan. This
research will be extended to Hongkong and the Philippines. In 1987, the first
large-scale, quantitative psychographic research was conducted in Malaysia.
This was the first research of its kind in Asia as a whole.[5]

Malaysia

In the Malaysian psychographic study consumers were clustered into seven
psychographic segments: "Yesterday People", "Village Trendsetters",
"Chameleons", "Loners", the "New Breed", "Yuppies" and "Sleepwalkers".

The "Sleepwalkers" appear to be predominantly Chinese. They are relatively
family-minded, moralistic, introvert, socially and physically inactive,
conforming, followers, non-doers and neurotic. They are not religious,

Figure 2 Four Japanese life models: attitudes towards life changes

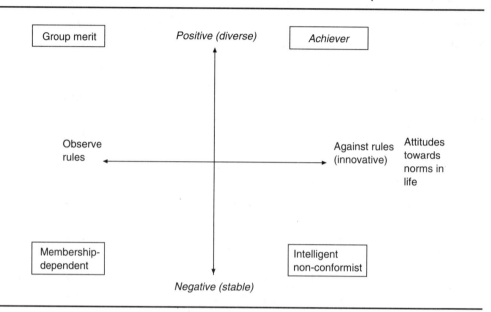

Source: Dentsu/Hiroe Susuki, "Japanese lifestyle, life models and applications to creative concepts", ESOMAR conference, June 1990.

adventurous or houseproud, and are less community spirited and patriotic. In order to understand why "Sleepwalkers" have such attitudes and values, it is necessary to understand Chinese culture and the influence on it of Confucianism, *Yin* and *Yang* and animism.

As an example, product buying behaviour of milk was compared for the Sleepwalkers and the Village Trendsetters, who are predominantly Malays. In the milk category, the penetration of fresh milk and evaporated milk on Sleepwalkers is only six per cent and two per cent, compared with seventeen percent and thirteen percent on Village Trendsetters. The relatively low penetration levels for the Sleepwalkers could be due to the Chinese belief in the *yin-yang* relationship. Refrigerated milk is still considered a "yin" food which will soothe and still the spirit — not a good way to start the day! Table 3 summarizes the findings.

In the branded biscuits, tomato sauce and chilli sauce categories, the penetration levels for Sleepwalkers are again significantly lower than for Village Trendsetters, as Table 4 shows.

The Sleepwalkers appear to be more price-sensitive and more interested in what the product does for them. They buy to fit in, not to stand out. The Village Trendsetters in contrast prefer established brand names and focus on attributes, image and status — anything that will give evidence of success.

Table 3 Penetration of fresh milk and evaporated milk among village trendsetters and sleepwalkers

Penetration	Village trendsetters %	Sleepwalkers %
Fresh milk	17	6
Evaporated milk	13	2

Source: Victor Kiu, Adasia conference, Lahore, Pakistan, 1990.

Table 4 Penetration of branded biscuits and sauces among village trendsetters and sleepwalkers

Penetration	Village trendsetters %	Sleepwalkers %
Branded biscuits	32	17
Branded tomato sauce	59	47
Branded chilli sauce	60	46

Source: Victor Kiu, Adasia conference, Lahore, Pakistan, 1990.

Singapore

In Singapore the Chinese and Malay population was clustered into ten psychographic groups. The Chinese were clustered into four groups and the Malays into six.

Figure 3 shows typology names and percentages with a vertical axis representing high v. low drive and a horizontal axis representing Eastern v. Western value expectations.

The four Chinese groups can be described as follows:

1. *The Brat Pack*: age 20–34, mostly single, with above-average education; Western oriented, youthful, individualistic and disinterested in most Eastern values; competitive, less materialistic, confident and quality conscious; light TV viewers, preferring English programmes; moderate radio listeners, preferring English channels; preferring English press to Chinese press.
2. *The Possession Paraders*: aged 20–44, married, well-educated; young optimists who have adjusted to the new society of Singapore; materialistic, status conscious, ambitious, upward striving; willing to spend on new and improved products; light TV viewers, preferring English programmes; moderate radio listeners, preferring English programmes; prefer English press to Chinese press; visit the cinema regularly.

Figure 3 Typologies found in Singapore

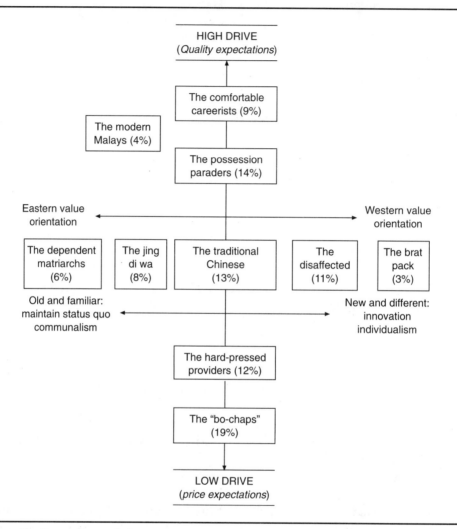

Source: The Survey Research Group.

3. *The Comfortable Careerists:* aged 25–44, married, well-educated; leaders in professions, corporate executives; visible success and affluence; appreciate value of education, go for luxury goods/services, like new and improved products; light TV viewers, preferring English programmes; moderate radio listeners, preferring English channels; avid English press reader, but also read Chinese newspapers.

4. *The Traditional Chinese:* aged 30–49 years, married, average education, mainly in Chinese; traditional, conforming, family-oriented, inward looking,

religious and superstitious; rational buyers who are brand loyal, preferring established brands; cautious about new things and ideas; average TV viewers, preferring Chinese programmes; light radio listeners, preferring Chinese programmes, frequent cinema goers, preferring Chinese movies.

The Malays were clustered in six groups, which can be described as follows:

1. *The Modern Malays*: below 45 years, married, average education; belong to the new breed of non-Chinese who have adjusted to the new society; combine the materialistic trappings of today with their traditional, religious and moral background; family-oriented; success-oriented; believe in good education; relatively carefree about money; would respond to sales promotions; prefer to stick to reasonably priced, established brand names; light TV viewers on weekdays but heavy on weekends; heavy radio listeners; prefer the Malay press, but also read the English press.

2. *The Jing Di Wa* ("Frogs in a well"): aged 35 years and over, married, primary education; traditional, family-oriented; narrow-minded, fatalistic and superstitious; follow norms; rational spenders, interested in what the product does for them, not what it says about them; heritage brand buyers; average on most things; heavy TV viewers and radio listeners; average press readership; low on cinema visits.

3. *The Disaffected*: age 20–34, mostly single, average education; come from traditional and conservative families but have been exposed to Western values through education; very status-conscious, materialistic; find life meaningless, do not know what to do with so much free time; bargain hunters, emotional spenders, seek new and improved products; heavy TV viewers especially at weekends; moderate radio listeners, average press readers.

4. *The Hard-Pressed Providers*: aged 35–39, married, primary education; law-abiding, good citizens; traditional and moralistic; family-oriented; materialistic, status-conscious; maintaining face is important; bargain hunters; image-oriented, but brand-loyal on established products; moderate TV viewers with low channel loyalty; moderate radio listeners; average readers of both English and Malay press; go to cinema occasionally.

5. *The "Bo-Chaps"*: diverse age groups, married, primary education; indifferent towards attitudes and values imposed by society; self-centred; low motivation; followers; fatalistic; emotional spenders; low brand loyalty; focus on benefits and good value for money; light TV viewers, preferring Malay programmes; light radio listeners, preferring Malay programmes; read Malay papers.

6. *The Dependent Matriarchs*: mostly women, aged 45 or over, married or widowed, primary education; out of the mainstream; resigned; relaxed,

contented; hold oriental attitudes, values and aspirations; price is the dominant factor; heavy TV viewers on weekdays but moderate on weekends; light radio listeners; light press readers.

Taiwan

SRG found eight psychographic clusters in Taiwan[7]. These may be described as follows:

1. *The Traditional Homebodies* (16 per cent of the population): solid citizens who take a fairly traditional view of life; not interested in trends; value and money conscious, open to bargains; like television and especially soap operas.
2. *The Confident Traditionalists* (12 per cent of the population): middle aged with a traditional outlook on morals and social virtues; competitive nature; not impulse buyers or bargain hunters; highly developed self-image and a keen sense of social expectations and norms.
3. *The Family-centred Fatalists* (13 per cent of the population): a female, family-oriented, older group; fairly content with the status quo, not interested in trendy goods but in traditional women's and family products.
4. *The Lethargic* (14 per cent of the population): this group does not stand out in any way, either in behaviour or product usage; their overriding characteristic is "ordinariness". Their buying and media habits make them difficult to reach. The key to selling to them appears to lie in distribution and media weight.
5. *The Middle-class Hopefuls*: down-to-earth; optimistic; male and middle-class; reasonable spenders; interested in new things, and willing to take a few risks with their money; important buyers of durables.
6. *The Discontented Moderns*: this group likes to follow new trends, but also retains a number of key traditional attitudes, and advertising should be careful not to offend these; heavy watchers of TV and cinema; looking for fun and a better quality of life.
7. *The Rebellious Young*: (7 per cent of the population): younger, discontented non-conformists; relatively affluent; seeming trend-setters in society; do not wait for a trend to be accepted; impulsive buyers; relatively individualistic, and therefore not impressed by any Western trend.
8. *The Young Strivers* (13 per cent of the population): a younger group of average affluence; competitive, materialistic; average TV viewers, but also users of cinema, radio, videos and magazines; not impulsive buyers or bargain hunters; look for specific goods that fit their self-image and needs.

Thailand[8]

In Thailand, psychographic research carried out in 1989 was restricted to Bangkok. A great diversity of lifestyles and values was found. The results suggested nine distinct segments: "Today's Women" (3 per cent), "The Comfortable Middle Class" (11 per cent), "We Got The Blues" (11 per cent), "Mainstream Belongers" (17 per cent), "Young Achievers" (11 per cent), "Young At Heart" (8 per cent), "Trying To Make It" (20 per cent), "The Left Outs" (7 per cent), and "Almost There" (12 per cent).

There are four groups which show brand loyalty and are readily influenced by advertising. "*Almost There*" consists of brand-loyal consumers, who are easily influenced by advertising. "*Trying To Make It*" is a group which is strongly conformist, but is also brand loyal and easily influenced by advertising. "*Mainstream Belongers*" support the status quo and the monarchy, are extrovert and brand-loyal, and, although they do not watch much television, are influenced by advertising. "*Young Achievers*" are materialistic, liberal and buy on impulse; they look for something new, and although they do not watch TV, they do pay attention to advertising. "*The Comfortable Middle Class*" consists of conformist, unambitious and unadventurous people who watch a lot of TV, but are neither greatly influenced by advertising nor very brand loyal. "*Today's Women*" are conformist, houseproud, family-oriented and watch a lot of TV, but are less strongly influenced by advertising. "*Young At Hearts*" are busy, socially-active people; they tend to be introvert, and are not impulse buyers; they watch less TV than others and are not greatly influenced by advertising. "*We Got The Blues*" are the least educated people of all segments. "*The Left Outs*" are the city's disadvantaged, low-income households.

NOTES

1. Kazuaki Ushikubo, 1986: "A method of structure analysis for developing product concepts and its applications", *European Research*.
2. Henry A. Murray, 1938: *Explorations in Personality*, Oxford University Press, New York.
3. Robert Wilk, "The new rich: a psychographic approach to marketing to the wealthy Japanese consumer", ESCOMAR Conference on: "America, Japan and EC '92; The Prospects for Marketing, Advertising and Research", Venice, Italy, 18–20 June 1990.
4. Hiroe Suzuki, "Japanese life-style, life models and applications to creative concepts", ESOMAR Conference on: "America, Japan and EC '92; The Prospects for Marketing, Advertising and Research", Venice, Italy, 18–20 June 1990.
5. Victor Kiu, "How advertising people in Asia interpret psychographic data", Adasia Conference, 18–23 February 1989, Lahore, Pakistan.
6. From findings of lifestyle research done by The Survey Research Group, kindly provided by Victor Kiu, Ogilvy & Mather, Singapore.
7. *Ibid.*
8. *Ibid.*

MARIEKE DE MOOIJ is Managing Director of the BBDO College, and World Secretary of the International Advertising Association Education Program.

WARREN KEEGAN is Professor of International Business at Pace University.

7 The Meanings of "YES" in the Far East

Carl R. Ruthstrom and Ken Matejka   B- relevance

Introduction

When does "yes" mean agreement? This paper will explore one possible reason for negotiation difficulties in the Far East. To improve their negotiating abilities, American negotiators must recognize some deficiencies in understanding language and cultural cues.

When presenting a contract proposal, the American presenter may find the Far Eastern listener(s) saying "yes" each time he or she pauses. The new American arrival may assume to be making great progress. But as the negotiations move forward, he or she may discover that "yes" does not have as clear-cut a meaning in the Far East as it does in the United States.

The four levels of "YES"

During the years we spent in Asian countries, four levels of meaning for the word "yes" were observed. These levels are:

1. *Recognition.* The first level acknowledges that you are talking to me, but I don't necessarily understand what you are saying. In many societies politeness demands that we recognize the words of the speaker either through a nodding of the head or uttering the word "yes" more out of instinct and focusing on the conversation than any real affirmation.

2. *Understanding.* The second level acknowledges that you are talking to me and adds that I understand you perfectly, but I may have no intention of doing what you propose. This is similar to "tacit agreement" in our American culture. The "yes" means that your words and meaning are clear

Reproduced with permission from *Industrial Marketing Management*, 19 (August 1990), pp. 191–192.

to me. Whether I agree with what you are saying cannot be determined unless it is specifically asked.

3. *Responsibility*. The next level of "yes" conveys that I understand your proposal, but I must consult with others and secure their agreement before your proposal can be accepted.

4. *Agreement*. The final level of "yes" means that I understand, we are in total agreement, and your proposal is accepted.

The American negotiator's lack of understanding of the people and customs of the Far East can easily result in a failure to understand which level of "yes" is operative and cause irreparable harm to the negotiations. The negotiator is considered a "guest," and the negotiation is a "quest." Considerable "loss of face" could be inflicted on the host if the guest were offended, embarrassed, or harmed in any way. Therefore, the traditionally courteous host says "yes" after each phrase or pause by the negotiator.

A real life example

One example of this potential communication problem occurred when an American organization shipped a telephone cable laying machine into a country to expedite the completion of a telephone system. The Americans involved had proposed that they obtain the machine for the project and improperly thought that the "yes" responses to the proposal meant total agreement of all parties involved. To the utter dismay of the Americans, the machine was parked and allowed to rust. Later conversations revealed that they were in total agreement that the cable laying machine was the best way to construct the system, but there were several overriding reasons for not using the machine. First, the host country had a large number of manual laborers who needed jobs. Second, the wages were extremely low in comparison to the cost of fuel. And third, the host country officials felt a moral obligation to provide the laborers with the means to be self-sufficient.

Besides communication, an ethical dilemma may arise. Oftentimes, consensus was thought to have been reached only to find weeks later that nothing was being done. When asked why no action had been taken on a specific task or recommendations, the host country officials often replied that their superior had not yet told them to do the task. To the uninitiated negotiator, these host country officials, whether government representatives or private businessmen, may appear to be acting in an unethical manner. This perceived ethical dilemma is really created by the inability of the negotiator to interpret which level of "yes" was involved.

Solution to the meanings of "YES"

The solution to this communication problem for companies attempting to do business in the Far East multifaceted. First, the negotiator must be aware of and sensitive to the culture and customs as they relate to business in the particular host country. Second, it is highly desirable to speak the language of the host country. Learning the language and customs are not only expeditious for understanding, but they symbolize respect for the partner. Finally, and perhaps more realistic in the short run, negotiators must be carefully taught to ask questions that cannot be answered by a simple yes or no. For the negotiators who were involved in our example of the cable laying machine, the questions could have included the following: (1) While we seem to agree on the usefulness of the machine, is there any reason why we might want to pursue another alternative?; (2) When should the machine arrive in your country?; (3) What is the earliest date that you intend to put the machine into operation?; (4) Is there anything else that we need to understand before we go forward? The answers to these questions could have immediately revealed the host country officials' level of meaning of "yes"!

CARL R. RUTHSTROM is from the Department of Management and Marketing at Stephen F. Austin State University, Nacogdoches, Texas.

KEN MATEJKA is from the School of Business and Administration at Duquesne University, Pittsburgh, Pennsylvania.

III Researching and Selecting Target Markets

The research and selection of appropriate target markets is a vital activity of marketing decision making. Hence, marketers in the Asia Pacific must be able to distinguish and cater to the different characteristics and needs of consumers in different segments in which they operate.

After reading the four articles in this part, you should derive a deeper insight into the following aspects of marketing in the region:

1   The differences between and application of mass marketing, market segmentation, and mass customization.
2   Consumer and industrial markets in Japan, South Korea, and Southeast Asia.

8   Mass Customization: Japan's New Frontier

Roy Westbrook and Peter Williamson

Mass customization — making products tailor-made for each individual buyer, in which even the base components are varied — sounds impossible. Yet it is a reality in Japan and represents a new Japanese competitive advantage.

Roy Westbrook and Peter Williamson, reflecting on many visits to Japan, identify a new generic strategy — mass customization — in the story of continuous growth fuelled by response to crisis, so revered in Japan.

The authors cite case studies of Melbo (men's clothing) and National Panasonic Bicycle as successful Japanese examples, underlining the fact that such achievement depends on a high degree of manufacturing competence. This is a serious competitive threat.

Copernicus would have smiled. The accountants claimed it defied the laws of economics. Industry experts pronounced it an impossibility. The shop floor workers were convinced that their bosses were taking tremendous risks which could only be the result of too much *sake*. The managerial ranks produced reams of careful argument explaining why the plans should be abandoned. The object of their scepticism was *mass customization*: the idea of producing mass volumes of tailor-made suits, bicycles or golf clubs manufactured to fit the shapes and tastes of their future owners. For years, progressive companies had offered the customer a wide range of cosmetic choice: automobile finish or upholstery, different engine sizes, or thousands of faces on Swatch® watches. But to produce a product which was customized to the core, so that even the base components were varied for each individual buyer, would require a daunting list of new capabilities. Worse still, such a change could render obsolete many of the very skills and processes of standardization, volume production a company had spent years honing to perfection. Mass customization suffered from almost every

Reproduced with permission from *European Management Journal*, 11 (March 1993), pp. 38–45.

imaginable problem from unacceptably high investment requirements to directly threatening company culture. Yet, in the most recent of our many visits to Japanese companies we have seen the emergence of mass customization as a reality. We believe it represents the new frontier of Japan's competitive advantage in a world of increasingly saturated markets and sluggish growth in demand for many manufactured products.

Thinking the unthinkable

After a prolonged period of remarkable economic success what has happened to cause Japanese companies to begin thinking about, experimenting with, and implementing an unthinkable like mass customization which threatens to turn their world upside down? The answer, we believe, lies in the fact that Japan "loves" a crisis.

We saw it with the oil shocks and again with Endaka. Japan emerged from those crises, which were assumed to spell the end of her economic miracle, with even greater competitiveness. Today the leaders of Japanese business and society are busily painting in the storm clouds of a new, traumatic scenario. They are pointing to the slowdown of Japanese market growth in recent years, to the demographic threat from a greying society, to the shortage of domestic labour, and to the changing attitudes to work among the new generation in Japan. The evidence is everywhere for those who care to look; they say, that Japan's progress risks being slowed to a crawl by the spectre of economic stagnation. They are quietly confident, of course, that the creativity and energy of the Japanese people, fuelled by fierce domestic competition, will again produce ways of solving these problems. At the same time, they know that simply entreating workers and management to expend greater and greater effort will not provide the way forward. They recognize that the strategies of Japanese companies must now take another step.

Take a look at the drivers of Japanese economic progress over the last 30 years, and it is clear why its major companies are now in need of a new growth tonic. During the initial period of Japan's post-war expansion, much of the growth was achieved through relentless lowering of the costs of reliable, standardized products. Manufactured goods which had previously been the novelties of the rich becomes affordable to an ever increasing proportion of an expanding population. Today this is known in Japan as the "product out" period.[1] The first oil crisis in 1973–74, combined with the beginning of saturation of the local market, rendered this "manufacturer push" strategy ineffective as an engine of further growth. For all their success the quality circles, value engineering and zero defect systems, which had underpinned dramatic cost reductions and increased reliability, were no longer enough.

Recognizing that new growth would come only from convincing Japanese consumers they needed not just one home air conditioner, but a different size, colour and specification for every room, for example, manufacturers began to add more variety to their product lines. Looking for overseas growth as a supplement, they added further models, with new gadgets, bells and whistles in order to differentiate their products as a way of wresting share from entrenched, local incumbents. This period, extending roughly from the mid 1970s through to the mid 1980s is known as "market in". While trying to lock in cost savings through component and process design, manufacturers added additional features to stimulate increased demand.

By the late 1980s, however, Japanese consumers were again reaching saturation, they not only had most types of products, they now had a range of each. Worse still, the gadgets, bells and whistles were losing their novelty. Quite simply, consumers were becoming bored. Manufacturers copied a trick the fashion industry had learnt a long time ago: if you want people to buy, keep changing what is on offer. Well before a product's technical life has run, ensure it is demonstrably out of date. Product life cycles were shortened, underpinned by simultaneous engineering and impressive reductions in product development times. Not only was the notoriously choosy Japanese customer offered a wide range of product varieties, new variations of each continually hit the market in the hope of exciting replacement demand. The skill of Japanese companies in resolving the contradictions between rapid turnover of a wide variety of models and low cost manufacture have enabled them to pull off this feat to a degree which has made many of their international competitors wince.

Yet there was little time for congratulation; by the early 1990s business leaders were pointing out that the old ghost of demand stagnation was already beginning to reappear. Domestic capacity was also being replaced by "plant export" to cheaper areas within the Asian region from where Japanese companies were shipping a variety of quality products back to Japan. High volume, low cost producers among the NIEs, like nearby South Korea, were increasingly supplying the Japanese market on which even leading companies were still dependent for over 75% of their sales. Luxury European brands, meanwhile, were capturing the high-end and even penetrating the mainstream market as a population of over 8 million Gucci handbags in Tokyo testifies. Many industries could see the writing on the wall for their strategic positioning in the Japanese market, but their problem was where to go next?

The available list of generic strategies had been exhausted. Japanese manufacturers had been cost leaders, they had become effective differentiators, they had then moved on to combine the benefits of both. They rejected the route chosen by many Western companies: to provide a specialized product variety to meet the needs of a particular segment by becoming focused, niche competitors. Instead they replicated many of the advantages of focus by combining flexible, multi-model production systems with a distribution network which feeds back very detailed information on the requirements of particular groups of buyers. Despite these achievements, the task master of continuous growth, so revered in corporate Japan, was demanding to see a new trick.

A new generic strategy is emerging to meet the need for growth through the 1990s by a process which is classically Japanese. Rather than being announced or codified, it is being developed out of practical necessity by a number of companies at once. To these firms it reflects a logic which is irresistible as a way out of the strategic *impasse* they would otherwise face. Given markets close to saturation and consumers who now regard very wide choice, low cost, high quality and fast delivery as the norm, what could possibly add more value and continue to stimulate demand? Answer: the widest variety of all — to personalize the product for each customer.

Of course this has been done before. We are all aware that customized products are available. In fact, many hark back to the days long before mass production was a gleam in Henry Ford's eye. But the tailored suits and hand-made shoes which respond exactly to our personal needs cost a premium over goods off the shelf which few of us could begin to afford for everyday purchases. Once or twice in a lifetime we may indulge in spending on a really special item combining a craftsman's skilled care with the "custom-made" cachet. The strategic innovation is that now Japanese companies have begun to offer a truly customized product — one made to the customer's precise specifications from the ground up — at only a small premium over goods in the store.

The trick lies in an alliance between their obsession with discovering the customer's needs with their highly responsive and flexible production methods to offer potentially *millions* of variants which are inherently, rather than cosmetically, different. As we detail in the case studies below, by creating just one of these variants in response to a customer's order they can provide a result which is virtually indistinguishable from old-fashioned customization processes at a cost normally associated with high volume manufacture of a standard range. What is more, they can do it with a response time that would cause the Savile Row tailor to lose a great deal of sleep. The capability to supply the mass market with products which are manufactured, not just finished, to meet a customer's individual requirements at prices and with lead times that market now expects, is allowing a new generic strategy — *mass customization* — to be born.

Here we have more evidence, if more were needed, of the pace of change in global competition. When Ohmae urged us to "get back to strategy" in 1988,[2] by listening to customers and finding ways to add value based on their needs, rather than competitor's actions, he was right. But he was still referring to new product design in which value was embodied in the product itself, a product which you bought in the store just like other goods. Now, only four years later, Japan's mass customizers are offering a new level of customer involvement in product design. Remember that Japan has long been the country in which you could create your own house, not by employing an expensive architect, but by choosing from a catalogue showing a range of prefabricated room units, mixing, matching, choosing colour schemes, and have it all delivered on trailers and assembled in just a few weeks. Now this principle is being extended to other products; from fishing rods to cosmetics, golf clubs, gent's suits and bicycles. For those firms who have recognized that mass production was a milestone along the road of the relentless improvement in the supply chain, rather than an end goal, mass customization becomes the obvious next step. (See Figure 1.)

Figure 1 Mass customization: the logical "next step"

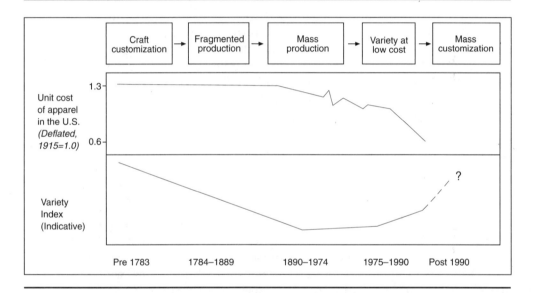

Sources: *One Hundred Years of Economic Statistics* (Economist Publications, 1989), *Statistical Tables of National Income, Expenditure and Output, 1855–1965,* C. H. Feinstein (Cambridge University Press).

Although the strategic idea seems simple enough, there is nothing inevitable about its successful implementation. This requires the complex combination of excellence in marketing, engineering and logistics. Just within the last two examples — suits and bicycles — there are varying degrees of success. For although mass customization has obvious market appeal, it can easily become a manufacturing and logistics nightmare. It is a strategy which critically depends on a high degree of manufacturing competence.

Suiting the customer

Up until the late 1970s the Melbo company made suits in much the same way as everyone else, and like all of their competitors, at the end of the season they faced the problem of unsold stock. Many companies simply shifted it by means of reduced price "sales". For a company building an exclusive brand image, however, this was anathema. Instead, Melbo was forced to swallow retailer returns from all over Japan. Because its brand strategy involved offering wide customer choice, however, stock obsolescence was high. Faced with this conundrum somehow the stock in the pipeline from factory to final customer would have to be reduced.

The germ of a solution came from an apparently unlikely source. As Vice-president Shimizu put it to us: "In the late 1970s the Toyota production system was becoming widely known, and we went to look at it. We were impressed by the idea of selling a car first, then making it; by the many colours and styles on the line; and by the very low inventory, especially since stock was such a problem to Melbo. So in 1978 we launched our Apollo project".

The name "Apollo" comes from the fact that the project was seen as a ten-year development effort. Like much of Japanese borrowing of ideas, the Apollo project was not simply a matter of transplantation. Automobile manufacture, for all its end variety, is based on a range of standard models and components which the customer mixes and matches. In bespoke tailoring, by contrast, customization has to begin right back at the cloth cutting stage; even the base "components" have to be unique. Melbo's goal was to move from the six days it took to make a suit to a lead time of just one day. Today, manufacturing lead time is three days. Measured solely in terms of its ambitious lead time goal, Melbo has fallen short. But in the course of its continuing quest, the Apollo project has taken the company in some unexpected directions, which have now placed Melbo within an arm's reach of mass customization.

Entering one of Melbo's own stores in Tokyo today, you will find the fine wood panelling of an up-market men's clothing emporium. What you will not find are the usual acres of racks, crammed with stock and occupying lots of phenomenally expensive Tokyo real estate. Instead the entire store carries less than a hundred suits, with a floor space requirement only a fraction of that needed by competitors. Melbo's customers do not come to fit themselves into a suit on the rack because the company's "Ready-Made Order System®" will guarantee that a suit designed by houses like Givenchy, Daniel Hechter, or Nina Ricci, but individually cut can sewn to fit them, with a choice of over a hundred fabrics, will arrive at their home or office within the week. In 1991 Melbo's sales of suits exceeded ¥18 billion, yet it provides a service almost as customized as a local tailor. At the same time it saves the costs of stock and the retail space in which to display it.

Behind the scenes at the Shiga plant you can see both the change in manufacturing thinking necessary to support mass customization and the practical difficulties in implementing it. Orders carrying the 18 details which define the customer's order arrive by fax from stores around the country. These are then input into the CAD/CAM system which will direct the automatic marking and cutting. Right at the cutting stage the differences in production philosophy are evident. Throughout the world engineers are working to produce machines which will cut more and more layers of fabric with a single pass. By cutting 50 or 100 suits at once, so the argument goes, production can be speeded up and costs pared. Instead, Melbo cuts only two layers of fabric, enough for a single suit, at once. The idea of using computer-controlled cutting for these "one-offs" departs so much from received wisdom in the industry that Melbo had to have machines specially designed for the purpose.

Cutting one suit at a time like this could hold up the entire production system, with every suit queuing to be cut. To prevent this cutting bottleneck, it was essential for Melbo to find ways of taking time out of the process. One method has been to increase the number of cutting machines relative to that in similar, mass production plants. The machines have also been designed so that while the automatic cutter is at work on one suit, the operator is setting the cloth in position for the next. This simple idea means that the cutting machines never stop: some of the loss in processing time has been won back by avoiding lost time in set-up.

Your local tailor would then begin to construct the suite sequentially. Instead, Melbo processes different parts of the suit, trousers, arms, collars and even sub-sections of the body itself, in parallel. Each individual suit is therefore being constructed virtually simultaneously by highly specialized operators and machinery. This should permit a dramatic reduction in lead time. The challenges, however, are obviously formidable: the work rates of every operator must be carefully timed and coordinated and every individual sub-assembly for the hundreds of suits passing through the factory each day must be precisely tracked. Getting it wrong could easily result in an output of patchwork quilts, his sleeves sewn to your shoulders, or a sorting operation at final assembly worthy of a major post office. Most other manufacturers solve the problem by sending large batches, much easier to keep track of, to each work-station in a sequence. At Melbo, shrewd coding and automatic transfer systems, including AGVs (automatic guided vehicles), make sure all of the sub-parts come together at final assembly. (See Figure 2.)

Despite these achievements, Melbo still has further to go. Although the JIT idea of a batch size of one has been attained, their mass customization system still buffers the different work rates of individual operators by allowing work in progress of between six to twelve items between each station. The accumulation of these small delays contribute to the current 3 day lead time. Lacking the

Figure 2 Melbo's Shiga mass customization plant

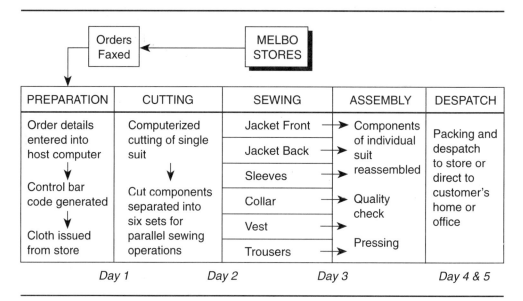

strong engineering presence on the shop floor which is so characteristic of many other Japanese manufacturers, it is not clear how the work flow will be improved. But the Apollo project may be only temporarily stalled. If other garment makers begin to embrace mass customization, as they almost certainly will, Melbo will doubtless press on with the engineering tasks necessary to reap the full potential of the strategy.

"The human bicycle"

National Panasonic Bicycle (NPB) has taken mass customization in still new directions in the drive to avoid the all too common spiral of sluggish demand and retrenchment associated with "mature" industries. Part of the giant Matsushita Electronics Industries, many Western parents would probably have sold NPB off years ago as a "dog" business in an otherwise high growth portfolio. From the early 1980s the outlook for the highly competitive Japanese bicycle industry looked bleak. Sales of all models were dropping and prices were being forced down across the board, trends aggravated by cheaper imports from the NIEs. Consumer demand was beginning to fragment as new segments emerged. NPB found itself on the wrong side of these trends with falling share in the "sports cycles" market. Even the fashion for mountain bikes seemed only to give NPB indigestion trying to cope with rising variety, a more complicated forecasting task, and increased inventory.

In 1987, NPB set itself a set of ambitious strategic targets which, to some, looked like a contradiction in terms:

- to create demand for high value-added products which met diverse individual needs
- to clearly distinguish themselves from the competition
- to avoid producing any unsold stock or obsolete products
- to prevent retail price cutting

Their secret weapons were a scheme to build a new pilot plant within their factory at Osaka combined with a marketing strategy deploying what is now known as the "Panasonic Order System".

The Panasonic Order System (POS) was based on a simple concept: if you can order a tailored suit, then why not a tailored bicycle? The customer enters any cycle shop in Japan on the USA which displays the "POS" sign and he or she is measured up on a special frame because, as Managing Director Hata puts it, "it is obvious that riders come in different proportions not just different heights" so the frame dimensions will be custom built, piece by piece. The customer can also choose from a wide variety of design elements (see Fig. 3),

Figure 3   Custom choices at National Panasonic bicycle: 11,231,862 total variations

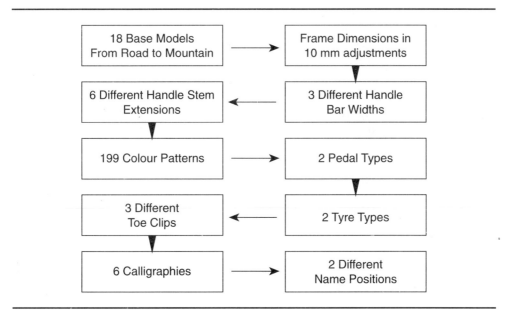

even down to five choices of script for the customer's name to be painted on the frame! The cycle will be in that customer's hands in under two weeks in Japan, or three weeks if the bicycle has to be shipped to a shop in America.

The POS marketing slogan is "be one of a kind". In fact, when the system was introduced in 1988 you would have been more like "one in 11,655". Back then, with a choice of 4 models, 44 frame sizes and 35 colour schemes, Stalk and Hout described the company as a "semi-custom" supplier in their popular book *Competing Against Time*.[3] Today the range is over 11 million; a one thousand fold step forward in mass customization. Tomorrow will see even more customization still as National Bicycle plans to offer 1 mm increments in frame dimensions instead of the 10 mm increments now available. But the point is that, despite the marketing advantage of offering a customized product, manufacturing is not being asked to deal with infinite variety. 199 surface finishes seems like a lot to most customers, but of course it could be far wider. To allow the customer to dictate his own personal hue and pattern, rather than to select from limited ranges, might invalidate the robotized painting process. It would tip the plant over the edge into traditional, hand-built customization.

Instead, the complexity is being controlled so that many of the mass production techniques are still applicable. Mass customization involves carefully mixing true individualization, with high variety and standardized processes. Customer perception guides the decision as to where customization can add real value versus where a wide choice will do. The riding comfort that can come only from the right frame dimensions demands true customization, down to the last 1 mm. For finish, however, true customization would have little more to add to customer satisfaction compared with the cost. Here a wide choice of standard colours and patterns is sufficient. This is the delicate balance which successful mass customization must find. The balance also shifts as new capabilities are developed. Mass customization is not a matter of "one shot" change. It is an incremental process, like so much in Japan. NPB is increasing the customized component as it learns to deliver ever greater individualization.

The basic specification POS custom bicycle is priced at the top of the standard range. Although certain choices cost extra, the average cost is only 15% above the best mass produced cycle. But the real advantage comes from the fact that salespeople can now encourage customers to trade up to an individualized version. NPB can thus break out of the destructive downward price spiral of comparisons with competitors and cheaper models by adding demonstrable extra value. A great marketing idea, but consider the production challenges.

Each bicycle is quite different at its most basic level: the dimensions of each piece of the frame. So when your order arrives at the factory by fax, minutes after you have left the store, there is no basic frame in stock, no pre-cut components, only 20ft lengths of metal tube. Your details are entered into the computer system (see Figure 4) which converts the specifications into a set of manufacturing instructions for each stage of frame manufacture. Then when a section of tube arrives at the first process, it has a bar code attached which identifies it as yours. The operator need only swipe his bar code reader across this label and the computer-controlled tube cutting machine can, drawing on your individual measurement data, automatically adjust the end stop of the cutting machine to suit and cut a tube to the precise length for you. The operator is liberated to deal with the ancillary processes grouped around him in the production cell which enables higher labour productivity and lower cost. In later production stages, several ex-professional cyclists in the workforce ensure that components are assembled with appropriate care.

Figure 4 Behind the "Panasonic order system" at National Panasonic bicycle

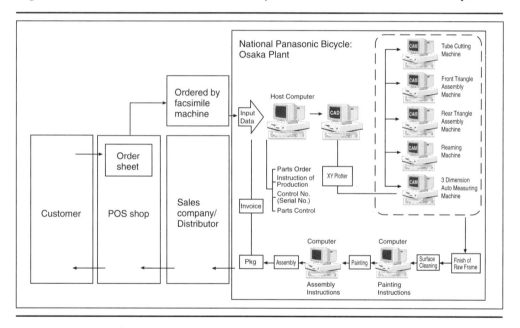

Last year NPB produced only 15,000 customized bicycles in its pilot plant, but already the experiment in mass customization has had a profound influence on the company. The customized product has regenerated the company's image so that sales of the 723,000 off-the-shelf bicycles it sold last year have enjoyed a boost. Its retailers are now focused on selling differentiated features, not just on price. It has also extended its capabilities by developing new equipment, methods, and acquiring new skills in CAD/CAM, the use of bar coding and production cells. The standard bicycle factory has directly benefited from the application of these systems and skills to its own production system.

Most important of all, National Panasonic Bicycle has proved that mass customization can be a reality, not just a pipe dream. When they floated their plan with industry experts just four years ago they were politely assured that mass customization was impossible. The accountants proved the numbers did not add up, but already the POS bicycle is profitable. The employees were sceptical, a feeling now reversed; today active groups refine and develop the new philosophy. Managing director Kotaro Hata has cause for some satisfaction. Not only was he the scheme's designer and champion against heavy odds, but, being a production engineer, he played the key role in designing the pilot plant and its facilities. Now NPB have developed the competence necessary to support mass customization. Having reached a new frontier, the only question is when the pilot plant will be scaled up to provide an unbeatable offering to an even larger market.

Where next?

How long before every car, easy chair, personal organizer or even video camera is made for an individual? In 1990 Motorola salesmen were sending orders (via computer link) for customized pagers through to the factory. Within 17 minutes of receipt production had begun for next day delivery. The manufacturing objections to mass customization are being overcome in industry after industry. The economic order quantity is breathing its last gasps. For decades our factories have been arguing that the goal of cost efficiency requires us to produce items that do not fit the customer's personal requirements at a time they are not wanted. As FMS, computer-integrated manufacturing and communication between the factory and the market all improve, and flexible plans render changeover time immaterial, these arguments lose whatever validity they had in the past. More and more companies will build the capabilities to deliver what might have seemed as unrealistic set of customer promises only a few years before.

The proliferation of mass customization will have profound effects on the roles of factories, designers and marketers. The factory will itself become a service centre with a much closer link to retailer and final customer. Finished goods inventory will increasingly become an anachronism as customers are offered products manufactured to suit them at a modest additional cost either in price or time delay. Designers will shift their focus from designing finished product lines to designing choices which allow the customer to complete the final design. Rather than designing a range of cosmetic finishes and after-thoughts, tomorrow's designers will have to consider how choice can be built in at the level of base components, like the frame of a bicycle. Marketing will have to shift its focus from "segment" to "individual". Customers will want to be "one of a kind". And the product catalogues of yesteryear, with reams of product listings, will be found wanting. Consumers will need marketing materials which educate them in designing something customized. Would you know which of the pedal styles or tyre types available on a National POS bicycle to choose? The job of marketing will increasingly be to predict or create the next new service the customer will demand from the factory.

Mass customization also has implications for channel strategy. National Panasonic Bicycle have had to select and train 15,000 dealers with the kind of facilities and staff necessary to communicate the advantages of customization. Each has to be equipped with both a "fitting" machine and a facsimile (a Panasonic, of course!). Once established, however, mass customization outlets act as a uniquely valuable source of up-to-the-minute market intelligence. Previously this information came in the rather expensive form of returned suits and bicycles unsold at the end of the period. Now exact and current information about what buyers are choosing comes down the Melbo or POS fax lines. Trends can be quickly spotted. New styles can be launched without the risk of writing off stock. It is no longer a matter of waiting for last period's aggregate sales data and then sitting down to interpret them. Mass customization gives the company a direct line to the market.

In the second half of the 1990s when personally customized products become more common, the generic strategies of the 1970s will look even more inadequate than they do today. The Japanese have already demonstrated that cost leadership and differentiation were not mutually exclusive alternatives. They are now poised on a new frontier. It will again join the forces of two old adversaries, this time mass production and customization. The union will undoubtedly be a powerful one, opening the way for product–service combinations as yet unheard of.

The Japanese stand to gain most from the rapid introduction of customized, mass market products. Their well-developed sub-contract relationships and *Keiretsu* networks, linking sales, assembly, component and raw material suppliers, will be even more potent sources of advantage in a world where variety and flexibility extended right back into the core of manufactured products. Since mass customization often means higher volatility in the demand for different types of components, such as specific styles of pedals or tyres, the fact that a company like National Panasonic Bicycle is tightly linked to its supplier, none located more than 40 minutes away, is a major advantage. Mass customization will also allow Japanese firms to lever off highly developed competences in optimizing workflow, in implementing flexible manufacturing and in the application of barcoding and IT to the factory floor. Their historically close links with retail distribution will give many Japanese manufacturers a head start in educating buyers to the possibilities mass customization offers. In Japan's drive to stay ahead of its next real or imagined crisis, mass customization looks set to be the next frontier territory into which it could be difficult for the competition to follow. There is no time to lose.

NOTES

1. Yamashina, H., *Competitive Manufacturing and Subcontracting Systems*, Kyoto University, Mimeo, 1991.
2. Ohmae, K. "Getting Back to Strategy", *Harvard Business Review*, November–December, 1988.
3. Stalk, G. and Hout, T. *Competing Against Time*, Free Press, 1990.

ROY WESTBROOK, *London Business School, Sussex Place, Regent's Park, London NW1 4SA* Assistant Professor of Operations Management at London Business School. Roy Westbrook worked with the Department of Health and Social Security before turning his attention to manufacturing management. His doctoral research was on design of information systems for production management. He has studied manufacturing methods in Japan and Europe, and developed a particular interest in the management of quality, in both manufacturing and service organisations.
He has published in various academic journals, and recent articles include "Time to Forget 'Just-in-Time'? Observations on a Visit to Japan" *and* "New Strategic Tools for Supply Chain Management".

PETER J. WILLIAMSON, *London Business School, Sussex Place, Regent's Park, London NW1 4SA*
Peter Williamson joined the Strategic and International Management Faculty at London Business School after a number of years with the Boston Consulting Group in London. He holds an MBA and Ph.D. from Harvard where he taught strategy and business economics. Dr Williamson has worked extensively in the Far East. His current research includes work on Japanese distribution systems and export strategy.

9 Seven Crucial Viewpoints to Understand the Japanese Consumer

Masaru Ariga

Japan is a rich market with promise. The world has watched in wonder the remarkable economic successes this nation has achieved in the past 30 years. With 122 million of the most affluent people in Asia, Japan wields enormous purchasing power. The combination of capital, growth and people attracts business from every continent of the world.

Although Japan may have many Western features, it is a unique blend of both Western and indigenous elements. Japanese eclectically assimilate these elements (including other cultures) into their own culture. However, it still retains strong Japanese values which make both the culture and the market different from any other.

During the high economic growth era, the Japanese united as one people in a race to catch up to Western standards of living — to create a new lifestyle. They have achieved that goal and the society has matured. Changes in lifestyles that we witness today go beyond mimicry of Western ideals. The result is a nation of people with many different values, ideals, aspirations and standards of living.

If Japan were to be described in one word, it would be "change." The rapid pace of change makes it all the more difficult for businesses to use marketing tools that were successful in other countries and even in Japan a few years ago. One example of macro-sociological change is that Japan's society is aging at a faster rate than in any other country. This alone will pose major challenges to businesses which must adapt to meet the needs of a society whose over-65 population will reach 20 per cent early in the 21st century.

Changes in the consciousness and lifestyle values of the Japanese themselves accompany changes in the social structure. For example, Japanese are striving to

Reproduced with permission from *Japan 1991 Marketing and Advertising Yearbook*, Tokyo: Dentsu, Inc., 1991, pp. 85–90.

shed the "workaholic" image. Family life is taking on more importance as a recent Dentsu Lifestyle Survey confirmed. This and other studies show that Japanese want to lead more enjoyable lives apart from work. Therefore, industries which enrich the quality of life, such as leisure, sports and travel are booming.

In order to succeed in the Japanese market, businesses must discern not only Japan's differences from other markets, but also the changing trends in present Japan.

This article highlights seven viewpoints of the changing lifestyles of the Japanese from the consumer perspective, and the implications that these viewpoints have on marketing in Japan.

Viewpoint 1: Condensed society

Japan is a "condensed society," a relatively large population situated on a comparatively small land mass. It is easy to overlook the extent to which this lack of space affects every aspect of Japanese life.

In comparison to Europe and the U.S., Japan is a relatively small country. It is also a mountainous country, and only 30 per cent of the total land area is habitable, making the population density of cities very high. Specifically, population density averages 322 persons per square kilometer, or 834 persons per square mile, including uninhabitable land. Counting only the habitable portion, the density of the population is considerably higher. As it is, the state ratio in Japan is more than 12 times that of the U.S., and more that three times that of France. As a result, living space is severely cramped. A family in Japan has only 60 per cent of the housing space that Americans enjoy. For this reason, space and convenience often take precedence over cost.

Overcrowding in the cities results in astronomically high land prices. On the average, a home in Tokyo that would be uncomfortably small by most Western standards costs about eight times a household's annual income, almost double that in America.

An increasing number of people are moving farther and farther out into the suburbs, lengthening the distance between home and work. Commuting time has risen, bringing stress to all who must travel these distances. In Tokyo, the average business person commutes more than an hour each way in crowded trains.

The "condensed society" aspect of Japan has spurred several "time-saving business" opportunities: Japanese are always on the lookout for more efficient uses of limited time and space. The "capsule hotel" is one extreme example. Guests at capsule hotels sleep in cubicles stacked one on top of the other. Each cubicles or "capsule," is equipped with a radio, television and alarm clock, and communal shower and sauna facilities are located down the hall. Capsule hotels

International comparison of living space (m²)

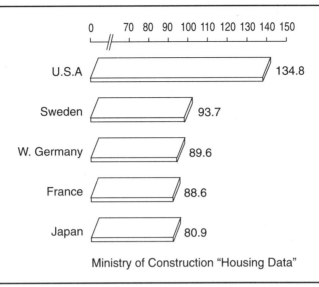

U.S.A — 134.8
Sweden — 93.7
W. Germany — 89.6
France — 88.6
Japan — 80.9

Ministry of Construction "Housing Data"

are an inexpensive alternative for those who, having missed the last train, would rather not wait up to two hours for an expensive taxi ride home, only to face a long grueling train ride back to work the next morning.

There is also a huge market for time-expanding, or 24-hour businesses, such as golf ranges, tennis courts and convenience stores. These give business people the flexibility to make their own schedules and fit several activities into the day rather than be restricted by limited business hours. It is not all pleasure; there are even all night schools for studying English for the particularly dedicated businessperson.

A third development is the "one-room mansion." Primarily popular among young singles, these "mansions" are usually 15 to 20 square meters or 130 to 200 square feet in area. The residents must go to extraordinary lengths to fit all their belongings into such a place. Businesses must take such living environs into account when designing new products. Product miniaturization, for one, is a big business.

Viewpoint 2: Tokyo concentration

For the Japanese, Tokyo is the center of the universe — the only place to be. This domineering influence affects all Japanese from Okinawa to Hokkaido.

One quarter of the population, or about 30 million people are concentrated in the greater Tokyo area. Tokyo is the center of Japanese finance, manufacturing, and government, as well as the birthplace of major cultural trends. Everything revolves around Tokyo. Tokyo could be compared to a black hole, attracting anything and everything. Because Tokyo is the source of all that is current throughout Japan, it may also be compared to an exploding star, a continual "big bang."

Tokyo is also the center of capital. It is no wonder that Tokyo citizens are the recipients and users of an abnormally large proportion of bank loans. Like a black hole, this capital formation grows and becomes more concentrated every year.

With regards to the concentration of business, foreign, along with Japanese companies are drawn to this city. Of the nearly 1,300 foreign firms in Japan, nearly 90 per cent are concentrated in greater Tokyo. Furthermore, Tokyo is the source of information for Japan. Not only are new ideas and trends born in Tokyo, but information from other regions of Japan also finds its way first to Tokyo and then wends its way throughout the nation. As Japan becomes a more advanced information society, being at the heart of this concentration of information will become increasingly important.

Percentage of population in Tokyo

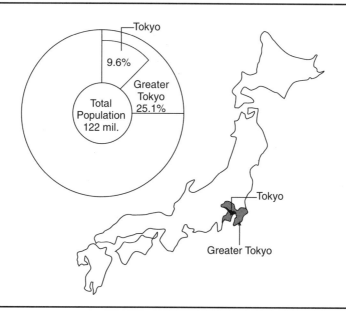

Source: Ministry of Home Affairs, "Population Census".

Also of importance is the enormous purchasing power of Tokyo's consumers, as large corporation headquarters and well paid jobs are found in the city. Look around: haute couture, Louis Vuitton bags, mink coats and high-priced accessories are everyday sights.

Tokyo contains what have become known as "antenna shops," established by such diverse business interests as beer brewers and auto markers. These unusual shops feature everything from clothing to restaurants to event halls. Why?

The Tokyo market is an accurate indicator of the total national market, as most changes in lifestyle begin in Tokyo. Businesses aiming to dominate or find a niche in the market ignore Tokyo at their peril. Young people in particular, start trends which, in time, will reverberate throughout Japan. To capture these trends, companies establish "antenna shops." The purpose of these shops is not high sales volume, but rather, to observe and to study the lifestyles and values of consumers. These observations become part of an integrated plan in the cycle of new product development.

Viewpoint 3: Difference among equals

Japanese are essentially of one nationality, one language and one culture. Few nations have the degree of homogeneity seen here. One aspect of this uniformity is that nearly 90 per cent of the Japanese feel they belong to the middle class. Although the recent skyrocketing of land prices have made people who own land in the cities very wealthy, on the whole, this middle class consciousness is likely to remain strong. That is, most Japanese feel they have similar standards of living, behavior and values. Because of this, it is not surprising that people are most comfortable when they look and feel similar to others. For example, if you went skiing wearing an old red sweater, blue jeans and yellow mittens, you might receive some strange glances, since everyone else is fashion coordinated from the hat down to the skis. Not wanting to be left behind, the Japanese pay close attention to their appearance in public. To behave conspicuously takes a lot of courage.

One aspect fueling this behavior is the overwhelming influence media has on the public in establishing norms or standard reference points. While people want to show that they are the same as everyone else, there is also the contradictory desire to express individuality. For this reason, many products whose basic functions are identical, yet which differ in subtle ways have a successful place in the market. The same manufacturer may produce several Walkmans, each model with different features. Finding the small differences through which people believe they can "feel their individuality" can make a big difference in sales.

The Japanese market creates an environment conducive to the emergence of super hit products. For instance, Asahi breweries introduced and promoted a new beer having a "dry" taste, Asahi Super Dry, the result of a slightly different brewing process. This small difference became a big hit. It propelled the brewery into the No. 2 spot in the fiercely competitive beer industry, the first change in ranking among the Japanese breweries in decades.

Viewpoint 4: Image consciousness

Japanese are very conscious of the image of the products or services they consume. Let us look at how image influences purchasing habits.

Value judgements of the Japanese are significantly affected by "established reputation." Being well known and highly evaluated leads to the gain of the consumer's trust and confidence. This applies to more than the product itself. A perfect example is a department store like Mitsukoshi. Gift giving is an important custom in Japan and the place where you buy the gift is as important as what you buy. Giving a gift bought and wrapped in an honored store like Mitsukoshi is a sign of the sender's sincerity, which the receiver appreciates. While "established reputation" does not come easily, it is essential for long-term business prosperity.

In many instances, "established reputation" is synonymous with "famous brands," where confidence backed by superior image runs very high. Japanese feel uneasy when they consider buying a product with which they are not familiar, and aspire toward famous brands. Because of this, image is critical for imported brands. One example is Chanel, popular among all income strata as a product which projects a luxurious image that is worth the expensive price tag. Put another way, the Japanese attach importance to what the ownership of a given product signifies to others. Choosing a brand is an expression of one's identity.

Along with the "famous brands" there are also the "hidden brands." They are "hidden" because most people have not yet discovered them. Hidden brands are usually imported and are of high quality and have a highly esteemed reputation, at least in the home country. Because of their achievement in another market, there is a higher potential to translate these elements into an image that will appeal to Japanese consumers. Some Japanese seek out these products for personal satisfaction, knowing that only those who are aware of them can appreciate their taste at this "hidden" stage.

In Japan, image often takes precedence over content. You may have the best product in the world, but unless it projects the correct image, it is not likely to succeed.

Similarly, projecting a clear total corporate image is also essential. It is especially critical in Japan where one survey revealed that "having no understanding of what a company does" was the second most common reason people held a company in low regard. The so-called "company without face" is more maligned by Japanese consumers than companies which "cause social problems" or whose presidents were judged to be of "poor character." Having a visible and familiar corporate face is the pillar of Japanese corporate strategy. Indeed, image affects acceptance in all of a corporation's activities from attracting new business and reinforcing existing business relationships to recruiting capable university graduates and even maintaining high employee morale.

Handicap of being unknown; worst 12 corporation images

1.	Poor product/service	87%
2.	No understanding of what company does	69%
3.	Character of the president is poor	59%
4.	Cause social problems	45%
5.	Poor taste in advertisements	41%
6.	Unstable business	30%
7.	Branch into any business	28%
8.	Play no role in society	27%
9.	Old-fashioned	23%
10.	No awareness of company	19%
11.	Too profitable	19%
12.	Too large	13%

Source: Dentsu Corporate Image Survey

Viewpoint 5: Quasi-affluence

This viewpoint explains the dichotomous circumstances in which those who are affluent cannot feel affluent.

The rise in the number of overseas travelers, primarily vacationers, is one characteristic of having achieved an affluent standard of lifestyle. Japan's stable economic growth has generally made the life of the Japanese an affluent one. Most can strive beyond merely making a living, and can lead a life in some measure of comfort. However, this affluence is not in terms of fixed assets such as real estate, but rather, it is in the form of liquid assets; cash for goods and services. People can afford to buy expensive goods. But because of the sharp increase in land prices, 76 per cent of the nation's renters have given up the hope of ever owning a home which meets all of their desires. An increasing number of those who used to save a portion of their income for purchasing a home can now divert this reserve of cash to other uses. They are accelerating the "cash-rich" phenomenon. These people are consuming now and the leading a life of affluence rather than saving in the hopes of buying a home several years in the future.

As a result, an increase in the sales of luxury goods has come about. Because people cannot own a satisfactory home, they want to have something that is luxurious. As soon as watches adorned with jewels, or high-class cars launch into the marketplace, they catch the public's attention and sell quickly. This is true even for "ordinary" items such as specially bottled milk from the renowned breed of Jersey cows. Though five times as expensive, the milk will sell out within a couple of hours of going on sale.

Wealth without property

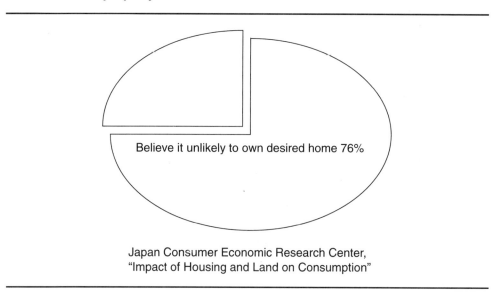

Believe it unlikely to own desired home 76%

Japan Consumer Economic Research Center,
"Impact of Housing and Land on Consumption"

Bleak views of ideal home ownership are accelerating the "cash-rich" phenomenon.

Another aspect of this new wealth is many people have satisfied their desire to own material things and are now showing greater interest in cultural activities. The popularity of classical music, the opera and ballet has been climbing significantly. For example, tickets for a recent tour by the Milan Opera were sold out within hours, regardless of the fact that seats were priced at ¥60,000 each.

In other words, people want to experience a "rich feeling." When the Queen Elizabeth II is in port, it is booked solid with people wanting to experience just a night or even a meal on this truly luxurious vessel, although it never actually leaves the pier. The consumption of these luxurious high-priced goods and services is directed not so much at ownership, but more at the feeling of wealth and affluence that this consumption gives.

Viewpoint 6: Ultra-quality consciousness

The high level of Japanese technology has gained a solid worldwide reputation. The unwavering high quality of goods made in Japan supports this reputation. Understandably, the Japanese have long been accustomed to consuming goods which match their feelings and are of high quality. Quality consciousness is so ingrained that it is generally taken for granted. Because of this attitude, it is crucial to ensure that there are no accidents. A serviceman may offer free maintenance check of his company's products. A company that incurs a quality problem even once, can lose consumer confidence. Similarly, Japanese products priced from the least expensive to the most expensive nearly always include a manufacturer's warranty. This guarantee of scrupulous after-sales service is an expression of the responsibility that companies take for their products.

Quality is important not only for goods, but also for service. Here is a scene that nearly everyone in Japan has experienced at least once: female department employees bowing at the entrance of the store as a greeting to customers. What is not so well known is that these employees have gone through extensive training to learn how to bow perfectly. Courteous and attentive employees are essential for winning consumer trust and business. Appearance must also be perfect. It is not good enough for a store to put different size fruit (strawberries, apples and oranges) together in a basket. Rather, packaging should reflect the high quality and care a company puts into its product.

Viewpoint 7: Infociety

The final viewpoint explains how the ever expanding growth and use of information has heralded the information society, or what we call "infociety."

This infociety affects people's lifestyles and forces companies to continuously revamp their marketing strategies. One important aspect of Japanese society is the sheer volume of information and the amount of time people devote to consuming this information. For example, customers often fill bookstores late into the night. People are eager to know something about everything. Along with the increase in reading material is an increase in the exposure to information, including airwaves.

A truly powerful medium of information is the television. Broadcasting time has risen considerably over the past 10 years to the point where 24-hour television is quickly becoming the norm. All the major networks locate their central studios in Tokyo and dominate most of the viewing time in every other city. They transmit the same information simultaneously throughout the country, and millions view the same programs. Needless to say, information carried this way has a tremendous impact.

Unlike the U.S., all major daily newspapers in Japan are nationals, again confirming the influence of Tokyo. The circulation of Japanese newspapers (due in large part to the structured home delivery system) is by far the largest in the world. If stacked on top of each other, one day's printing would reach 10 times the height of Mount Fuji. One reason for the power of the printed word is Japan's nearly 100 per cent literacy rate.

The dramatic advancements in and dissemination of word processors have brought about an informationalization of the Japanese language. Until a few years ago, the country had to rely on writing with pen and paper. This revolution of information is not confined to the office. People are now using this equipment freely in their own homes.

Information is also used as a value-added asset. A manufacturer may successfully obtain information concerning the desires of consumers and integrate this desire into the product idea. design, name and marketing approach. Companies often compete to attach news worthiness to their product or service so that it will ride the strength of media power and stimulate people's attention. Given a good product, this information asset will translate into large sales.

Companies must always keep up with trends in consumer lifestyles. This means constantly replenishing old information with new, fresh ideas. Consumers demand this, and successful companies are able to continually introduce new products with new image values.

These seven viewpoints should be kept in mind when developing marketing strategies for Japan. With these viewpoints, a clearer picture of the Japanese market can be drawn. The key to success in Japan is consumer-oriented marketing, taking into account the different aspects of the Japanese consumer as covered in this brief article. While pricing must not be ignored, it is crucial to pay extra attention to the values and the lifestyles of consumers.

Many say the Japanese market is the most difficult market in the world in which to succeed. However, rewards await those with a precise marketing strategy and an enterprising spirit. Sometimes the returns exceed expectations many times over.

MASARU ARIGA is Analyst & Planner in the Marketing Division of Dentsu Inc.

10 Consumer Power Sets Standards

Neal McGrath

Reputations increasingly depend on paying attention to customers.

Asia is steadily making the shift from export-driven manufacturing to consumer goods and services targeted at local markets.

As this trend gathers pace, companies that make it a priority to provide quality goods and services for local consumption are gaining increasing admiration.

That's the conclusion that stands out from the results of *Asian Business'* fourth annual survey to identify Asia's Most Admired Companies (AMAC).

The survey, which covers nine Asian countries, illustrates trends and qualities that give companies particular prominence in Asia, in the eyes of their peers — the readers of *Asian Business*.

This year the clearest message is that, in the mind of Asia's business leaders, good service and reliable products are a direct reflection of a well-run, respectable — and therefore admirable — business.

The gradual consumer revolution is a double-edged sword for Asian companies. As consumers gain influence, they are becoming more demanding. Manufacturers who once enjoyed a certain amount of immunity from consumer sentiment by anonymously exporting to distant markets must now become more attuned to popular sentiment.

Companies that treat their customers and the community well will enjoy solid reputations, while those that neglect or abuse the consuming public will suffer.

Where's the beef?

In the Philippines, local upstart Jollibee has shown how a small player can compete with the giants. A newcomer to the AMAC survey (it only recently

Reproduced with permission from *Asian Business*, 31 (May 1995), pp. 24–32.

listed; the survey covers only listed companies), Jollibee ranked seventh Asia-wide and second among Philippine companies for overall admirability, nipping at the heels of long-time leader San Miguel.

Founded in 1975 as an ice-cream parlour by Tan Cat Tiong, by 1978 Jollibee had evolved into a fast food corporation. Today it boasts 152 outlets across the Philippines and commands a 70% share of the nation's hamburger business — beating the otherwise undisputed king of hamburgers, McDonald's. The company ranked third of the companies polled in the Philippines for the quality of its products and services, behind only San Miguel and Del Monte.

Analysts say Jollibee scores high because of its management quality, its aggressive marketing and advertising and food that caters to Filipinos' sweetish palates.

Republic Flour Mills (RFM) — another Philippine company — also boosted its standing in the AMAC ranking through its high-profile activities, climbing 45 places from 120 to 75.

Over the past few years, RFM has acquired companies such as Selecta Ice Cream and Cosmos Bottling, helping it stage a strong recovery in 1994. The big boon came because RFM was successful in relaunching these products, quickly grabbing market share from established competitors. Selecta even gave San Miguel's Magnolia ice cream a beating in Metro Manila sales, capturing 40% of supermarket sales.

"Customers who have faced San Miguel products all their lives are attracted by RFM's aggressive advertising," says one market analyst.

Companies in the service business are also making a name for themselves by going upmarket and acquiring new brand names. Thai hospitality company Dusit Hotels & Resorts scored when its parent, the Dusit Group, finally reached its goal of becoming a world player in the hotel industry with the purchase of Kempinski Hotels, one of Germany's largest hotel chains. The hospitality group ranked third among Thai companies for overall admirability, and sixth among all Asian companies for the quality of its goods and services.

Dusit executive director Chanin Donavanik has been on an expansion spree for the past few years, both in Thailand, where the group now has 25 hotels, and overseas. The US$165 million deal to buy a 63% stake in Kempinski from Germany's national airline Lufthansa adds another 18 properties to Dusit's international network.

Kempinski is a plum pick: The five-star hotel chain boasts properties across Germany, Hungary, Turkey, Russia, the US, Canada, Argentina, Chile, China, India, Hongkong and one boutique operation in Bangkok.

Industry sources have wondered aloud about this strange management marriage of German efficiency and Thai hospitality, although, to some extent, their reservations are mooted by the fact that the two chains will continue to keep completely separate identities, and will only partially merge certain management and administrative functions.

For example, Chanin is now joint chairman of both Dusit and Kempinski, and the companies will make efforts to find synergies in marketing and reservations operations. But Dusit says that the management mix won't go any further than that.

"There are certain things every company that wants to succeed has to do," says Chanin, explaining his expansion strategy. "They have to be aggressive and expand while maintaining the quality of their operations and services. And they have to take care of their own people and take care of the customer. Whatever industry you're in, I think it's the same."

Philippine property developer Ayala Land also climbed the ranks of admired companies on the back of several high-profile deals, rising 22 places from 46th in 1994 to 24th in 1995. Ayala Land's prominence can be credited to its launch of three prestigious luxury condominium projects, Asia Tower, 3 Salcedo Place and Ayala Triangle. The latter is a 35-storey block that is home to half of the Philippine Stock Exchange, adding a further boost to the company's prestige.

Company president Francisco Licuanan takes pride in employee relations. "We foster a great deal of family feeling. We capture the employees' loyalty by demonstrating we're also loyal to them." Ayala ranked third among Philippine companies as being a good employer.

No resting on laurels

But companies must be careful not to become complacent with their high standing in the public eye. Even the best reputation can be easily tarnished by questionable business practices — a lesson that Malaysia's Edaran Otomobil Malaysia (EON) learned the hard way.

EON is a hugely successful company. Set up in 1985 to distribute Malaysia's national car, the Proton, EON boasts a 75.5% share of the automobile market and has introduced a string of successful models, most recently the Proton Wira.

"EON has had an overwhelming success with the Wira," says Aishah Ahmad, chairwoman of the Malaysian Motor Traders Association (MMTA). "We don't expect their market share to fall this year or next."

EON is clever. Just distributing the national car doesn't make it much money, so it loads cars with extras that Malaysians like to buy. The trouble is that EON has been too clever — too clever by a half.

The company's success has been supported largely by heavy restrictions on the local market that keep foreign competitors out. Until recently, consumers didn't seem to mind as long as the company continued to serve its role of filling the nation's need for new automobiles and providing jobs for Malaysians. But recent events aroused complaints that the company is abusing its market position at the expense of the consumer.

In November the local press whacked EON after Malaysia's Domestic Trade and Consumer Affairs Ministry unearthed evidence that syndicates within the company were selling new cars as "used" in a bid to milk extra cash from the tight market.

Strong demand has created a six-month waiting list for a new Proton, but some dealers discovered that customers could jump the queue by opting to buy a used car instead. The ministry found that dealers were conniving with outsiders to reserve blocks of new Protons, and then re-classify these cars as used — thus diverting them from the normal distribution chain and into their hands.

Able to make delivery immediately, the dealers could sell these "used" cars at a substantial mark-up. In the public's eye, EON appeared to be in cahoots with its dealers, exploiting the advantage it has over other distributors.

EON's public image suffered heavily in the wake of the scandal, as reflected in the results of the AMAC survey. The company's overall admirability ranking tumbled precipitously from 53rd in 1994 to 102nd this year.

Thailand's Siam Cement knows the value of a good reputation, and works hard to maintain its image for ethics and in the process showed that being ethical is not bad for business. After loosing some of its lustre in the past few years as the Thai economy slowed, the group restored its image among stock investors in a big way in 1994. At year-end it reported consolidated profits of Baht 5,398 million (US$216 million), a 53% climb over 1993.

The strong performance was a ringing endorsement of the group's virtues. From 8th place in 1994, Siam Cement climbed to 5th in 1995 for overall admirability among all Asian companies, and ranked highest for being honest and ethical.

Siam Cement's current president Chumpol Nalamlieng, who took full control of the group in 1993, rewrote the Siam Cement Group Code of Ethics in 1994 to spell out more clearly what ethics means for business. Some might argue that excessive concern for ethics gets in the way of competitiveness and profits, but Chumpol is convinced that the two goals aren't necessarily contradictory. "You can push competitiveness while at the same time reminding people to play fair," Chumpol insists.

Chumpol wanted to define exactly what "fair play" constitutes in his revised ethical code. For instance, Siam Cement employees are broadly warned to avoid questionable activities such as disclosing sensitive information as a favour to a particular party at the expense of others, seeking business gains by providing false information or enticing others to violate agreements that have already been made with a customer.

"Actually we didn't make this code up," says Chumpol. "Any Thai who reads it would agree with it. It's just that in Thai culture there is also a high degree of tolerance." Siam Cement hopes its clear-cut ethical code will help eliminate tolerance of ethical breaches.

Siam Cement's code of conduct has not stopped it from expanding both at home and abroad, but the company does admit it may limit where and in what industries it invests. "For instance, when we look at China we end up in the northern half," says Chumpol with a smile. "Now, if you ask me how come, I would tell you it's because there are a lot of activities in the South already, or because the North has a deeper industrial heritage, but the fact is the South is kind of . . . difficult. But Shanghai and upwards is pretty straightforward."

Maintain momentum

Ethical issues aside, even failing to maintain the pace of introducing hit products can sour a fickle public's perception of a company. Japanese consumer product powerhouse Sony slid from the number five slot to number 30 this year as a series of events took their toll on the company's image.

Sony has, in recent years, experienced a serious drought in new product introductions. What's worse, it seems to be heading down a familiar path as it seeks to force its format for digital video disks on the market, going against the rest of the industry.

This brings to mind the brutal 1980s battle for control of the video cassette recorder market, in which Sony's Betamax lost out to the now standard VHS format.

Management issues are closely tied with a company's performance and standing in the public eye. A professional approach to running the business is one of the hallmarks of many of the companies that rank highly.

Jollibee executive vice-president and chief operating officer Ernesto Tanmantiong, brother of the founder, says that although the firm is still family-controlled, it is managed by professionals. "We have a clear focus in our business," says Tanmantiong. "We empower our people to deliver the goals that we have set."

Jollibee also places a premium on human resources development. "In the food business, you rely on people to deliver customer satisfaction," Tanmantiong notes. "You have to motivate people on a daily basis, so you need a lot of training."

Jollibee spends the equivalent of 10% of sales on human resource development and workers' benefits. Its quality of management has been bolstered by a participatory system. "We encourage people to speak out, we listen to suggestions and we have individual counselling," says Tanmantiong.

Like Jollibee, RFM relies on professionalism to maintain its quality of management, bringing outside management skills into a family-controlled business. The company has also de-centralised into several business units, each with a separate corporate service.

"We started improving the system because we want to get accredited for the ISO 9000, the world standard certificate," says RFM president Joey Concepcion III.

Japan's Toyota Motor Corp, which ranked number one in Japan for overall admirability and quality of management, also places a strong emphasis on management issues. "Our managers are serious about sticking to the firm's guiding principles," says Yukitoshi Funo, general manager of planning for Asia/Oceania and the Middle East, adding that lower-level employees are also given access to people making the decisions. "Top management is quite ready to accept suggestions from middle management and lower."

Malaysia's Hong Leong Industries is another example. Hong Leong is the parent company of Malaysian businessman Quek Leng Chan's stable of nine listed companies. Since starting as an outpost of the Singapore Hong Leong empire, Quek's outfit in Malaysia has grown to more than 200 companies employing 27,000 and boasting turnover of US$1.32 billion.

"Working for Hong Leong you know you are working for the best managed company in Malaysia," says the general manager of one of the 200 companies. "It's a very tight ship, but you get autonomy and you are very well rewarded."

Management issues are closely tied to a company's public image. Consumers often assume that if a company offers quality products and good service, that it is a well-managed organisation. Shoddy service and ethical breaches often lead the public to believe that management is slack.

When the charges against EON came to light, the company did not respond quickly enough to the public's grievances. By the time it did investigate the situation, its image had already suffered considerable damage. True or not, the perception was that EON management knew about the scam but did nothing about it. Not only did EON's score for being honest and ethical fall, but the ranking for its quality of management also suffered.

HOW THE SURVEY WAS DONE

The fourth annual survey by *Asian Business* to identify Asia's Most Admired Companies covers 250 companies, most of them from Asia, but also including a variety of multinational firms from the US and Europe that have achieved a high profile in the region.

Companies chosen for inclusion are all major players. In the case of the Asian companies, all rank among the top 50 listed companies, by turnover, in their home country. So in a very real sense, there are no losers in the survey; the highest scorers are the best of the best.

The overall list of companies was split into smaller lists, with about 30 being surveyed in each of nine countries: Hongkong, Indonesia, Japan, Malaysia, the Philippines, Singapore, South Korea, Taiwan and Thailand.

Survey respondents were chosen at random from *Asian Business'* circulation database, with 1,000 senior business people being picked from each of the same nine countries.

The respondents were asked to score companies in terms of how admirable they thought each was in overall terms, and also in terms of six attributes: Quality of management; quality of products/services; contribution to the local economy; being a good employer; potential for growth; and being honest and ethical.

The respondents were also asked to rank these attributes in terms of how important each was to their overall perception of a company's admirability.

Polling took place between mid-November 1994 and mid-January this year, during which time 2010 reponses were received, giving a return of just over 22%.

The survey, including analysis and compilation of results, was conducted by the Hongkong office of the independent research company Asia Market Intelligence (AMI).

Reported by Peter Janssen in Bangkok, Sid Astbury in Kuala Lumpur, Abby Tan in Manila and David Hulme in Tokyo.

The 10 companies that climbed the most in 1995 (in terms of score)

	1995	Change
Acer	7.81	0.69
Tokai Bank	6.52	0.61
Indosat	7.78	0.54
Astra International	7.62	0.51
NYK Line	6.62	0.48
Volkswagen	6.22	0.47
Apple Computer	7.35	0.45
Ricoh	6.34	0.45
Cycle and Carriage	7.32	0.43
Northwest Airlines	6.11	0.43

The 10 companies that fell the most in 1995 (in terms of score)

	1995	Change
Dong Ah Construction	5.53	−1.17
China Airlines	5.53	−1.09
Yeo Hiap Seng	5.21	−0.74
Atlas Mining	4.68	−0.71
Philippine Airlines	5.25	−0.70
Singapore Telecom	7.86	−0.66
Esso/Exxon	7.12	−0.47
Amcol	5.64	−0.43
Mitac International	6.26	−0.43
Digital Equipment Corp	5.89	−0.43

Best products and services

Company	Score
1. Mandarin Oriental	4.37
2. Singapore Airlines	4.36
3. Daimler-Benz	4.24
4. San Miguel Corp	4.22
5. Sony Corp	4.20
6. Dusit Thani Hotel	4.19
7. Hewlett-Packard	4.18
8. Samsung Co	4.18
9. McDonald's	4.15
10. Shangri-La Hotels	4.15

Best managed

Company	Score
1. Singapore Airlines	5.00
2. Samsung Co	4.99
3. San Miguel Corp	4.89
4. Siam Cement	4.83
5. McDonald's	4.75
6. Toyota Motor Corp	4.73
7. Jollibee	4.61
8. Formosa Plastic	4.61
9. DBS Bank	4.60
10. Charoen Pokphand	4.58

Most honest and ethical

Company	Score
1. Siam Cement	4.03
2. Singapore Airlines	3.93
3. DBS Bank	3.92
4. San Miguel Corp	3.92
5. AT&T	3.87
6. McDonald's	3.86
7. Hewlett-Packard	3.86
8. China Steel	3.82
9. Honda Motor	3.80
10. Acer	3.80

Greatest potential for growth

Company	Score
1. Charoen Pokphand	4.43
2. Indosat	4.41
3. AT&T	4.38
4. Samsung Co	4.38
5. Acer	4.34
6. Dacom	4.29
7. Bank of China	4.27
8. Shinawatra	4.27
9. Hongkong Telecom	4.26
10. Asia Pacific Breweries	4.25

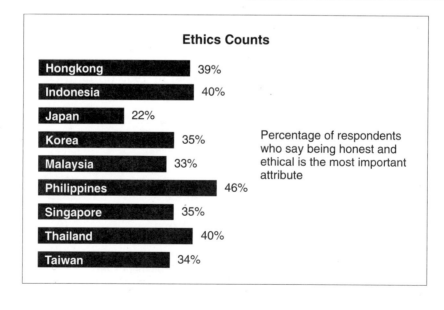

Ethics Counts

Hongkong	39%
Indonesia	40%
Japan	22%
Korea	35%
Malaysia	33%
Philippines	46%
Singapore	35%
Thailand	40%
Taiwan	34%

Percentage of respondents who say being honest and ethical is the most important attribute

The top 10 companies in each industry group

Airlines

Company	Score
1. Singapore Airlines	8.83
2. Cathay Pacific	7.75
3. KLM	7.18
4. Thai Airways	7.17
5. Korean Air	6.85
6. Lufthansa	6.80
7. United Airlines	6.77
8. Swiss Air	6.73
9. Malaysian Airlines	6.57
10. Northwest Airlines	6.11

Retail/Consumer

Company	Score
1. San Miguel Corp	8.62
2. McDonald's	8.34
3. Jollibee	8.23
4. Coca-Cola	8.10
5. Asia Pacific Breweries	7.80
6. Nestlé (Malaysia)	7.78
7. Colgate-Palmolive	7.75
8. Shoe Mart	7.73
9. Del Monte	7.71
10. Fraser And Neave	7.65

Heavy Industry

Company	Score
1. Siam Cement	8.25
2. Pohang Iron And Steel	8.23
3. Toyota Motor Corp	8.15
4. Formosa Plastic	8.05
5. BMW	8.00
6. Daimler-Benz	7.99
7. Shell	7.89
8. China Light & Power	7.82
9. Boeing	7.81
10. Honda Motor	7.78

Banking/Finance

Company	Score
1. DBS Bank	8.03
2. Hongkong Bank	8.01
3. Shinhan Bank	7.87
4. Citibank	7.76
5. Bangkok Bank	7.51
6. Malayan Banking	7.35
7. Bank Niaga	7.27
8. Standard Chartered	7.22
9. Chase Manhattan	7.22
10. American Express	7.19

Shipping and Transport

Company	Score
1. DHL	7.49
2. Evergreen Marine	7.46
3. Saha Union	7.30
4. Federal Express	7.03
5. C Itoh (Itochu)	6.87
6. Sumitomo Corp	6.77
7. East Asiatic	6.77
8. NYK Line	6.62
9. Berli Jucker	6.59
10. Malaysian Intl Shipping Corp	6.53

Light Manufacturing

Company	Score
1. Hewlett-Packard	7.99
2. Motorola	7.92
3. Acer	7.81
4. Sony Corp	7.79
5. Toshiba Corp	7.72
6. Shinawatra Computer & Communication	7.69
7. IBM	7.59
8. Formosa Chem. Fibre	7.43
9. Siemens	7.43
10. Matsushita Electric	7.41

Conglomerates

Company	Score
1. Samsung Co	8.63
2. Charoen Pokphand	8.21
3. Genting	7.70
4. Astra Int'l.	7.62
5. Hyundai Corp	7.50
6. Sime Darby	7.45
7. Swire Pacific	7.45
8. Lucky Gold Star Int'l.	7.32
9. Cycle And Carriage	7.32
10. General Electric	7.23

Property/Construction

Company	Score
1. Ayala Land	7.86
2. Keppel Corp	7.66
3. Sun Hung Kai Prop.	7.43
4. Cheung Kong	7.34
5. Bechtel	7.06
6. ABB	6.93
7. Sembawang Shipyard	6.84
8. Kuok Philippine Prop.	6.67
9. Hopewell Holdings	6.50
10. First Capital Corp	6.47

Hotels

Company	Score
1. Shangri-La Hotels	7.80
2. Hyatt Hotels	7.78
3. Dusit Thani Hotel	7.75
4. Mandarin Oriental	7.67
5. Hilton Intl'. Hotels	7.27
6. Resorts World	7.24
7. Sheraton Hotels	7.19
8. Westin Hotels	6.99
9. Holiday Inns	6.90
10. New World Dvlpmnt.	6.81

Telecoms/Media

Company	Score
1. Hongkong Telecom	8.12
2. ABS-CBN	8.02
3. AT&T	7.90
4. Singapore Telecom	7.86
5. Indosat	7.78
6. Post Publishing	7.39
7. Dacom	7.26
8. Telekom Malaysia	6.77
9. United Daily News	6.49
10. NTT Corp	6.48

Greatest contribution to the local economy

Company	Score
1. Hongkong Telecom	4.52
2. Pohang Iron And Steel	4.44
3. Siam Cement	4.43
4. DBS Bank	4.40
5. Samsung Co	4.39
6. Singapore Telecom	4.39
7. China Light & Power	4.35
8. Charoen Pokphand	4.28
9. San Miguel Corp	4.27
10. Singapore Airlines	4.23

Best employer

Company	Score
1. Samsung	4.20
2. Siam Cement	4.14
3. San Miguel Corp	4.10
4. Pohang Iron And Steel	4.04
5. China Light & Power	4.03
6. Hongkong Bank	3.99
7. Singapore Airlines	3.98
8. Astra International	3.94
9. McDonald's	3.93
10. Hongkong Telecom	3.91

Rank (Last year)		Company	Score
1	(2)	Singapore Airlines	8.83
2	(3)	Samsung Co	8.63
3	(1)	San Miguel Corp	8.62
4	(10)	McDonald's	8.34
5	(8)	Siam Cement	8.25
6	(14)	Pohang Iron And Steel	8.23
7	(-)	Jollibee	8.23
8	(9)	Charoen Pokphand	8.21
9	(6)	Toyota Motor Corp	8.15
10	(26)	Hongkong Telecom	8.12
11	(11)	Coca-Cola	8.10
12	(19)	Formosa Plastic	8.05
13	(13)	DBS Bank	8.03
14	(18)	ABS-CBN	8.02
15	(12)	HongkongBank	8.01
16	(34)	BMW	8.00
17	(30)	Daimler-Benz	7.99
18	(28)	Hewlett-Packard	7.99
19	(41)	Motorola	7.92
20	(23)	AT&T	7.90
21	(15)	Shell	7.89
22	(45)	Shinhan Bank	7.87
23	(4)	Singapore Telecom	7.86
24	(46)	Ayala Land Inc	7.86
25	(32)	China Light & Power	7.82
26	(84)	Acer	7.81
27	(29)	Boeing	7.81
28	(7)	Shangri-La Hotels	7.80
29	(56)	Asia Pacific Breweries	7.80
30	(5)	Sony Corp	7.79
31	(25)	Nestlé (Malaysia)	7.78
32	(70)	Indosat	7.78
33	(31)	Hyatt Hotels	7.78
34	(52)	Honda Motor	7.78
35	(33)	Citibank	7.76
36	(22)	Colgate-Palmolive	7.75
37	(43)	Dusit Thani Hotel	7.75
38	(60)	Cathay Pacific	7.75
39	(54)	Shoe Mart	7.73
40	(62)	Toshiba Corp	7.72
41	(16)	Del Monte	7.71
42	(21)	Genting	7.70
43	(27)	Shinawatra Computer	7.69
44	(48)	Mandarin Oriental	7.67
45	(20)	Keppel Corp	7.66
46	(61)	Fraser And Neave	7.65
47	(44)	Nan Ya Plastic	7.64
48	(38)	Pepsi Cola	7.63
49	(86)	Astra International	7.62
50	(39)	Procter & Gamble	7.62
51	(59)	IBM	7.59
52	(67)	Fuji Xerox	7.56
53	(17)	Bangkok Bank	7.51
54	(74)	Hyundai Corp	7.50
55	(47)	DHL	7.49
56	(50)	China Steel	7.49
57	(40)	Evergreen Marine Corp	7.46
58	(66)	Sime Darby	7.45
59	(42)	Swire Pacific	7.45
60	(80)	Pure Foods	7.45
61	(93)	Formosa Chemical Fibre	7.43
62	(36)	Sun Hung Kai Properties	7.43
63	(65)	Siemens	7.43
64	(58)	Mobil	7.42
65	(64)	Matsushita Electric	7.41
66	(75)	Post Publishing	7.39
67	(51)	Kia Motors	7.36
68	(69)	Malayan Banking	7.35
69	(118)	Apple Computer	7.35
70	(37)	Cheung Kong	7.34
71	(79)	Multi Bintang Indonesia	7.34
72	(68)	Hitachi	7.33
73	(92)	Lucky Goldstar Int'l.	7.32
74	(119)	Cycle And Carriage	7.32
75	(120)	RFM Corp	7.30
76	(24)	Unilever Indonesia	7.30
77	(49)	Saha Union	7.30
78	(55)	President Enterprises	7.29
79	(91)	Philips	7.29
80	(73)	Saha Pathanapibul	7.28
81	(95)	Hilton International	7.27
82	(77)	Bank Niaga	7.27
83	(101)	Hong Leong Industries	7.26
84	(88)	Dacom	7.26
85	(63)	Texas Instruments	7.26
86	(85)	Resorts World	7.24
87	(90)	Canon	7.24
88	(112)	Gudang Garam	7.23
89	(129)	General Electric	7.23
90	(82)	Standard Chartered	7.22
91	(124)	Chase Manhattan	7.22
92	(76)	Du Pont	7.21
93	(78)	Sheraton Hotels	7.19
94	(110)	Fujitsu	7.19
95	(100)	American Express	7.19
96	(71)	Wharf	7.19
97	(81)	KLM	7.18
98	(104)	Thai Airways Int'l	7.17
99	(97)	NEC Corp	7.17
100	(94)	Hero Mini Supermarket	7.17
101	(96)	Ford Motor Company	7.16
102	(53)	Edaran Otomobil Nasional	7.15
103	(83)	Yukong	7.15
104	(57)	Hutchison Whampoa	7.13
105	(-)	Johnson & Johnson	7.12
106	(35)	Esso/Exxon	7.12
107	(72)	Hongkong And China Gas	7.11
108	(122)	Carlsberg	7.07
109	(131)	Singapore Petroleum Corp	7.07
110	(99)	Bechtel	7.06
111	(137)	Korea Electric Power Co	7.05
112	(106)	Mitsubishi Heavy Industries	7.04

Rank (Last year)		Company	Score
113	(133)	Federal Express	7.03
114	(98)	Sunkyong	7.02
115	(125)	Westin Hotels	6.99
116	(132)	Minolta	6.99
117	(143)	Guinness Anchor	6.98
118	(141)	Eastman Kodak	6.98
119	(109)	Hoechst	6.98
120	(87)	Volvo	6.98
121	(108)	Ssangyong Corp	6.97
122	(89)	Bayer	6.96
123	(114)	United Tractors	6.96
124	(128)	ABB Asea Brown Boveri	6.93
125	(154)	Holiday Inns	6.90
126	(-)	Yaohan	6.90
127	(134)	C Itoh (Itochu)	6.87
128	(163)	Cerebos	6.85
129	(148)	Korean Air	6.85
130	(102)	Sembawang Shipyard	6.84
131	(153)	International Cosmetics	6.84
132	(149)	Shanghai Commercial Bank	6.83
133	(164)	Kentucky Fried Chicken	6.83
134	(166)	3M	6.82
135	(116)	New World Dvlpmnt.	6.81
136	(160)	Lufthansa	6.80
137	(156)	General Motors	6.79
138	(115)	Dairy Farm	6.79
139	(126)	AST	6.79
140	(139)	ICI	6.78
141	(138)	United Airlines	6.77
142	(111)	Sumitomo Corp	6.77
143	(150)	East Asiatic	6.77
144	(105)	Telekom Malaysia	6.77
145	(157)	Taiwan Cement	6.76
146	(169)	Fuji Bank	6.76
147	(140)	Bank of America	6.74
148	(170)	Inchcape	6.74
149	(136)	Swiss Air	6.73
150	(162)	Perlis Plantation	6.73
151	(117)	Dai-Ichi Kangyo Bank	6.73
152	(168)	Sanyo Electric Co	6.72
153	(152)	Deutsche Bank	6.70
154	(135)	Philippine National Bank	6.70
155	(146)	Magnum Corp	6.69
156	(113)	Precision Electronics	6.69
157	(192)	Kolon Industries	6.68
158	(159)	Lotte Co	6.67
159	(165)	Int. Nickel Indonesia	6.67
160	(195)	Kuok Philippine Properties	6.67
161	(158)	Bakrie and Brothers	6.62
162	(205)	NYK Line	6.62
163	(103)	Jardine Matheson	6.62
164	(185)	Thai Plastic and Chemical	6.61
165	(130)	Cartier	6.61
166	(204)	Aiwa	6.60
167	(167)	Berli Jucker	6.59
168	(-)	China Motor	6.59

Rank (Last year)		Company	Score
169	(155)	Indocement	6.58
170	(121)	Malaysian Airlines	6.57
171	(107)	Padaeng Industry	6.57
172	(144)	American Insurance Group	6.56
173	(172)	Natsteel	6.53
174	(7)	Malaysian Int'l. Shipping Corp	6.53
175	(175)	Jakarta International Hotel	6.53
176	(222)	Tokai Bank	6.52
177	(182)	United Engineers (Malaysia)	6.52
178	(147)	Daewoo Corp	6.51
179	(191)	Pacific Electric Wire	6.50
180	(123)	Hopewell Holdings	6.50
181	(189)	Hanjin Shipping Co	6.49
182	(181)	McDonnell Douglas	6.49
183	(188)	United Daily News	6.49
184	(127)	NTT Corp	6.48
185	(-)	First Capital Corp	6.47
186	(200)	First Pacific	6.46
187	(197)	Tan Chong Motors	6.44
188	(193)	Federal Flour Mills	6.44
189	(184)	Gadjah Tunggal	6.44
190	(178)	Neptune Orient Lines	6.42
191	(211)	Summarecon Agung	6.40
192	(201)	Tatung	6.40
193	(179)	Metro Drug	6.39
194	(196)	Nomura Securities	6.38
195	(-)	BHP	6.36
196	(206)	Kumpulan Guthrie	6.36
197	(177)	Thai-Asahi Glass	6.36
198	(114)	Ricoh	6.34
199	(180)	Ambassador Hotel	6.32
200	(187)	Consolidated Plantations	6.32
201	(173)	United Parcel Service	6.32
202	(176)	Far Eastern Textile	6.28
203	(226)	Alcatel	6.27
204	(145)	Mitac International	6.26
205	(183)	Pan Pacific	6.26
206	(174)	National Steel Corp	6.25
207	(232)	Volkswagen	6.22
208	(198)	Far Eastern Department Stores	6.21
209	(186)	Cathay Construction	6.20
210	(-)	Bangkok Steel Industry	6.19
211	(212)	Philippine Appliance Corp	6.19
212	(-)	Henderson Land	6.18
213	(-)	CITIC	6.18
214	(217)	Intraco	6.13
215	(171)	Nissan Motor	6.12
216	(-)	Shimizu	6.12
217	(202)	Teijin Indonesia Fibre	6.12
218	(239)	Northwest Airlines	6.11
219	(194)	Amalgamated Steel Mills	6.09
220	(228)	Garuda Indonesia	6.08
221	(203)	Daelim Industrial	6.06
222	(218)	Miwon Co	6.05
223	(215)	Hyosung Corp	6.04
224	(216)	Haw Par	6.04

Rank (Last year)		Company	Score	Rank (Last year)		Company	Score
225	(240)	Wearne Brothers	6.00	238	(225)	Brother Industries	5.79
226	(235)	Indah Kiat	5.98	239	(210)	Amcol	5.64
227	(-)	Japfa Comfeed	5.98	240	(237)	Mazda Motor Corp	5.62
228	(209)	Nikko Hotel	5.97	241	(221)	Delta Airlines	5.61
229	(233)	Philex	5.95	242	(236)	Japan Airlines	5.56
230	(199)	Tjiwi Kimia	5.92	243	(161)	China Airlines	5.53
231	(190)	Digital Equipment Corp	5.89	244	(142)	Dong Ah Construction	5.53
232	(230)	Phil Long Distance Telephone	5.89	245	(238)	Benguet Corp	5.40
233	(207)	Caterpillar	5.89	246	(245)	Fiat	5.34
234	(234)	Bangkok Rubber	5.87	247	(220)	Philippine Airlines	5.25
235	(227)	Mitsui OSK Lines	5.84	248	(219)	Yeo Hiap Seng	5.21
236	(-)	Bank of China	5.83	249	(248)	Unicord	4.91
237	(214)	Marsman and Co	5.82	250	(247)	Atlas Mining	4.68

1995 most admired companies, alphabetical order

Company	Rank (Last year)		Score	Company	Rank (Last year)		Score
3M	134	(166)	6.82	Dacom	84	(88)	7.26
Asea Brown Boveri	124	(128)	6.93	Daelim Industrial	221	(203)	6.06
ABS-CBN	14	(18)	8.02	Daewoo Corp	178	(147)	6.51
Acer	26	(84)	7.81	Dai-Ichi Kangyo Bank	151	(117)	6.73
Aiwa	166	(204)	6.60	Daimler-Benz	17	(30)	7.99
Alcatel	203	(226)	6.27	Dairy Farm	138	(115)	6.79
Amalgamated Steel Mills	219	(194)	6.09	DBS Bank	13	(13)	8.03
Ambassador Hotel	199	(180)	6.32	Del Monte	41	(16)	7.71
Amcol	239	(210)	5.64	Delta Airlines	241	(221)	5.61
American Express	95	(100)	7.19	Deutsche Bank	153	(152)	6.70
American Insurance Group	172	(144)	6.56	DHL	55	(47)	7.49
Apple Computer	69	(118)	7.35	Digital Equipment Corp	231	(190)	5.89
Asia Pacific Breweries	29	(56)	7.80	Dong Ah Construction	244	(142)	5.53
AST	139	(126)	6.79	Du Pont	92	(76)	7.21
Astra International	49	(86)	7.62	Dusit Thani Hotel	37	(43)	7.75
AT&T	20	(23)	7.90	East Asiatic	143	(150)	6.77
Atlas Mining	250	(247)	4.68	Eastman Kodak	118	(141)	6.98
Ayala Land Inc	24	(46)	7.86	Edaran Otomobil Nasional	102	(53)	7.15
Bakie And Brothers	161	(158)	6.62	Esso/Exxon	106	(35)	7.12
Bangkok Bank	53	(17)	7.51	Evergreen Marine Corp	57	(40)	7.46
Bangkok Rubber	234	(234)	5.87	Far Eastern Department Stores	208	(198)	6.21
Bangkok Steel Industry	210	(-)	6.19	Far Eastern Textile	202	(176)	6.28
Bank Niaga	82	(77)	7.27	Federal Express	113	(133)	7.03
Bank of America	147	(140)	6.74	Federal Flour Mills	188	(193)	6.44
Bank of China	236	(-)	5.83	Fiat	246	(245)	5.34
Bayer	122	(89)	6.96	First Capital Corp	185	(-)	6.47
Bechtel	110	(99)	7.06	First Pacific	186	(200)	6.46
Benguet Corp	245	(238)	5.40	Ford Motor Company	101	(96)	7.16
Berli Jucker	167	(167)	6.59	Formosa Chemical Fibre	61	(93)	7.43
BHP	195	(-)	6.36	Formosa Plastic	12	(19)	8.05
BMW	16	(34)	8.00	Fraser and Neave	46	(61)	7.65
Boeing	27	(29)	7.81	Fuji Bank	146	(169)	6.76
Brother Industries	238	(225)	5.79	Fuji Xerox	52	(67)	7.56
C Itoh (Itochu)	127	(134)	6.87	Fujitsu	94	(110)	7.19
Canon	87	(90)	7.24	Gadjah Tunggal	189	(184)	6.44
Carlsberg	108	(122)	7.07	Garuda Indonesia	220	(228)	6.08
Cartier	165	(130)	6.61	General Electric	89	(129)	7.23
Caterpillar	233	(207)	5.89	General Motors	137	(156)	6.79
Cathay Construction	209	(186)	6.20	Genting	42	(21)	7.70
Cathay Pacific	38	(60)	7.75	Gudang Garam	88	(112)	7.23
Cerebos	128	(163)	6.85	Guiness Anchor	117	(143)	6.98
Charoen Pokphand	8	(9)	8.21	Hanjin Shipping Co	181	(189)	6.49
Chase Manhattan	91	(124)	7.22	Haw Par	224	(216)	6.04
Cheung Kong	70	(37)	7.34	Henderson Land	212	(-)	6.18
China Airlines	243	(161)	5.53	Hero Mini Supermarket	100	(94)	7.17
China Light & Power	25	(32)	7.82	Hewlett-Packard	18	(28)	7.99
China Motor	168	(-)	6.59	Hilton International	81	(95)	7.27
China Steel	56	(50)	7.49	Hitachi	72	(68)	7.33
Citibank	35	(33)	7.76	Hoechst	119	(109)	6.98
CITIC	213	(-)	6.18	Holiday Inns	125	(154)	6.90
Coca-Cola	11	(11)	8.10	Honda Motor	34	(52)	7.78
Colgate-Palmolive	36	(22)	7.75	Hong Leong Industries	83	(101)	7.26
Consolidated Plantations	200	(187)	6.32	Hongkong and China Gas	107	(72)	7.11
Cycle and Carriage	74	(119)	7.32	Hongkong Bank	15	(12)	8.01

Company	Rank (Last year)		Score	Company	Rank (Last year)		Score
Hongkong Telecom	10	(26)	8.12	Neptune Orient Lines	190	(178)	6.42
Hopewell Holdings	180	(123)	6.50	Nestlé (Malaysia)	31	(25)	7.78
Hutchison Whampoa	104	(57)	7.13	New World Dvlpmnt.	135	(116)	6.81
Hyatt Hotels	33	(31)	7.78	Nikko Hotel	228	(209)	5.97
Hyosung Corp	223	(215)	6.04	Nissan Motor	215	(171)	6.12
Hyundai Corp	54	(74)	7.50	Nomura Securities	194	(196)	6.38
IBM	51	(59)	7.59	Northwest Airlines	218	(239)	6.11
ICI	140	(139)	6.78	NTT Corp	184	(127)	6.48
Inchcape	148	(170)	6.74	NYK Line	162	(205)	6.62
Indah Kiat	226	(235)	5.98	Pacific Electric Wire	179	(191)	6.50
Indocement	169	(155)	6.58	Padaeng Industry	171	(107)	6.57
Indosat	32	(70)	7.78	Pan Pacific	205	(183)	6.26
Int. Nickel Indonesia	159	(165)	6.67	Pepsi Cola	48	(38)	7.63
International Cosmetics	131	(153)	6.84	Perlis Plantation	150	(162)	6.73
Intraco	214	(217)	6.13	Phil Long Distance Telephone	232	(230)	5.89
Jakarta International Hotel	175	(175)	6.53	Philex	229	(233)	5.95
Japan Airlines	242	(236)	5.56	Philippine Airlines	247	(220)	5.25
Japfa Comfeed	227	(-)	5.98	Philippine Appliance Corp	211	(212)	6.19
Jardine Matheson	163	(103)	6.62	Philippine National Bank	154	(135)	6.70
Johnson & Johnson	105	(-)	7.12	Philips	79	(91)	7.29
Jollibee	7	(-)	8.23	Pohang Iron and Steel	6	(14)	8.23
Kentucky Fried Chicken	133	(164)	6.83	Post Publishing	66	(75)	7.39
Keppel Corp	45	(20)	7.66	Precision Electronics	156	(113)	6.69
Kia Motors	67	(51)	7.36	President Enterprises	78	(55)	7.29
KLM	97	(81)	7.18	Procter & Gamble	50	(39)	7.62
Kolon Industries	157	(192)	6.68	Pure Foods	60	(80)	7.45
Korea Electric Power Co	111	(137)	7.05	Resorts World	86	(85)	7.24
Korean Air	129	(148)	6.85	RFM Corp	75	(120)	7.30
Kumpulan Guthrie	196	(206)	6.36	Ricoh	198	(114)	6.34
Kuok Philippine Properties	160	(195)	6.67	Saha Pathanapibul	80	(73)	7.28
Lotte Co	158	(159)	6.67	Saha Union	77	(49)	7.30
Lucky Goldstar Int'l.	73	(92)	7.32	Samsung Co	2	(3)	8.63
Lufthansa	136	(160)	6.80	San Miguel Corp	3	(1)	8.62
Magnum Corp	155	(146)	6.69	Sanyo Electric Co	152	(168)	6.72
Malayan Banking	68	(69)	7.35	Sembawang Shipyard	130	(102)	6.84
Malaysian Airlines	170	(121)	6.57	Shanghai Commercial Bank	132	(149)	6.83
Malaysian Int'l Shipping Corp	174	(151)	6.53	Shangri-La Hotels	28	(7)	7.80
Mandarin Oriental	44	(48)	7.67	Shell	21	(15)	7.89
Marsman and Co	237	(214)	5.82	Sheraton Hotels	93	(78)	7.19
Matsushita Electric	65	(64)	7.41	Shimizu	216	(-)	6.12
Mazda Motor Corp	240	(237)	5.62	Shinawatra Computer	43	(27)	7.69
McDonald's	4	(10)	8.34	Shinhan Bank	22	(45)	7.87
McDonnell Douglas	182	(181)	6.49	Shoe Mart	39	(54)	7.73
Metro Drug	193	(179)	6.39	Siam Cement	5	(8)	8.25
Minolta	116	(132)	6.99	Siemens	63	(65)	7.43
Mitac International	204	(145)	6.26	Sime Darby	58	(66)	7.45
Mitsubishi Heavy Industries	112	(106)	7.04	Singapore Airlines	1	(2)	8.83
Mitsui OSK Lines	235	(227)	5.84	Singapore Petroleum Corp	109	(131)	7.07
Miwon Co	222	(218)	6.05	Singapore Telecom	23	(4)	7.86
Mobil	64	(58)	7.42	Sony Corp	30	(5)	7.79
Motorola	19	(41)	7.92	Ssangyong Corp	121	(108)	6.97
Multi Bintang Indonesia	71	(79)	7.34	Standard Chartered	90	(82)	7.22
Nan Ya Plastic	47	(44)	7.64	Sumitomo Corp	142	(111)	6.77
National Steel Corp	206	(174)	6.25	Summarecon Agung	191	(211)	6.40
Natsteel	173	(172)	6.53	Sun Hung Kai Properties	62	(36)	7.43
NEC Corp	99	(97)	7.17	Sunkyong	114	(98)	7.02

Company	Rank (Last year)		Score	Company	Rank (Last year)		Score
Swire Pacific	59	(42)	7.45	Unicord	249	(248)	4.91
Swiss Air	149	(136)	6.73	Unilever Indonesia	76	(24)	7.30
Taiwan Cement	145	(157)	6.76	United Airlines	141	(138)	6.77
Tan Chong Motors	187	(197)	6.44	United Daily News	183	(188)	6.49
Tatung	192	(201)	6.40	United Engineers (Malaysia)	177	(182)	6.52
Teijin Indonesia Fibre	217	(202)	6.12	United Parcel Service	201	(173)	6.32
Telekom Malaysia	144	(105)	6.77	United Tractors	123	(114)	6.96
Texas Instruments	85	(63)	7.26	Volkswagen	207	(232)	6.22
Thai Airways Int'l	98	(104)	7.17	Volvo	120	(87)	6.98
Thai Plastic and Chemical	164	(185)	6.61	Wearne Brothers	225	(240)	6.00
Thai-Asahi Glass	197	(177)	6.36	Westin Hotels	115	(125)	6.99
Tjiwi Kimia	230	(199)	5.92	Wharf	96	(71)	7.19
Tokai Bank	176	(222)	6.52	Yaohan	126	(-)	6.90
Toshiba Corp	40	(62)	7.72	Yeo Hiap Seng	248	(219)	5.21
Toyota Motor Corp	9	(6)	8.15	Yukong	103	(83)	7.15

11 Stop and Go in Korea

Bruce Cheesman

Doing business in South Korea is easier than before, but it's still tough.

American businessman Jay Tunney doesn't pull any punches when it comes to advising foreign companies on how tough it is to succeed in South Korea.

After five years of frustration and hair-pulling in the Korean market, Tunney, the son of Gene Tunney, world heavy-weight boxing champion from 1926 to 1928, has carved out a successful retail business for himself. The hurdles he had to climb in order to introduce Hobson's ice-cream to Korea have given him a unique insight into the thinking of the local business community.

Ostensibly, Korea is clearing many of the market barriers that formerly gave the country a reputation for being second only to Japan in terms of the hurdles placed in the way of foreigners. In fact, say observers, the hurdles are still there. They're just not quite as obvious or as official as they used to be.

Tunney knows all too well how the Koreans can smilingly fling open their markets and hold out a welcoming hand, while at the same time placing so many hidden trip-wires in the way that the foreign company ends up on its knees.

The liberalisation has mostly been forced on Korea. Tough talking, by Washington in particular, accompanied by threats of retaliation in the form of restrictions on Korean goods coming into the US, has led to many of the nation's markets being opened to foreigners. More than 300 items have been removed from the list of import restrictions, and markets ranging from finance and insurance to telecommunications and advertising have been liberalised.

The Koreans, again under pressure from the US, have also considerably cleaned up their investment laws and done away with some of the red tape that used to reduce foreign managers to tears.

Reproduced with permission from *Asian Business*, 26 (April 1992), pp. 46–47.

But doing business in Korea still requires considerable inventiveness and a great deal of toughness. Take Tunney: Almost immediately after he brought Hobson's ice-cream to Korea in 1987 under a franchise, he ran into problems.

His main difficulty was government restrictions. Officials ordered him to give 25% of his enterprise to a Korean partner and to make his ice-cream locally instead of importing it.

Fed-up with government interference and red tape, he closed his ice-cream parlour and concentrated on wholesale deals, supplying ice-cream to hotels and to the country's largest bakery chain. To stay in the retail business he bought a Korean hamburger joint and continued to sell his ice-cream from there.

Since then Koreans have been queuing up to buy franchises from him. "I am happy to see them put their money where my mouth is," says Tunney. "It makes me know I am on the right track."

Despite his run-ins with the South Korean government, he still believes foreign companies can succeed in Korea. "There is a tremendous market here. With the right approach and a lot of patience, foreigners can succeed."

Apart from Tunney, the other big foreign success story these days is the growing presence of American fast-food outlets in Seoul.

One American burger chain, Hardee's, which set up its first store in Seoul last year, has used a unique formula to penetrate the Korean market. Cleverly side-stepping Seoul's prohibitive real estate prices, it set up a joint venture with a high-street shoe retailer, Kumkang.

This incongruous partnership gave Hardee's access to prime sites in key business and shopping areas by converting Kumkang's shoe shops into restaurants.

Most of the fast-food retailers have entered the market through franchises or joint ventures to circumvent officialdom and overcome the hurdle of foreign companies not being able to own property for retail purposes.

Companies in other sectors are finding the going rather tougher. One problem is that even where government policy has changed for the better, officials don't respond to it.

"The mid-level bureaucrats all seem to have their own agenda as to what the fatherland should or should not have. And it bears no relation to what the minister says or what official government policy is," says one foreign businessman.

Some of Korea's more enlightened government officials agree that in many cases the difficulties foreign companies encounter are caused by over-zealous lower echelon officials. "Quite often officials go well beyond their duties," said Yu Deuk-hwan, an assistant minister of trade.

For example, foreign cars are hit by import duty as high as 300%. As if this were not enough to discourage local buyers, eager tax officials have begun noting down foreign car registration numbers. Special offer: Buy a foreign car and we'll track you down and give you a free tax audit.

Distributors of Scotch whisky — again, highly taxed — have found *lack* of government action highly effective in clobbering their sales efforts. They have been battling competition from black-market whisky from US bases, selling at a third of the price. "High tariffs and government inaction on black marketing have scuppered what should be a unique market for UK companies," says a diplomat at the British embassy in Seoul.

As if all this were not enough, there's the government's austerity campaign. South Koreans have been on a massive spending spree over the last few years. They have a growing appetite for foreign products and the money to spend on them. The austerity campaign is aimed at persuading them that a love of designer labels is unhealthy and against Confucian ethics.

The campaign's success has been patchy. But a number of sectors have been particularly hard hit. There has been a marked drop-off in consumption of so-called "luxury" goods, mainly because the government has taken steps to enforce austerity by using its most insidious weapon — tax audits — against big spenders.

Likewise, domestic tourism, an area opened to foreign investment at the end of last year, has been hit by the campaign. The growth of outbound travel has fallen almost 30% over the same period last year because, again, Koreans who show too great a taste for travel become targets for the tax man.

The once booming credit card industry suffered a double blow last year. First, limits on overseas spending were reduced from US$5,000 to US$3,000. Then credit card companies were "asked" to submit the spending records of all travellers for a six-month period last year.

"Confidentiality is vital to us," says Kevin Kneebon, American Express managing director in Seoul. "[The campaign] has affected all our business at a time when the market should be exploding."

Most observers believe the austerity campaign cannot last forever, as it is also beginning to stifle domestic production — many local companies are reluctant to invest in manufacturing at a time when people are being told not to buy.

But foreign companies will undoubtedly encounter other problems stemming from one factor: The perception by most Koreans that, once the doors are open, many local companies will go to the wall.

The argument that foreign competition will improve the productivity of local firms and the level of service to consumers does not seem to convince many people.

Despite their many complaints, however, most foreigners admit that the business climate is now much better than it was. One foreign businessman concedes that Korean-style market opening, unofficial barriers and all, is still better than nothing. "At least we are here and can set up shop on our own."

IV Developing Marketing Strategies

This part covers various aspects of developing marketing strategies and how these impact organizations and companies operating in the Asia Pacific region. These strategies set the direction for detailed development of the marketing mix programs.

After reading the three papers in this part, you should acquire a better understanding of the following aspects of marketing in the Asia Pacific:

1   The different ways in which organizations organize themselves to compete successfully around the world.
2   Sun Tzu's military principles and their marketing applications.
3   Localization and globalization of marketing strategy.

12 Managing across Borders: An Empirical Test of the Bartlett and Ghoshal [1989] Organizational Typology

Siew Meng Leong and Chin Tiong Tan

This paper reports an empirical test of the Bartlett and Ghoshal [1989] organizational typology. Some 131 senior executives of corporations with worldwide operations classified their organizations as being multinational, global, international, or transnational in nature and evaluated their organizations' configuration of assets and capabilities, role of overseas operations, and development and diffusion of knowledge. Results provide partial support for the typology. As expected, transnational corporations were least frequently reported by the respondents. The hypothesized practices associated with multinational and global organizations were more consistent with the typology's predictions relative to those of the international and transnational types.

> The multinational of the 1970s is obsolete. Global companies must be more than just a bunch of overseas subsidiaries with executive decisions made at headquarters. Instead, a new type of company is evolving. It does research wherever necessary, develops products in several countries, and promotes key executives regardless of nationality.
>
> *Business Week* [1990: May 14, front cover]

Several recent conceptualizations of global business management seem to suggest the emergence of stateless organizations operating in a borderless world. Accelerating this trend has been the lowering of transportation costs and the advent of modern communications networks [Reich 1991]. Such developments have encouraged businesses to get the most value from the least cost for their output. This shift in focus from volume to value production can be observed worldwide and across products and industries. Indeed, Ohmae [1989, 1990] has documented that successful corporations were those with such global-minded management.

Reproduced with permission from *Journal of International Business Studies*, 24 (No. 3, 1993), pp. 449–464.

However, many of these arguments have been founded on the observations and views of business people, academics, and management consultants. There has been a relative scarcity of empirical work verifying the extent of globalization among corporations. A major exception to this has been the stream of research by Bartlett and Ghoshal [1986, 1987a, 1987b, 1989]. Using a clinical approach, they conducted an in-depth study of nine companies from three countries operating in three industries with worldwide interests. Both personal interviews and survey questionnaires of key personnel were employed to develop a typology of organizations operating in the international business environment. Based on their results, these scholars identified four forms of organizations used to manage international businesses. They labeled these the multinational, global, international, and transnational corporations. Specific characteristics associated with the four forms of international organizational structures that differentiated their management practices were also proposed. Further, it was argued that businesses with a transnational structure and mindset would be most effective and efficient in future. This thesis is thus consistent with the view that a new, stateless corporate identity with a network of systems and activities in different parts of the world, deriving value from whichever location provides it at the lowest cost, is emerging (cf. Hedlund [1986]; Perlmutter and Trist [1986]; Prahalad and Doz [1987]).

Bartlett and Ghoshal's [1989] typology represents a significant contribution to the literature in international business. These scholars furnished a more fine-grained delineation of the evolution, structure, and orientation of the four organizational types not heretofore accomplished. The typology also offered prescriptive insights for a transnationalistic perspective for future international business organizations. Clearly, it also provides propositions for empirical testing necessary for theory building and extension.

We address two issues pertaining to the typology in this article from an international sample of executives of corporations with worldwide interests. These include: (1) the prevalence of the transnational corporation in contemporary international business relative to the other three organization types identified in it; and (2) whether the characteristics purported by it to distinguish one organization type from the others are demarcations employed by executives managing such enterprises. Empirical evidence on these issues would furnish some tentative insights regarding the relevance of the typology for international business organizations and perhaps suggest aspects of it that require additional conceptual attention. In addition, the larger sample studied here would augment the empirical basis for the typology by incorporating companies from a wider array of national origins operating in a more diverse range of industries than those investigated by Bartlett and Ghoshal [1989].

In the remainder of this article, we first discuss the evolution of corporate structure in the international business context. In particular, the Bartlett and Ghoshal [1989] organizational typology, which forms the foundation for our empirical investigation, will be described.[1] Based on this literature review, hypotheses are advanced to examine the extent to which (1) the four organizational structures are adopted among companies, and (2) the various characteristics noted by Bartlett and Ghoshal [1989] correspond to their respective organizational types. The research method employed is then detailed followed by the presentation of our survey results. Finally, we discuss the implications of the findings and provide some directions for future research.

Evolution of international corporate structure

Corporations are constantly seeking better ways of managing their businesses. Over time, every company is likely to evolve an organizational structure that facilitates its growth and international expansion (see, e.g., Stopford and Wells [1972]). According to Bartlett and Ghoshal [1989], different types of organizational structure evolve as a function of two key determinants. The first factor is the need for firms to match their capabilities to the strategic demands of their businesses. Hence, companies that manage a portfolio of multiple national entities perform well when the key strategic requirement is a high degree of responsiveness to differences in national environments around the world. Where global efficiency is vital, more centralized strategic and operational decisionmaking and the treatment of the world market as an integrated whole appeared most suitable. Finally, where transfer of knowledge is crucial, a structure that leveraged learning by adapting the parent company's expertise to foreign markets was preferred.

Bartlett and Ghoshal [1989] labeled these three types of organizations that operate in the international business environment as: (1) multinational companies, which build a strong local presence through sensitivity and responsiveness to national differences; (2) global companies, which build cost advantages through centralized global-scaled operations; and (3) international companies, which exploit parent company knowledge and capabilities through worldwide diffusion and adaptation.

The second factor influencing the organization of worldwide operations is the company's administrative heritage. Defined as its existing organizational attributes and way of doing things, it is shaped by the company's founder or key executive, the norms, values, and behaviors of managers in its national companies, and its historical context. Bartlett and Ghoshal [1989: 33] argue that a company's administrative heritage can be a major asset, the underlying source of its key competencies, as well as a significant liability, since it resists change and thereby prevents realignment or broadening of the firm's strategic capabilities. They further detail how this internal force produces strategic and organizational consequences in a firm's expansion overseas [Bartlett and Ghoshal 1989: 48–52].

Briefly, a multinational company reflects a decentralized federation with distributed resources and delegated responsibilities. Such structures are impacted by the enduring influence of family ownership, personal relationships, and informal contacts upon which organizational processes are built. Rather than relying on formal structures and systems, such processes reinforce the delegation of operating independence to trusted appointees in offshore subsidiaries. In contrast, the global organization can be construed as a centralized hub, a structural configuration based on group-oriented behavior requiring intensive communication and a complex system of personal interdependencies and commitments. This in turn produces a dependence of overseas subsidiaries on the parent headquarters for resources and direction. The international form may be described as a coordinated federation suiting companies with a reputation for professional management. This implies a willingness to delegate responsibility while retaining overall control via sophisticated management systems and specialist corporate staffs.

Bartlett and Ghoshal [1989] caution that no particular organization type is best suited for specific industries or countries. Rather, they propose that the three organizational forms vary based on their (1) configuration of assets and capabilities, (2) role of overseas operations, and (3) development and diffusion of knowledge. Specifically, multinational corporations are seen to (1) be decentralized and nationally self-sufficient, (2) have their overseas operations sense and exploit local opportunities, and (3) develop and retain knowledge within each individual unit. In contrast, global corporations are those that (1) are centralized and globally scaled, (2) have their overseas operations as implementing tools of parent company strategies, and (3) develop and retain knowledge at headquarters level. International corporations are characterized by (1) having some of their sources of core competencies centralized, others decentralized, (2) adapting and leveraging parent company competencies, and (3) developing knowledge at parent level and transferring it to overseas units.

Beyond these organizational types, Bartlett and Ghoshal [1989] go further in arguing that with the growing complexities of conducting international business, such traditional management modes cannot effectively respond to the multidimensional and dynamic demands of contemporary industries and markets. They propose a fourth model based on the notion of a transnational corporation. Such companies seek to be globally competitive through multinational flexibility and worldwide learning capability. Their organizational characteristics include (1) being dispersed, interdependent, and specialized, (2) having differentiated contributions by national units to integrated worldwide operations, and (3) developing knowledge jointly and sharing it worldwide.

Hypotheses

The Bartlett and Ghoshal [1989] framework thus offers some interesting propositions for empirical testing. To the extent that the transnational structure is considered a new form and ideal structure for international business management, it can be predicted that it would be the least prevalent form observed in the marketplace today. Hence, H1 states:

H1: Relative to other organizational types, the transnational corporation will be the least prevalent form for organizing international business activities.

The other predictions stated in H2, H3, and H4 arise directly from the assertions of their framework concerning the practices associated with each type of organization. These hypotheses compare characteristics of organizing international activities among the three other types of structures — multinational, global, and international.

H2: Relative to global and international organizations, multinational corporations are more likely to (a) be decentralized and nationally self-sufficient, (b) have their overseas operations sense and exploit local opportunities, and (c) develop and retain knowledge within each individual unit.

H3: Relative to multinational and international organizations, global corporations are more likely to (a) be centralized and globally scaled, (b) have their overseas operations as implementing tools of parent company strategies, and (c) develop and retain knowledge at headquarters level.

H4: Relative to multinational and global corporations, international corporations are more likely to (a) have sources of core competencies centralized and others decentralized, (b) adapt and leverage parent company competencies, and (c) develop knowledge at parent level and transfer it to overseas units.

Given its special status in the Bartlett and Ghoshal [1989] typology, the transnational structure should be assessed against all the other organizational types. Thus, a final test of the typology is that:

H5: Relative to all other types of organizations, transnational corporations are more likely to (a) be dispersed, interdependent, and specialized,

(b) have differentiated contributions by national units to integrated worldwide operations, and (c) develop knowledge jointly and share it worldwide.

Method

Sample

A major consideration in research of this nature is that respondents be willing and able to provide the necessary information (cf. Campbell [1955]). Clearly, respondents should be executives of sufficiently high corporate standing to posses the likely expertise and bird's eye view required to furnish an informed perspective of their organization's international management structure. Moreover, they should represent companies with worldwide interests. Finally, they should provide input almost simultaneously so that enhanced comparability is possible within a given time frame [Sekaran 1983].

One opportunity presented itself that enabled these criteria to be satisfied. A Global Strategies Conference was organized in 1990 by the Singapore Economic Development Board. Top officers of MNCs around the world were invited to participate in the seminar. Some 151 executives participated in the meeting and formed the sample for this study. Of these, 131 provided complete and usable returns for the analyses. The modal designation of respondents was managing director (38.4%). Of the remainder, such titles as president, director, chairman, and CEO were common. Their companies were engaged in a wide range of operations, with electronics, computers, and chemical industries most frequently mentioned (45.7%). The large scale of their operations was reflected in annual parent company sales exceeding US$10 billion for 78.5% of the respondents' organizations. All but 22.2% also had at least 1,000 employees worldwide.

In summary, these statistics seem to suggest that respondents were well qualified to make informed judgments in the survey and represented large corporations with worldwide interests. The sample profile seems to fit well with the four organizational types posited by Bartlett and Ghoshal [1989] to be tested in this study. However, as the sample does not include domestic and probably just-internationalizing firms, more comprehensive validity assessment of the typology is precluded. To the extent that such firms can be shown not to possess the characteristics associated with the four corporate forms in the typology, greater evidence of discriminant validity can be accorded to it.

Measurement

A survey questionnaire was designed that required respondents to (1) categorize the international management structure of their organization into one of four types as defined by Bartlett and Ghoshal [1989], and (2) indicate the extent of agreement with twelve statements on 5-point scales regarding the three dimensions of configuration of assets and capabilities, role of overseas operations, and development and diffusion of knowledge in their organizations.

Specifically, respondents were asked to indicate how their company achieved competitiveness in the global market on one of four forced choices: (a) by building a strong local presence through sensitivity and responsiveness to national differences among countries; (b) by building cost advantages through global-scaled operations; (c) by exploiting their parent company's knowledge and capabilities through worldwide implementation and adaptation; or (d) by building interdependent resources with specialized subsidiary roles while maintaining flexible and joint operations among countries. Each option reflected one of four international management structures in the Bartlett and Ghoshal [1989] framework. In particular, options (a), (b), (c) and (d) reflected the typical multinational, global, international, and transnational type of organization, respectively.

Note that the self-typing approach used by respondents in this study to classify their organizations is not without shortcomings (cf. Snow and Hambrick [1980]). Managers may be reluctant to categorize their own organizations. However, the number who did not do so in this study was a mere 13%. There may be possible variance among managers' perceptions within the same organization. However, this possibility can be discounted given that only one respondent per organization provided the classification in this research. The approach used also lacks external confirmation of the respondents' categorization. However, by using key informants who were willing and able to furnish their perceptions, this possibility is also minimized. Another limitation of this method is executives' tendency to report their organizations' intended rather than realized international management structure. Most serious is that if none existed, an arbitrary one may be created for the benefit of the researchers. However, this is a common problem in the social sciences [Nisbett and Wilson 1977], although use of an "other" category to allow respondents to fill in their own classification could have alleviated it somewhat.[2]

Given four organizational types to be evaluated on three dimensions, the minimum of twelve statements was created to assess the individual characteristics of respondents' organizations. These were modified from Bartlett and Ghoshal's [1989: 65] summary table, the conclusions of which were reported in the literature review. The modifications to improve comprehension were based on a pre-test with twelve specialists working in the area of global investment and business. All items were also consistent with the group's views of operations of the various types of organizations.

Results

H1 stated that relative to other organizational types, the transnational corporation will be the least prevalent form for organizing international business activities. Consistent with expectations, only twenty-three respondents considered their organizations as being transnational in character. Of the remainder, some fifty-one respondents considered their organizations as being multinational in nature, twenty-six deemed theirs as being global, and thirty-one classified their organizations as international corporations. The observed frequencies differed statistically from a uniform distribution of firms across the four organizational forms (*chi square* = 14.55, df = 3, p < .01). More importantly, the actual proportion of transnational firms (17.6%) was significantly lower than the 25% expected under the null hypothesis of an equal proportion of firms in each category (z = -1.97, p < .05). Hence, the evidence appears to support H1 as transnational corporations were observed to be the least prevalent organizational structure in international business management. Furthermore, the 38.9% of multinational firms significantly exceeded the 25% level (z = 3.67, p = <.01). This bears out Bartlett and Ghoshal's [1989] observation that most worldwide operations are of the multinational organization type.

Descriptive statistics concerning respondents' evaluation of the hypothesized practices of the four organizational forms are contained in Table 1. On the average, respondents most strongly agreed with the statements concerning (1) the primary role of overseas units is to find and take advantage of opportunities within the countries in which they operate, and (2) their organization being integrated worldwide, with overseas units playing an important role by contributing their individual strengths and know-how towards their operations. In contrast, they most strongly disagreed with the statements regarding (1) new knowledge developed in overseas units tending not to be transferred to other locations in which their organization operates, and (2) R&D activities conducted and retained at parent company level without being disseminated to overseas units.

To test H2 through H5, the mean agreement score for the target organizational type in each hypothesis was compared against the average score of the other organizations of concern for each of the three characteristics (statements) with which it was associated.[3] Given the a priori nonothogonal nature of the contrasts, t-tests were performed using the Dunnett procedure (see Kirk [1982] for details). Table 2 reports the results.

H2 stated that relative to global and international corporations, multinational organizations are more likely to be decentralized and nationally self-sufficient, have their overseas operations sense and exploit local opportunities, and develop and retain knowledge within each unit. As Table 2 shows, multinational corporations differed from their global and international counterparts on two of

Table 1 Mean agreement scores of international organizational structures[a]

Statement	Overall	Multinational	Global	International	Transnational
1. The skills and resources of my organization are located around the world, but each overseas unit conducts its own operations without relying on the expertise of other units located elsewhere.	2.75 (1.16)	2.72 (1.10)	2.73 (1.15)	2.69 (1.17)	2.81 (1.33)
2. The main role of our overseas operations is to implement parent company strategies.	3.49 (.88)	3.41 (.76)	3.81 (.63)	3.63 (.93)	3.00 (1.14)
3. New knowledge (e.g., product improvements) is developed at the parent company and then transferred to overseas units.	3.43 (.89)	3.36 (.85)	3.42 (.86)	3.45 (.96)	3.48 (.93)
4. The most vital and strategic skills and resources of my organization tend to be located at parent company headquarters, while less important activities are located in our overseas units.	2.91 (1.04)	2.75 (1.06)	3.12 (1.07)	3.24 (.87)	2.50 (1.06)
5. The primary role of our overseas units is to find out and take advantage of opportunities within the countries in which they operate.	3.94 (.86)	4.09 (.83)	3.72 (1.06)	3.80 (.71)	4.05 (.84)
6. Research and development activities are conducted, and the results retained, at parent company headquarters with little dissemination to our overseas units.	2.45 (.97)	2.20 (.87)	2.67 (1.01)	2.66 (1.04)	2.45 (1.00)
7. Our skills and resources are centralized and globally scaled.	3.04 (.94)	2.68 (.86)	3.48 (.99)	3.25 (.89)	3.00 (.89)
8. Research and development activities are typically conducted jointly by parent company and overseas units with the knowledge gained shared worldwide in my organization.	3.68 (.87)	3.74 (.88)	3.79 (.72)	3.52 (.99)	3.68 (.89)
9. Our overseas operations receive and adapt products and services offered by our parent company to the best advantage in the countries in which they operate.	3.92 (.66)	3.95 (.68)	3.68 (.69)	4.03 (.50)	3.89 (.74)
10. My organization locates specialized skills and resources around the world, but our overseas units often cooperate with and depend upon each other.	3.64 (.82)	3.70 (.88)	3.58 (.72)	3.48 (.87)	3.84 (.76)
11. The new knowledge (e.g., product improvements) developed in our overseas units tends not to be ransferred to other locations in which my organization operates.	2.38 (.82)	2.09 (.60)	2.83 (.96)	2.52 (.74)	2.26 (.81)
12. My organization is integrated worldwide and our overseas units play an important role contributing their individual strengths and know-how towards its operation.	3.95 (.77)	4.02 (.79)	3.75 (.68)	4.00 (.85)	4.00 (.56)

[a]standard deviations in parentheses

Table 2 Results of hypotheses testing (*t*-statistics)

Statement	H2 MNC vs GC & IC	H3 GC vs MNC & IC	H4 IC vs MNC & GC	H5 TC vs Others
1. The skills and resources of my organization are located around the world but each overseas unit conducts its own operations without relying on the expertise of other units located elsewhere.	.064	–	–	–
2. The main role of our overseas operations is to implement parent company strategies.	–	1.775[b]	–	–
3. New knowledge (e.g., product improvements) is developed at the parent company and then transferred to overseas units.	–	–	.360	–
4. The most vital and strategic skills and resources of my organization tend to be located at parent company headquarters while less important activities are located in overseas operations.	–	–	1.632[c]	
5. The primary role of our overseas units is to find out and take advantage of opportunities within the countries in which they operate.	1.898[b]	–	–	–
6. Research and development activities are conducted and the results retained at parent company headquarters with little dissemination to our overseas units.	–	1.285[c]	–	–
7. Our skills and resources are centralized and globally scaled.	–	2.671[a]	–	–
8. Research and development activities are typically conducted jointly by parent company and overseas units with the knowledge gained shared worldwide in my organization.	–	–	–	–.024
9. Our overseas operations receive and adapt products and services offered by our parent company to the best advantage in the countries in which they operate.	–	–	1.277	–
10. My organization locates specialized skills and resources around the world but our overseas units often cooperate with and depend upon each other.	–	–	–	1.130
11. The new knowledge (e.g., product improvements) developed in our overseas units tends not to be transferred to other locations in which my organization operates.	3.763[a]	–	–	–
12. My organization is integrated worldwide and our overseas units play an important role by contributing their individual strengths and know–how towards its operation.	–	–	–	.272

[a]significant at .01
[b]significant at .05
[c]significant at .10

the three hypothesized characteristics. These included: viewing the role of overseas operations as uncovering and exploiting local opportunities, as well as new knowledge developed overseas tending not to be transferred elsewhere. On the remaining item regarding the autonomy of overseas units and their non-reliance on expertise from other units, the difference in agreement was in the predicted direction but was not statistically significant. Considered collectively, these results furnished some support for H2.

H3 posited that relative to multinational and international organizations, global corporations are more likely to be centralized and globally scaled, have their overseas operations as implementing tools of parent company strategies, and develop and retain knowledge at headquarters level. The survey findings also provided support for H3. Executives of global corporations more strongly agreed with the three statements concerning the characteristics of their organizational type vis-à-vis those from multinational and international corporations. Specifically, they held more strongly to the view that the role of overseas operations was to implement parent company strategies, that results from research and development activities were retained at headquarters, and that their companies' skills and resources were centralized and globally scaled.

H4 proposed that relative to multinational and global corporations, international organizations are more likely to have sources of core competencies centralized and others decentralized, adapt and leverage parent company competencies, and develop knowledge at parent level and transfer it to overseas units. Executives from international organizations also reported stronger agreement (than those of multinational and global corporations) on all three hypothesized characteristics regarding their categorization. However, only one such difference — that pertaining to the most strategic skills and resources being maintained at parent company level while less important activities were located overseas — was found to be statistically significant.[4] Overall, the results do not furnish much support for H4.

H5 stated that, relative to all other types of organizations, transnational corporations are more likely to be dispersed, interdependent, and specialized, have differentiated contributions by national units to integrated worldwide operations, and develop knowledge jointly and share it worldwide. Even less empirical evidence was obtained supporting H5. In no case did executives from transnational corporations differ from their counterparts in the other three organizational types on the hypothesized characteristics. In two cases, however, differences obtained were in the predicted direction. These included location of specialized skills and resources worldwide and overseas units contributing their individual strengths and know-how towards their operations. On the remaining item of joint conduct of research and development, the difference was in the direction opposite to that hypothesized.[5]

Discussion

This study produced two principal findings. First, the results showed that executives perceived their companies to vary in international organization type. Multinational corporations dominated, followed by the international and global forms. The transnational form, as expected, was found to be the least evident structure. Second, the evidence in general furnished partial support for the differences in characteristics predicted across the four organization types of Bartlett and Ghoshal [1989]. In particular, the demarcations between multinationally and especially globally organized corporations relative to other organizational types were more evident than those expected for international and transnational corporations. Prior to discussing these results, due qualification must again be made of the sample and questionnaire limitations in this research.

Implications

In general, corporations appeared to be trying to 'think global' and 'act local.' The strong levels of agreement towards the expanded and proactive role of overseas units coupled with worldwide integration of activities and free transfer of knowledge to all locations tended to support this contention. More interestingly, the results suggested variations existed in the practice of managing across national borders. Specifically, it was found that multinational and global corporations seemingly followed a particular mode of organization for managing their international operations by adopting practices consistent with those stipulated by Bartlett and Ghoshal [1989]. However, it was found that executives who typed their organizations as being international and transnational in nature did not appear to endorse many of the behaviors predicted by the typology.

Our findings thus indicate that a reformulation of the Bartlett and Ghoshal [1989] typology appears necessary. Specifically, they imply that the practices of international and transnational forms may be distinguished from other organizational types as well as from each other on a more selective basis than previously conceptualized. Hence, international corporations may differ from multinational and global organizations on the role accorded to their overseas operations. Transnational corporations seem to be marginally differentiated from international organizations on their configuration of assets and capabilities, and from global enterprises on the role of their overseas operations.

In addition, the minimal differences obtained regarding the characteristics of transnationals versus the other organization types in the framework seems disturbing. Several explanations may be advanced to refute the inference that this represents a critical contradiction of the typology. One rationale may be that executives from the three other types of organizations have misclassified their corporations. This appears unlikely given the generally consistent differences obtained from examination of characteristics reflective of their respective types relative to others.

A more possible explanation concerns the finding that the transnational organization category received the fewest proportion (18%) of mentions. Bartlett and Ghoshal [1989], by comparison, noted that *none* of the companies they surveyed had reached this ideal. This may imply respondents misclassifying their organization as being transnational. It may also suggest that simply deeming one's organization as being transnational does not necessarily result in its adopting the characteristics normatively prescribed to such an entity. Potentially, the desired mindset of their executives may be one that has not truly absorbed the underlying managerial mentality of transnational organizations. If so, more effort is needed to cultivate this perspective to enhance the global competitiveness of their organizations.

The lack of differences in activities between the transnational and other types of organizations also may be due to the evolving nature of corporate structures in international business. Being the preferred option in the competitive global environment, the transnational structure is likely to be the one most companies are attempting to adopt. Given that they are likely to be operating in the multinational, global, or international mode, they are likely to resemble these existing organizational types. Moreover, the path towards transnationalism appears to be a difficult one. Indeed, Hu [1992] argues that international organization forms were mainly national firms with international operations.[6] Using secondary data, he found that the geographic spread and scope, ownership and control, management and workforce, and legal nationality and tax domicile of several well-known companies with worldwide operations were concentrated in their home countries.

Future research

Several useful directions for future research emanate from this study. First, only single-item measures were employed here given the limited time the participants had to complete the questionnaire. The development of multi-item, internally consistent measures would allow for a more complete explication of these complex constructs in future research. As alluded to earlier, it would also be instructive to include domestic and just-internationalizing firms in future samples to more completely assess the typology's discriminant validity.

Third, it may be beneficial to perform a study using customers of the organizations. This will provide an external validation of the findings. Moreover, factors other than those suggested by Bartlett and Ghoshal [1989] accounting for differences in organizational types may be theorized and tested (cf. Egelhoff [1991]); Hu[1992]). Indeed, such research may lead to the uncovering of omissions and misrepresentations of the typology, possibly leading to added conceptual refinement and extension. In a similar vein, added effort may be directed towards furthering the conceptual development of the transnational and international organization types as well as more precisely delineating them from other structural configurations.

Perhaps the most important area meriting research attention is whether transnational do indeed outperform the other organizational types across countries and industries over time. Such an analysis would require longitudinal, rather than the present cross-sectional, data to empirically examine how differences in customer requirements and key success factors have an impact upon the movement towards transnationalism.

NOTES

1. This exposition is necessarily brief for economy of presentation. Interested readers may find a more detailed and comprehensive account of the framework directly from Bartlett and Ghoshal [1989].

2. Nonetheless, using more open-ended categories is not without drawbacks. Errors may arise in researcher classification of such responses unless appropriate coding schemes are developed to categorize them reliably.

3. While from a strict psychometric perspective, the dependent variables were measured on ordinal scales, the Likert-type items employed here have been treated as though they were interval in nature in most social science research (cf. Guilford [1954]). One exception would be when *gross* inequality of the intervals exists [Kerlinger 1973: 441, his emphasis], a possibility that does not appear to hold here. Consequently, our data have been subjected to parametric tests to extract the most information from them.

4. A one-tailed t-test showed that it was the difference between executives of international corporations and those from multinational enterprises ($t = 2.57, p < .01$) that accounted for this result. Another test revealed that executives of international corporations also more strongly agreed that their overseas operations received and adapted products and services to the best advantage where they operated relative to those from global corporations ($t = 2.22, p < .05$). All other pairwise comparisons were not significant (t's < 1, p's > .10).

5. Pairwise comparisons using one-tailed t-tests revealed only two marginally significant findings (p's < .10). Transnational managers agreed more strongly than those of international corporations that they located specialized skills and resources worldwide, with overseas units often cooperating and depending on each other ($t = 1.59$). They also agreed more strongly than those of global enterprises that their organizations were integrated worldwide with overseas units playing an important role by contributing their individual strengths and know-how in operations ($t = 1.39$). All other pairwise comparisons were not significant (t's < 1.23, p's > .10).

6. The two exceptions cited were binational companies that were owned, controlled, and staffed in two home nations and firms from small nations, for which the home nation accounts for a small percentage of total assets and operations [Hu 1992: 121–22].

REFERENCES

Bartlett, Christopher A. & Sumantra Ghoshal. 1986. Tap your subsidiaries for global reach. *Harvard Business Review*, 64: 87–94.

_____ . 1987a. Managing across borders: New strategic requirements. *Sloan Management Review*, 28: 7–18.

_____ . 1987b. Managing across borders: New organizational responses. *Sloan Management Review*, 29: 43–54.

_____ . 1989. *Management across borders: The transnational solution*. Boston, MA: Harvard Business School Press.

Business Week. 1990. The stateless corporation. May 14: 52–60.

Campbell, Donald T. 1955. The informant in quantitative research. *American Journal of Sociology*, 60: 339–42.

Egelhoff, William G. 1991. Information-processing theory and the multinational enterprise. *Journal of International Business Studies*, 22(3): 341–68.

Guilford, Joy P. 1954 (second edition). *Psychometric methods*. New York: McGraw-Hill.

Hedlund, Gunnar. 1986. The hypermodern MNC: A heterarchy? *Human Resource Management*, Spring: 9–35.

Hu, Yao-Su. 1992. Global or stateless corporations are national firms with international operations. *California Management Review*, Winter: 107–26.

Kerlinger, Fred N. 1973. *Foundations of behavioral research*. New York: Holt, Rinehart and Winston.

Kirk, Roger E. 1982 (second edition). *Experimental design*. Monterey, CA: Brooks/Cole Publishing.

Nisbett, Richard E. & Timothy D. Wilson. 1977. Telling more than we know: Verbal reports on mental processes. *Psychological Review*, 84: 231–59.

Ohmae, Kenichi. 1989. The global logic of strategic alliances. *Harvard Business Review*, 67: 143–54.

_____ . 1990. The borderless world. *Harvard Business Review*, 68: 32–42.

Perlmutter, Howard & Eric Twist. 1986. Paradigms for social transition. *Human Relations*, 39(1): 1–27.

Prahalad, C.K. & Yves Doz. 1986. *The multinational mission: Balancing local demands and global vision*. New York: Free Press.

Reich, Robert B. 1991. *The work of nations*. New York: Knopf.

Sekaran, Uma. 1983. Methodological and theoretical issues and advancements in cross-cultural research. *Journal of International Business Studies*, 14(2): 61–74.

Snow, Charles C. & Donald C. Hambrick. 1980. Measuring organizational strategies: Some theoretical and methodological problems. *Academy of Management Review*, 5: 527–38.

Stopford, John M. & Louis T. Wells, Jr. 1972. *Managing the multinational enterprise*. New York: Basic Books.

SIEW MENG LEONG and CHIN TIONG TAN are Senior Lecturer and Associate Professor, respectively, in the Department of Marketing, National University of Singapore. The authors thank the Singapore Economic Development Board for its assistance in data collection, the National University of Singapore for funding this research, and the three anonymous JIBS reviewers for their helpful comments.

13 Sun Tzu's Strategic Thinking and Contemporary Business

Min Chen

[handwritten: (C-) relevance, has 5 personality traits for generals/ CEOs.]

The Chinese expression *"Shang Chang Ru Zhan Chang"* is translated into English as "The marketplace is a battlefield." This is how Asians view success or failure in the business world. From the Asian perspective, the success or failure of a family business directly influences the survival and well-being of the family. The success or failure of a nation's economy affects the survival and well-being of a nation. Therefore, many Asians treat business competition as life-and-death warfare.

Many Western business people, for example, have observed that the Japanese conduct business as if they were waging a war, using the term "waging business" to describe the intensity of Japanese competitive strategies. Because the marketplace, in the eyes of Asians, is a battlefield, military strategy is held to be very useful in guiding business activities. Many Asian business leaders have attached great importance to the classical Chinese military strategies. Many of the principles behind these strategies are even commonly applied to daily life.

Military strategies and business competitions

In Chinese, the word military strategy consists of two parts: *Bing* ("soldier") and *Fa* ("doctrine"), which together can also be translated to mean "the art of war." The golden era in the development of classical Chinese military strategy was the few hundred years between the beginning of the Spring-Autumn period and the end of the Warring States period in Chinese history (772–221 B.C.). Many of the classic strategies were written during this period, because it was a time of constant warfare and of the famous "hundred flowers blooming" and "hundred schools debating." Many of the greatest Chinese philosophers — Confucius,

Reproduced with permission from *Business Horizons*, 37 (March–April, 1994), pp. 42–48.

Mencius, Lao Tzu, Zhuang Tzu, and Han Fei Tzu — lived during this period. Their philosophies left an indelible imprint on classical Chinese military strategy.

Sun Tzu Bing-Fa, allegedly written by the master Sun Tzu in the fourth century B.C., is the most complete and reputable book of military strategy that has survived to date. It is still difficult to determine the biography of the author, who supposedly was a subject of Kingdom Qi and a contemporary of Confucius. Around 512 B.C., he traveled to Kingdom Wu and was appointed general. In the ensuing 30 years, he won numerous wars and eventually helped Wu achieve a sort of hegemony by replacing the traditional hegemonic Kingdom Jin. It was at this point that he came to be regarded as a genius of military strategy.

As were other philosophical and strategic texts, Sun Tzu's strategies were heavily influenced by Taoist thought, which emphasizes the interrelatedness and relativity of everything in the world. As one quotation of Taoist thought goes:

The Tao gives birth to the one.
One gives birth to two.
Two gives birth to three.
And three gives birth to ten thousand things.
The ten thousand things carry *yin* and embrace *yang*.
By combining these forces, harmony is created.

Tao not only deals with the truth of Oneness, but also the propensity for change of the Oneness. All things in the world originate at one source; all things are different but also interrelated, changing constantly in accordance with the laws of nature. There is no difference between goodness and evil, ease and difficulty, high and low, long and short. Contrasting motivating factors influencing human behavior, such as love and hate, arise from the same place, as two sides of the same coin. One can turn love into hate and hate into love, as they are not essentially different and depend on the circumstances. The same logic is applied to courage and fear, generosity and miserliness, and extroversion and introversion.

The famous story of Top Horse, Middle Horse, and Weak Horse in the Warring States Period (476–221 B.C.) exemplifies the advantages of the Taoist dialectic. Sun Bin was a master strategist who served General Tian of the Kingdom Qi. General Tian raced horses with the princes of Qi as a hobby, often wagering large sums of money. One day, General Tian came up to Sun for advice on an upcoming horse race, which seemed to be at a draw. As the usual practice went, the contest consisted of three races. The traditional strategy for victory was to pit one's best, middle, and worst horse against the similar horses of his rival. Sun Bin advised General Tian to race his worst horse against his rival's best horse, to pit his best horse against his rival's middle horse, and finally to use his middle horse to compete against his rival's worst horse. General Tian followed Sun's advice; after one loss and two wins, General Tian was declared the final winner of the contest. As a good strategist, Sun Bin saw the larger picture and understood that the goal was to win the contest, not each race.

The story clearly illustrates the Taoist concept of interrelatedness and relativity, according to which there is no absolute good or bad thing in the world. One should always use one's strong points in competing against weak points in others. The story of the Liangxiang computer company shows how ancient strategic thinking has influenced the Chinese in commercial dealings. On the whole, the Liangxiang company's computers are no match for Japanese, American, or even Taiwanese computers. But the company has adopted a strategy of selling its medium-range computer in the bottom-of-the-range international market, because the costs of the medium-range model are still low enough to allow the company to remain competitive in the bottom-of-the-range market.

Certain comparisons can be made between enterprise competitions and military warfare:

- Enterprises and armies strive for a favorable position by defeating their competitors while defending themselves.
- Competitions and wars are confrontational activities.
- Organizations must be well-organized and well-managed.
- Organizations and wars require strategies and tactics.
- The leadership of an army and an enterprise has an important influence on the shaping of success.
- They both need high quality and committed people.
- They both thrive on information.

There does exist a fundamental difference between business and war. The former is an act of construction; the latter an act of destruction. As such, the two are diametrical.

With this in mind, we should be able to expand on those aspects of business that more closely resemble war — business competition and competitiveness. Where business and war overlap, the comparison is sound, the strategies interchangeable.

The principle of strategies

According to the opening statement of Sun Tzu's work, "War is a matter of vital importance to the state; a matter of life and death, the road either to survival or to ruin. Hence, it is imperative that it be thoroughly studied."* This enunciates the importance of one aspect of Sun Tzu's principle of strategies:

prudence and the need for good planning. Before a decision to wage war is made, one must engage in detailed planning. This is manifested in many parts of his writings:

> With careful and detailed planning, one can win; with careless and less detailed planning, one cannot win. How much less chance of victory has one who does not plan at all! From the way planning is done beforehand, one can predict victory or defeat.

The same is true for business competition, which concerns the survival or death of the company and the fate of shareholders, employees, customers, and the community in which it operates. Therefore, careful strategic planning is very important.

Sun Tzu emphasized first and foremost the importance of avoiding bloody conflicts as much as possible. Therefore, the highest form of victory is to conquer by strategy. To win a battle by fighting is not the best strategy; to conquer the enemy without having to resort to war is the highest, most admirable form of generalship. The next best form of generalship is to conquer the enemy with an alliance — by borrowing strengths from one's allies. This is followed by the strategy of conquering the enemy by fighting on open ground, where one can attack and withdraw easily. The worst form of generalship is to conquer the enemy by besieging walled cities. This is bound to be the most costly of endeavors. As Sun Tzu said, "For this reason, to win a hundred victories in a hundred battles is not the culmination of skills. To subdue the enemy without fighting is the supreme excellence."

To achieve this goal, one has to grasp the total picture of the situation:

> Know your enemy, know yourself, and you can fight a hundred battles with no danger of defeat. When you are ignorant of the enemy but know yourself, your chances of winning and losing are equal. If you don't know both your enemy and yourself, you are bound to perish in all battles. . . . Know the terrain, know the weather, and your victory will be complete.

Sun Tzu further described the necessity of appraising the following seven elements:

- the moral influence of the ruler;
- the ability of the general;
- the conditions of climate and terrain;
- the implementation of laws and rules; ~ *not covered below?*
- the comparative strengths of troops;
- the training of officers and soldiers; and
- the use of rewards and punishments.

Moral influence

By moral influence, Sun Tzu meant the way in which the people are able to be in good accord with their ruler, for whom they are willing to fight through all the pitfalls involved in war. If the ruler is wise, he must first acquire the moral support of his subjects, without which he will not be able to win. To achieve this, the ruler should take care of the interests of his subjects, exercising benevolent rule and treating them as his own family members.

In the context of a war, this moral influence refers to the principle of "fighting as one man" (*tong-xin*). By this Sun Tzu meant that generals and soldiers share the same goals and difficulties. He wrote:

> Troops directed by a skillful general are comparable to the Shuai Ran. The Shuai Ran is a snake found in Mount Heng. Strike at its head, and you will be attacked by its tail; strike at its tail, and you will be attacked by its head; strike at its middle, and you will be attacked by both its head and its tail . . . The principle of military administration is to achieve a uniform level of courage.

To achieve this goal, Sun Tzu emphasized one important principle: If a general treats his soldiers as his own beloved sons, they will stand by him until death. Many Chinese generals paid attention to this advice. Qi Ji-guang, a general in the Ming Dynasty, once said, "Although soldiers are not very smart, they are most easily moved." Because the majority of soldiers were peasants, they could be easily motivated by a little care from their generals. The famous general Yue Fei of the Song Dynasty, for example, personally prepared medicine for his soldiers.

In an extremely competitive business world, managers should endeavor to formulate a common corporate goal to be shared by all employees, so that all in the company come to view themselves as members of the group crossing the river in the same boat. They would more likely consider company affairs as their own and be willing to make personal sacrifices when needed. Only in this way can a company survive fierce competition and make full use of its competitive advantage. As Sun Tzu said, "He whose ranks are united in purpose will win."

The ability of generals

A good general, according to Sun Tzu, should possess five important qualities: wisdom (*zhi*), sincerity (*cheng*), benevolence (*ren*), courage (*yong*), and strictness (*yan*). By wisdom, he meant the ability to observe changing circumstances and act accordingly, and the ability to discern and judge situations. Sincerity concerns the ability to win the complete trust of subordinates. Sun Tzu's benevolence implies deep love for one's soldiers, the ability to sympathize with their problems, and a true concern for their well-being. Courage requires a general to be brave, decisive, and able to gain victory by taking advantage of opportunities without hesitation. Strictness concerns the ability to implement discipline and mete out punishments so troops dare not violate commands or rules.

Having explained the positive qualities of a general, Sun Tzu also listed five common negative qualities that a general should discard to avert disaster:

> If reckless, he can be killed; if cowardly, he can be captured; if quick-tempered, he can easily be provoked; if sensitive to honor, he can easily be insulted; if overly compassionate to the people, he can easily be harassed.

These desirable and undesirable qualities of generalship can be used to measure corporate leadership. A corporation is similar to an army organizationally. A powerful and efficient leader is indispensable to the success of a corporation. The five positive qualities of Sun Tzu's generalship are those also needed by CEOs, whereas the five negative qualities should be avoided by any CEO. A good CEO can be expected to have a combination of the following qualities:

- Broad knowledge with the capability to identify business trends and opportunities;
- The ability to establish mutual trust between management and employees;
- The capability to delegate power, while knowing how to tolerate subordinates' unavoidable mistakes;
- Benevolence that understands the problems of subordinates and cares about their well-being;
- Moderate amounts of compassion, to avoid easy harassment from trifles;
- The boldness to make risky decisions, while not making hasty or reckless decisions; and
- The ability to combine strict discipline, meting out punishment decisively and fairly.

Sun Tzu emphasizes the basic qualities and cultivations of a military leader — his generalship rather than his military and technical background. According to Sun Tzu, "It is the business of a general to be quiet and thus ensure depth in deliberation; and to be impartial and upright, and thus keep good management." These requirements contrast commonly accepted standards on the ability of enterprise leaders in the West, which emphasize specialized and outward abilities in such areas as manufacturing, management, finance, marketing, and creativity. For many Chinese, the technical backgrounds of a candidate can always be improved through training, but the qualities of generalship are not easy to acquire. That is why the Chinese say that "it is easier to acquire a large troop with thousands of soldiers than a good general."

(3) **Climate and terrain**

By climate, Sun Tzu meant the changing seasons, weather, temperatures, days, and hours. Although climatic conditions represent an uncontrollable aspect of military situations, a good general knows how to use these uncontrollable components advantageously. A good general would choose the right time to fight and turn bad weather to the disadvantage of his enemy. The Russian general Kuznetzov, for example, defeated Napoleon's troops with the help of a severe Russian winter. General Zhou Yu of the Chinese Three Kingdoms Period borrowed one night's east wind to burn down his rival Cao Cao's camp. In business, a CEO also has to grapple with climatic conditions, such as the "economic climate" and the "business climate." Among these conditions are:

- Political situations, such as stability, ethnic conflicts, and wars;
- Economic cycles, such as booms, recessions, and stagnation;
- The investment climate, such as government policies, regulations, incentives, the state of technology, the protection of intellectual property, and changes in market structure; and
- Other related social and cultural factors, such as changes in demography and consumer attitudes.

To be competitive, a company has to capitalize on the various changes in the economic and business environment and formulate its strategies accordingly. As in military situations, a company must realize that these environmental variables are beyond its control. It can neither command the fluctuations of economic or business environments nor dramatically affect social or cultural norms. A general must know how to fight within the constraints of climatic conditions, and a CEO of a company also has to adapt strategies for environmental constraints. On the other hand, a good general or CEO knows how to choose the best time and turn these conditions into advantages. An import substitution policy, for example, may hamper market entrance but at the same time provide opportunities for investment, which can result in access to the closed market.

Terrain refers to the area for military operation. It can be classified as accessible (we and the enemy can traverse it with equal ease); entangling (easy to reach, but difficult to exit); temporizing (equally disadvantageous for both the enemy and us to enter); precipitous and constricted (advantageous for whichever side occupies it first); or distant. It is the highest responsibility of a general to inquire into these various terrains with the utmost care, because these conditions will determine the chances of life and death in battle.

We should note that the word "terrain" has two dimensions: the geographical features of the battlefield and the chosen ground for fighting. The geographical features of the battlefield are largely the uncontrollable variables. Once an army is engaged in a battle on specific terrain, it will have to face the consequences incurred as a result of the terrain. Although the terrain is hard to change, a good general can decide where to fight — the battleground most favorable to the army and least favorable to the enemy. Again, as with climatic conditions, one can make a choice and turn the uncontrollable into controllable.

The same logic is also applicable for the business context, where a company has to deal with such physical and infrastructural variables as the location of its business operation. The variables include:

- the supplies of industrial and raw materials, as well as abundant cheap or high-quality labor;
- infrastructural characteristics, such as transportation systems, tele-communications, and water and power supplies; and
- access to domestic and international markets.

Again, these uncontrollable variables can be made controllable, as one can choose the best location according to one's needs. If, for example, one needs to tap cheap labor, one should move operations to a developing country. The mass migration of Taiwan's sunset industries to mainland China exemplifies this.

In sum, to cope with different climate and terrain, one should understand the general picture. As Sun said, "If one knows the place and time of the coming battle, his troops can march a thousand *li* and fight on the field." Although climate and terrain are for the most part unalterable, one can make a wise choice.

To cope with ever-changing situations, one should maintain a high degree of mobility and flexibility. This is the principle of "coping with change by adapting quickly." For example, the tastes and priorities of consumers change concurrent with economic changes. In an economic downturn, they tend to choose the most price-competitive goods, whereas in an economic boom many may shift their attention to designs and styles. Enterprises should change their competition strategies accordingly. Sun Tzu said:

Of the five elements, none is ever predominant; of the four seasons, none last forever; of the days, some are long and others short; and of the moon, it sometimes waxes and sometimes wanes. Hence, there are neither fixed postures nor constant tactics in warfare. He who can modify his tactics in accordance with the enemy situation and thus succeed in winning may be said to be divine.

Why don't you cover Laws here?

(4) Strengths

Strength, for Sun Tzu, is a relative concept. There is no absolute superior strength nor absolute inferior strength. It all depends on how one can arrange it. According to Sun Tzu, "In war, number alone confers no advantage. If one does not advance by force recklessly, is able to concentrate his military power through a correct assessment of the enemy situation, and enjoys full support of his men, that would suffice." This is the principle of concentrating one's strength on the most needed area.

The principle can be applied to business, too. Sheer size may be an advantage for major enterprises, but it can also lead to an unnecessarily large organization and low efficiency. Medium and small enterprises, though restricted by limited resources, can compete with major enterprises if they can take full advantage of talents, maintain high efficiency as well as flexibility, and develop their unique products in a market niche.

For Sun Tzu, a small army may be small in comparison to a large one, but if it knows how to concentrate its small force for various battles, it may look large and eliminate the big armies one by one:

> When outnumbering the enemy ten to one, encircle him; when five times his strength, attack him; when double his strength, engage him; when evenly matched, be capable of dividing him; when slightly weaker than the enemy, be capable of defending oneself; when greatly inferior to the enemy, elude him. For no matter how obstinate a small force is, it will succumb to a larger and superior force.

Another way to enhance one's own strength is to resort to deception to confuse the enemy's perception of that strength:

> All warfare is based on deception. Therefore, when able to attack, we must pretend to be unable; when employing our forces, we must seem inactive; when we are near, we must make the enemy believe we are far away; when far away, we must make him believe we are near.

An enterprise should also hide its own real strength so its competitors do not know its real situation and direction of development. The enterprise can prepare stealthily and launch an attack where its competitors are unprepared and take action when it is unexpected.

A third method is to use spies. Sun Tzu expressed the following regarding spies:

> The reason that the enlightened sovereign and the wise general conquer the enemy whenever they move and their achievements surpass those of ordinary men is that they have foreknowledge. This "foreknowledge" cannot be elicited from spirits, nor from gods, nor by analogy with past events, nor by any deductive calculations. It must be obtained from the men who know the enemy situation.

To be competitive, an enterprise also needs information regarding its competitors, such as the development plan of its new products, operational plans, and financial situations. In this regard, Silicon Valley has learned its lessons; many Asian firms, having benefited from technologies through all possible channels, have become fierce competitors within the shortest possible time.

Sun Tzu also pointed to the importance of borrowing energy from the environment as a way to enlarge one's strength. For him, a skilled commander always uses the situation to the best advantage.

> He who takes advantage of the situation in fighting uses his men as rolling logs or rocks. It is the nature of logs and rocks to stay stationary on the flat ground, and to roll forward on a slope. If four-cornered, they stop; if round-shaped, they roll. Thus, the energy of troops skillfully commanded is just like the momentum of round rocks quickly tumbling down from a mountain thousands of feet in height.

The same principle can be applied in a business context, where a company should be able to create a favorable external environment. A trading company, for example, can consolidate its position by securing good relations with suppliers or investing directly in suppliers.

Doctrine and training

This element stresses the importance of a whole set of regulations and rules, designation of ranks, allocation of responsibilities, and organizational structure. According to Sun Tzu, "If the army is confused and suspicious, the neighboring states will certainly cause trouble. As a saying goes: 'A confused army predicts victory for the enemy.' "

One important principle of Sun's organizational ideas is to delegate one's subordinates with necessary power. He explains one of the five preconditions for victory: "He whose generals are able and not interfered with by the sovereign will win." This is the principle of "not using the suspectable at all and using the trustworthy with full confidence" (Li and Ma 1991). He advised a good balance between an authoritarian leader and unorganized decentralization, because either of the extremes is harmful to an organization. In a highly competitive environment, corporate managers should have sufficient power to be able to coordinate their strategies and tactics based on the changing environment. CEOs should have confidence in their subordinates and give them enough power to carry out their assignments.

For Sun Tzu, training is very important for ensuring organizational efficiency. If soldiers do not know how to follow signals, they cannot act accordingly. In a business context, companies with well-trained employees can be managed with great efficiency. Successful business organizations all over the world have good on-the-job training problems.

⑥ Discipline

According to Sun Tzu, a good army always has stringent discipline, which it can achieve with an efficient reward-and-punishment system. Nevertheless, a good general should know how and when to mete out rewards or punishment. Soldiers must be treated with humanity but kept under control by iron discipline.

> If troops are punished before they have grown loyal, they will be disobedient. If not obedient, it is difficult to employ them. But if troops have become loyal, but discipline is not enforced, the general can't employ them either.

In addition, orders should be consistently carried out under strict supervision. Otherwise, troops will still be disobedient. Sun Tzu also advised a proper balance of reward and punishment: "Too frequent rewards indicate the running out of ideas; too frequent punishments indicate dire distress."

The combination of strictness and benevolence is the key to guaranteeing loyalty and discipline. This is evidenced by many examples in Chinese history. With tears in his eyes, Premier Kung Ming of the Three Kingdom Period beheaded his most beloved general when the general disobeyed his orders and lost a battle. In another example, after giving the order that soldiers not trample on crops, Cao Cao cut his own hair to show his determination to instill discipline when his own startled horse ran into the crop field.

A company that has an effective disciplinary system will be geared toward higher performance and a better competitive position. When employees are well aware of what they will receive, they will perform accordingly. Strict discipline is a reverse incentive. By introducing the system of "high rewards and severe punishment," the joint venture of Fujian-Hitachi TV Ltd. of China raised productivity. Top management members were not exempted. The chronic problem of late arrival and early departure was rooted out within a short period. Employees became more identified with the company.

Sun Tzu's strategic ideas can contribute to business competitiveness in the following areas. First, Sun Tzu emphasized the importance of moral influence within an organization. A successful manager should be able to mobilize subordinates to work as a team. Second, he stressed the importance of a broadly defined generalship for military leaders as opposed to merely their technical background. In many Asian businesses, a manager's general qualities are often viewed as much more important than technical qualifications. Third, according to Sun Tzu's views on relativism, there is no absolute superiority and inferiority in competition. One must know where one's competitive edge lies, and when, where, and how to engage in competition.

NOTE

*All the translations of Sun Tzu's work are quoted from Wu (1990).

REFERENCES

"The Chinese Art of Management," *The Economist*, October 26, 1991, p. 41.

Chin-ning Chu, *The Asian Mind Game* (New York: Rawson Associates, 1991).

Samuel B. Griffith, *Sun Tzu: The Art of War* (New York: Oxford University Press, 1971).

Ji-xing Guo, *Three Kingdoms and Management Strategies* (Nanning: Guanxi People's Press, 1988).

Fe Li and Ma Hong, *Military Strategies and Enterprise Competitions* (Nanning: Guanxi People's Press, 1991).

Shi-zun Li, Xian-ju Yang, and Jia-rei Tan, *Sun Tzu Art of War and Business Management* (Nanning: Guanxi People's Press, 1986).

Jian-shu Min, "The Competition Model of Sun Tzu Art of War," *The Ancient Management Philosophies and Chinese-Style Management* (Beijing: Economic and Management Press, 1989), pp. 11–26.

Haichen Sun, *The Wiles of War: 36 Military Strategies from Ancient China* (Beijing: Foreign Language Press, 1991).

Chow Hou Wee, *Sun Tzu: War and Management* (New York: Addison-Wesley Publishing Co., 1991).

Jiu-long Wu, ed., *Sun Tzu Art of War* (Beijing: Military Science Press, 1990).

MIN CHEN is a professor of international studies at the Thunderbird American Graduate School of International Management, Glendale, Arizona.

14 How Honda Localizes its Global Strategy

Hideo Sugiura

In recent years management scholars have developed a dazzling array of matrices and models intended to answer the often difficult questions raised by international management. Mr. Sugiura, retired chairperson of Honda Motor Company, brings decades of practical experience to bear on those same questions in this paper, which is adapted from a speech delivered at MIT last fall. He describes Honda's undeniably successful localization strategy, discusses the firm's early experiments in international management, and proposes a new definition of "customer": the entire society in which a firm operates.

Advances in information technology and increased exchanges of information in all fields are making nations more dependent on each other than ever before. This interdependence is creating a solid foundation for global economic development.

However, interdependence is also increasing the impact nations are having on each other, weakening their economies and making the global economy less predictable. As trade frictions between industrially advanced nations intensify and the economic gap between developed and developing nations widens, governments are leaning heavily toward economic nationalism, seeking quick, unilateral, political solutions to economic problems.

But economic problems must be discussed at the global level, not at the level of individual countries or even regions. It is extremely important to build interdependent relationships among nations, and in doing so to restore mutual trust. This will open the way to stable development of the world economy. Such development will require international efforts of various kinds at the government level. At the same time, industrial activities at the corporate level, including investment, assume great significance. Yet the uncertainty of the world

Reproduced with permission from *Sloan Management Review*, 32 (Fall, 1990), pp. 77–82.

economy makes international corporate activity very risky.

The Pacific Basin must be a key focal point in any discussion of the evolving world economy. The countries in the Pacific Basin have grown increasingly important, both politically and economically. Their share of global trade has also risen every year. More important, industrial products account for a fast-growing portion of their exports — proof that they are making dramatic progress in industrialization. A mutually trusting relationship must be established between the region's relatively advanced countries and its rising nations to ensure further growth and prosperity in the Pacific Basin, which I think is indispensable for revitalization of the world economy.

There are many ways in which the advanced countries can support the region's development. The most important is the creation of new business and employment opportunities by private enterprises. Specifically, the two key means by which corporations from the advanced nations can contribute are *investment* and the *transfer of technology*. Such corporate activities should, of course, be different from government assistance programs.

The cultural diversity of the Pacific Rim countries presents major obstacles that must be overcome before the economic sphere can be solidified through investment and technology transfer. (In my view, such solidification has already occurred in the Mediterranean and Atlantic spheres — and indeed, the cultural diversity was less remarkable there to begin with.) Two factors are prerequisite to overcoming such cultural differences. First, the countries involved must clearly understand the goals to be attained through mutual cooperation. Second, each country's role must be recognized and agreed upon. Unless these two conditions are met, one cannot expect any cooperation program to succeed.

These beliefs are based on Honda's experience during its many years of international activities. It may be useful, then, to look at specific examples of Honda's overseas strategy.

The four localizations

Since its modest beginning in 1948, Honda has grown into a corporation with $25 billion in sales, largely because of its successful international activities. More than 60 per cent of our total sales take place outside of Japan; our products are marketed in well over one hundred countries. Moreover, we manufacture products at seventy-seven plants in forty countries outside Japan, and our cumulative total investments abroad have surpassed $1 billion, not counting over $2 billion reinvested locally by our overseas subsidiaries, which I will describe in detail later.

Honda is often described as an international enterprise. But in promoting internationalization, we place the utmost importance on *localization* — adapting our activities to those practices in the countries where we operate. This overseas strategy consists of four target concepts: localization of *products*, *profit*, *production*, and *management*.

Localization of products

This means developing, manufacturing, and marketing the products best suited to the actual and potential needs of the customers *and* to the social and economic conditions of the marketplace. While it is true that a good product knows no national boundaries, there are subtle differences, from country to country and from region to region, in the ways a product is used and what customers expect of it. If a corporation believes that simply because a product has succeeded in a certain market, it will see well throughout the world, it is most likely destined for large and expensive errors or even total failure.

Take our motorcycles as an example. North Americans use motorcycles primarily for leisure and sports; a racer looks for high horsepower output and speed. Southeast Asians, on the other hand, use motorcycles as a basic means of transportation, so they want ease of maintenance, at low cost. In Australia, shepherds use motorcycles to drive sheep they look for low-speed torque, rather than high speed or ease of maintenance. So, while we do use a common basic technology, we develop different types of motorcycles for different regions. Such differences apply not only to cars and motorcycles, but to most industrial products as well. Corporations must be capable of accurately grasping such differences and producing appropriately targeted products.

To localize products, corporations must invest in research and development of both products and constantly increasing production efficiency. Honda earmarks 5 per cent of the parent company's unconsolidated gross annual sales for R&D of products and production techniques regardless of fluctuation in profits. In addition, we have established R&D centers in North and South America, Western Europe, and Southeast Asia. Japanese and local engineers work together to understand local market conditions and to develop the products best suited to each market.

Localization of profits

This means reinvesting as much of the profits as possible in the local market. A company investing abroad must regard itself as a local company and endeavor to prosper together with the host country. Reinvestment effectively addresses the concern that multinational enterprises are interested only in sending profits home and not in benefiting the host country.

In 1959, for example, Honda established a wholly owned marketing subsidiary, American Honda, in Los Angeles with a capital investment of $250,000. This sum has now grown 800 times to $200 million, a dramatic increase achieved through the reinvestment of American Honda's profits. More than $1.7 billion in reinvested American Honda profits has gone into the construction and expansion of motorcycle, automobile, and engine manufacturing plants in Ohio. Meanwhile, automobile production began at our new plant in Allison, near Toronto, in November 1986. Most of the $200 million Canadian investment represents reinvestment of profits earned by Honda Canada, our marketing strategy.

1 c) Localization of production

A corporation does not merely make profits by exporting completed products; it carries out production activities where major markets exist, thereby contributing to the development of the host nation and achieving mutual prosperity. Normally, a corporation explores a new market by establishing a marketing base and importing completed goods. Yet, whenever the host country needs the product manufactured locally, the corporation should as soon as practicable set up a manufacturing base; this is the best way to assure acceptance of both the product and the corporation, and achieve long-term prosperity. There are two ways to make local production activity most effective. One is to increase the ratio of local content, which gives added impetus to related industries. The other is to increase the value added in local production, which not only expands employment opportunities, but also gives employees a great sense of responsibility for and pride in manufacturing their own products.

Establishing local production can mean entering into a technical collaboration agreement with a local partner for technological transfer, setting up a joint venture with local capital, or establishing a wholly owned manufacturing subsidiary. A corporation must choose the method best suited to the requirements and conditions of the host country. In so doing, it should consider such factors as level of industrialization, market size, restraints arising from local economic and social needs, and the needs and capabilities of the local partner. Honda, for example, has chosen to establish wholly owned manufacturing subsidiaries in the United States and Canada, while in Europe, we are collaborating with the Rover Group of Britain. In Thailand, we produce motorcycles in a joint venture with local capital, and cars through a technical collaboration. In Indonesia, we produce motorcycles and cars, their engines, and other components through joint ventures and technological tie-ins.

1 d) Localization of management

This goes beyond transferring knowledge about management systems operations. Local managers and employees must understand the corporate philosophy. Managers dispatched from the head office should be encouraged to become part of the community by understanding local culture and ways of thinking; to delegate authority to local personnel; and to create a sense of unity between management and labor so that everyone is working toward a common goal. In implementing these measures, managers should avoid forcing local people to accept management know-how or corporate philosophy in its original form, which may be foreign to them. Every effort must be made to modify it, where feasible, to suit local conditions. These efforts create a sense of unity that is essential for the achievement of common goals.

Through years of experience in many parts of the world, we have become convinced that good communication between management and labor, as well as delegation of authority, elevate the employees' sense of participation in decision making. This, in turn, gives the employees a stronger sense of responsibility and motivation, which leads to improved productivity and maintenance of high quality standards.

I would like to emphasize that management initiatives are essential to achieving these ideals. Success or failure depends on management. Good management and good labor-management relations go hand in hand.

The four kinds of localization represent our fundamental international philosophy. We developed this philosophy by way of repeated successes and failures. We fully realize that pursuing this philosophy is not the easy way, and that it sometimes requires sacrificing short-term profits. Yet we are convinced that it is the best way to conduct business on a long-term basis.

How this corporate philosophy works

Our activities in North America are perhaps the best examples of localization of production. In 1974 we started studying the feasibility of production in the United States. At that time, there was very little auto trade friction between Japan and the United States, and nobody was talking about restricting Japanese car imports, let alone local content. I wish to emphasize that our decision to produce in the United States was not meant to circumvent trade restrictions. We started producing motorcycles in Ohio in 1979 and automobiles in 1982. Automobile production there has now reached 360,000 units per year, more than double the original capacity. We also produce motorcycle and car engines in Ohio and began manufacturing lawn movers in North Carolina in 1984. Our dealers and customers tell us that the quality of our American-made products is equal to or better than that of the cars produced in Japan, and we have found that our North American employees are as diligent and hard working as any in the world.

In September 1987, we announced our "Five-Part Strategy," which was intended to make the automobile manufacturing operation in Ohio a fully integrated, self-reliant entity. The strategy consists of the following:

• By 1991, 70,000 Ohio-built cars will be exported to various world markets, including Japan.

- The number of engineers engaged in research and development activities in North America will be increased to 500 by 1991, compared with 200 in 1989. Another 200 engineers will design and develop new production equipment and machinery.
- A new automobile production plant will soon start operating adjacent to the existing factory. It will ultimately produce 150,000 cars a year, bringing Honda's total car production capacity in Ohio to 510,000 units annually.
- The engine plant located in Anna, Ohio, will be expanded to produce half a million engines per year.
- The domestic content of the Ohio-built cars will reach 75 per cent in the near future.

The Five-Part Strategy will bring the total investments made in Ohio to more than $2 billion and create more than 11,000 jobs.

In administering the plants in Ohio, Honda attaches particular importance to three policies. The first is to establish good human relations between the management and the workforce. Any production activity requires a good deal of coordination and cooperation among various departments. This is possible only through teamwork that encompasses the entire company. One cannot expect to develop that capacity without close labor-management communications, initiated by management. Management encourages employees to communicate problems directly and then promptly seeks solutions through discussions with them. The management staff wears the same white work clothing and eats at the same cafeteria as the other employees. Much effort has gone into creating a safe, clean, pleasant, friendly work environment. These and other measures have contributed to intracompany unity and to an employee sense of responsibility for and pride in their own work.

The second policy is to maintain and promote harmony with the local community. An important factor in producing high-quality goods is securing high-quality labor. For this reason, Honda has gone beyond just educating and training its employees. It has worked at creating a good understanding with the local community, which is the source of its labor. We now release information through newspapers and other mass media and invite local families to factory tours, test rides, Honda festivals, and field days.

The third policy is to give top priority to maintaining high quality standards in our products. I believe that quality level is determined primarily by the actual design of the product itself, not by quality control in the production processes. Still, assuring high quality standards requires good production equipment and technology. This is why our plants in Ohio are equipped with sophisticated machinery, some of which does not even exist at our Japanese factories. Even with such good equipment and technology, however, assuring high quality standards is not possible without quality consciousness on the part of all individuals concerned. Such consciousness can be generated only where there are good human relations. For this reason, our Ohio plants promote dialogues between the management and the workforce, as well as providing employees with an extensive training program, including classroom training on product design and engineering and intensive on-the-job training in production techniques. The employees now have a broad understanding of how to perform their jobs and meet quality expectations, and they are committed to the corporate policy of winning customer satisfaction by supplying quality products.

One episode at our Ohio plant is a good example of quality consciousness on the part of employees. Shortly after our motorcycle production started, I visited the plant. After landing in Columbus sometime after 6:00 p.m., which was already after the plant's working hours, I was driven directly to the plant. When I walked through it, I was surprised to see six or seven American employees polishing motorcycle fuel tanks with compound wax so late in the evening. When I asked them why they were doing that, they told me that earlier in the day, following a change in the fuel tank paint material, minor defects had appeared on the surface finish of some tanks. Although these defects were of the kind that could easily be rectified in the final inspection area after the vehicles were completed, the employees in the painting section decided that they could not send substandard fuel tanks to the assembly line. They voluntarily worked overtime so that the motorcycles to be assembled the following day would be fitted with tanks free of defects.

Up until that time, I had been given to understand that such voluntary overtime would never be practiced at U.S. plants. Generally speaking, that is probably still true. What I witnessed at our Ohio plant, however, clearly shows that individual employees understand and accept the management policy of achieving top quality standards, that both management and the workforce share the goal of winning maximum customer satisfaction, and that employees are fully aware of their roles and are prepared to fulfill their responsibilities completely. You may think this a minor incident. But I think it is of great importance because it could not have happened without a well-formulated management policy. I have rarely been more impressed by employee enthusiasm and motivation.

A well-formulated management policy serves to unify the members of the corporation, which, in turn, adds to corporate vitality. Such a policy requires that management establish goals that the employees can fully understand, appreciate, and commit themselves to. It also requires that management take the lead in motivating the workforce.

These three policies — establishing good human relations, maintaining harmony with the local community, and placing highest priority on quality standards — represent the embodiment of Honda's philosophy of localization.

A less successful attempt at localization occurred in Belgium, where, in 1962,

Honda began the production of mopeds. This is said to be the first instance of direct Japanese investment in a manufacturing venture in an industrially advanced country. Japan's economy in those days was not what it is today, and there was apparently considerable opposition in the Japanese government to Honda's investment in Belgium.

But Europe was a big market; it accounted for 85 percent of the world's non-Japanese motorcycle ownership. The motorcycle was firmly established and widely used by Europeans as a means of transportation. Honda decided to manufacture mopeds in Belgium because it had confidence in its technical process and believed that a good product knows no national boundaries.

In spite of this confidence, our manufacturing venture turned into a series of mistakes and miscalculations. The plant in Belgium was in the red for more than ten years.

Our early failure was caused by several problems: the model we developed with so much confidence did not match European users' needs; we had put too much of Honda's distinctive technology and design into the model and were thus unable to find local manufacturers who could supply us with parts that met our specifications; and our inadequate comprehension of local labor practices led to misunderstandings between management and local employees, resulting in unexpected disruptions of routine production activities.

In other words, the difficulties we encountered in Belgium were caused by our failure to understand and respond to the differences in history, culture, and values.

The lesson we learned was that to invest and do business overseas, it is not enough to have abstract knowledge about the host country. It is essential to develop a deeper understanding. This can be achieved only by immersion in local society and by working with the people of the country.

We learned the importance of adopting a locally oriented approach and building up a new way of doing work in the host country. It took us a long time to make our factory in Belgium pay, but we do not think that the cost of the lesson was too high. From that experience, we learned how difficult it is and how much time and patience it takes to establish mutual understanding between different cultures. Our Belgian experience gave us the valuable know-how essential for launching Honda's subsequent overseas activities, and this know-how has become a valuable asset.

Conclusions

Two points are particularly critical when discussing Honda's localization policy. First, as the degree of localization rises, the amount of investment naturally increases in proportion. As I mentioned at the outset, this is an inevitable result of the growing interdependence between countries and regions. Increased investment is a manifestation of commitment. This must be clearly recognized by the host country.

Second, localization of production through investment is not confined to the transfer of technology. It involves the transfer of a philosophy, that is, the corporate culture that constitutes the basis of technology and management, developed within a corporation since its founding.

In this connection, I believe it important that both the investing party and the host party should make efforts to overcome, intelligently and flexibly, the difficulties that might eventually arise, so that the cultural background of the host country and the investor's transplanted corporate culture will blend in a proper way. It is essential to solve problems arising out of differences in culture, ways of thinking, and values. A corporation seeking to be globally active must be capable of creating a new corporate culture that results from the blending of two different cultures.

I am convinced that the success or failure of investment depends on whether the enterprise can build mutual understanding and trust. International investment at the corporate level will contribute greatly to expanding interdependence, revitalizing the world economy, and bringing about stable development. To invigorate corporate investment, every effort must be made, on private, national, and international levels, to create an environment that will convince the potential investor that investment will result in mutual prosperity.

I think it is fair to say that today Honda's activities in many corners of the world are accepted and appreciated. I attribute this to the policy of localization. Through this policy, we have been able to generate new corporate cultures in different parts of the world by directing the minds of all concerned to common goals, while respecting the traditional cultures of Japan and of the host countries. In so doing, we have paid maximum attention to taking good care of our human resources in order to consolidate the labor-management partnership.

Let me close by noting that Honda's strategies and policies are aimed at achieving maximum customer satisfaction. In a narrow sense, this means satisfying individual customers by providing high-quality products that meet their needs at reasonable prices. But it is also essential for a corporation to interpret the word "customer" in a broader sense — to cover the whole society in which it operates. Corporate behaviors must be such that the corporation itself and all of its activities are satisfactory to the community, society, and country. In other words, the corporation must be a good citizen. The four types of localization represent Honda's strategy for achieving this broader sense of customer satisfaction.

HIDEO SUGIURA is retired Chairperson of Honda Motor Company. He currently serves as an adviser to the company.

V Planning Marketing Programs

Once the marketing strategy is established, the company designs its marketing mix. This is the tactical phase of marketing decision making. Asia-Pacific marketers must thus have a thorough knowledge to develop appropriate product, price, place, and promotion programs to effect their chosen marketing strategy.

After reading the six articles in this part, you should have a better understanding of the following aspects of marketing in the Asia Pacific:

1 Managing brands successfully in the Asia Pacific.
2 The Zaibatsu approach to OEM/supplier relationships which is being transplanted to the region as Japanese firms relocate their manufacturing elsewhere in the Asia Pacific.
3 The complexities and choices of distribution in Asia.
4 Advertising strategy alternatives for the Asia Pacific.

15 Managing Corporate and Brand Identities in the Asia-Pacific Region

Bernd H. Schmitt and Yigang Pan

A common Chinese idiom describes territory which is unknown but full of great treasures as "a place of hidden dragons and tigers." Western companies, seeking to establish themselves in the Asia-Pacific Region are finding that the Region fits this description. Consider the following facts:[1]

- The newly industrialized nations in the Asia-Pacific Region — the four Asian Dragons (Hongkong, Singapore, South Korea, and Taiwan) — have enjoyed growth rates between 5 per cent and 10 per cent over the last decade. In 1992, the per capita GDP of Hongkong and Singapore was higher than that of Canada, Australia, and New Zealand. Meanwhile, the People's Republic of China (PRC) — with its 1.3 billion consumers — is undergoing a radical transformation toward a consumer society.
- The percentage of people living below the poverty line in the Region has decreased from 33 per cent to 10 per cent, even though the region's population has surged by 40 per cent since 1970. The number of non-Japanese Asian households earning US$18,000 annually is expected to increase fourfold to 75 million by the year 2000.
- In 1992, annual trade between the U.S. and the Asia-Pacific Region exceeded US$360 billion — more than four times the figure from 15 years ago and nearly 40% more than America's two-way trade with Europe. For the remainder of this decade, investors will be more enthusiastic about Asian emerging markets than about any other emerging markets. Hongkong, Malaysia, the Philippines, and Indonesia were some of the top performing stock markets in U.S. dollar terms in 1993 — all up more than 100 per cent.

Reproduced with permission from *California Management Review*, 36 (Summer 1994), pp. 32–48.

As *Business Week* put it, "under way is nothing less than a massive shift in the global economic balance of power, as the economies of East Asia catch up with Japan and the West. The emerging powerhouse combines Hongkong, Taiwan and China with the blossoming economies of Southeast Asia — whose business classes are dominated by ethnic Chinese. Throw in South Korea, and gross domestic product totals $2 trillion. East Asia will surpass Japan in purchasing power within a decade."[2]

Most of this growth will occur in the domain of consumer goods — from soft drinks and computers to discretionary products and services, such as entertainment, home and leisure, convenience services, restaurants, consumer financial services, communications, apparel, health care, and fitness. High economic growth in the Region has translated into a rapid rise in people's income and a surge in consumer spending. While disparities in the distribution of wealth in Asian societies are common, consumption trends have continued to move up-market. Even in the PRC, one of the less developed countries in the Region, more than 70% of city households already own a telephone, at least one TV, and a refrigerator. For companies in consumer markets, but also for those in the industrial and services industries, establishing and managing viable corporate and brand identities is therefore the major challenge. To quote *Fortune* magazine, "brand equity may be buffeted at home, but across Asia, from Beijing to Bombay, American brands are commanding big premiums over inferior hometown competitors."[3]

For example, Nike used to only manufacture its shoes and sportswear in the Asia-Pacific Region; now it is increasingly selling there as well. In fiscal year 1993, US$500 million of the company's total revenues of $4 billion were contributed by Asian markets, an increase of 66 per cent from 1992. IBM has about 300 people dedicated to the China market alone and is forecasting 40 to 50 per cent annual growth in its PRC sales over the next few years. Both Coca Cola and Pepsi-Cola International have discovered the thirst for American-style soft drinks in the Asia-Pacific Region, the fastest growing beverage market in the world today. Along with other U.S. companies, the two soft drink giants are getting ready to target consumers in Indochina's most attractive market: Vietnam. Both Coca Cola and Pepsi have announced plans to produce there.

However, managers are also beginning to sense the intricacies and complications involved in operating in the territory of dragons and tigers. M&M managers were surprised to run into W&W candy bars, a brand that a manufacturer in Central China coined to confuse consumers and take advantage of M&M's strong image in the market. Moreover, many companies had to change the names of their company and their brands as they moved between Asian markets because the names had different connotations in each market. Finally, some U.S. firms are getting frustrated at their lack of success in establishing positive relationships with customers and in persuading Asian consumers of the quality of their products.

In addition, competition among Western multinationals and with regional conglomerates is intensifying. Indonesia, at 180 million, is Asia's third largest market, and has become the battleground in a struggle between Procter & Gamble, Anglo-Dutch Unilever, and other multinationals. The Chinese government is in the process of following the Japanese examples of creating industrial conglomerates that are able to compete in international markets. Korean companies such as Samsung, Daewoo, Hyundai, and Lucky Goldstar spend heavily to develop their own brand names. Finally, Taiwan has started an ambitious Image Enhancement Program to upgrade the country's economic identity and encourage companies to produce high-quality, brand-name products.

To meet these challenges, U.S. firms must develop increasingly sophisticated techniques for building and managing the identities of their companies and brands in Asian markets. Most importantly, U.S. managers must develop a sense for the unique way in which consumers respond to corporate and brand identities in the Region.

These are three major tasks involved in building and managing corporate and brand identities in the Asia-Pacific Region. Each management task requires a different focus and approach in the Asia-Pacific Region than it does in the West. Across Asian societies, it is thus possible to identify characteristics of corporate-identity building and brand management that differentiate, in degree or in kind, the Asia-Pacific Region from the West. Most of the management literature has focused in its analysis on Japan.[4] However, because of China's growing importance and cultural dominance in the Region, most of the illustrations in this article focus on Chinese culture, using examples from the PRC, Hongkong, and Singapore.

Corporate identity and brand equity

Corporate identity is concerned with the impressions, the image, and the personality projected by an organization.[5] The task of creating a corporate identity begins with the selection of an appropriate corporate name. Other factors that contribute to corporate identity include the logo of the organization, marketing communications, and the image projected by various corporate activities.

Brand equity has been defined as "a set of brand assets and liabilities linked to a brand, its name and symbol, that add to or subtract from the value provided by a product or service to a firm and/or to that firm's customers."[6] Brand equity thus refers to the *differential* effect of brand knowledge as a result of the marketing of the brand. Brand knowledge, in turn, consists of brand awareness (brand recall and recognition) and brand image/associations.[7] One of the most important associations is quality. Brand management thus includes the key tasks of selecting a viable brand name, surrounding the brand with appropriate symbolism and associations, and enhancing consumers' perceptions of quality.

The concepts of corporate identity and brand equity are related. In fact, corporate identity has been viewed as branding at the corporate level, and in many service industries (e.g., airlines, hotels, car rentals, and financial services), branding activities are almost synonymous with corporate-identity activities.

In sum, building and managing corporate and brand identities may be seen as comprising the following interrelated tasks: selecting viable corporate and brand names; establishing the right image for the corporation and its brands; and enhancing quality perceptions of the company and its products.

Due to differing linguistic and cultural contexts, each management task must be approached differently in Asia-Pacific than in Western markets.

Task 1: Selecting corporate and brand names

Names (corporate and brand) serve several functions. First, they identify the company and its brands. Second, they serve as cues for remembering information about the company and its brands. Finally, names express the positioning of the company and its products in the market.

What is a good name? Brand-naming research conducted in the West has shown that a brand name should be short, distinctive, memorable and indicative of the product's functions.[8] Similar criteria apply to corporate names. While these factors also matter for selecting corporate and brand names in Asia, there are additional considerations that complicate naming decisions. In research conducted in the PRC, the writing of the name and whether or not the name is a "lucky name" were found to be significant predictors of brand attitudes.[9]

Linguistic and cultural aspects of naming-decisions

To understand the features of a good name in the Asia-Pacific Region better, it is necessary to examine pertinent linguistic and cultural aspects of corporate and brand naming.

LINGUISTIC ASPECTS

Many languages in the Region, e.g., Chinese (Cantonese, which is spoken in Hongkong and in Southern China; Mandarin, the official Chinese dialect; and Hokkien, the most common dialect spoken among Chinese in Southeast Asia, as well as in Taiwan, southern Fujian and Hainan), Japanese, and Korean are ideographic in origin and largely based on Chinese characters. Vietnamese also uses Chinese characters, though to a smaller extent. Chinese characters are sign-symbols composed of strokes. In contrast to letters in an alphabet, characters are inherently meaningful linguistic units, consisting of smaller units called radicals. There is a total of approximately 50,000 Chinese characters, of which 7,000 are in general use. Chinese characters are pronounced differently in Cantonese, Mandarin, Hokkien, Japanese, Korean, and Vietnamese. Yet, although people in Hongkong, Beijing, Taipei, Tokyo, Seoul, and Hanoi may not be able to talk to one another, they can communicate to a certain extent in writing.

In comparison to Western languages, languages of the Asia-Pacific Region have a large number of homonyms (words with distinct writing but identical pronunciation). For example, the Chinese pronunciation of "gong" corresponds to at least ten distinct characters with equally distinct meanings, which include "work", "bow", "public", "meritorious service", "attack", "supply", "palace", "respectful", and a surname. In addition, some languages in the Asia-Pacific Region such as Cantonese and Mandarin are tonal. That is, the same phonetic pronunciation has different meanings depending on how the word is pronounced, for example, with a falling, rising, or flat tone.

IMPLICATIONS FOR CORPORATE AND BRAND NAMING

First, the ideographic nature of Asian languages must be taken into account in the creation of corporate and brand names and in marketing communications created to promote the company and its products. The way as Asian perceives and evaluates writing differs significantly from the way a Westerner views writing.[10] A name is like a work of art, and the art of writing — "shu-fa" (calligraphy) — has had a long tradition all over Asia. A name should therefore "look good" and be rendered in appealing writing. It functions like a logo or trademark. Whereas advertisers in the West try to improve memorability for a corporation or a brand by means of jingles, marketing communications to Asian consumers should create distinct writings for the corporate and brand names and for product benefits. Indeed, in Asian marketing communications the corporate/brand name or the key benefits often stand out in the center of the ad to attract consumers' attention.

Volkswagen's ad campaign for its Shanghai Cheep exemplifies this approach. In different ads, Chinese characters, meaning "value", "solid", and "dependable", rendered by famous Chinese calligraphers, were placed in the middle of the ad. In one ad, a calligraphy stroke was used as an imaginary slope that the jeep had to climb, creating a highly memorable interactive imagery. The campaign was a big success and widely copied by other Western firms. In the case of a Delta Airlines ad, however, artistic expression went too wild. Delta Airlines used a map of its Asian destinations to suggest a novel, mock-Chinese character. Although the ad was visually striking, Asian consumers, searching for meaning in the mock-Chinese character, were confused.

Second, as sign-symbols, characters are inherently meaningful and even their smaller units, the radicals, consisting of two to five strokes, carry meaning. Therefore the connotations and meanings of a two/three character-name must be analyzed at different levels (e.g., the meaning of the name as a whole, of its constituent characters, and of the radicals) to create an appropriate name and avoid negative associations.

Third, since Chinese characters are pronounced differently in different languages (e.g., the same character is pronounced as *Toyota* in Japanese but as *feng-tian* in Chinese), companies must examine whether a corporate or brand name sounds good in all its markets. Because of the large number of homonyms, it is possible that the spoken name has a homonym with undesirable meanings. Therefore, the full range of sound associations must be carefully examined, especially with respect to negative meanings that could hurt the corporate and brand images.

Finally, the tonal nature of some Asian languages further increases the chance of undesirable associations and confusions. To be sure, speakers of a tonal language pay attention to tones because they signify meaning. However, corporate and brand names are often novel names, consisting of two or three characters which are meaningful on their own but not necessarily meaningful as a unit. As a consequence, consumers may search for meaning and mistakenly associate the name with a a character of a different tone, especially when they are exposed to the name through oral communications (e.g., radio or personal recommendations). Therefore, managers are well advised to make sure that such tonal confusions do not occur.

CULTURAL ASPECTS OF NAMING-DECISIONS

When choosing a name, aside from these linguistic aspects Asians also consider certain cultural factors such as the impact of the particular type of writing system. As mentioned earlier, Chinese characters are the common basis of the writing systems of Japanese and Korean. Yet, over the centuries, new writing systems have been invented in these languages and are used in addition to or interchangeably with Chinese characters. Japanese is a particularly complex example. Modern Japanese uses four writing systems: Chinese-character based *kanji*, two phonemic systems called *hiragana* and *katakana*, and the Western alphabetic writing system called *romaji*. Everyday Japanese writing is mostly a combination of *kanji* and *hiragana*. Yet, corporate names are typically spelled in *romaji* (and sometimes, in the case of foreign firms, in *katakana*), and brand names may be spelled in any of the four writing systems. For cultural and historical reasons, writing systems carry associations and are therefore more or less appropriate for certain product categories.

Specifically, brands that use the oldest writing system, *kanji*, are perceived to be "traditional"; as a result, kanji may be appropriate for tea products but not for high-tech products. For high-tech products, the most "modern" language system, katakana, is the best. The *katakana* system was introduced into the Japanese language in the nineteenth century and designed specifically for foreign loan words. It is most appropriate for foreign products and products associated with foreign lifestyles. *Hiragana*, used exclusively for the first time in the famous novel *Genji Monogatari* ("The Tale of Genji"), written in the eleventh century by a courtesan, has a somewhat feminine image. It is frequently used for beauty products, hair salons and kimono stores. Clearly, companies entering the Japanese, and other Asian markets, should be familiar with the impact of different writing systems and writing styles on brand perceptions.

Another cultural aspect of brand-naming concerns the concept of a "lucky name". Pepsi Cola is a lucky name in Chinese (meaning "hundred happy things"). Also, to qualify as a lucky name, a name should have an appropriate balance of *yin* and *yang* — roughly, feminine and masculine qualities. *Yang* characters are made up of odd number of strokes in Chinese characters while *yin* words are made up of even number of strokes. In a name, consisting of two or three characters, the combination of *yin/yang* elements matters, too. *Yin Yin Yang* is better than *Yin Yang Yin*. Finally, the total number of strokes should be auspicious. In lucky names, the total number of strokes equals a lucky number, such as 8, 11, 13, 15, 16, 17, 18, 25, 29, 31, 32, and 39.

An analysis of actual name selections in the region

Asian firms spend an extraordinary amount of time and resources on selecting corporate and brand names. Some of the resources are spent on research. Others are spent on metaphysical inquiries: there are hundreds of "nomology" books on the market that interpret the "fate" of a name, and many companies consult fortune tellers as part of the naming decision. Most Western companies, in contrast, consider those practices as irrational. They rarely consider the linguistic and cultural complexities involved in brand naming and spend little effort and few resources on research.

The Intel Corporation is a notable exception. The company selected the Chinese name for its flagship processor, the Pentium, after carefully analyzing 500 entries submitted by Intel staff in Hongkong, the PRC, Malaysia, Singapore, and Taiwan. Such a thorough, localized process can produce excellent results. Another example of a careful selection that resulted in a superb Chinese name is Coca Cola. Its Chinese name sounds like Coca Cola (*Ke-kou-ke-le* in Mandarin and *ho-hau-ho-lohk* in Cantonese) and means "tasty and happy". The Chinese name thus expresses the essential positioning of the brand. Other successful applications include Mercedes Benz (the Chinese name means "striving forward fast"), Boeing ("wave of sound"), and Sharp ("treasure of sound").

Most companies, however, end up with suboptimal solutions, perhaps out of necessity, or, worse, out of lack of thorough research. For example, some Western firms have kept the Western name and Western spelling. This approach may be appropriate in Japan where consumers are familiar with the Roman alphabet, but it is less appropriate in a fast-growing market such as the PRC, where only a minority of consumers knows the Roman alphabet. Keeping the original, alphabetic name seems to work, however, for companies or brand names that are short and catchy such as 3M, IBM, AT&T, and M&M. In that case, the name becomes a visual symbol or logo and is remembered by its graphic qualities rather than as a linguistic unit.

Most companies that have translated their names have done so by sound (e.g., Ford or Winston), without considering the Asian name's meaning. Because of the structure of Asian languages, this implies that the name must be written differently in different languages. Other companies have translated their names by meaning (e.g., United, Northwest, SAS, as well as General Electric, Digital Equipment, and Westinghouse Electric), irrespective of how the name sounds in different languages.

Finally, branding decisions in Asian-Pacific markets are often made on an *ad hoc* basis as the company enters market after market rather than on a pan-Asian basis. As a result, the company may have chosen a name which works in one market but the name does not transfer well to another market. For example, name awareness and positive associations may be established with a Cantonese name in Southern China but, as the company expands to Northern China, it discovers that the name has negative associations in Mandarin. Similar problems occur as the company enters the Japanese, Korean, and Vietnamese markets. Ultimately, the company may end up with a multitude of names, a different one for each market, which may hurt its perception as a global enterprise. Even Japanese companies operating in the Asia-Pacific Region are not immune to this phenomenon. Matsushita has adopted National for its brands in most Asian-Pacific markets but Panasonic for its brands in Western markets. When Matsushita first entered the PRC market through the South, *le-sheng* meaning "merry sound" was used for National in the Southern provinces. Later, in the North, *song-xia* was used; the character-combination *song-xia* is a meaningless name but the characters correspond to the corporate name pronounced *Matsushita* in Japanese. Johnson & Johnson provides another example. When it entered the Hongkong market, the name *zhuang-cheng* was used, meaning "an official or lord during feudal times." This traditional, upper-class association was seen as inappropriate for communist China. So, in the PRC *qiang-sheng* ("active life"), a name with a more upbeat, modern tone that matches well with the PRC's drive for modernization was adopted. Nonetheless, Johnson & Johnson ended up with two names in the same culture.

To further illustrate the complexities of the naming-process, we now turn to the example of an individual firm.[11]

The Robert Bosch case

Robert Bosch, a German vehicle-parts and electrical-appliance giant with a long history of innovative, high-quality products and successful marketing, had been using the Cantonese name displayed as A1 in Table 1 since 1986 in Hongkong and the South of China. In 1988, the name was registered as a trademark. At the same time, A8 had been widely accepted in the PRC, especially among clients

Table 1　Translation of the BOSCH corporate name into Chinese

Character	[BO] Mandarin	Cantonese	Character	[SCH] Mandarin	Cantonese
A　波	bō	bō	1　殊	shū	syùh
B　博	bó	bok	2　士	shì	sih
C　保	bǎo	bóu	3　世	shì	sai
D　寶	bǎo	bóu	4　逝	shì	sīk
			5　時	shí	sìh
			6　西	xī	sāi
			7　施	shī	sī
			8　許	xǔ	héui

Note: Letters A to D display the four characters considered for the first syllable [BO], with the corresponding pronunciations in Mandarin and Cantonese listed next to it; numbers 1 to 8 display the possible characters and corresponding pronunciations for the second syllable [SCH].

The Pinyin transliteration system is used for Mandarin and Cantonese. The four tones in Mandarin are indicated in the following way: ‾ = flat; ` = falling; ′ = rising; ˇ = falling/rising. The tones in Cantonese are indicated in the following way: ` = high-falling; ′ = high-rising; `h = low-falling; ′h = low-rising; h = low-level; ‾ = high-level. Middle level has no accent. Pronunciations ending in "k" or "h" indicate clipped tones.

in the diesel-fuel injection-equipment field, one of Bosch's core business sectors. When Bosch considered opening an office in Beijing during the same year, a name unification seemed necessary.

The options (displayed in Table 1) were considered carefully. The objective was to select a name (i.e., a combination of characters) that

- sounds like Bosch when pronounced in Mandarin and Cantonese;
- has positive meanings that relate to Bosch's core business or image as a company;

- has no negative sound associations; and
- is distinct from other corporate names and therefore does not pose any registration problems.

All of the options displayed in Table 1 sound like Bosch in Mandarin (but less so in Cantonese). Also, each option involves trade-offs. For example, A1 had established name recognition in the South of China but negative connotations in the second character (the first radical means "death"). C5 does not sound as good in Cantonese as in Mandarin. It means "save time" or "time as a value" which is a positive association, although it does not refer directly to Bosch; also the first character (C) has a homonym that means "insurance." The word as a whole has a homonym in Mandarin that means "jewel". B2 is used for the doctoral degree and has the association of "academic education" — a positive association but not appropriate for an industrial firm. B2 had also been registered by several other firms, including one firm selling generators and oscilloscopes, thus potentially contributing to customer confusion. D6 means "valuable from the West" but does not sound good in Cantonese.

B3 was ultimately chosen, even though Bosch felt that the new name sounded less good in Cantonese than A1, the original name used in Hongkong and in the south of the PRC. However, those names that would have sounded better in Cantonese would not have sounded like Bosch in Mandarin or would have had associations of a welfare organization. The word's connotations are favorable (B means "win", "knowledgeable", and "rich" and 3 means "world"; so the name may be interpreted as "winning all over the world"). In terms of luck, B3 is a twelve strokes/five strokes character-combination and thus a yin-yang word which does not have the most favorable condition of luck.

Of course, in other markets, e.g., Korean and Japanese, B3 would be pronounced differently (e.g., "bank se" in Korean and "Hakuse" in Japanese). Aside from the fact that both names do not sound good in either Korean or Japanese, the Chinese writing would be seen as old-fashioned and thus inappropriate. In Korea, the *hangul* writing system is commonly used for foreign corporate names and in Japanese, as discussed earlier, *romaji* or *katakana*.

Task 2: Establishing the right image

Asians are perhaps the most image-conscious consumers in the world. Three image-enhancement strategies have been quite successful with Asian consumers: associating the corporation or brand with prestige and an upscale image; capitalizing on Asians' beliefs in the supernatural; and providing appealing aesthetics.

Creating a prestigious image

With regard to image, "right" often means classy, upscale, and prestigious. The marketing of liquors, cars, and fragrances provide good examples. Johnny Walker's most recent line extension, *Honour*, has been developed specifically for the east Asian markets, using the classy British spelling, a proprietary bottle shape and distinctive box design (an embossed box with seal and satin lining) to enhance the high-end positioning of the brand. Mercedes Benz, using upscale image advertising, is in big demand in Hongkong and in the south of China. Champagne, the new fragrance by Yves Saint-Laurent, is making a fortune in Asia.

A prestigious image is an important asset not only for brands but also for companies. For Asian consumers, it is not only important that products be perceived as reliable and prestigious. The manufacturers should also have a positive image. It is therefore important for overseas manufacturers to promote not only their brands but also the image of the corporation.[12]

In Japan and other Asian countries, every television commercial from a consumer giant ends with a shot of the company's logo. Because brands are most successful if they are linked to companies with a respectable image, a company's image may be leveraged in the form of brand extensions. In the West, a diaper by the Japanese cosmetics firm Shiseido may be judged primarily in terms of whether cosmetics and diapers go together; in Asia the image of Shiseido provides enough justification for giving the product a try. Therefore, companies operating in the Region need to be very concerned about their company image because corporate identity is a major asset for marketing products.

Capitalizing on beliefs in the supernatural

As McDonald and Roberts have noted, "in contemplating the symbolic impact of a brand, prudent marketers in the Asia Pacific region would be well advised to probe folklore, taboos, and superstitious and religious connotations by colors, numbers or symbols,"[13] Indeed, from ghosts in Japan to card-reading in China and healing techniques in the Philippines, the supernatural attracts most Asians. Managers should capitalize on Asians' beliefs in the supernatural strategically to the benefit of their companies and brands.

Feng-shui is a particularly good example.[14] *Feng-shui*, which is widely applied in Chinese culture but also in Japan and Vietnam, means "wind and water" and refers to the ancient art of geomancy — a calculated assessment of the most favorable conditions for any venture. Many Westerners believe *feng-shui* defies logical or scientific explanation. The PRC outlaws it, but it is nonetheless very common. In practice, a company's image and reputation as well as the success of its brands can depend crucially on whether or not the company takes *feng-*

shui seriously — not necessarily because of the usefulness of the advice but because of consumers' perceptions. A company that consults a *feng-shui* expert (and publicizes it in the media) tells customers and employees that it cares for their prosperity and well-being. In Hongkong, *feng-shui* is a multibillion dollar business, and it is spreading to other parts of the globe. City planners in Vancouver, Canada, have reportedly consulted a *feng-shui* expert as have executives at the Hongkong and Shanghai Bank in London and at Motorola Semiconductor in Phoenix.

Feng-shui may be used primarily to enhance the image — and fate — of the corporation's headquarters building and offices. To have good *feng-shui*, a corporate building should face the water and be flanked by mountains. At the same time, the building should not block the view of the mountains. At the same time, the building should not block the view of the mountain spirits. That's why a number of major office buildings in Hongkong such as the famous headquarters of the Hongkong and Shanghai Banking Corporation, designed by well-known architect Norman Foster, have see-through lobbies to keep the spirits happy. Sharp angles give off bad *feng-shui*. That's why the Bank of China in Hongkong, designed by I.M. Pei, is perceived by many people as having bad *feng-shui*. Similar principles apply to the design and layout of hotels, restaurants, department stores, and corporate offices.

The concept of "lucky numbers" is related to the *feng-shui* system. Eight is a lucky number. To compensate for its bad geomancy, the Bank of China in Hongkong opened its doors on the eighth of August 1988 (8/8/88), probably the luckiest day of the century. When the Hongkong stock market closed on December 31, 1993, 115 per cent higher than the year before, most of the computer screens in town showed the Heng Seng index at 11,878. But when the official figure came from the stock exchange, it was 11,888, the triple eight being regarded by Chinese investors as a sign of further prosperity and good fortune in the new year.

The role of aesthetics

A general concern for aesthetics — i.e., for an attractive look, touch and feel, and attention to detail — is widespread in the Asia-Pacific Region; and, despite regional variations, the Region as a whole seems to share a common aesthetic style. Specifically, aesthetic expressions — whether in the arts or in the form of corporate aesthetic output (e.g., packaging, brochures, advertisement, store designs) — are guided by three aesthetic principles. First, Asians value complexity and decoration: they love the display of multiple forms, shapes and colors. This feature is most pronounced in Chinese, Thai, Malay, and Indonesian aesthetics. Second, beauty means balancing various aesthetic elements; harmony in aesthetic expression is seen as one of the highest goals.

Third, Asian aesthetic expression values naturalism. In China, symbols and displays of natural objects — of mountains, rivers, and phoenixes prevail and are frequently found in packaging and advertising. From "Dragon Air" to "Tiger Beer" naturalism abounds in brand names and logos. In Japan, gardens, trees, and flowers are prime objects of aesthetic symbolism.

Finally, colors seem to have different meanings and aesthetic appeal in the Asia-Pacific Region than in the West. In Chinese culture, red has been appreciated for centuries as the most appealing — and most lucky — color. Blue, on the other hand, is considered to be a cold color and carries associations of being evil and sinister. Yellow is seen as pleasant and associated with authority, and white is associated with death. Whereas blue is clearly the favourite corporate color in the U.S., it is found less frequently in East Asia. Instead, red is the winning corporate color. In Singapore, prominent enterprises such as Singapore Telecom, Singapore Technologies, Wuthelam Holdings, and the Urban Redevelopment Authority use red. Blue is almost exclusively found in logos of companies whose business is related to the sea. The logo of the Sembawang Group, a diversified conglomerate with core business in the marine and process engineering industries, is blue. So is the logo of the Navy. Other companies use the professional blue only in the writing of the corporate name but not in the actual logo. For example, the name of Singapore Airlines is written in blue but the crane logo is brownish-yellow.

Task 3: Enhancing quality perceptions

Whether or not a company is able to convince customers that it provides quality products is the key factor for determining customer loyalty and repeated purchase. Name recognition and a positive company or brand image may be established via mass media communications. But quality is affected by consumption experiences, and determined in Asia by what others think about the company and its products. Also, quality is closely tied to service. Asian consumers always expect a certain level of service, even if they are price-conscious, and the service concept in Asia seems to be different from the West. There are two ways of enhancing quality perceptions: using reference groups and social relations; and providing the appropriate level of service.

Reference groups and quality perceptions

Individualism versus collectivism — the extent to which an individual considers group concerns, as compared to individual concerns, in making decisions — has been identified as one of the major cultural differences between Western and Asian cultures.[15] Americans are said to be individualist and to resent conformity. Because Confucianism is part of their cultural background, Asians are said to be collectivist and motivated toward conforming to the norms of their reference groups. Indeed, Asians care greatly about others' perceptions of themselves and are very concerned about *guanxi*, i.e., establishing social relations and connections. In turn, they are strongly influenced by the opinions of others in their reference group and concerned about "not losing face," i.e., maintaining their social prestige and standing in the relevant reference group. Asians show how much they have embodied the group ideal by being like others.

The cultural dimension of individualism/collectivism has been applied mostly to the analysis of work-related values and negotiations. It also has important consequences for consumer behavior and for enhancing the perceived quality of a company and its products.[16] For example, friendship circles or people living in the same area (e.g., an apartment building) often consume similar product categories, select the same brands within a category and purchase them in the same department store.[17] Asians are less likely to complain when they receive defective products or inappropriate service; instead they change companies and products silently. Group acceptance of the company and its brands determines whether or not the products will be accepted in the marketplace. Häagen Dazs ice cream, promoting its ice-cream with a European premium-quality image all over Asia, is primarily relying on word of mouth to expand its sales. Opinion leaders play major roles in promoting the quality of a product on TV. Comparative advertising and quality-comparisons, on the other hand, are seen as "bad-mouthing" the competition; a company that does it loses face.

Monitoring the societal and communal role is also significant in terms of promoting the company and its products. Every year, the magazine *Asian Business* nominates Asia's company of the year. The following criteria are used to evaluate the companies in the Region: quality of management; quality of products/services; contribution to the economy; size and type of charitable donations and establishment of educational foundations; concern shown for the environment; the image projected of being honest, ethical, and a considerate employer; and potential for growth. Note the heavy emphasis on social/communal activities and responsibilities. For building corporate reputations, a company's communal activities, sponsorships, and public relations are extremely important.

Providing the appropriate level of service

Asia is, by its very traditions, a service culture. The service concept has been institutionalized, for example, in the rituals surrounding the serving and drinking of tea, in host-guest relations, and in the packaging rituals found all over Asia. Service is often crucial for enhancing quality perceptions.

What constitutes good service "Asian style"? First, service must be people-oriented. Personal characteristics matter: Asian customers find it strange to be served by an older person unless the person is the owner. Also, efficiency and time-savings are less important than personal attention. Customization rather than efficient standardization is the key. As a recent Sheraton ad, run in the Region, put it, "Service is what you want it to be."

Asia's profitable airlines are good examples of this aspect of the Asian service concept. Rather than focusing on schedules, number of destinations, baggage handling, and frequent-flyer bonus programs, Asian airlines have positioned themselves primarily as providing superior inflight service, centered around the flight attendants. Singapore Airlines took the lead years ago by creating the icon of the Singapore Girl as an idealized version of the young, gracious, and courteous Asian hostess. The campaign has been copied by other airlines in the region (e.g., Malaysian Airlines, Thai Airways, Hongkong's Cathay Pacific), which have also positioned themselves by superior inflight service and used the stewardess as the focal point of their ad campaigns. When Virgin Atlantic tried to engage Cathay Pacific in a price competition on the profitable Hongkong-London route, Cathay responded with "inflight service enhancements."

In addition to personal attention, Asian consumers value the ritualistic aspects of service — e.g., the movement, the pose, and the look of the service personnel. Although present all over the Region, the ritualistic element is the most pronounced in Japan. For example, Japanese women speak in a higher-pitched voice in customer-contact situations than in private situations. Every salesperson is trained in elaborate gift-wrapping techniques. In five-star hotels, the bellboy accompanies the guest to the departing bus or car and waits until the guest has departed. Even in the fast food outlets, ritualized service is quite common.

Conclusions

Table 2 summarizes the unique features of corporate-identity and brand management in the Asia-Pacific Region and our key recommendations concerning each management task. Some of our recommendations (e.g., use prestige or communal activities) are of a more general strategic nature because they define a broader range of objectives and activities for a company while others may be seen as tactical (e.g., present names in attractive calligraphy). Moreover, although we have discussed the unique features of Asian cultures as independent from one another, with occasional cross-references, they are in fact highly interrelated. For example, *feng-shui* and *yin-yang* concepts refer to names, numbers, colors, and other facets of the material and immaterial world, thus creating unifying concepts and themes that form the basis for other concepts. As a result, corporate identity and branding decisions such as the choice of a name and logo should not be approached in a sequential fashion (first considering the sound of a name, then the meaning, then the number of strokes, then the color of the logo etc.), but in a parallel fashion in which the overall *gestalt* of the end-product as well as its various components are considered. As stated earlier, Asian

Table 2 Strategic/tactical recommendations for the three management tasks

Unique feature	Strategic/tactical recommendation
Selecting corporate and brand names	
Ideographs	Choose name with desirable connotations
Homonyms	Choose name with desirable sound associations
Multiple tones	Choose name with desirable tonal associations
Writing as art	Present names in attractive calligraphy
Multiple writing systems	Use writing system appropriate for product category
Lucky names	Choose name associated with luck based on stroke number and *yin-yang*
Establishing the right image	
Prestige	Create prestige associations, promote the image of the corporation and leverage corporate image in brand extensions
Mysticism	Check for mysticism and *feng-shui*
Aesthetics	Focus on complexity, balance and naturalism
Enhancing quality perceptions	
Collectivism	Use reference groups as influencers
Societal role of company	Engage in community projects and sponsorships
Personal service	Customize service elements
Service rituals	Attune to movement, gestures and rituals

consumers appreciate balance and harmony of different elements in the final product.

Building and managing corporate and brand identities in the Asia-Pacific Region is, in many respects, similar to corporate identity and brand management anywhere else in the world. At the same time, there are subtle, yet crucial differences related to linguistic and cultural factors, which require that managers pay close attention to local conditions. Some of the issues that we have discussed (e.g., the linguistic issues) are likely to be permanent factors because they reflect intrinsic differences in consumer perceptions and information processing. Other differences may diminish over time. For example, in the consumption of some product categories such as clothing, entertainment, and consumer electronics, there seems to be a convergence of lifestyles and preferences, at least among certain strategically important market segments such as city dwellers. Managers must be sensitive to both and must be able to distinguish which is which: the unchanging aspects of consumer perceptions and behaviors deeply rooted in language and cultural traditions, and the ephemeral preferences resulting from changing lifestyles and sometimes consumer fads.

NOTES

1. The following information as well as the company examples in the remainder of the article are based on research by the authors; newspaper articles in 1993 and 1994 in The *Asian Wall Street Journal, China Daily, The Economist, The World Executive's Digest, The Far Eastern Economic Review, The South China Morning Post, The Straits Times*; and the following major articles and special reports: "Asia/Pacific: The New Consumers," *The International Herald Tribune*, February 1, 1994, I-XII; "Asia's Wealth," *Business Week*, November 29, 1993, 100–112; "Brands, It's Thrive or Die," *Fortune*, August 23, 1993, 32–36; "China Speeds on to Market," *The Economist*, November 20, 1993, 35–36; "Go East Young Man," *Far Eastern Economic Review*, November 4, 1993, 40–44; "Korea goes for quality," *Fortune*, April 18, 1994, 153–159; "Marketing Brand Names in Singapore, Malaysia, and Taiwan," *Hongkong Trade Development Council Research Report* (January 1992).

2. "Asia's Wealth," *Business Week*, November 29, 1993, p. 10.

3. "Asia, Where the Big Brands are Blooming," *Fortune* (August 1993), p. 35.

4. For recent examples, see David Aaker, "How Will the Japanese Compete in Retail Services," *California Management Review*, 33/1 (Fall 1990): 54–67; Jeremiah J. Sullivan, "Japanese Management Philosophies: From the Vacuous to the Brilliant," *California Management Review*, 32/2 (Winter 1992): 66–87; Chalmers Johnson, "Comparative Capitalism: The Japanese Difference," *California Management Review*, 35/4 (Summer 1993): 51–67; Toyohiro Kono (Guest Editor), "Special Issue: Competing and Cooperating with the Japanese," *Long Range Planning*, 26/4 (August 1993).

5. For overviews of corporate identity, see Wallis Olins, *Corporate Identity: Making Business Strategy Visible Through Design* (Cambridge, MA: Harvard University Press, 1989); Veronica Napoles, *Corporate Identity Design* (New York, NY: Van Nostrand Reinhold, Motoo Nakanishi, *Building a New Form of Corporate Identity: Japan's CI Revolution.* (Tokyo, 1993.)

6. David Aaker, *Managing Brand Equity* (New York, NY: The Free Press, 1991), p. 15. See also David A. Aaker and Alexander L. Biel, *Brand Equity and Advertising: Advertising's Role in Building Strong Brands* (Hillsdale, NJ: Lawrence Erlbaum, 1993); David Arnold, *The Handbook of Brand Management* (Reading, MA: Addison-Wesley, 1992); Leslie de Chernatony and Malcolm H.B. McDonald, *Creating Powerful Brands* (Oxford: Butterworth Heinemann, 1992); and the special issue of the *Journal of Marketing Research* (May 1994) on brand management.

7. Kevin Lane Keller, "Conceptualizing, Measuring, and Managing Customer-Based Brand Equity," *Journal of Marketing*, 57, 1–22.

8. Kim R. Robertson, "Strategically Desirable Brand Name Characteristics," *Journal of Consumer Marketing*, 6 (Fall 1989): 61–71; Leslie Collins, "A Name to Conjure With," *European Journal of Marketing*, 11 (1977): 339–362.

9. Yigang Pan and Bernd H. Schmitt, "What's in a Name? An Empirical Comparison of Chinese and Western Brand Names," *Asian Journal of Marketing* (forthcoming).

10. Bernd H. Schmitt, Yigang Pan, and Nader Tavassoli, "Language and Consumer Memory: The Impact of Linguistic Differences between Chinese and English," *Journal of Consumer Research* (forthcoming).

11. The authors thank the Beijing office of Robert Bosch Corporation for providing these materials.

12. "Marketing Brand Names in Japan," *Hongkong Trade Development Council Research Report*, June 1992.

13. Gael M. McDonald and C.J. Roberts, "The Brand-Naming Enigma in the Asia Pacific Context," *European Journal of Marketing*, 24/8 (1990): 6–19.

14. Evelyn Lip, *Feng Shui for Business* (Singapore: Times Books International, 1989).

15. Much has been written on individualism/collectivism. Classic references include Michael Bond, K. Leung, and K.C. Wan, "How Does Cultural Collectivism Operate?" *Journal of Cross-Cultural Psychology*, 13/2 (1982): 186–200; and Geert Hofstede, *Culture's Consequences: National Differences in Thinking and Organizing* (Beverley Hills, CA: Sage Press, 1980).

16. David K. Tse, "Chinese Consumers: Characteristics and Research Propositions," in Michael Bond, ed., *Handbook of Chinese Psychology* (Oxford: Oxford University Press, forthcoming).

17. Chol Lee and Robert T. Green. "Cross-Cultural Examination of the Fishbein Behavioral Intentions Model," *Journal of International Business Studies*, 22/2 (1991): 289–305.

BERND H. SCHMITT is Associate Professor of Business at Columbia University's Graduate School of Business.

YIGANG PAN is Assistant Professor at the College of Commerce, DePaul University.

16 What It Takes to Supply Japanese OEMs

David L. Blenkhorn and A. Hamid Noori

The Japanese worldwide success with products in virtually every field they have entered has caused much concern to industrial marketers who wish to do business with Japanese firms. Although much has been written about Japanese management techniques and their role in the success of Japanese business and products, little has been written about the supplier side of the equation and how it can be a critical input in understanding Japanese business. This article reports on two research projects, one carried out in Japan and the other in North America, which contrast OEM/supplier relationships in the two geographic areas. With the increase in the number of transplant Japanese manufacturing firms in North America, Europe, and other parts of the world, a prerequisite to successfully marketing to Japanese business is surely an understanding of their OEM/supplier relationships.

Introduction

New technologies and new approaches in product design are resulting in end products having fewer and fewer components. In the manufacturing of sewing machines, for example, one microprocessor has replaced 350 mechanical parts! These developments are having fundamental impacts on the final assembly, manufacturing of subassemblies, and production of parts [4].

The assembly of end products now requires less time (because of the integration of components) and contains less added value. At the same time, the subassemblies and particularly the parts area are playing a much more direct representation in terms of added value and "know how" of the endproducts. This implies that the suppliers of parts and components are now playing an ever increasing role in supporting the activities of the Original Equipment Manufacturers (OEMs).

Reproduced with permission from *Industrial Marketing Management*, 19 (February 1990), pp. 21–30.

Crucial to the success of the final assembler in any industry is its supply base, which becomes its lifeblood; and the automobile industry is no exception. In fact, one factor accounting for the differing levels of success between the Japanese and North American auto industries may well be the relationships with their supply bases.

It is well documented that the structures of the auto parts industries in North America and Japan differ significantly [see 5,8,9]. However, is the structure a prime determinant of the success of the Japanese auto industry, or are there other key discriminating variables?

Cognizant of the fact that industrial structure differs in North America and Japan, by examining the auto industry supply bases in the two geographical areas, this research seeks to uncover key factors that might account for the greatly differing degrees of success exhibited by the two industries. Based on the research findings a blueprint for action for the North American supply base is laid out.

Background

In order to understand manufacturer/supplier relationships in Japan, it must be recognized that industry in Japan is structured quite differently than in North America. To illustrate, Toyota is part of a group that includes petroleum, insurance, banking, construction, and machinery companies. This is not to say that large North American firms are not diversified into often unrelated fields, but Japanese firms differ in that most large manufacturers have an "extended company" that reaches far down the supply network. Toyota has a large direct interest in many of its suppliers, which are not labeled as Toyota "divisions," and exerts indirect control over the firms which in turn supply them. In aggregate they may be referred to as the Toyota "family" of companies and a special relationship exists among them. Similarly, Nissan has an interest in at least 34 firms supplying to the auto industry.

The Japanese Zaibatsu structure

The notion of extended company allows a large manufacturer (the OEM) to form the nucleus of a relationship with primary suppliers which in turn deal with their own suppliers. This is based on historical Zaibatsu relations that have dominated Japanese culture for centuries (see Figure 1). The first tier suppliers are often controlled by the OEM or if not controlled, there is a very close relationship between them. An example would be Aisin-Warner, which supplies automatic transmissions to Toyota and is indirectly controlled by Toyota to the extent of 90% ownership. The first tier suppliers provide major parts and subassemblies. Aisin-Warner also supplies to other auto assemblers such as

Mitsubishi, Isuzu, and Volvo, but does not supply to Toyota's arch-rival Nissan. This sequence of relationships then follow between first tier and second tier, and so on. Generally, the further down in number of tiers, the more likely will be the use of home workers or entrepreneurs as suppliers.

Typically, any changes in suppliers are likely to come between tiers 1 and 2, and at lower levels, and not between the large manufacturer and its suppliers at tier 1. This is because of the close, long-term relationship between manufacturer and top tier suppliers. The Zaibatsu relationship is often not as straightforward as presented above. For example, a second tier supplier may supply directly to a major manufacturer and also supply to a first tier supplier. McMillan [7] and Bryant et al. [3] further elaborate on these relationships.

Figure 1 The Zaibatsu approach to OEM/Supplier relationships

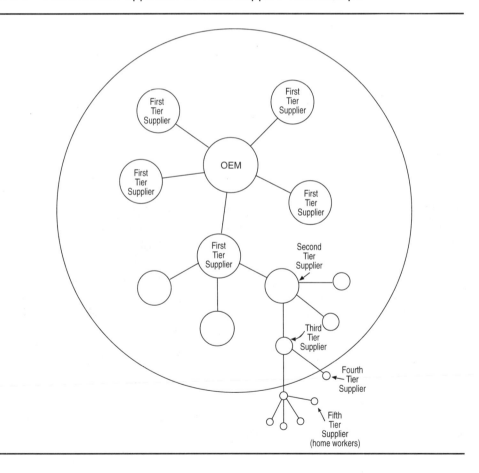

A comparison study

To compare the relationships between OEMs and suppliers, two separate studies were undertaken, one in North America and one in Japan.

The North America study was conducted during fall 1986 and winter 1987, and consisted of visits to five parts-makers and two major assemblers (OEMs). In May and June of 1987, 13 parts-makers and two major assemblers (OEMs) were visited in Japan. A typical visit lasted half a day, including interviews with the CEO and several other executives and a plant tour followed by a question and answer period.

The Japanese research

The following nine criteria were perceived as being crucial to the Japanese respondents in the manufacturer/supplier relationship.

WELL-DEFINED MANDATES, GOALS, AND OBJECTIVES: The intense competition from both domestic and offshore parts-makers, as well as continual pressure from their major customers to reduce prices, has forced firms to concentrate on well-defined mandates, goals, and objectives. The firms visited seemed to have clear ideas of what they had to do. The payoff in firms being focused was more teamwork, employees exhibiting greater reliability, less confusion, and more communication resulting in a much more efficient operation.

FOCUSED CUSTOMERS: Outsourcing, historically a well-practiced mandate, is being pushed to new limits as the OEMs and suppliers struggle to reduce their fixed costs even further. In many situations, the unique Zaibatsu relationship results in OEMs having single sources for their parts, thus enabling better communication, easier coordination of production processes, and compatibility of just-in-time (JIT) philosophies. In addition, suppliers are often located close to major manufacturers in order to better coordinate their deliveries with the OEM's production schedules.

There may be occasions for adding to the supplier base as new vendors with new technology and new products can provide extra capacity for growth. For an existing supplier, however, to be cut off by the OEM would be an uncommon event as the two are expected to work closely together. In return for such stability, the OEM has access to almost all the supplier's information, can demand high loyalty, can influence whomever else the vendor may sell to, can insist on a nearby location, and can exercise extreme pressure to conform to quality, delivery, and quantity expectations.

SUPPLIER AGGRESSIVENESS: Suppliers at all tiers appear to be working on very low profit margins. Typically, they share their cost figures with their customers, with the quoted price for a part or a subassembly being very close to their actual costs of production. The incentive for profits puts pressure on the supplier to reduce costs through production process efficiency and economies of scale. Workers in supplier firms fully recognize the necessity for cost reduction and efficiency in their employer's ability to survive and approach this very aggressively.

USER/PRODUCER INTERFACE: There is usually close technical cooperation in product development between large manufacturers and first-tier suppliers. This cooperation may take different forms. For example, design engineers from both firms may work as part of a team on a new product, or the supplier firm may be permitted to use the research facilities of the OEM.

The exhibited high level of user/producer interface usually results in more integration of ideas and faster communication; hence greater adaptability and flexibility is produced in the organization. Japanese suppliers appear to invest heavily in new product development and in making their production processes more efficient. The OEM and its suppliers often form joint task forces to address specific problems resulting in better understanding of the OEM's production processes.

SELECTION OF SUPPLIERS BASED ON EQUIPMENT COMPATIBILITY: Many firms have in-house facilities for producing machine tools, designing and producing their own robots, and modifying existing machines, which facilitates synchronization of their production processes with those of their major customers. Supplier selection is often based on equipment capability and compatibility rather than price. Machines are not only grouped for easier access by workers, but typically each process is handled by a single worker controlling up to eight machines. The firms' experience with process control has shown that its effective utilization results in high efficiency, low down-time, and lower maintenance costs.

ZERO DEFECT POLICY: This terms is ubiquitous in Japanese firms' description of their corporate objectives and their attitudes toward the products they produce. Many firms espouse the "zero defects" principle, and producing a quality product is the job description. Workers' commitment to zero defects resulting in quality products was evidenced in all of the firms visited. In one case, a firm that set a target of 72 suggestions per worker for process/product improvement for the year ended up with 92 suggestions per worker over the year!

JUST-IN-TIME DELIVERY: Just-in-time (JIT) delivery, as part of the more encompassing JIT philosophy was stressed by all the firms visited. Most firms interviewed have had JIT for a number of years (up to 15) and for them this is a way of life. Many firms use JIT in obtaining their raw materials and components parts, and all firms use JIT delivery to their major customers.

Full implementation of the JIT philosophy has given firms lower inventory costs, lower per unit costs, and increased quality of products, which has made the user firms more competitive.

ENCOURAGEMENT OF INNOVATIVE THINKING: A thrust for innovative thinking is evident because new product design engineering is often the responsibility of the parts-maker. As mentioned, it is not unusual to have engineers from suppliers working side-by-side with the OEM's design engineers in its R&D units. Also, the widespread successful use of quality circles produced many suggestions for increased production and design of products, which helped manufacturers produce a more innovative final product. The firms as a group seemed receptive and completely open to discovering new approaches and methods of doing almost anything.

CULTURE, PEOPLE AND ATTITUDE: Good performance or nonperformance would be viewed from a societal perspective. Japanese cultural norms appear to play a large role in the expectations of manufacturer/supplier relationships.

Without exception, the firms visited elaborated on their unique corporate culture which they felt permeated to their suppliers and their major customers. Typically, active quality circles programs provide the opportunity for employee involvement accompanied by an "open-door" policy practiced by senior executives. Even junior employees seemed completely at ease with senior people who spent much time communicating with employees on the factory floor. The firms believe that the biggest payoff from employees' positive attitude is their flexibility, willingness to change, and their teamwork efforts.

The corporate culture and attitude of workers in the firms visited were reflected in one firm referring to its employees as associates rather than workers, and another having no classification of employees, a common locker room, and everyone starting work at the same time in the morning.

The North America research

In a study reported in Automotive Industries [1] on the North American parts industry, it was found that top on the list of concerns voiced by suppliers was their lack of success in supplying the Japanese OEM transplants opening plants in North America. This finding prompted the authors to further examine the North American supply base and contrast it to the Japanese model. In the study reported here, the following six criteria reflect major differences between the North American and Japanese suppliers. Upon the completion of interviews with five parts-makers and two OEMs, a pattern of consistency appeared. This was corroborated through discussions with several industry experts which prompted the researchers to limit the North American sample size to seven firms.[1]

INDEPENDENCE OF SUPPLIERS FROM OEM: The North American parts suppliers typically do not design and manufacture their own equipment nor do they have as many design engineers on staff. The driving force in their process equipment is not synchronization with their major customers or suppliers, but demonstration of their desire to retain a high degree of independence from their OEM customers.

SELECTION OF SUPPLIERS BASED ON PRICE QUOTATION: Historically North American OEMs have done less outsourcing and more in-house parts production (with degrees of difference among the OEMs). When outside suppliers are sought, multiple sourcing is still the accepted norm with "price" still a prime criterion in supplier selection. This tends toward a "them-us" confrontational, atmosphere (rather than a supplier/OEM "team" approach to problem solving) resulting in less efficiency for both parties.

LESS USER/PRODUCER INTERFACE: The user/producer interface experienced by North American parts-makers is often limited to the order at hand rather than a long-term R&D relationship, and coordination of efforts. While parts-makers admit that closer relationships with OEM customers are necessary and important, there is less evidence that they establish trust and close communication ties. Little or no exchange of technical staff means a lower level of adaptability by the parts-maker and minimal design to cost criteria utilized.

ZERO DEFECT POLICY: Conventionally, North American auto parts suppliers have emphasized "quality control" rather than "built-in quality." Typically, quality was checked after the production process was completed rather than being an integral part of the process itself. Lack of concrete steps toward a zero defect policy and its accompanying higher level of overall quality management often results in higher per unit costs.

A FORCED JUST-IN-TIME DELIVERY: In most cases JIT delivery was commenced in response to a demand by the firm's major OEM customer(s). One firm's major reason for starting JIT deliveries was stated as being a preemptive move to match expected incoming Japanese competition. Another firm adopted JIT to remain competitive with the rest of the auto industry. Still another firm adopted the concept "to try something new."

The lack of a JIT policy or a half-hearted one by suppliers has resulted in lower efficiency for all concerned. It was evident that some of the firms interviewed seemed to overlook the real point behind the whole JIT philosophy. For example, some firms felt that their customers only wanted on-time delivery from JIT. One firm stated that they felt the OEM didn't really care if they adopted JIT, just as long as the parts-maker was able to supply the parts on time to the OEM's schedule.

LESS EMPHASIS ON INNOVATION: Encouragement of innovative thinking is also present in the North American parts industry but to a lesser degree than in Japan. Due to the lack of full fledged emphasis on design engineering, there exists much less opportunity for demonstration of innovative thinking for parts designers when contrasted to their Japanese counterparts.

Japanese and North American suppliers' practice: A comparison

The attitudes measured and feedback received on important criteria in supplier/ OEM relations differed greatly between the two studies. Table 1 compares the two groups on a number of criteria considered important by respondents in each study.

In addition, Tables 2 and 3 depict criteria (inputs) considered important by the companies interviewed and the resultant outputs based on the current supplier/OEM relationships in Japan and North America respectively. The differing inputs and attendant outputs partly account for the vast differences between the two groups. These tables are structured around the ideas presented by [2].

As summarized in Table 2, just-in-time delivery, which has been a fact of life for Japanese suppliers for many years, has resulted in lower inventory cost because usually everyone in the supply chain is utilizing JIT. This eventuates in a lower per unit cost which improves supplier competitiveness. The zero-defect policy implemented voluntarily by the suppliers originates a higher quality product being delivered to them. Suppliers' emphasis on process control produces higher efficiency, lower down time, and subsequently lower maintenance costs. The unique corporate culture pervading the supplier/OEM firms with emphasis on the human side with a very positive attitude results in successful quality circle implementation, more reliably employees, and a greater demonstration of teamwork. The encouragement of innovative thinking results in more innovative products. Firms' well-defined mandates, goals, and objectives produce less confusion and more focus on the task at hand when everyone is cognizant of the firm's stated direction. Focusing on a few well-identified customers facilitates better communication with them, often resulting in a better understanding of their needs and a superior product being produced. Close and

Table 1 A comparison of Japanese and North American suppliers

Criterion	Attribute	
	Japan	North America
Quality	Part of the process	Monitored after production
JIT Delivery	Not a new phenomenon: part of the total supply/delivery system	Imposed by external forces — customers or threat of competition from the Japanese
Process/Equipment	Synchronized with their major customer(s) and suppliers	Firm specific centered rather entire system centered
Culture/People/ Attitude	Team playing, job enlargement, attempts to play down rank or hierarchy on job	Union centered them — us attitude
Innovative thinking	Mandatory to survive as auto assemblers demand innovative, cost saving solutions	Encouraged but historically not mandatory to survive as parts maker
Efficiency	Efficiency enhanced through manufacture of robots or modification of purchased equipment	Often look to external sources to increase efficiency
Competitiveness/ Price	Other Japanese firms seen as major competitors and in-house capability of auto assemblers	Offshore parts makers viewed as major competitors
User/producer interface	An ongoing R&D thrust with regular exchange of personnel	Often limied to the order at hand
Degree of computer linkage/sophistication	The supplier/assembler interface perhaps is very similar in both Japan and North America	
	Extensive use of CAD/CAM in design engineering	Much less use of CAD/CAM
JIT necessity	Pressure to adopt came from the auto assemblers	
	Much more commonly utilized and understood	Being adopted by those suppliers that wish to remain suppliers
Design-to-cost criteria	Historically a common occurrence in the Japanese auto industry, but the rise in the yen has intensified its use	No data
Outsourcing	More outsourcing often offshore cause principally by increased value of the yen	More outsourcing precipitated by OEM's desire to reduce fixed costs
	More for both groups but for different reasons	

Table 2 Supplier/OEM Practice in Japan

Inputs	Outputs
• Well-defined mandates, goals and objectives • Focused customers • User/product interface (R&D engineering) exchange • Process control/selection of suppliers based on equipment compatibility • Zero-defect policy • The just-in-time concept • Encouragement of innovative thinking • Culture/people/attitude	• Low inventory cost • Low per unit cost • Improved competitiveness • High quality products • High efficiency • Low down time • Low maintenance cost • Quality circles implemented more successfully • Reliability of employees • Teamwork • Flexibility of employees to change • High efficiency of the operations • Less confusion and more concentration • Better communication • Better products • Lower cost products • More innovative products • higher integration • Faster connection/communication • Higher adaptability • Higher flexibility of the organization • Design-to-cost criteria • More efficient product

Table 3 Supplier/OEM Relationships in North America

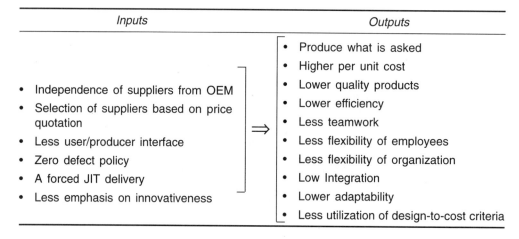

Inputs	Outputs
• Independence of suppliers from OEM • Selection of suppliers based on price quotation • Less user/producer interface • Zero defect policy • A forced JIT delivery • Less emphasis on innovativeness	• Produce what is asked • Higher per unit cost • Lower quality products • Lower efficiency • Less teamwork • Less flexibility of employees • Less flexibility of organization • Low Integration • Lower adaptability • Less utilization of design-to-cost criteria

frequent user/producer interface fosters a higher degree of integration of the OEM's specifications and suppliers' perceptions of them. Related to this close interface is R&D and engineering exchanges which enable the supplier to be more flexible in its design and production with greater organizational flexibility. This total integrative approach extends to the selection of suppliers based on the degree of OEM/supplier equipment compatibility, which can assist design-to-cost criteria, producing the product within cost constraints.

As depicted by the inputs and attendant outputs in Table 3, for North American suppliers a zero defect policy or specified quality level is fulfilled by producing to minimum specifications. Just-in-time delivery in North America is usually a sporadic event which is forced on suppliers by the OEM and lacks integration and coordination in the whole supply chain. Adherence to a JIT delivery schedule without fully understanding its philosophy often results in a lower quality product and higher per unit cost. Selection of suppliers based on price quotation rather than mutual information sharing causes suppliers much additional time and expense in producing prototypes for an unsuccessful contract bid. This inevitably lowers the supplier's efficiency in obtaining contracts. The independence of North American suppliers from OEMs results in a less harmonious supplier/OEM relationship and less teamwork. Because suppliers traditionally produce to OEM-generated specifications, there is less emphasis on the supplier being innovative.

The lesser user/producer interface ensues in a lower degree of intercompany integration, and the lack of communication causes the supplier to be less adaptable than the Japanese counterpart. Due to lower emphasis on outsourcing by North American OEMs, there has been less utilization of design-to-cost criteria by suppliers.

Japanese diagnostic approach to parts manufacturing

Figure 2 depicts the sequential steps that both the OEM manufacturer and the parts-maker typically follow in arriving at a finished product. The OEM manufacturer begins with a marketing research stage whereby the perceived needs of the marketplace are examined. This triggers the formulation of product plans (e.g., car types and models needed), leading to R&D work on the attendant parts and assemblies. The R&D process results in design of the necessary parts and components which are then tested for suitability. Satisfactory testing completed, the part or component specifications are set followed by production either in-house or by a supplier. The parts are then assembled and shipped to the final user.

The parts-maker goes through a similar series of steps commencing with recognition of a functional need that can be satisfied with the properly designed part or assembly. The R&D function takes over in coming up with the required parameters, followed by the design stage to produce a feasible part or assembly.

Figure 2 Japanese diagnostic approach and North American traditional
approach to parts manufacturing

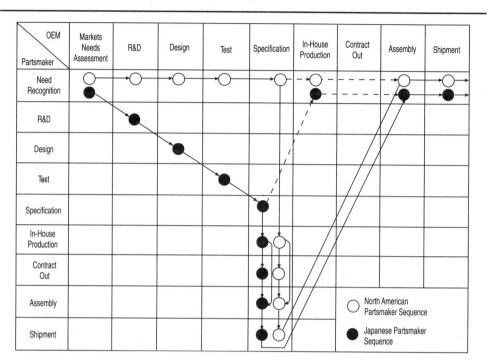

[Original idea from: R. A. More, Developer/Adopter Relationships in New Industrial Product Situations, *Journal of Business Research*, 501–517 (1986)].

The prototype is tested, and when proven satisfactory, specifications are agreed to, often in conjunction with the parts-maker's major OEM customers. Production may be carried out in-house or contracted out. The resulting parts are then assembled and shipped to waiting OEM customers. As displayed in Figure 2, the sequence of events for both the OEM assembler and the parts-maker differ considerably in North America and Japan.

In North America the OEM assembler carries out the product marketing research, R&D work, design stage, and testing, and sets the specifications in most cases in isolation from the supplier, which enters the scene after the specifications have been set. If outsourcing is used by the OEM, the parts are produced by the parts-maker under contract, assembled into assemblies if required, and shipped to the OEM where they form part of the OEM's product.

In contrast, the Japanese parts-maker participates in the process at need-recognition stage, often in advance of the OEM. Typically Japanese OEMs look to their suppliers for leading edge technology in their parts/assembly specialty.

To do this the Japanese parts-maker maintains a strong design engineering/ R&D presence. The R&D, design, testing, and specification setting are carried out in conjunction with their major OEM customers often as partners in a project design team. This contrasts with the process of their North American counterparts. The next stages of contracting out or producing in-house, assembly, and shipment to the OEM customers parallel those of their North American counterparts.

It is posited that the different routes followed in North America and Japan are a prime factor contributing to their differing degrees of performance. The critical difference with the Japanese diagnostic approach to parts manufacturing is the early time frame where the Japanese supplier gets involved with the OEM and the close ensuring relationship. This process is enhanced when long-term, trusting relationships are the norm, not the exception.

Differing management styles — a critical determinant?

Pascale and Athos [10] partially explain the differing levels of performance between North American and Japanese industry through the "7S's" model. They posit that North American industry is similar to Japan on the "hardball" S's — strategy, structure, and systems. However, on the "softball" S's (i.e. skills, style, staff, and superinordinate goals), there exists a wide disparity between North American and Japanese management techniques. Their observations are paralleled in the findings of the studies reported here in that their culture appears to give Japanese suppliers advantages in the softer S's. Nevertheless, Japanese managers do not have a monopoly on the softer S's — North American managers merely must put increased serious emphasis on them, which has been lacking in the past.

Implications

The prescription that the authors are advocating does not imply that the North American auto industry simply duplicate Japanese methods — this would be a simplistic approach and clearly would not work. However, there are lessons to be learned from the Japanese success and this forms the foundation for this prescription for survival.

The reason for the Japanese success does not appear to be their technology per se but the way they manage their affairs and the organization they build to achieve their goals. The Japanese integrative approach within their own organization and with the supplier base seems to be the key to their success and the major reason for distinguishing them for the way they do business in North

America. Japanese OEM success in establishing supplier relationships is based on trust, integration and sharing of goals, and the back-up support that exists in the system. To what extent these factors can be incorporated to a high degree in the North American system remains to be seen. There are examples of success — GM Canada's Autoplex, Chrysler's Eagle Premier plant.

The philosophy that North American firms in general and the auto industry in particular have historically followed has to be changed and should be based on doing business successfully together. It should not be based on a zero-sum game — "I win at your expense" — but on "mutual prosperity," which is part of the Toyota philosophy. North American managers must put more emphasis on the softer side of management, e.g., developing worker skills, modifying their confrontational "them-us" management style, and putting more emphasis on employee relationships and how employee's individual goals can be coordinated with those of the firm to achieve realistic objectives.

While the structure of the auto industry in North America is quite different than in Japan, this should not be regarded as a prime determining factor in their differing levels of performance. It is rather the contrasting management styles and philosophies in North America and Japan that have caused the vase difference in their levels of success.

In the typical North American OEM/supplier liaison the lack of long-term relationships, close interaction, information sharing, and trust manifests itself in many ways. One such fallout which is currently coming to the forefront is that suppliers have not taken the initiative in design engineering and new product development, thus putting them at a distinct disadvantage to their Japanese counterparts.

In order for North American firms to break into the Zaibatsu "inner circle" (as depicted in Figure 1) and become successful suppliers to the Japanese North American transplants, they not only must be cognizant of and practice the points made above but they must be willing to substantially change their corporate culture and the way they have traditionally conducted their business operations. This is the price of admission to the inner circle and the authors posit it is a price that few firms are willing to pay.

NOTE

1. Since the completion of this study, several North American companies have moved to rectify some of the deficiencies pointed out in this report.

REFERENCES

1. Supplier-Side Economics: The Silent Majorities Speak, *Automotive Industries* (December), 56–87 (1986).
2. Bache, J., Carr, R., Parnaby, J. and Tobias, A.M., Supplier Development Systems, *International of Technology Management* 2(2), 219–228 (1987).
3. Bryant, Murray J., D'Cruz, Joseph R. and Kelly, Paul S., Managing the Supplier Relationship: The Automobile Industry in Japan, unpublished working paper, University of Toronto, (1984).
4. Kumpe, T. and Bolwijn, P.T., Trends and Issues in Improving Productivity of Industrial Organizations Engaged in Medium to High-Volume Manufacture of Discrete Products, in *Proceedings of World Productivity Forum*, International Industrial Engineering Conference, Washington, D.C., 1987, pp. 48–50.
5. Leenders, Michiel R. and Blenkhorn, David L., *Reverse Marketing: The New Buyer–Supplier Relationship*. The Free Press, New York, 1988, p. 143.
6. Leenders, Michiel R. and Blenkhorn, David L., *Supplier Relations and Supplier Development by Japanese Manufacturers*. Working Paper Series No. 84–17, School of Business, The University of Western Ontario, 1984.
7. McMillan, Charles J., "Production planning and organization design at Toyota, *Business Quarterly* (Winter), 22–30 (1981).
8. McMillan, Charles J., *The Japanese Industrial System*. Walter de Gruyter, Berlin, 1984.
9. Murray, J. Alex and Blenkhorn, David L., Japanese Suppliers Are Coming With Just-In-Time, *Cost and Management* (July–August), 36–38 (1984).
10. Pascale, Richard T. and Athos, Anthony G., *The Art of Japanese Management*, Warner Books, New York, 1981, p. 326.

DAVID L. BLENKHORN is an associate professor of Marketing in the School of Business and Economics at Wilfrid Laurier University in Waterloo, Ontario, Canada.

A. HAMID NOORI is an associate professor of Operations Management in the School of Business and Economics at Wilfrid Laurier University.

Address correspondence to Professor David L. Blenkhorn, School of Business and Economics, Wilfrid Laurier University, Waterloo, Ontario, Canada N2L 3C5.

This research was funded by a grant from the Social Sciences and Humanities Research Council of Canada.

17 Asia Joins the Franchising Bandwagon

Kin Gatbonton

What was once the preserve of hamburgers and doughnuts now extends to a whole variety of services and products. In the United States, franchises for fax and copier services, carpet cleaners, window treatments, day care centers and homes for the aged, are promoted and pursued as vigorously as more traditional franchises: ice cream parlors, cookie stalls and family restaurants in the Kentucky Fried Chicken mold.

Although established franchisors like Dunkin' Donuts and McDonald's remain the pillars of the franchise establishment, money makers now include more esoteric franchises, those which are highly specialized and innovative. One American sourcebook for franchise opportunities lists over 2,000 franchises by type of business.

The West — particularly the United States — is witnessing a veritable explosion in franchise concepts and revenues. In 1983, franchising accounted for more than $150 billion, or 10% America's GNP. A decade later, franchising accounts for nearly $600 billion in sales in the United States, roughly one-third of all American consumer purchases, and 34% of the country's GNP. Employment in franchising, both at the part-time and full-time level in 1990, totalled over 7 million. More significantly, despite the deepening '80s recession, franchising actually grew at a rate (5%) almost double that of the economy as a whole. By the end of 1992, there were an estimated 430,000 franchises in America.

In Asia, the figures are considerably smaller — franchising being a relatively young phenomenon which took-off in the early '80s. But for an industry that did not exist in the region until just 20 years ago, franchising has come of age.

Asia's biggest and most profitable franchises remain largely American. One just has to read the signs to see that America has secured for itself a firm toehold

Reproduced with permission from *The Asian Manager*, (October 1993), pp. 18–22.

in the region. In almost every Asian capital, it has become virtually impossible to travel more than a few blocks without running into a neon sign that says McDonald's, Carl's Jr., Mrs. Fields, or Toys-R-Us. Each outlet doing brisk business to dozens upon dozens of ravenous locals eager to sample a slice of Americana. Interestingly enough, a Filipino participant to a recent conference on franchising listed what he termed, "American magic," along with low cost as one success factor for local franchises.

Asia tastes

Happily, this is becoming less and less true as the venerable American fastfood institutions have begun to take into consideration local tastes and preferences. Throughout the Philippines, for instance, McDonald's recently introduced *longaniza* (Spanish-style pork sausages) and fried rice for breakfast. In Singapore, spicy *rendang* burgers — although hardly Burger King's bread and butter — do very well, while Pizza Hut restaurants in Hongkong allow its customers to create their own pizza Chinese-style which amounts to a concoction no self-respecting Italian would dare call "pizza."

Perhaps because the love for food is the same in any language and because tastebuds are easily manipulated (KFC Malaysia introduced its "hot and crispy" recipe to win over chicken aficionados who felt their traditional recipe too bland for these parts), fast food is probably the most successful foreign franchise in Asia. Both franchisors and franchisees of such companies as Wendy's, Pizza Hut or Shakey's, say they have had very little trouble transplanting their operations in the region.

Although franchising success in Asia is often associated with household names, this, too, is slowly changing. Entrepreneurs are queuing up for smaller, homegrown franchises whose most obvious advantages are lower costs and less exorbitant royalty fees. Service oriented franchises are a case in point.

While borrowing Western franchise concepts, a large number carry local names and are largely indigenous. Launderettes and shoe repair stores are two examples. Shoe-repair stores found their way to Asia in the early and mid-'80s, replacing the itinerant cobbler in the suburban Philippines or the odd shoesmith and shoe shine boy that one could find on either end of the Harbour in Hongkong in the '70s. Nowadays, service shops like Mister Minit in Singapore, or Mr. Quickie in the Philippines allow you to have your shoes shined and repaired while you wait, sitting gingerly on high stools in flimsy leather slippers three sizes too large.

Franchising in Asia

In Asia, franchising is still in its infancy. Few figures exist to quantify franchising's impact on the region, but Tan Thuan Seng of the Singapore

International Franchise Association (SIFA) estimates that in Singapore — where the majority of franchises are master franchises — franchising accounts for 3.5% of the island-state's GNP.

Already a whole range of homegrown companies are starting to give the more established foreign companies a run for their money. In the Philippines, world-famous McDonald's is scrambling to catch up with Jollibee Foods Corporation. Jollibee has a 57% share of the local hamburger market — by contrast, McDonald's has only 25% — and is the largest fast food restaurant chain in the Philippines with close to US$38 million in sales as well as a secure place in the nation's Top 50 Corporations — the first and only fastfood chain to win that distinction.

Jollibee operates 117 stores, 26 of which are company-owned. The remaining 91 are franchises which operated under an agreement which provides for the payment of an initial franchise fee and royalty fees equal to a fixed percentage of a particular store's gross sales. In addition, the chain holds five other franchises in Indonesia and Brunei, with plans to open 16 other stores both in the Philippines and abroad before the end of the year.

Since the company went public in June 1993, plans to open additional franchises have been temporarily put on hold. Jollibee's focus, says licensing officer, Lillian Reventar, is to develop more company-owned stores. "We've suspended franchise applications for the time being because although franchisees increase sales and help broaden our consumer base, management feels that the company has sufficient resources to expand operations on its own," Reventar says.

One example of a western franchise which has done spectacularly well in Asia is Pizza Hut Hongkong, owned by the Jardine Group and a Marketing Management winner of the Asian Management Awards. Unlike most entrepreneurs who own the odd store here or there and whose entire life savings are sometimes sunk into one store (in Jollibee's case, a franchise requires from US$370,000–$500,000. Rival McDonald's requires US$300,000–$500,000), Jardine Pacific is into franchising in a big way. Having identified restaurants and food service as a growth business early on, Jardine has acquired the master franchise for Pizza Hut in Taiwan, Sizzler, a "steak-seafood-salad" chain in Australia, and Taco Bell in Hawaii. At present, the company now oversees more than 260 restaurants and fastfood outlets in the Asia-Pacific region.

From Hongkong, Jardine Pacific controls Pizza Hut franchises in Canada, Hawaii, Guam, Taiwan, Macau and Australia. With its 50 Pizza Hut franchises in Hawaii, Jardine Pacific easily dominates the local pizza market.

In Malaysia, Kentucky Fried Chicken is probably the country's most successful franchisor. The local franchise is owned by KFC Holdings Bhd., a publicly-listed company on the Kuala Lumpur Stock Exchange which, at last count, runs a chain of over 110 KFC restaurants throughout Peninsular and

East Malaysia.

KFC Holdings' sales are $39 million and return on sales is a staggering 9.4%. By contrast, McDonald's, its closest competitor, can only claim 1% return on sales.

In many ways, KFC Malaysia is vastly more successful than its franchisor in the United States. Judging by the company's numerous innovations in both products and marketing efforts, the KFC Malaysia experience is a classic example of technology transfer in reverse. Not one to submerge its innovativeness, the company recently introduced so-called "second generation restaurants," scaled-down versions of fastfood outlets especially designed for locations in semi-urban areas with smaller populations. It also introduced mobile restaurants known as "Meals on Wheels." The concept its currently taking hold in other countries where KFC holds franchises.

Something for almost everyone

"The good thing about franchising," says one housewife who owns a Smokey's Sausage World trailer stationed at a petrol station near her home, "is that it works for everybody. Franchising is an option for someone like me who has a little extra money to spend, good business sense and a bit of time on her hands. But it is also a viable venture for huge conglomerates who are looking to diversify their business holdings."

For many, like this housewife, the traditional advantages of franchising — a proven system, extensive research and training (a McDonald's franchise applicant anywhere in the world is required to attend a 10-day to four-week training session at the company's Hamburger University in Illinois), and an established identity, are enough to convince entrepreneurs that franchising is a solid concept.

And for the most part, it is. It's been known to fail however — as most things — when the franchisee or the franchisor enter an agreement with their eyes closed. For instance, a growing number of franchisees these days are former company executives who, tired of the rigors of corporate life, have chosen to do it on their own. Often, says Miguel Zosa, the man largely responsible for bringing the California-based Pollo Loco and Round Table Pizza franchises to the Philippines, these executives are convinced that their considerable business experience automatically makes them good franchisees.

Not so. "They don't realize," he says, "the amount of work that goes into opening a franchise. They don't realize that in the beginning at least, they have to be everything — janitor, patty-maker, accountant."

"Unlike working in a company where there are always other people to fall back on, a franchise's success," says Zosa, "is almost always equal to the franchisee's efforts and determination. Although you are given a blueprint on how to run a business, you're ultimately on your own."

A caveat for the entrepreneurial

Reventar of Jollibee says, "Some franchisees think that by opening one of our restaurants they are leaving behind a world in which they were constantly dictated upon. What they don't realize is that they aren't entirely escaping this sort of life. Because what you're essentially paying for when you buy a franchise is a *proven system*, one that doesn't allow for too much deviation." To get around the problem of feeling restricted, one management magazine suggests that all rugged, highly-individualistic types who enjoy conquering new ground, make a bee-line for service oriented franchises or lesser-known franchises rather than mature fast food chains, where there is less room to maneuver.

Nevertheless, at the top of many a franchisor's wish-list for the ideal prospective franchisee is "entrepreneurial spirit." The McDonald's prospectus for franchisees, for example, lists this qualification ahead of other such qualities as "a strong business background" and "people-handling skills."

It takes two

A franchisor can also make serious miscalculations. For instance, Taco Bell made the mistake of entering the Philippines in 1983 when the national economy was beset with a deepening recession. The chain's owners and franchisees also misjudged local tastes. Having become more cosmopolitan in terms of cuisine only in the last decade, Filipinos then weren't quite ready to indulge wholesale in tacos, burritos and tamales. In Singapore, franchises that have failed for similar reasons include Wendy's, Baskin-Robbins and Blue Rooster. Says Tan Thuan Seng, "I attribute their failure to a combination of factors: inadequate investment and managerial commitment on the part of the franchisees as well as the lack of willingness of the franchisor to adjust to local market taste or cultural requirements."

It is also important to keep in mind, says Reventar, that when franchising does succeed, it is a shared success. Franchisors sometimes believe their franchisees succeed because of what the franchisor has done — that the franchise's success is a result of years research, routinized operating procedures and management services only *they* can offer.

On the other hand, the franchisee may "fall into the trap of believing that his franchise has succeeded in spite of the franchisor." (*Entrepreneur*, April 1993) Says one franchisee, "It's so easy to forget that it was the franchisor that brought you into the business in the first place. I used to resent having to issue royalty cheques because I thought, well, it's *my* hard work and energy that's gone into this business. When I feel this way, I try to remind myself why I got into franchising in the first place. Which, of course, is for the relative security it offers. My franchise is successful because of the franchisor's existing quality control systems, training programs and rigorous market research as well as other support services such as advertising."

Says Reventar, "We treat franchisees as our clients and provide them everything we feel they need, from developing systems and corporate staff to providing them forms that may be useful in meeting production targets. We work everything out with them to the last detail and most importantly, we see the franchise in terms of a partnership. And at the end of the day, it is essentially that. Our franchisees are helping us expand and we are giving them the chance to succeed with limited capital and know-how."

Although there is plenty of room for conflict in franchising, both franchisors and franchisees agree that franchising will continue to be a vital economic force not just in the United States, but in Asia, where newly-prosperous entrepreneurs are finding franchising a viable and extremely attractive concept.

Regulation

In the Philippines, where laws governing technology transfer arrangements are now less restrictive than ever before, new franchisors are likely to join the ranks of the 20 existing franchises registered with the Bureau of Patents Trademarks and Technology Transfer (BPTTT). Leo G. Dominguez, a Filipino lawyer with the law firm Quisumbing, Torres & Evangelista and an authority on the legal aspects of franchising, says that under the new laws, foreign franchisors will have greater incentive to set up shop in the Philippines.

"Under the new amendments governing technology transfer arrangements, franchisors are guaranteed royalties of 5%. Previously, the payment of royalties could not exceed 1–2% of a franchise's gross sales. Industry norms elsewhere in the region are much higher."

Another plus, says Dominguez, is government's decision to extend the maximum allowable term of technology transfer arrangements to 10 years, from the previous five years as well as its efforts to establish clearer guidelines. At present, licensing and distributor agreements, often resulting in royalty disputes, because royalty payments are only permitted under franchising agreements.

Singapore, which now has 30 different foreign franchisees in the food industry alone, has no specific franchise legislation. Says SIFA president Tan Thuan Seng, "All franchising activity is regulated by the Singapore Companies Act. And because Singapore believes in a free market, we have no restrictions on foreign ownership or payments of franchise fees, which makes us more attractive to franchisors who shy away from Thailand and Indonesia whose governments promote policies restricting foreign ownership in the retail trade."

A new maturity

The new retail environment will be far more complex, competitive and uncertain. For many, franchising offers a formula that is tried and tested. For an entrepreneur reflecting the uncertain and fragmented character of the future enterprise landscape, the franchising format that can best assure an enterprise's survival. Once an upstart industry, franchising is on its way to attaining a hard-won maturity.

WHY FOOD?

Among all the obvious franchising industries — ranging from service-oriented businesses to automotive products, the food industry has cash tills ringing up and down practically every major Asian city. Judging by robust sales figures, franchisors and franchise operators are on a roll.

Why then does food provide such attractive opportunities for franchisors? Part of the answer lies in changing demographics. A quick look at fastfood these days easily tells you just who is buying. Certainly, a younger Asian population (in contrast to the growing "grey market" in West Europe) and accelerated urbanization have helped the burgeoning food industry. Asians today are richer and have more leisure time than they did two decades ago.

Another factor is simply the unrelenting demand for what many consider a basic need. The fastfood format provides customers essential nourishment (although doctors, parents and the health-conscious may dispute this) at affordable prices in convenient and attractive settings.

In 1991, Filipinos spent close to US$18.5 billion on food alone, representing more than half of total household expenses for the year — proof enough that a stable and extremely lucrative market exists. For many food franchises, the potential for growth is there too, beckoning in the mid-distance.

Statistics show that the annual food intake of the average Asian is considerably lower than his American or western counterpart. For instance, while the Filipino consumes 3–4 kilos of chicken or beef a year, his twin across the Pacific consumes at least 36 kilos. And while a Filipino will drink close to 16 liters of softdrinks a year, an American will easily pour 75 liters down the hatch. Given a growing penchant for things American, fastfood franchisors are hoping that the average Asian will be up to the challenge of narrowing the East-West consumption gap.

What it costs in the Philippines

Greenwich (Pizza)	P1.5 million
Chow King (Chinese)	P3.5–4.5 million
Shakey's Pizza	P7.5–8 million
Jollibee	P12 million
McDonald's	P14–15 million

(Figures were provided by the companies concerned.)

FRANCHISING WITH YOUR EYES OPEN

Be knowledgeable. It should go without saying that the potential franchisee must thoroughly evaluate and investigate the various companies under consideration. Some of the things to pay extra careful attention to? Apart from scrutinizing the franchise agreement, ("Read carefully and take nothing for granted," says Smokey's Sausage World Franchisee.) Evaluate the company's promises to you as the franchisee vs. actual historical performance. Consider the demographics of the particular market area. Potential franchisees who approach Jollibee's licensing officer, Lillian Reventar, often own choice real estate. Apart from interviewing prospects, Reventar's job is to determine and evaluate whether the site will attract substantial customer traffic.

Be aware of your own strengths and weaknesses. Mike Zosa says, "Any aspiring franchisee should examine his own strengths and weaknesses. Does he have the drive to make the franchise work? Is he willing to work within the system, without trying to modify or improve the franchise? "Franchising", Zosa says, "requires a different kind of entrepreneur, one who is willing to curb his own business instincts and accept the professional guidance — everything from operations to marketing techniques — that franchisors have to offer." Any individual considering taking out a franchise, says one owner of a small Dunkin' Donut outlet in a Manila suburb, "should do a personal audit or inventory on his personal strengths and weaknesses." This leads to the corollary:

Be sure you have adequate working capital. Inadequate working capital is a common reason for business failure. A source book for franchise opportunities says it better, "Never underestimate the period needed before you achieve breakeven. Always be realistic about the potential need for additional funds." Jose P. Pardo, president of Philippine Seven Properties Corporation, a company which awards franchises for Wendy's hamburger restaurants and 7-Eleven convenience stores, considers access to capital one of the most important qualities required of prospective franchise holders.

Comparative success rate: franchised businesses vs. independent businesses

	Franchised Businesses	Independent Businesses
After 1st year of business	97%	62%
After 5th year in business	92%	23%
After 10th year in business	90%	18%

* Bond, Robert E., *The Source Book of Franchise Opportunities*, Dow Jones-Irwin, (Illinois, 1988).

18 Nihon-Mart

Louise do Rosario

A Wal-Mart of Japan? The idea is not as for-fetched as it once seemed. Discount houses are challenging established retailers as the Japanese become more price conscious.

In Kashiwa, a densely populated suburb of Tokyo, Japanese tradition is under siege. Here, Japan's top retailer — Sogo, Marui, Takashimaya and Ito-yokado — and dozens of small, family-run shops have co-existed happily for decades in a prime shopping area near the train station.

But today Kashiwa's cosy business community faces a challenge. Matsumo tokiyoshi, a discount pharmaceutical chain, has built in its midst a five-storey Home Centre selling everything from cosmetics to golf clubs — and at prices 30–40% below those of its competitors.

"Our rivals have seen sales drop by 20–30% since the Home Centre was opened in 1990," says Takeo Oki, a spokesman for the chain. The evidence behind Oki's figures is anecdotal, but he keeps a sharp eye on the competition. "Look," he says, "people are just window-shopping in the department stores. They're not buying, because the goods are too expensive."

Matsumotokiyoshi is among the hundreds of discount stores in Japan that at waging — and winning — a price war against traditional retailers. Thanks partly to deregulation and partly to increasingly price-conscious consumers, discounters now form Japan's fastest-growing retail sector. That is good news for price-conscious shoppers, but a threat to the decades-old and carefully controlled network of manufacturers and distributors whose collusion and inefficiencies make Japanese retail prices the world's highest.

It is also good news for foreign companies trying to penetrate the Japanese market: the bigger discounters are sourcing directly from overseas, bypassing the byzantine domestic distribution system. Foreign producers stand to profit

Reproduced with permission from *Far Eastern Economic Review*, (16 September 1993), pp. 62–64.

further: Japanese consumers, like their US counterparts, are growing accustomed to discounted imports — belying the long-held protectionist argument that Japanese tastes value lavish service and high quality above competitive prices.

Matsumotokiyoshi was an unimpressive concern until it began to discount aggressively back in 1985. Since then, sales have grown by double digits annually. In the year to 31 March, revenue surged 29%, the fastest growth among any of Japan's drug retailers.

Recession may be dogging other businesses, but not discounters. According to a survey by *Nikkei Ryutsu Shimbun* (Distribution News), a specialist publication, sales growth among the sector's top 134 concerns averaged 9.5% in the 12 months to 31 March 1992, the latest year for which figures are available.

Kawachiya, a discount liquor chain in metropolitan Tokyo, is doing so well that "during weekends we have to shut the gates of our shops to limit the number of customers," says chairman Yukio Higuchi. By contrast, sales by department stores and supermarkets have hit new lows every month since early 1991.

While these established names are busy cutting costs, discounters are opening new shops, advertising themselves variously as "wholesale clubs," "home centres," and "DIY" (do-it-yourself) outlets. Mr Max, which claims to be the Wal-Mart of Kyushu (in southern Japan), plans to open half a dozen new outlets next year. Marutomi, which runs small discount stores selling shoes, toys and apparel, is to add 260 stores next year to the 1,608 it already has.

Deregulation partly explains the proliferation. Amendments to the Large-Scale Retail Law in the late 1980s made it easier to open bigger shops. Even for foreigners: Toys 'R' Us, the US discount retailer, has opened six outlets in Japan since 1989. With floor space averaging 3,000 square metres, Toys 'R' Us outlets are many times larger than the typical Japanese retailer, and they undersell the competition by 10–20%.

But Japan's three-year-old recession is also responsible. Consumers are more price-conscious now than during the booming 1980s. "There is so much excess inventory around," says Victoria Melendez, a retail specialist for Jardine Fleming Securities.

And while Japanese exporters bemoan the surging yen, discounters smile. The *Endaka*, as the strong yen is known here, simply lowers the price of their imports. Free from the ossified cost structures that bind their competitors, discounters are freer to pass the savings on to consumers. Prices of American beer, French bags and Italian apparel, to name several conspicuous examples, have fallen 20–30%, in recent months.

"The potential for discounters is enormous," says Melendez. Discount stores account for a mere 1.8% of Japan's total retail sales, compared with 13.5% in the US. "The retail discount industry is still in its infancy in Japan, like the US in the 1960s," she says.

Thirty years ago, Wal-Mart and K-Mart were setting up their first outlets. Today, both are discount giants, something Japan has yet to produce. Japan's biggest discounter, Daikuma, posted sales of only ¥162 million (US$1.5 million), a fraction of the average department store's volume.

But Japan's discounters have already created upheaval in the country's complex distribution system. Their first victims are manufacturers, who for decades have enjoyed high margins by keeping prices fixed, uniform and high. Their technique is the old carrot-and-stick approach: manufacturers provide retailers with rebates and other incentives to participate in the system of controlled prices, but refuse to ship to those who do not.

By opting for price autonomy and abandoning the low-risk support system provided by manufacturers, discounters disrupt the whole game. Buying in bulk and dispensing with elaborate wrapping and other services, they pass their savings directly to consumers. The trade-off is austerity. Discount shops typically employ small staffs; customers get little attention but enjoy bargain prices.

"There are now retailers who say 'we don't need the fat margins because we are meaner and leaner and are willing to take 20–30% off the standard price'," says Larry Blagg, who heads the distribution committee of the American Chamber of Commerce.

One such retailer is Kawachiya, the liquor chain. In July it started selling cosmetics, at a discount of 20–30%. Chairman Higuchi says Shiseido, Japan's leading cosmetics maker, offered to pay his company ¥120 million a year as a "public-relations fee" in return for maintaining Shiseido's "suggested retail prices." He refused, and Shiseido has stopped shipment to his chain. The Fair Trade Commission, regarded by many as a toothless watchdog, is investigating the case.

To be sure, discounters face some formidable competition, particularly in markets dominated by a handful of manufacturers — high-end electronics and cosmetics, for example. Fortunately for discounters, however, the number of manufacturers who can dictate pricing terms as easily as Shiseido is dwindling. Small makers of apparel, cameras, toys, toiletries and low-end electrical appliances have succumbed to the increased purchasing power of the discounters.

And manufacturers are not the only ones under threat. Discounters bypass the numerous layers of wholesalers, the middlemen who push paper, add costs and make Japan's distribution sector among the world's most inefficient. Chiba-based Step, buying directly from the US processor, retails coffee at about ¥118 per 100 grams, half the price of domestically processed coffee.

"As prices go down, some commodities will no longer be attractive to marginal distributors who can only survive in a controlled system," says Blagg,

Tradition-Bound
How they compare; retail patterns in Japan and the US
(1991)

	% of total sales	
	Japan	US
All discount stores	3.1	13.5
Full-line discounters	1.5	7.7
Specialty discounters	1.6	2.1
Warehouse clubs	—	2.1
Off-price & catalogue showrooms	—	1.6
Department stores	9.9	13.8
Superstores	8.3	22.0
Others	78.7	50.7

Source: Jardine Fleming Securities

of the American Chamber, who also represents several US food concerns in Japan. "There will be a consolidation, and the small guys will be absorbed."

The small guys include 1.6 million mom-and-pop shops which sell everything from groceries to toys. Once the backbone of the manufacturer-controlled system, these shops are dwindling in number because of severe competition and a dearth of young people willing to carry on the business.

Specialty discounters, costing less to open and offering fewer product types, are "filling the vacuum created by the small shops very quickly," says Jardine Fleming's Melendez. For example, the number of Marutomi's discount shoe stores grew 45% between 1988 and 1991, while the number of small, family-run shoe stores fell by 7.9%.

"Any retailer that does not cut costs fast enough will lose out to another," says Toshiko Binder, a retail specialist at S. G. Warburg Securities. Even established department stores, with their prime locations, have to adapt fast to cut-throat competition increasingly shaped by discounters. "Department stores should consolidate and move upmarket. They can't sell air-conditioners or fridges in the expensive Ginza area when a discounter is offering the same products," she says. Supermarkets are fighting back too, launching private brands and special sales for cheap imports, ranging from beef to orange juice.

The biggest winner in this retail shake-up is the Japanese consumer, whose purchasing patterns have changed greatly in the last few years. "The mistrust over high prices is very strong now, and this is just the beginning," says Binder. "In the past, Japanese consumers said prices were high because of this and that reason. They were passive and not discriminating."

Discrimination, however, means the erosion of brand loyalty. "When I first came to Japan 10 years ago," says Blagg, "Japanese were very brand-conscious. Today, they are brand-switchers. People are saying 'We don't need the perfect product any more.' They are returning to the basics." Adds Kiyoshi Kuniyuki, vice-president of Matsumotokiyoshi: "Young customers don't care whether it's Shiseido cosmetics or not; the most important thing to them is price."

In the long run, though, discounters will need more than low prices to survive. Many of them are small, thinly capitalised and poorly managed. "About 20% of the newcomers go bankrupt each year," says Mamoru Takayama, a managing director of the Tokyo-based Institute of Distribution Research. Without economies of scale, cost control is a top priority. Matsumotokiyoshi, for example, has seen management costs rise from 19.4% of sales in September 1990 to 20.6% in March 1993.

Small discounters also suffer from irregular supplies — often excess and outdated inventory from large retailers or other second-hand sources. "It doesn't work if you sometimes have the product and sometimes you don't," says Hideo Amemiya, a retail specialist at *Nikkei Ryutsu Shimbun.*

Manufacturers can make supplies hard to come by. Kawachiya cannot secure local supplies of liquor for its new store in Yamanashi, which is two hours by train from Tokyo. Local breweries are boycotting Kawachiya, so it must buy supplies from the capital.

Perhaps the biggest challenge to discounters is competition among themselves. Retail conglomerates like Daiei and Ito Yokado are muscling into the discounting business, forcing out smaller concerns. Daiei has just built a so-called wholesale club and factory outlet in Kobe, offering discounts as large as 90%.

ONLY IN JAPAN

Japan's big retailers may be struggling, but you wouldn't know it looking at Toto, the country's largest seller of toilet equipment. Its secret: the "washlet." Developed by Toto, the washlet features, among other things, a user-controlled stream of water to do what more primitive cultures still accomplish with mere toilet paper.

Frivolous perhaps, but the washlet remains a recession-beater. "Let's face it. You still need to wash your bottom no matter what happens to the economy," says Toto spokesman Yuji Watanabe.

Toto, which commands 60% of Japan's washlet market, expects sales to grow by 10% in 1993 — no small feat in a land piled high with unsold consumer goods. "We think the market can eventually accommodate 2 million units a year, half-a-million more than now," says Watanabe. The washlet accounts for 10% of Toto's sales.

The washlet's success demonstrates how technology and clever marketing can transform mere gadgetry into an indispensable household item. The washlet is essentially a detachable toilet seat with control panels for easy manipulation while sitting on the toilet. Touch a button, and a small nozzle extends. One can adjust both the position and the intensity of the water. Other functions include warming the toilet seat and drying the user.

Outsiders may laugh — and so may Toto. The washlet is becoming a common feature of Japanese homes. "Toto created the market," says Eve Gordon Anderson, a marketing manager for American Standard, a leading US toilet maker. "It promotes the idea that to be a really clean and good person, you need to use a washlet. Once you've created that need, everybody wants it. It's like flossing your teeth."

"People told us that once they have tried the product in the toilets of hotels or offices, they want one for their home. It's a habit that can't be dropped easily," says Watanabe. At ¥100,000–140,000 (US$950–1,330) each, the washlet costs as much as a short overseas holiday.

As with many other products popular in Japan, the washlet originated in the US, where the "super toilet," a modified bidet, was developed mainly for use in hospitals (if flopped with consumers). Toto imported the first super toilet in 1964, marketing it as the "washing air seat." Says Watanabe: "The early models broke down very easily and were not too safe."

In the 1980s, Toto replaced the awkward wiring with computer chips, an improvement that came just in time for the 1980s consumption boom. The housing explosion helped too, as property buyers equipped new homes with fancy installations.

Why is the washlet popular in Japan but not elsewhere? One answer may be Japan's fondness for electronic products. But tradition is also a factor. Because most Japanese apartments still lack central heating, toilet-seat and dining-table warmers are already common. A user-friendly toilet seems only a natural extension — particularly for a nation so obsessed with cleanliness.

Toto, a 76-year-old manufacturer of sanitary ware, promotes the washlet not by heavy advertising but by making it as convenient as possible to use. With an easy-to-attach top, the user simply removes the old toilet seat without replacing the entire toilet.

And the next generation of washlets will look positively sleek, eliminating the bulky panels that house the electronics. Meanwhile, Toto is selling a new washlet with a deodoriser and another that measures urine content.

19 The Challenge of Global Communications in the Pan Asian Market Decision Heuristics for Advertising Operations

Charles Y. Yang

Four aspects of advertising operations are essential for marketing communications to be fully globalized — product, product concept, advertising message, and media. Five cases ranging from no-order globalization (DHL Courier Services) to full-scale globalization (XO Cognac) are illustrated. Based on the analysis of these cases, some rules-of-thumb can be used to assist marketing management as to when and how to globalize their advertising. Included in the list are such guidelines as the product itself being the easiest item to globalize, that the functional message and particularly the symbolic message are difficult to unify, and that the target market must be tightly defined to utilize global media.

The launching of the Asia satellite TV system in 1991 has made adoption of global communications in Asia a realistic goal. With five channels available to advertisers, in addition to three Japanese channels already in operation, exposure to global media has increased dramatically. The effective use of such advertising opportunities, however, hinges on how well advertisers can globalize the product itself, the concept behind the product, the product's communication message, as well as how the message can be transmitted via these global media.

The heuristics of globalization in marketing communications

Globalization of marketing communications is neither a catch-all term nor a magic word. Its many facets must be understood and application modes developed before the term becomes meaningful to executives of multinational corporations. Through case illustrations these different dimensions of global communications are shown and subsequently offer some useful guidelines for advertising operations.

Reproduced with permission from *The Singapore Marketer*, 1 (November 1993), pp. 21–23.

For marketing communications to be fully globalized, four aspects of advertising operations must be fully operationalized. These aspects, when fully realized, encompass a globally identical *product* with a globally acceptable *product concept* having a globally unified *advertising message* that can be transmitted via global *media*. In general, these four phases of operation run in a hierarchical order. The degree of globalization, therefore, hinges on the extent to which these dimensions are fulfilled in advertising operations.

Five cases are used to illustrate globalization which runs from zero-order, where none of the aforementioned phases is being realized, to full-scale globalization, in which all the conditions are fully met.

CASE 1
Zero-order globalization: DHL Courier Services

Product	Product Concept	Advertising Message	Media
x	x	x	x

When DHL's advertising agency in Japan was considering the possibility of a joint advertising campaign for Taiwan and Japan, it raised the basic question of whether such an operation was feasible. Furthermore, in the future, it would be ideal to be able to come up with a global campaign for the Pan Asian market.

While DHL in Taiwan offered excellent courier services which are backed up by a system of monitoring and tracing, the scope of services offered is quite different from that in Japan, where the company offered, in addition to all the services available in Taiwan, a sophisticated logistic planning service.

Consequently, the product concepts in the two countries were also different. While the concept in Taiwan centred on "product care", the concept of "total planning" was being used in Japan. Furthermore, in some areas of the Pan Asian market where communication and computer facilities were less adequate for monitoring operations, the product concept still remained "world-wide delivery network".

The difference in the product concepts in Japan and Taiwan also led to the necessity of adopting different advertising messages. In contrast to "problem solving" for Japan, the message in Taiwan would still have to emphasize "reliability of delivery".

This is a case in which diverse product features made it impractical to globalize the product, the product concept, and the advertising message, not to mention the use of global media.

CASE 2
First-order globalization: Honda's new civic

Product	Product Concept	Advertising Message	Media
o	x	x	x

The new Civic was launched in the fall of 1991 in Japan and Australia, and in May of 1992 in Taiwan. Its sporty styling, fuel economy, high performance, and safety features are present in all the models launched in the three markets. The product concepts that have been developed in these markets are, however, quite different. In Japan, the concept of "two-couple car" was introduced to emphasize the roominess that is generally absent in most economy-type sedans. This led to an advertising message depicting enjoyment of social life among young couples. Thus, the concept of "from enjoyment of having to enjoyment of doing" was established.

In Australia, however, a product concept of "benchmark car" was advanced to emphasize the new standards set for a family sedan. That is, the new Civic set new standards in every respect (performance, safety, comfort, etc.) for this class of cars. The advertising message was then tuned to this theme with the slogan: "A revolution is coming".

In Taiwan, "revolution" was not only out of the question because of political sensitivities, but also because the basic concept of a benchmark car was abandoned in favour of safety and environmental concern. Thus, a concern for safe driving and the environment was emphasized. This product concept led to an advertising message that stresses a fusion of personal happiness with social concern.

The Honda Civic case demonstrates a situation in which the product can be made global, but the product concept and the advertising message have to be geared to local situations. Since the advertising message cannot be unified, the use of global media would also not be possible.

CASE 3
Second-order globalization: NEC mobile phone

Product	Product Concept	Advertising Message	Media
o	o	x	x

NEC has developed the smallest mobile phone. It weighs only 22g and measures 215mm in width, so it can be conveniently tucked into a suit pocket or carried in a lady's handbag. The product was simultaneously launched in Japan, Taiwan, and Hongkong. Since the product was manufactured in Japan, the same quality standard was maintained for all the markets. The product concept was also kept global because of its uniqueness as the smallest and the lightest available on the market.

The advertising message, however, was varied to fit into the lifestyles of target consumers in each country. Since this generation of mobile phone was likely to attract a younger socially active target in Japan, a communication theme was developed to project a chic image of the product. In Taiwan and Hongkong, however, the practical aspect of the product was brought forward instead, particularly for a business lifestyle, since businessmen were selected as the main target.

In this case the product and the product concept are both global, but the communication messages are geared to the local settings and therefore, global application to both the advertising message and media would not be practical.

CASE 4
Third-order globalization: Carlton cigarettes

Product	Product Concept	Advertising Message	Media
o	o	o	x

Carlton brand of cigarettes is known to have the lowest nicotine and tar contents among all the cigarettes that are available on the Pan Asian market. Naturally, there is no need to alter this distinct product quality locally. The product concept based on low risk in smoking is also universal and requires no modification.

Although advertising execution may be allowed to vary somewhat from country to country, its basic theme of being light in comparison to other brands remains unified for all the countries the product is being marketed. Thus, the opportunity for a full-scale globalization does exist were it not for the fact that global media is not likely to offer needed cost efficiency, since the target for the cigarettes appears to be spread out thinly across all the vehicles of global media. In other words, the best media selection can at most cover only a small fraction of the total target.

CASE 5
Full-order globalization: XO Cognac

Product	Product Concept	Advertising Message	Media
o	o	o	o

This is a case where the product, its concept and advertising message can all be unified, while the use of global media is not economically justified.

XO Cognac is perhaps the most preferred alcoholic beverage among Chinese with high incomes. It has just the required snob appeal for those who wish to identify with upscale society. The product itself for any given brand, Hennessy for instance, is identical everywhere, and its concept is generally represented by a symbol of success. With a touch of sex appeal, the advertising message can be developed to project a successful man in either a business or social setting. In this case both the product concept and advertising message can be made global. Furthermore, there are sufficient opportunities for the product to be exposed to the well-defined target (i.e., Chinese with high incomes who can usually understand English, and who prefer to play golf in their leisure time) via such international media as Time Asia edition, Asia Magazine, STAR TV's Prime Time Sports Channel, and STAR TV's Chinese language station financial reports.

This case demonstrates the type of product for which full scale globalization of marketing communications is possible for the Pan Asian market.

Heuristic rules of globalization in advertising

An examination of the above cases offers an opportunity to draw some useful guidelines for advertising operations. The rules of thumb are as follows:

1 The *product* itself is the easiest item to be globalized. Product modification seems unnecessary unless there is a significant difference in either purchasing power, demographic or geographical backgrounds. For example, local version of VTR without recording feature.

2 Since the *product concept* is generally linked to the prevailing consumption experience in each market, globalization would be difficult if there is a variation in such experiences. For example, Halls as a quick remedy for sore throats or as a refreshment candy.

3 Generally speaking, the lower levels on the Maslow hierarchy of consumer motives offer a better opportunity for globalizing the *product concept*, since the concept is likely to be functional in nature and is linked more directly to the product features. For example, "Attack" concentrated detergent marketed by Kao.

4 *Advertising message* is greatly influenced by personalities, lifestyles and cultural backgrounds of consumers in different countries, and is therefore far more difficult to globalize. For example, IBM's use of Chaplin in "Modern Times".

5 In general, the *functional message* is less difficult to unify except for the language barrier. While an image message might avoid such a barrier, it may encounter psychological obstacles in a different country. For example, VW's black humour.

6 A *symbolic message* is the most difficult one to globalize because of its cultural roots. For example, Japanese symbols of boys and girls.

7 The corporate image campaign for a multinational company is most suited for a full-scale globalization. For example, NEC corporate ad.

8 To utilize *global media*, the target must be tightly defined in terms of language, income, as well as readership and program preferences of the target consumers in the countries to be covered. For example, Hennessy XO Cognac.

Looking forward

There are three factors which will impact the globalization of marketing communications in the coming years. First, value perceptions and lifestyles of consumers in the Pan Asian market are becoming more similar as a result of rising standards of living and increased cross-cultural contacts. Second, the cost of advertising production has sky-rocketed to the level that advertises are compelled to consider cost sharing among different countries. Finally, the increase in the number of intercountry media has made globalization a realistic goal.

As the 21st century draws nearer, the challenge will be to make advertising operations relevant to the new environment in the Pacific Rim.

CHARLES Y. YANG is Chairman of H & Y Communications System and Advisor of Hakuhodo, Inc.

20 Content Analysis of Major Mass Media Advertising in the United States, Japan, South Korea and China

Charles F. Keown, Laurence W. Jacobs, and Kyung-Il Ghymn

Approximately 50 television, 30 radio, 30 magazine, and 30 newspaper ads were content analyzed from each of four countries: United States, Japan, South Korea, and China. Specifically, the items analyzed were type of product advertised, intent and basic strategy of the ad, length, format, music, announcer and cast, product information, price citations, and informational content. Differences were found among countries, leading to the conclusion that most advertising has not been globally standardized in the countries under study.

Introduction

The basic objective of this research was to compare and contrast television, radio, newspaper and magazine advertising in three Asian countries. Advertising in Japan, South Korea and China (People's Republic of China) was compared with the United States. Such cross-cultural relationships have both academic and pragmatic value to marketing academicians and advertising practitioners.

Advertising appeals among countries may vary from mood or image designs to a straightforward presentation of facts. The types of products frequently advertised in certain media may change from country to country. Advertising executions can vary in time or size, primary intent and basic strategy.

This pilot study utilizes content analysis as its primary tool. This technique has been widely used in advertising research (Kassarjian 1977, Wheeler 1988). Due to the number of issues that can be addressed by content analysis, most research has focused on specific topics, with information content being the most popular topic. Studies have reported advertising appeals (Mueller 1987), role stereotyping of women (Courtney and Lockhertz 1971), Black minority (Berkman 1963), the elderly (Gantz et al 1980), cultural values (Hong et al

Reproduced with permission from *Asian Journal of Marketing*, 2 (December 1993), pp. 31–43.

1987), time orientation (Gross and Sheth 1989), use of humor (Weinberger and Spotts 1989), and <u>information content (Aaker and Norris 1982</u>, Lackniak 1979 and Madden et al 1986).

Research pertinent to this paper on Asian advertising are studies on Chinese advertising (Rice and Lu 1988, Tse et al 1989, Stewart and Campbell 1986 and 1988), and Japanese advertising (Belk et al 1985, Hong et al 1987, Kishii 1988, Madden et al 1986, Mueller 1987 and 1991). There are no studies in the literature involving content analysis of South Korean advertising.

The present study employs content analysis with a broad focus. Various elements of television, radio, magazine and newspaper ads were assessed. Specifically, the items analyzed were the type of product, intent of ad, format, music, place, persons (voice-over announcer, spokesperson, cast), brand and manufacturer's names, price citations and information content. The results first compare advertising among the four countries, while major differences are highlighted in the conclusions.

Methodology

Television, radio, magazine and newspaper ads were collected in each of the four countries during March 1988, except the American radio ads that were taped in November 1988. All TV ads were recorded during prime time on Friday evening in Japan and South Korea and Thursday evening in the U.S. A video recorder for the Chinese broadcast system was not available, so the Chinese Television Bureau (CCTV) taped one week of prime time ads specifically for this study. Radio ads were taped during prime time on Friday, except in the United States where recording was done during morning and evening weekday drive times.

Copies of leading consumer magazines and newspapers were collected for each country during the same November week. Since Chinese magazines typically contain fewer than four pages of advertising per issue, several magazines were used to provide an adequate sample. Details of the ads from each country are given in Table 1.

Bilingual native speakers (Japanese, Chinese and South Korean graduate students) were used to analyze and code the foreign ads. An American graduate student evaluated the American ads. All coding was done by graduate students, one from each country. A supervisor and a professor of linguistics, both with knowledge of the languages, were used to oversee the coding process.

Each coder watched, listened, or viewed each ad several times to become familiar with the contents. Then a check-list type of code sheet was completed. The coder was able to review the ad as many times as necessary to be sure that the answers were complete. Since many of the areas tested did not require language skills, the American graduate student was able to supervise this data

Table 1 Advertising media by country

	U.S.	Japan	S. Korea	PRC
TELEVISION				
Station	NBC	Fuji	Korean Broad.	CCTV
Time	Thursday pm	Friday pm	Friday pm	One week pm
No. of Ads	44	50	50	50
RADIO				
Station	KHVH	Nippon Radio	Moonwha Broad.	Beijing Radio
Time	drive time	Friday pm	Friday pm	Friday pm
No. of Ads	29	30	23	31
MAGAZINE				
Publication	Reader's Digest	Bungeishunjun	Sin-Dong-A	Popular Cinema and others
No. of Ads	30	30	30	23
NEWSPAPER				
Publication	New York Times	The Yomiori Shinbun	The Chosun Ilbo	People's Daily
No. of Ads	30	30	30	27

collection. A professor of linguistics, who was familiar with all of these languages, was available for coding help. He also spot checked the data for accuracy and consistency.

Each coder was trained in the same method. Individual and group sessions were held to resolve any questions or problems. Each ad was content analyzed using a standardized coding sheet.

Comparison by product, intent and strategy

Product category

As shown in Table 2, the majority of sampled television ads in the United States, Japan and South Korea were for consumer nondurables. In China, however, a large portion of the sampled ads in TV and magazines were for consumer durables. China also had a substantial number of ads for industrial products.

Most radio ads in Japan (73%) and South Korean (74%) were for consumer nondurables, while in the United States there was almost an equal split among consumer durables, nondurables and services. In China, one-third of the ads were for industrial products.

In the United States, Japan and South Korea, consumer nondurables were the most popular product category for magazine advertising; for China, it was

Table 2 Product category

| | Per cent of sampled ads by country | | | |
	U.S.	Japan	S. Korea	PRC
TELEVISION				
Product Category				
consumer durables	37	40	28	48
consumer nondurables	67	60	72	36
consumer services	0	0	0	2
industrial	0	0	0	14
RADIO				
Product Category				
consumer durables	31	27	17	3
consumer nondurables	35	73	74	39
consumer services	34	0	9	26
industrial	0	0	0	32
MAGAZINES				
Product Category				
consumer durables	4	30	33	35
consumer nondurables	83	37	57	26
consumer services	13	33	10	22
industrial	0	0	0	17
NEWSPAPERS				
Product Category				
consumer durables	33	50	27	25
consumer nondurables	43	33	30	15
consumer services	23	17	43	4
industrial	0	0	0	56

consumer durables. Newspaper advertising varied by country. In the U.S. sample, the most-used product category was consumer nondurables; in Japan, consumer durables; in South Korea, consumer services; and in the PRC, industrial goods.

Type of product

Table 3 provides data on the types of products advertised in each country by sampled media. For television, packaged food/beverage was the most popular type of product in all countries, except China. Health and beauty aids also were popular in all countries, except the United States. For radio, health and beauty advertised often.

The type of products advertised in print media is related to the target

Table 3 Type or product

| | Per cent of sampled ads by country | | | |
	U.S.	Japan	S. Korea	PRC
TELEVISION				
Principal types of products				
automobiles	30	14	*	*
clothing	*	*	*	*
health and beauty aids	*	12	22	20
home appliances/furnishings	*	*	12	29
home electronics	*	10	*	12
home and garden	*	*	10	*
jewelry	*	*	*	*
packaged food/beverage	30	44	40	*
restaurant food/beverage	23	*	*	*
services	*	*	*	*
RADIO				
Principal types of products				
automobiles	*	23	*	*
clothing	*	*	*	*
health and beauty aids	21	23	17	16
home appliances/furnishings	17	*	*	26
home electronics	*	*	*	*
home and garden	*	10	*	*
jewelry	*	*	*	*
packaged food/beverage	*	32	*	*
restaurant food/beverage	*	*	*	*
services	35	*	*	*
MAGAZINE				
Principal types of products				
automobiles	*	10	*	17
clothing	*	*	30	*
health and beauty aids	33	10	10	13
home appliances/furnishings	*	*	*	*
home electronics	*	10	10	17
home and garden	*	*	*	*
jewelry	*	10	13	*
packaged food/beverage	43	20	20	*
restaurant food/beverage	*	*	*	*
services	*	*	*	*
NEWSPAPER				
Principal types of products				
automobiles	*	30	*	*
clothing	20	*	17	15
health and beauty aids	10	23	47	*
home appliances/furnishings	*	*	*	*
home electronics	17	3	17	11
home and garden	*	17	*	*
jewelry	*	*	*	*
packaged food/beverage	*	*	*	*
restaurant food/beverage	*	*	*	*
services	*	*	*	*

*Less than 10% of total ads

audience of the specific magazine and newspaper. For this study, the most frequently advertised products were packaged food/beverage (all countries except China), health and beauty aids (all countries), home electronics (all countries except the U.S.), jewelry in Japan and South Korea and clothing in South Korea. For newspapers, health and beauty aids were advertised most often in all countries except China; clothing and home electronics in all countries except Japan.

Primary intent

Obviously advertising is very complicated. Few ads attempt to do only one thing at a time. It has been argued, for example, that every ad is an image ad in that every exposure to the company or product builds an impression in the mind of the customer. Table 4 is an attempt to classify the primary strategies of the advertising when this was possible. The "Other" category was reserved for the ads that the research group (graduate students, research directors and professors) could not classify. These classifications are by primary motive only.

The primary intent of most of the ads studied was, as expected, to encourage purchase at the retail level. That is, relatively few of the ads surveyed were primarily image ads. None of the Chinese ads encouraged mail or phone orders; in China, both the phone system and the mail service preclude this type of distribution. Likewise in Japan, mail and phone ordering is not a major distribution channel. In South Korea, on the other hand, newspaper ads do promote a mail or phone ordering system. In the United States, all media contained some ads for mail or phone orders.

Interestingly, many U.S. ads (20% of newspaper, 14% of radio, 7% of magazine, 0% of television) had "to appreciate merits of firm" as their primary intent. Chinese ads using this same intent were 30% magazine, 19% radio, 8% television and 7% newspaper.

Basic strategy

The basic strategy of television ads in the United States, South Korea and China was dominated by a desire to inform the public of both the existence of the product as well as its attributes. This strategy is also carried into other media. The basic strategy of most Japanese advertising was to inform the consumer of the existence of various products, and not consider information about attributes or function. This reflects the brevity of most Japanese advertising copy. Short radio and television commercials as well as a lack of copy in print ads appear to create this phenomenon.

Table 4 Primary intent of ad and basic strategy

| | Per cent of sampled ads by country | | | |
	U.S.	Japan	S. Korea	PRC
TELEVISION				
Principal intent of ad				
to buy by mail or telephone	2	0	0	0
to buy in retail outlet	96	100	100	92
to appreciate merits of firm	0	0	0	8
other	2	0	0	0
Basic strategy of ad				
inform of existence	40	48	12	41
inform of attributes	47	38	46	47
inform of functions	4	10	36	0
convince by association	2	4	4	0
reminder	7	0	0	0
other	0	0	2	12
RADIO				
Principal intent of ad				
to buy by mail or telephone	3	3	0	0
to buy in retail outlet	62	94	91	52
to appreciate merits of firm	14	0	5	19
other	21	3	4	29
Basic strategy of ad				
inform of existence	10	47	5	7
inform of attributes	38	0	61	32
inform of functions	3	43	22	19
convince by association	3	10	4	0
reminder	5	0	0	0
other	41	0	8	42
MAGAZINES				
Principal intent of ad				
to buy by mail or telephone	7	3	3	0
to buy in retail outlet	83	77	93	61
to appreciate merits of firm	7	0	3	30
other	3	20	1	8
Basic strategy of ad				
inform of existence	20	53	40	26
inform of attributes	60	13	43	22
inform of functions	0	0	13	22
convince by association	3	17	0	0
reminder	0	0	0	0
other	17	17	4	30
NEWSPAPERS				
Principal intent of ad				
to buy by mail or telephone	7	0	20	0
to buy in retail outlet	60	70	50	93
to appreciate merits of firm	20	0	0	7
other	13	30	30	0
Basic strategy of ad				
inform of existence	43	70	40	48
inform of attributes	17	7	3	33
inform of functions	20	3	17	11
convince by association	3	0	3	0
reminder	10	0	0	0
other	7	20	37	8

Length of ads

As shown in Table 5, most American and Chinese television ads sampled were 30 seconds long, while 94% of Japanese ads were only 15 seconds. South Korean ads were about 15 seconds, and half 30 seconds. Many South Korean and Chinese ads did not follow the standard times and varied in length.

Table 5   Length of ads

	Per cent of sampled ads by country			
	U.S.	Japan	S. Korea	PRC
TELEVISION				
0–29 seconds	18	94	44	30
30–59 seconds	80	6	56	70
60 or more seconds	2	0	0	0
RADIO				
0–14 seconds	0	23	5	0
15–29 seconds	3	57	90	26
30–59 seconds	83	13	5	38
60–89 seconds	14	7	0	23
90 or more seconds	0	0	0	13
MAGAZINES				
less than 1 page	0	0	0	0
1 page	93	87	77	100
more than 1 page	7	13	23	0
NEWSPAPERS				
less than 1/2 page	20	60	90	100
1/2–<1 page	53	17	10	0
1 page or more	27	23	0	0

The length of radio ads also varied by country. Most American ads were 30 seconds, most Japanese and South Korean ads were 20 seconds and Chinese ads ranged between 20 and 60 seconds. As with television, there was no standardized time for many South Korean and Chinese radio ads.

Table 5 shows that the Japanese use shorter broadcast ads. This is in marked contrast to the United States where only 18% of television and 3% of radio ads were less than half a minute. The South Korean and the Chinese advertisement length was more in the middle, with the South Korea showing a greater affinity for shorter broadcast ads than the Chinese.

Most of the newspaper ads in all countries were less than one page. The majority of the magazine ads were one page, but the United States, Japan and

South Korea showed examples of advertisers using more than one page advertising (i.e., "spreads").

Comparison of advertising content

Television advertising

Most American (80%) and Chinese (96%) ads dramatized real situations as their basic format. Testimonials were used occasionally in American and Japanese ad formats, but very little in South Korean or the Chinese ads. In contrast, demonstrations were used by most Japanese (80%) and South Korean (70%) advertisers.

Music was used in most ads, and was a major element in American and Japanese ads. By contrast, Chinese and South Korean ads used music for background sound. Jingles were used to a high degree in all but Chinese commercials.

The product was shown in virtually all ads in each country. The advertiser's logo was shown mostly in South Korean (84%) and Japanese (80%) ads, as contrasted with American (57%) and Chinese (29%) ads. The price was given in less than 20% of all TV ads. Prices were quoted in 18% of the Japanese ads, 16% of South Korea, 14% in America and 4% in China. In most instances, price was printed once on-screen toward the end of the ad.

Voice-over announcers (heard but not seen) were used in most ads in all four countries. The gender of the voice-over announcers varied by country: 75% male in the United States, 68% male in South Korea and 55% male in Japan and China.

Celebrity spokespeople (seen and heard) were used in 32% of the Japanese and 9% of the American ads. The balance of TV ads in each country used a cast, ranging from 1 to more than 100 people. The average cast size by country was 4 in South Korea, 5 in Japan, 6 in U.S. and 20 in China. Six Chinese ads used more than 100 people, and two ads had about 50 people.

Informational content of advertising, using Resnik and Stern's (1977) classification system of fourteen information cues, also varied by country (Keown et al 1990). American ads had the highest average number of cues per ad (2.9), followed by Japanese ads (2.1), Chinese (1.9) and South Korean (1.9).

Radio advertising

Radio ad formats also varied by country. In the U.S., 55% of the ads used real situations and 35% of the ads used testimonials. In Japan, 97% of the ads used a testimonial format, while in China 97% of the ads used real situations. In South Korea, 48% of the ads were real situations and 43% were demonstrations.

Table 6 Comparison of electronic media

| | Per cent of total by medium and country* | | | | | | | |
| | Television | | | | Radio | | | |
	U.S.	Japan	S. Korea	PRC	U.S.	Japan	S. Korea	PRC
Format								
real situation	80	34	26	96	55	27	48	97
testimonial	18	24	4	2	35	97	4	0
demonstration	18	80	70	7	0	0	43	4
problem/solution	10	0	8	6	0	0	4	0
interview	0	2	0	0	7	0	17	0
other	2	0	0	0	7	0	17	0
Music								
major element	43	46	8	18	10	40	30	0
background	34	48	70	77	38	40	65	61
jingle	25	26	36	6	20	17	39	3
Product information								
product shown/named	100	100	98	100	100	100	100	99
logo seen/spoken	57	80	84	29	–	–	–	–
price given	14	18	16	4	7	7	0	29
Voice-over announcer								
used	57	74	92	96	88	93	83	94
male	75	55	68	55	83	67	65	71
Spokesperson								
celebrity	9	32	2	0	10	7	4	0
foreigner	2	6	0	0	0	0	0	0
Cast/people								
speak	25	32	50	2	45	26	8	0
no. in cast								
no cast	39	28	10	33	46	70	83	100
1	7	26	26	12	17	20	4	0
2–5	23	30	52	14	31	7	13	0
6–10	11	6	6	8	6	3	0	0
11 or more	20	10	6	33	0	0	0	0
average size	6	5	4	20	2.5	1.7	2.0	0
Informational cues number	2.9	2.1	1.9	1.9	2.7	2.1	1.6	2.0

*Totals may not add to 100% due to multiple response

Music was used as a major ad element in 40% of Japanese radio ads, 30% of South Korean ads and 10% of American ads. None of the Chinese ads used music as a primary feature. There was background music used in 38% of U.S. ads, 40% of Japanese ads, 61% of Chinese ads and 65% of the South Korean ads. Jingles were used frequently in South Korean ads (39% of total ads), but less often in American (20%) and Japanese (17%) ads. Only one Chinese ad (3%) used a jingle.

The product's brand name was cited in virtually all ads. The brand name was typically given two to three times in each ad. Price was quoted in 29% of the Chinese radio ads, and less than 10% of the time in the other three countries.

More than 80% of all radio ads in each country used an announcer (anonymous person rather than an identifiable spokesperson). In all countries most announcers were male. Celebrities were used in 10% of the American radio ads, 7% in the Japanese ads and 4% in the South Korean ads. The Chinese radio commercials did not use celebrities.

Casts were used in all countries, except China. The average cast size was 2.5 persons in the United States, 2.0 in South Korea and 1.7 in Japan.

Information content of radio ads was higher in American (2.7 average number of cues per ad), Japanese (2.1) and Chinese (1.94) ads, than in South Korean (1.6) ads (Keown et al 1990).

Magazine

The majority of headlines in China, South Korea and Japan used plain straightforward language. Many mentioned the product name in the headline. Double meaning and unusual construction (cute) headlines were popular in the United States and Japan and to a lesser degree in South Korea. This attention-gaining technique was not found in Chinese magazines.

Most ads used a realistic picture of the product. In the United States and South Korea the illustration often showed the product in use. Most ads showed people, often depicted as customers or users of the product. By contrast, 78% of the Chinese magazine ads showed no people.

Copy occupied less than 25% of ad space in 66% of American, 70% of South Korean and 53% of Japanese magazine ads. Chinese ads showed the most copy. Thirty percent of the Chinese ads had more than 75% space devoted to copy.

Price was given in 63% of the South Korean ads and 40% of the Japanese ads; this compares to 9% in Chinese ads and 7% in American ads. Special offers, such as coupons, were not popular. Ten percent of the U.S. ads contained a special offer, and the percentages were lower for the other countries.

Slogans were most popular in American (73%), Japanese (60%) and Korean (40%) ads, while only 17% of Chinese ads used a slogan. Less than one half of the slogans used the product name. The information content for magazine advertising by country was 3.27 average cues per ad for China, 3.23 for South Korea, 3.03 for Japan and 2.87 for the United States (Keown et al 1990).

Newspaper

The majority of newspaper headlines used straightforward language. Headlines, having double meanings or unusual construction (cute), were used in Japan (44%), America (45%), South Korea (22%) and China (26%). Most ads had an illustration of the product, except in Korea where the smaller size ads utilized only copy. People were used in the illustrations of American (59%) and Japanese (87%) ads, but not as frequently in South Korean (27%) and Chinese (4%) ads.

About 25–75% of the total ad space was devoted to copy for the majority of American, Japanese and Chinese ads. By contrast the majority of South Korean ads had copy covering more than 75% of total space.

The majority of the Japanese (83%) and South Korean (60%) ads contained either a price or a special offer or both. Only 11% of Chinese and 37% of American ads contained these elements.

Slogans were used primarily in the American newspaper ads (60%), and less so in Japan (35%), South Korea (23%) and China (7%). However, all the Chinese ads and 57% of the South Korean ads used the product name as a part of the slogan.

The average number of information cues for newspaper advertising by country was 3.27 for China and Japan, 3.00 for the U.S. and 2.13 for South Korea (Keown et al 1990).

Limitations

This pilot study has several major limitations. The analysis may be more meaningful if the data had a significant number of ads for the same product for each country, rather than comparing random ads. Content analysis, using pencil-and-paper code sheets as in this study, may mask or ignore significant differences among ads, particularly for television.

Advertising is evolving in all of these countries. For example, there are a growing number of joint venture and foreign ad agencies bringing a sophistication to Chinese advertising. The data of this study represent one point in time. It is left to future research to provide a longitudinal perspective so direction can be discerned. It should be recognized that this study is merely one picture.

A final potential limitation is that every possible effort was made to collect similar advertising examples from each country. However, it is always possible that some unknown or unrecognizable influence might bias the sample. While no such factors have been detected, this does pose a potential limitation.

Managerial implications

The major implication of this analysis is that advertising in the mass media varied significantly in the countries under study. The types of products

Table 7 Comparison of print media

	Television				Radio			
	U.S.	*Japan*	*S. Korea*	*PRC*	*U.S.*	*Japan*	*S. Korea*	*PRC*
Headline								
straight forward	40	57	63	87	66	60	78	85
double meaning	53	43	27	0	35	40	22	15
unusual construction	13	10	0	0	10	4	0	11
Product								
shown	77	77	97	65	80	70	27	62
in use	50	37	50	22	53	33	4	8
Cast								
males only	20	40	27	9	13	37	10	4
females only	23	20	7	4	23	50	7	0
both	7	0	27	9	23	0	10	0
no people	50	40	39	78	41	13	73	96
% Space for copy								
less than 25%	66	53	70	26	33	20	17	16
25–75%	27	40	23	44	57	63	27	50
more than 75%	7	7	7	30	10	17	56	34
Price								
given	7	40	63	9	27	60	50	7
special offer	10	3	0	4	10	23	10	4
Slogan								
used	73	60	40	17	60	35	23	7
uses product name	40	10	17	4	18	7	57	100
Information cues								
number	2.9	3.0	3.2	3.3	3.0	3.3	2.1	3.3

*Per cent of total by medium and country**

*Totals may not add to 100% due to multiple responses

frequently advertised deviated by country and by media. For example, industrial products were advertised on Chinese television and radio but not in the other countries. The length of ads also varied. Chinese and South Korean ads do not follow standardized time increments. The overall information content of advertising is greater in the U.S. and Japan, where advertising is relatively unregulated. This compared with China and South Korea with less information content and a highly regulated advertising industry.

Each country has its idiosyncrasies. For advertisers planning to use global or cross-culturally standardized advertising, this study provides areas of similarity as well as difference. In all four countries, the intent of most ads was to encourage the consumer to buy the product in a retail outlet rather than to build a company or product image. The basic strategy of the majority of the ads was to provide information about the existence, attributes or functions of the product. The execution of ads is somewhat similar. For example, voice-over announcers were used in all four countries.

By contrast there are several important elements that differed from country to country. The type of product advertised in each medium varied. Consumers may come to expect certain types of product ads in a particular medium. For example, packaged food/beverage ads are commonly found on U.S. television but not so often on U.S. radio. This is not the case in China.

Another implication of this study is that ads in China tend to emphasize the merits of the company (quality of their products, acceptability of their products, etc.) Ads in the other countries tended to focus more on the products and stress attributes.

The appropriate length of an advertisement in broadcast media may also be important. A longer radio or television ad may seem endless in a country (like Japan) that is accustomed to shorter commercials. Likewise American ads have a higher number of informational cues than the other cultures. This may mean that more complicated messages are possible. South Korean broadcast advertising had about half the informational cues of U.S. commercials.

There are several interesting specific differences in execution. These may have managerial implications for advertisers who plan to promote in these countries.

1. Demonstrations are used more commonly on Japanese and South Korean television than in the other countries.
2. The advertiser's logo is commonly shown in South Korean and Japanese ads, but not as much in Chinese and American ads.
3. 14% of television and 32% of radio ads in China are for industrial products.
4. Most television ads in Japan are 15 seconds long compared with 30 seconds or more in the other countries.
5. Many South Korean and Chinese radio and television ads do not follow standard lengths of time.
6. Information content of U.S. and Japanese ads is higher than in South Korean and Chinese television.
7. Prices are cited in 29% of Chinese radio ads, compared with less than 10% in the other countries.
8. Prices are commonly presented in Japanese and South Korean newspaper ads but rarely in Chinese ads.
9. Newspaper and radio is used more to promote automobiles in Japan while television is more widely used in the United States.
10. Clever headlines, having double meanings and unusual construction, are widely used in newspaper and magazine advertising in the U.S. and Japan.

Finally, standardized advertising does not occur in these countries and probably will not happen soon. Although advertising execution is similar in some areas, there are major differences among countries in their creative styles and informational content. Successful advertising must be presented in a fashion that is acceptable and familiar to the target market.

REFERENCES

Aaker, D.A. and D. Norris (1982). "Characteristics of TV Commercials Perceived as Informative," *Journal of Advertising Research*, 22, 2: 61–70.

Belk, R.W., W.J. Bryce and R.W. Pollay (1985). "Advertising Themes and Cultural Values: A Comparison of U.S. and Japanese Advertising," In: K.C. Mun (ed.), *Proceedings of the Southeast Asia Region*, Hongkong, Academy of International Business: 11–20.

Berkman, D. (1963). "Advertising in 'Ebony' and 'Life': Negro Aspirations vs. Reality," *Journalism Quarterly*, 40, 53–64.

Courtney, A.E. and S.W. Lockhertz (1971). "A Woman's Place: An Analysis of the Roles Portrayed by Women in Magazine Advertisements," *Journal of Marketing Research*, 8, 1: 92–95.

Gantz, W., H.M. Gartenberg and C.K. Rainbow (1980). "Approaching Invisibility: The Portrayal of the Elderly in Magazine Advertisements," *Journal of Communication*, 30, 1: 56–60.

Gross, B.L. and J.N. Sheth (1989). "Time-oriented Advertising: A Content Analysis of United States Magazine Advertising," *Journal of Marketing*, 53, 4: 76–83.

Hong, J.W., A Muderrisogln and G.M. Zinkhan (1987). "Cultural Differences and Advertising Expression: A Comparative Content Analysis of Japanese and U.S. Magazine Advertising," *Journal of Advertising*, 16, 1: 55–62.

Keown, C.F., L.W. Jacobs, R.W. Schmidt and K.I. Ghymn (1990). "Information Content of Advertising in the United States, Japan, South Korea, and the People's Republic of China," H. Muhlbacher and C. Jochum (eds.), Proceedings of the European Marketing Academy, *Advanced Research in Marketing*, Volume II: 1417–1428.

Kassarjian, H.H. (1977). "Content Analysis in Consumer Research," *Journal of Consumer Research*, 4: 8–18.

Kishii, T. (1988). "Message vs. Mood — A Look at Some of the Differences Between Japanese and Western Television Commercials," *Japan Marketing/Advertising* 51–57.

Madden, C.S., M.J. Caballero and S. Matsukubo. (1986). "Analysis of Information Content in U.S. and Japanese Magazine Advertising," *Journal of Advertising* 15, 3: 38–45.

Mueller, B. (1987). "Reflections of Culture: An Analysis of Japanese and American Advertising Appeals," *Journal of Advertising* 27, 3: 51–59.

_____ (1991). "Multinational Advertising: Factors Influencing the Standardized vs. Specialized Approach," *International Marketing Review*, 8, 1: 7–18.

Resnik, A. and B.C. Stern (1977), "An Analysis of Information Content in Television Advertising," *Journal of Marketing* 41, 1: 50–53.

Rice, M.D. and Z. Lu (1988). "A Content Analysis of Chinese Magazine Advertisements," *Journal of Advertising*, 17, 4: 43–48.

Stewart, S. and N. Campbell (1988). "Advertising in China and Hongkong: A Preliminary Attempt at Some Comparisons of Style," *International Journal of Advertising*, 7, 2: 149–154.

_____ (1986). "Advertising in Mainland China: A Preliminary Study," *International Journal of Advertising*, 5, 4: 317–323.

Tse, D.K., W.B. Russell and N. Zhou (1989). "Becoming a Consumer Society: A Longitudinal and Cross-cultural Content Analysis of Print Ads from Hongkong, the People's Republic of China, and Taiwan," *Journal of Consumer Research* 15, 4: 457–472.

Weinberger, M.G. and H.E. Spotts (1989). "Humor in U.S. versus U.K. TV Commercials: A Comparison," *Journal of Advertising*, 18, 2: 39–44.

Wheeler, D.R. (1988). "Content Analysis: An Analytical Technique for International Marketing Research," *International Marketing Review*, 5, 4: 34–40.

CHARLES F. KEOWN, University of Hawaii at Manoa, LAURENCE W. JACOBS, University of Hawaii at Manoa and KYUNG-IL GHYMN, University of Nevada at Reno. We would like to extend our sympathies to the family of Professor Charles F. Keown who recently passed away.

VI Organizing, Implementing, and Controlling the Marketing Effort

The administrative aspects of marketing comprise the organization, implementation, and control of marketing programs. These occur as the final stage for marketing managers in the Asia Pacific.

After reading the five papers in this part, you should have a better understanding of the following aspects of marketing:

1 How Asian and non-Asian marketing executives differ in decision making and risk taking.
2 Asian marketing institutions such as the *keiretsu* and the trading house.
3 Future trends in the Asia Pacific and global economy which may impact marketing managers in the region.

21 Does Culture Matter? A Cross-Cultural Study of Executives' Choice, Decisiveness, and Risk Adjustment in International Marketing

David K. Tse, Kam-Hon Lee, Ilan Vertinsky, and Donald A. Wehrung

The authors investigate whether a manager's home culture significantly influences his or her international marketing decisions. They also examine whether the impact of home culture diminishes in an open economy with intense exposure to international markets, giving way to a process of "globalization." Decision making in four simulated international marketing situations was studied with executives from the People's Republic of China, Hongkong, and Canada. The findings confirm that home culture has predictable, significant effects on the decision making of the executives from the People's Republic of China and Canada. Chinese executives from Hongkong were influenced by a combination of Western and Chinese cultural norms.

An understanding of how cultural differences affect international marketing decisions is important to a firm's external operation. It can be used to predict strategic moves and responses of competitors and hence to design effective competitive strategies. This understanding is also salient to international sales negotiations (e.g., Pye 1983).

In addition, a knowledge of the impact of culture on marketing decisions is important to the internal conduct of multinational firms. Internal coordination in these firms requires well-orchestrated responses from executives with different cultural backgrounds. Even in organizations with elaborate standard operating procedures, the interpretation of environmental cues may vary among executives from different nations as a result of their cultural differences. A knowledge of cultural influences enables the firms to accommodate and adapt to such differences, hence reducing "noisy" communications among executives and errors in decision making (Montgomery and Weinberg 1979). In the past multinational firms were dominated by "Western managerial culture." Recent

Reproduced with permission from *Journal of Marketing*, 52 (October 1988), pp. 81–95.

trends in international trade and foreign direct investment have increased significantly the global role of Asian multinational firms and North American subsidiaries operating in Asia, thus increasing the salience of understanding cultural impact on a firm's internal operations.

We describe a study of the effects of a manager's home culture on the marketing decisions of Chinese and Western (Canadian) executives. The study also provides some preliminary indications of whether cultural effects on marketing decisions diminish as a consequence of intercultural exposure, interdependence, and learning. To accomplish this, two populations of Chinese executives, one from the People's Republic of China (PRC) and the other from Hongkong were studied. PRC business executives have been relatively isolated from contacts with international markets for many years. Hence, cultural effects on their marketing decision processes, if present, would represent a relatively pure form of cultural influence on business behavior. The Chinese executives in Hongkong represent an Oriental business community with intense and continuous interactions with the Western business world. If globalization of markets has eroded the impact of ethnicity on marketing decision making, one would expect Hongkong executives to behave similarly to North American executives. The Canadian executives, whose decision processes in risky situations have been found to be similar to those of U.S. executives (MacCrimmon and Wehrung 1986), represent the Western managerial culture.

The executives were asked to respond to four hypothetical marketing situations. An "in-basket" format (Frederiksen, Saunders, and Wand 1957; Gill 1979) was selected to investigate the impact of culture on executives' decision making because of its realism and its rich context (see Appendices A through D). In comparison with conventional tools for studying executives' decisions, such as belief statements, this approach provides more relevant decision variables to the respondents. In addition, because executives representing different cultural backgrounds and organizations are responding to some common decision situations, their behavior can be compared. In the past researchers have used the technique to study executive decisions toward trade unions and customer threats (e,g., MacCrimmon and Wehrung 1986).

In the four hypothetical marketing situations, the outcome variables of prime concern were (1) choice, (2) decisiveness, and (3) adjustment of the decision environment. The decisions involve elimination of a current product line, mode of entry into a new market, new product design, and response to a malfunctioning product. The cultural traits addressed include some of those commonly cited in the literature as distinguishing Western from Chinese managers, in particular (1) individual face saving (Lee 1982; Redding 1982), (2) repayment of "dues" and attitude toward competition (Meade and Barnard 1973; Redding 1982; Tung 1981), (3) participation in decision process (Cascio

1974; Han 1983; Meade 1969; Tung 1981), (4) pan-ethical orientation to problems (Ch'ien 1973; Yin 1976), (5) quest for harmony, and (6) fatalistic views (Chan 1967). ·

Culture and decision making

Some recent studies reported in the marketing literature have confirmed the importance and dynamics of cultural influence on consumer behavior (e.g., Erickson, Johansson, and Chao 1984; Tse, Belk, and Zhan 1988). Other studies such as the work of Wallendorf and Reilly (1983) have focused specifically on ethnic differences. Studies using Singaporean subjects found that traditional Chinese values were fading slowing because of Western influences (e.g., McCullough, Tan, and Wong 1986; Tan and Farley 1987). We examine how home cultural values affect managerial decisions in risky situations.

Hofstede (1980, p. 19) defined culture as " . . . the interactive aggregate of common characteristics that influence a group's response to its environment." Culture may be reflected in general tendencies of persistent preference for particular states of affairs over others, persistent preferences for specific social processes over others, and general rules for selective attention, interpretation of environmental cues, and responses. It is generally known that culture may provide detailed prescriptions (norms) for specific classes of situations while leaving other domains relatively unregulated. National and ethnic cultures are thus distinguished in their degree of regulation of behavior, attitudes, and values, the domain of regulation, and the consistency and clarity of regulation and tolerance of other cultures.

Comparative studies of Chinese and North American cultures have underscored several distinctive general norms that are dominant in one culture and absent in the other. Hence it is possible to find distinctions among societies having the same ethnic but different national cultures, such as those in the PRC and Hongkong.

The prime distinction between Chinese and North American cultures appears to be the collective orientation of the former and the individualistic orientation of the latter (see e.g., Chan 1986; Ch'ien 1973; Moore 1967; Yin 1976). A collective orientation implies (1) an emphasis on diffused relationships, that is, relationships not limited to a particular domain or function, (2) a pan-ethical approach to action, emphasizing social objectives in decisions, (3) an intergenerational time perspective that considers the rights of both current and future generations, and (4) an emphasis on collective harmony and discipline. In contrast, an individualistic orientation implies (1) the specific or functional definition of relationships, (2) a utilitarian concept of problem solving, (3) a shorter time perspective, and (4) an emphasis on freedom of choice and competition. A collective orientation also implies a tendency to submit to one's individual fate — fatalism (Chan 1967) — whereas the individualistic orientation, in the quest for freedom, implies a desire to seek control over one's fate.

Specific norms have been proposed in the literature as dominant in one culture and absent in the other. Four such norms that are relevant to the decision situations are discussed next.

Face saving

"Face" refers to the respect, pride, and dignity of an individual as a consequence of his or her position in society. This principle influences many facets of Chinese life and is regarded as a means for fostering harmony (Moore 1967). The norm regulates responsibilities and interpersonal relationships in the family and society. It prescribes that the dignity of the individual, even in trivial matters, must be defended and respected (Chan 1967). This responsibility for the preservation of dignity ensures the maintenance of hierarchies and elucidates the responsibilities of persons within the hierarchy. To a large extent this norm is similar to the notion of shame in Japanese culture.

In a marketing context, a product represents part of the person who initiated it. Hence the initiator is psychologically tied to the product and any criticism of the product would mean damage to his or her "face." It is reasonable, therefore, to expect Chinese executives to be more inclined to persist in investing in their products even if weakness is demonstrated. Studies of how Japanese managers react to product failures have found this characteristic in Japan (Johansson 1986).

Repayment of "dues" and attitude toward competition

Exchange relationships are present in both cultures. In Western culture they are based on principles of balance, clearance, and specific relationships. In Chinese culture exchanges create long-term moral obligations. This intricate system of long-term moral obligations of repayment, without explicit rules for termination of the obligations, buttresses collective survival and increases harmony.

In the marketing context, the Chinese system may place limits on destructive competition and may induce certain market imperfections. For example, some preferential treatment may be given to the "insiders" and barriers may be erected against the "outsiders."

Participation in decision making and the significance of consensus

Closely related to the Chinese face-saving norm is subordinates' lack of involvement in key decisions. Within the Chinese value system a subordinate is expected to obey, sometimes without question. A leader is consistently regarded as the most intelligent member of the group (Wu 1967). Consequently a question — or worse, a difference of opinion — may bring about loss of face of superiors. Authoritarian behavior by superiors and passive obedience by subordinates are expected. In contrast, consensus and participation in key decisions are valued in most Western cultures. They are also important elements of the Japanese system through the *ringi* (Cascio 1974).

In the marketing context, this tighter coordination is important to both the effectiveness of the marketing department and its contribution to the firm. It may lead to a quicker product development process and more effective brand management.

Pan-ethical versus utilitarian approach to problems

The key paradigm guiding behavior in the West is utilitarianism. In an extreme form, utilitarianism encourages a cost-benefit approach to the decision by the decision maker based on his or her own preferences. The alternatives are assessed from an individual's perspective rather than from a societal point of view. This approach tends to shorten the time horizon considered and increase the time discount rate. Ethical obligations are sometimes viewed more as social costs and constraints to be satisfied than as objectives to be fulfilled. In contrast, Confucian teachings emphasize moral ideals and place the virtue of social justice above any considerations of utility (Wu 1967, p. 223). This virtue is also emphasized in PRC's organizational guidelines (Tung 1981).

In the marketing context, the pan-ethical approach implies a concern for consumers that exceeds the usual rational considerations of costs and benefits (the basic decision criterion of the utilitarian approach). It may mean that a "moral" product warranty is stronger than either legal obligations or requirements for maintaining the firm's reputation.

Effects of cultural norms

The prime question we address is to what extent these cultural characteristics are reflected in the marketing decision process. The "ideal" business decision model in Western culture presumes rationality — a choice among feasible alternatives so as to maximize the decision maker's utility. In a risky situation the choice must reflect the risk-taking tendency of the decision maker, that is, the tradeoff between risks and returns.

Culture may affect the validity of such a model as a prescription for behavior in several ways.

1.   Cultural norms may influence problem definitions. What appears in the functional orientation to be a generic marketing problem may be interpreted as another type of problem because of the presence of features that trigger distinct cultural interpretations.

2.   Cultural norms may affect problem definition by providing standard operating procedures and programs for processing information. Thus, for example, some cultures promote the absorption of uncertainty by encouraging a "black and white" external description of uncertain situations.

3.   Cultural norms that regulate control beliefs may influence the generation of alternatives before and after a choice.

4.   Some cultures may encourage individuals to take strong positions on alternatives whereas other cultures may value caution and ambiguity in positions.

5.   Some cultures emphasize the processes of decision making (e.g., obtaining a consensus) more than the quality of the decisions reached.

6.   A culture may affect business decisions by generally influencing risk-taking patterns (e.g., promoting caution and discouraging gambling) or prescribing a pattern of tradeoffs between risk and return.

7.   A culture also may prescribe patterns of reward and punishment that affect what executives do to make the decision situation more favorable (i.e. risk adjustment) before and after the choice is made. Thus, if the Chinese culture tightly regulates how Chinese executives make decisions in the international marketing domain, a diffused orientation would imply susceptibility of problem definitions to concerns outside the scope of "risks and returns." Face saving may dominate functional organizational objectives related to risks and returns in certain decision situations. Fatalism may reduce willingness to generate alternatives and other risk-adjustment activities of Chinese executives in comparison with North Americans. A quest for harmony may decrease decisiveness among Chinese executives (i.e., strength of preference between alternatives).

Hypotheses

The basic hypothesis of this study is that general cultural differences significantly affect marketing decision making. We expect to find differences between PRC and Canadian executives in (1) choice, (2) decisiveness, and (3) adjustment of decision environment — the dependent variables investigated. A corollary to this hypothesis is that, as international contacts intensify (as in the case of Hongkong executives), the influence of ethnic culture diminishes. Hence we hypothesize that the behavior of Hongkong executives will be between that of PRC and that of Canadian executives. This hypothesis and the others discussed in this section are summarized in Table 1.

Table 1 List of hypotheses[a]

Decision situations and other dependent variables	Cultural norm investigated	Hypothesis
H_{1a}: Eliminating an unprofitable product line	Face saving	PRC executives: Continue HK executives: Between CND executives: Eliminate
H_{1b}: Joint venture with competitor who is in trouble	Repayment of "dues"	PRC executives: Joint venture HK executives: Between CND executives: Enter alone
H_{1c}: Adoption of a new design without subordinates' consensus	Leader authority	PRC executives: New design HK executives: Between CND executives: Standard design
H_{1d}: Recall malfunctioning product	Pan-ethical view	PRC executives: Recall product HK executives: Between CND executives: Send reminder
H_2: Decisiveness	Harmony	PRC executives: Least decisive HK executives: Between CND executives: Most decisive
H_3: Willingness to adopt risk-adjustment strategies	Fatalism or control of the environment	PRC executives: Least willing HK executives: Between CND executives: Most willing
(a) Willingness to control decision environment		PRC executives: Least preferred among all adjustment stratagies CND executives: Most preferred among all adjustment strategies
(b) Willingness to consult superiors		PRC executives: Most preferred among all adjustment strategies

[a]PRC denotes People's Republic of China, HK denotes Hongkong, and CND denotes Canadian.

On the basis of the cultural effects discussed in the preceding section, we hypothesized that the choices adopted by Canadian and PRC executives would differ in several ways. In comparison with Canadian executives, PRC executives would choose decision alternatives involving (1) greater face saving, (2) longer term repayment of obligations, (3) more authoritarian and less consensual decision processes, and (4) greater focus on a pan-ethical viewpoint. This hypothesis (H_1) was examined in four decision situations designed to allow cultural effects to influence the decision options under consideration, as described in the next section.

Most marketing decisions involve a choice among alternatives. An individual executive may (1) choose among the alternatives presented or (2) engage in what MacCrimmon and Wehrung (1986) call "risk adjustment" before making a choice. If one of the alternatives is clearly superior to other alternatives, the decision maker is likely to have a stronger preference for that decision. Similarly, in screening the options, a decision maker may find alternatives that can be rejected with strong confidence. The degree of conviction held for a particular alternative or, as Wehrung et al. (1988) termed it, "decisiveness," could be a function of the choice situation (e.g., its riskiness) or the culture of which the individual is a member.

The literature on decision making of PRC executives emphasizes their slowness in reaching a decision (Hendry 1986; Pye 1983), which could be explained as a result of either the executives' indecisiveness or the necessity of deferring the decision to consult with superiors (one of our subsequent hypotheses). We chose to hypothesize that culture affects the executive's individual decisiveness (H_2) and that PRC executives would be less decisive than the Canadians.[1] As a corollary to this hypothesis and as a test of the presence of globalization effects of decisiveness, we expected Hongkong executives to be similar in their responses to the Canadians (this corollary is general to all our hypotheses about cultural differences and is not repeated).

Managers frequently try to modify the situations they face to make them more favorable as part of their decision process. Four important types of adjustment identified by MacCrimmon and Wehrung (1986) are (1) gaining control of the environment, (2) gaining information, (3) gaining time, and (4) reducing one's personal exposure to risk. Chinese, like other Orientals, tend to accept their environments rather than seeking to change them (Chan 1967; Moore 1967). They seek to fit or harmonize with the environment. In contrast, Western cultures reject fatalistic perceptions, encouraging executives to seek means for controlling their environment. These control beliefs are part of the North American myth about the unlimited possibilities open to each individual.

Thus we hypothesized that PRC executives would be less inclined than Canadians to engage in risk-adjustment strategies (H_3). Among the four adjustment strategies, the PRC executives would avoid the use of risk-adjustment strategies to increase control over the decision environment, gather information, or develop alternative courses of action (H_{3a}). They would be most likely to reduce both their personal and the firm's exposure to risk by consulting superiors. (H_{3b}).

Research design

We used three subject groups (i.e., executives from three cultures) and four international marketing decisions as repeated measures. Two independent variables — country (i.e., manager's home culture) and situation (i.e., type of international marketing decisions) — were investigated.

The "in-basket" instrument

An in-basket format was used to ascertain how executives behave in risky marketing situations. In this method, developed first by Frederiksen, Saunders, and Wand (1957), hypothetical scenarios solicit managerial decisions. The method has been used in studies of decision making (e.g., MacCrimmon and Wehrung 1984) and other managerial topics. See Gill (1979) for a review.

The executives were asked to play the role of a newly promoted vice-president of a large multinational corporation based in their home country — in Shenzhen (one of the four experimental economic zones in the PRC) for PRC executives, Hongkong for Hongkong executives, and Toronto for Canadian executives. The decision problems each subject considered consisted of four international marketing situations. These problems were described by memoranda in the subject's in-basket and required immediate response. The decisions were whether to (1) continue or drop an unprofitable product line, (2) enter a new market alone or through a joint venture with a competitor, (3) adopt a new product design or use a current one, and (4) recall a malfunctioning product or send warning letters to buyers of the product. Appendices A through D are the memos used for the four situations.

The participants were asked to respond using the materials at hand. No outside information was allowed. To discourage delay, the exercise stated that the participant was scheduled to leave for an important business meeting in San Francisco within a couple of hours and would not return for a week, before which decisions would have to be made. None of the materials could be taken on the trip. Each participant was instructed to read through the materials and use his or her own experience as the basis for decisions.

As each situation presented a choice between two alternatives whose expected values were the same, the basis for a choice involved consideration of factors other than expected returns. This method has been used and tested by MacCrimmon and Wehrung (1984). In the decision to continue or drop an unprofitable product line, dropping the product could involve a "loss of face for the decision maker" because the executive had developed the product him- or herself. In the decision to enter a new market, either alone or through a joint venture with a financially troubled competitor who had helped the firm before, going alone might destroy a competitor whereas a joint venture would repay an obligation. The adoption of an innovative product design could be interpreted as making an authoritarian decision because there was no consensus on the design among subordinates, whereas the current design would promote continued harmony in the firm. Finally, in the decision whether to recall a malfunctioning product or send reminders, a pan-ethical orientation would require a complete correction of the problem through recall and a utilitarian orientation would permit a partial, short-run solution. See Table 1 for a summary of the specific hypotheses examined in each of these situations.

The entire questionnaire was translated into Chinese by a doctoral student from the PRC. The translated questionnaire was reviewed by a panel consisting of another PRC doctoral student and two of the authors whose mother tongue is Chinese. The Chinese version was used in a pretest conducted in the PRC and in the major study for PRC executives, whereas the English version (with appropriate changes in names of characters and addresses for each location) was used in Hongkong and Canada.

The in-basket instrument seemed appropriate for investigating the impact of cultural differences on decision making. In contrast to belief scales (e.g., Anderson and Coughlan 1987) and descriptive techniques (e.g., Lazer, Murata, and Kosaka 1985; Naor 1986), the in-basket instrument provides a rich contextual narrative for each stylized marketing problem, thus permitting cultural influence to be studied across subjects from different cultures. Special care was taken in the design of the instrument to ensure that the tasks were familiar and within the competence of the subjects (see Chakravarti, Mitchell, and Staelin 1981; Little 1970; Little and Lodish 1981). The situations were designed to provide a broad cross-section of marketing decisions that did not require detailed, specific know-how.

Pretest

Three pretests were conducted, with (1) 45 PRC teachers in business, (2) 16 MBA students enrolled in a West Coast Canadian university, and (3) 20 Canadian Chinese executives from Vancouver's Chinatown. The first and second pretests were designed to show whether the decision situations were perceived as appropriate for PRC and Canadian subjects. The third pretest assessed whether the situations and the amount of investment involved in each situation were realistic. The first pretest used the Chinese language version of the instrument and the latter two pretests used the English version. Subsequent to the pretests, the situations and some questions in the questionnaire were modified.

Sample

A total of 145 executives from Canada, Hongkong, and the PRC formed the sample. The PRC sample consisted of 50 working executives from the PRC who participated in an executive training program in international marketing management in Hongkong. The Hongkong sample consisted of 45 working executives from Hongkong who participated in an executive program in marketing and international business at a major university in Hongkong. The Canadian sample was pooled from two sources. It consisted of 34 executives attending an evening MBA program at a West Coast university and 16 executives identified by a local international trade association who agreed to participate in the study. Aside from differences in age and work experience, the two Canadian samples showed no marked differences in the dependent measures and hence were combined.

Research procedure

Each participant was asked to respond to each in-basket memorandum presenting the decision situations without consulting others. Once the subjects had read a memorandum they were asked to write a memorandum in response, describing what they would do and the reasons for their actions. After completing each memorandum the subjects were asked to provide additional judgments on 9-point bipolar scales. They were instructed to respond completely to one decision situation before beginning the next one.

The six scales can be divided into three types. The first type assessed the subject's perception of the riskiness of the situation to the organization (from 1 = very risky to the company to 9 = not risky to the company). The second type consisted of four scales measuring the participant's inclination to engage in four types of risk-adjustment strategies. They included the participant's inclination to (1) use resources to change the environment (from 1 = accept whatever outcomes occur from the decision to 9 = try to influence situation through bargaining and spending resources), (2) collect additional information (from 1 = use the available information to make the decision to 9 = gain as much additional information as possible), (3) develop more options (from 1 = decide among the options currently available to 9 = try to develop new options), and (4) consult superiors (from 1 = make decision by myself without consulting my superiors to 9 = make decision in consultation with my superiors).

The third type of scale measured the strength of the participant's preference between the two decision options specified in each situation. These alternatives formed the two ends of a 9-point scale. Higher values corresponded to a preference for the alternative consistent with the hypothesized Chinese perspective as summarized in Figure 1. Some additional scales indicated sociodemographic characteristics of participants. The entire response to the four decision situations took about one hour to finish.

Figure 1   Choice in four situations by subject groups

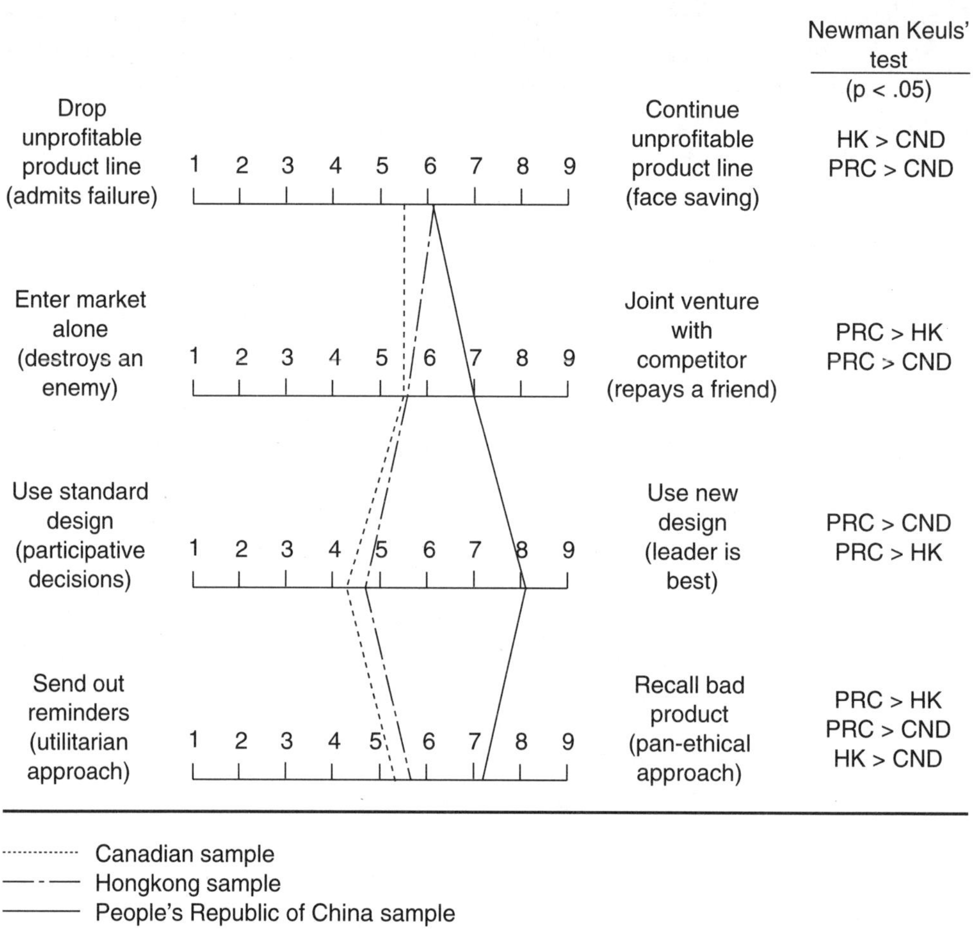

------------- Canadian sample
— - — Hongkong sample
———— People's Republic of China sample

Findings

Manipulation checks

The data first were checked to ensure that (1) each situation connoted similar levels of riskiness to the executives across cultures so that comparisons among the executives were meaningful and (2) the four situations represented different levels of riskiness so that a wide range of risky marketing decisions were considered.

Subjects' perceived riskiness for each situation was used as a manipulation check. Analysis of variance was performed with subjects' perceived riskiness as the dependent variable and country (i.e., subjects' home country) and situation as independent variables. The country effect and the country by situation interaction were insignificant, whereas the situation effect was highly significant (P < .01). The mean perceived riskiness ratings for the four situations were, respectively, 5.1, 6.9, 6.0, and 4.4 on a scale that ranged from 1 (very risky) to 9 (not risky to the company). The Newman-Keuls tests indicated that each situation was perceived to be significantly (P < .05) different from another. Hence, though the four situations differed in their perceived riskiness, executives from all three cultures perceived about the same degree of riskiness in each situation.

The data were analyzed mainly by ANOVA with country and situation as independent variables. Table 2 is a summary of the tests of the three formal hypotheses and some of their corollaries.

Table 2 Results of ANOVA on different dependent variables

	Dependent variables						
Effects	Choice (n = 144)	Decisiveness (n = 144)	Use resources to change environment (n = 141)	Gather information (n = 144)	Develop alternatives (n = 142)	Consult superior (n = 143)	Overall[a] (n = 140)
Country (C)							
Sum of squares	406.97	128.07	590.54	173.76	550.45	23.14	3650.11
F-value	19.16**	33.00**	22.42**	6.87**	27.74**	1.02	23.40**
Situation (S)							
Sum of squares	8.94	20.11	84.98	39.97	433.05	212.36	3519.54
F-value	.38	8.03**	5.98**	19.32**	24.39**	11.09**	29.41**
C × S							
Sum of squares	187.08	3.94	35.64	84.46	12.86	70.80	434.29
F-value	3.96**	.79	1.25	2.04	.36	1.85	1.82
r^2	.39	.55	.57	.45	.49	.41	.53

[a]Sum of all four types of risk adjustment.
*p < .05.
**p < .01.

Choice

The ANOVA results on the subjects' choices are summarized in the first column of Table 2. As expected, the country effect is significant, confirming H_1 that cultural difference affects subjects' decisions. The situation effect, which was not a central theme in the study, is insignificant. The country by situation interaction is significant at the .01 level, suggesting that a situation by situation analysis is necessary. A closer examination suggests the significance of this interaction probably is caused by the choices of Hongkong executives in situation 1 (see Figure 1).

Figure 1 displays the subjects' mean choice scores in the four situations with the results of the Newman-Keuls tests on the right. In summary, all the corollaries in H_1 that pertain to Canadian and PRC executives are confirmed; Hongkong executives differ from the other two groups, depending on the situation.

The first situation involved the influence of face saving on decision making. Both Hongkong (mean score 6.21) and PRC (6.10) executives were more sensitive to saving-face concerns than Canadian executives (5.35), and hence persisted with the unprofitable product line. Similar persistence was reported by Johansson (1986), who described Japanese reactions to product failures.

In the second situation, PRC executives (7.00) were significantly more inclined to maintain long-term exchange relationships by agreeing to a joint venture with a competitor than either the Hongkong (5.64) or Canadian (5.47) executives, who were less inclined to repay their friends.

The results for situation 3 confirm our hypothesis about the impact of preferences for different decision processes. PRC executives (8.06) reflected in their choices a preference for authoritarian decision styles, whereas Canadian (4.37) and Hongkong (4.70) executives revealed a preference for participative management.

Situation 4 involved a test of the impact of cultural differences stemming from pan-ethical versus utilitarian orientations. PRC executives (7.10) were more inclined to follow a pan-ethical approach to the problem and take complete remedial action when a faulty product was discovered than were Hongkong executives (5.71), who were in turn significantly more inclined to do so than the Canadian executives (5.28).

Except in situation 1, where Hongkong executives had a greater though insignificant tendency to continue an unprofitable product line, Hongkong executives always scored between their PRC and Canadian counterparts. Three of the four situations studied, however, showed Hongkong executives to be more similar to Canadian executives than to PRC executives. This finding suggests the important impact of continuous interactions with the Western business world in contrast to the influence of the ethnic culture. However, the significance of the country by situation interaction suggests that the globalization process is uneven along different cultural norms. Hongkong executives appear to adhere to the "face-saving" norm as strongly as the PRC executives but are similar to the Canadian executives on other norms investigated.

Decisiveness

An executive was regarded as decisive if one of the two decision alternatives specified in a situation was clearly chosen. An executive's degree of decisiveness therefore was operationalized as the absolute difference between the score given on the choice scale and the midpoint of that scale. Hence the decisiveness variable ranges from 0 (totally indecisive) to 4 (strongly committed to a particular course of action).

The ANOVA result (Table 2, second column) with decisiveness as the dependent variable shows that both the country and situation effects are significant but the interaction effects are not. The Newman-Keuls test results indicate that the PRC executives were significantly more decisive (mean score 3.6) than either Hongkong (mean score 2.8) or Canadian (mean score 2.5) executives, whereas the latter two show no significant difference.

This findings contradicts H_2 and the common views in the literature. It can be explained by the PRC executives inclination to classify the world into extremes — "black or white," "evil or good" (Moore 1967) — which implies a tendency to resolve ambiguity quickly and hence be more decisive.

Adjustment of the decision environment

Three indicators were used to understand how the subjects adjust their decision environment: the strength (or magnitude), the number, and the type of adjustment used.

First, each subject's responses to four adjustment scales in four situations were used as dependent variables in an ANOVA. The independent measures were country, situation, and type of adjustment. Table 3 shows that all three main effects and three two-way interactions are significant at .01 but the three-way interaction is not. The significant country main effect confirms H_3 and its corollary. PRC executives were significantly (Newman-Keuls test $P < .05$) less inclined to adjust their environment (mean score 3.94 on a 9-point scale) than those from Hongkong (5.17) and Canada (5.46). The latter two groups show no significant difference. Though they are not the principal foci of the study, types of adjustment, situation, and all two-way interactions of the three main effects are also significant in understanding the executives' risk-adjustment behavior.

The results of the ANOVA with total adjustment scores as the dependent variable are given in the last column of Table 2. They show that the sum of the four adjustment strategies depends significantly on country and situation effects but not on interaction between them. This sum ranges from 4 to 36, with higher values corresponding to a greater use of risk adjustments. Examining the country effect, we find that PRC executives (mean score 15.7) were significantly (Newman-Keuls test $P < .05$) less likely to try to adjust their environment than Canadian (mean score 20.7) and Hongkong (21.9) executives. Similar results are

Table 3 ANOVA on risk adjustment with country, type of adjustment, and situation as independent variables (N = 143)[a]

Effects	Sum of squares	F-value
Country (C)	991.95	25.21**
Type of adjustment (A)	276.31	13.91**
Situation (S)	971.86	48.93**
C × A	418.25	10.51**
C × S	130.70	3.29**
A × S	151.87	2.55**
C × A × S	71.65	0.60
r²		.29

[a]Here subjects' responses to four adjustment scores in four situations were used as repeated measures in the dependent variable; hence the number of observations is 143 × 4 × 4 = 2288.
**$p < .01$.

obtained when the four adjustment scores are analyzed by MANOVA, confirming H_3. No significant differences are found between Hongkong and Canadian executives. As found in the preceding test, the situation effect also is significant in explaining this measure of executives' risk-adjustment behavior.

When the four adjustments are analyzed separately (Table 2, columns 3 to 6), similar results are obtained for three adjustment strategies, namely using resources to change the environment, gathering information, and developing additional alternatives. Again the main effects are significant but the interaction is not. The mean score also reflects the fact that PRC executives were less likely than other executives to adopt these three risk-adjustment strategies (Table 4), as predicted by H_{3a}. The insignificant country main effect on consulting superiors disconfirms H_{3b} and suggests that PRC and Canadian executives preferred this mode of adjustment at similar levels. The Newman-Keuls test on types of adjustment among the PRC executives (Table 4, last row) suggests that consulting superiors was the most preferred among the four risk-adjustment strategies.

Number of adjustment strategies

A related measure for the degree of adjustment is the number of adjustment strategies adopted by an executive. An indicator variable was developed that recorded an adjustment as having been adopted (scored 1) if the corresponding raw score (from 1 to 9) exceeded the midpoint value of 5. The sum of these indicator variables across the four adjustments then was analyzed by ANOVA with country and situation as independent variables. These results confirm that PRC executives adopted significantly ($P < .001$) fewer adjustment strategies

Table 4 Mean score on types of adjustment across three countries

	Country groups[a]			
	Canada	Hongkong	People's Republic of China	Newman-Keuls Test
	(n = 50)	(n = 45)	(n = 50)	(p < .05)
Use resources to change environment (B)	5.69	5.91	3.52	CND > PRC HK > PRC
Gather information (I)	5.31	5.75	4.44	CND > PRC HK > PRC
Develop alternatives (A)	4.99	4.96	2.89	CND > PRC HK > PRC
Consult superior (S)	4.75	5.24	4.91	No sig. difference
Nweman-Keuls test (p < .05)	B > A, B > S I > S	B > A, B > S I > A	S > B, S > A I > B, I > A B > A	

[a]Mean score averaged across four situations on a scale ranging from 1 = least likely to 9 = very likely to engage in the particular risk-adjustment strategy.

Table 5 Zero, single, and multiple risk-adjustment strategies across three countries (number of responses = 640)

Number of strategies committed	Canada (%)	Hongkong (%)	People's Republic of China (%)
Zero	27	13	33
One	15	22	30
Multiple (2–4)	58	65	37
Total	100	100	100

$\chi^2 = 43.62$ with 4 d.f., significant at .001.
[a]A strategy was recorded as a 1 if the raw score (from 1 to 9) on the adjustment strategy was more than 5.

(1.32) than Hongkong (2.23) and Canadian (2.18) executives. The latter two do not differ significantly (P < .05).

More importantly, results in Table 5 show that more than half of Hongkong and Canadian executives used multiple risk adjustments, in contrast to only slightly more than a third of PRC executives (the chi square score is significant at .001).

Preferences among adjustment strategies

Table 6 reports the ANOVA result with the scores on all four adjustment strategies in each situation as dependent variables and type of adjustment and situation as independent variables. In general, both main effects (types of adjustment and situation) are significant for all countries whereas the interaction is marginally significant only for Canadian executives. The results reconfirm H_3. As shown in the first column of Table 4, the Canadian executives ranked highest the spending of resources to change the environment (Table 4, last row), followed by information gathering and development of new alternatives. Consulting a superior was the least preferred adjustment.

Hongkong executives also rated highest the strategy of spending resources to change the environment (Table 4, last row). This alternative was followed by gathering information. Like the Canadian executives, Hongkong executives show no significant differences in their preferences for consulting superiors to the options of developing new alternatives. In contrast, the PRC executives rated the option of consulting superiors as the most preferred, confirming H_3b. They rated the option of developing new alternatives as the least preferred whereas gathering additional information and the use of resources to change the environment were rated between these two options.

Table 6 ANOVA on risk adjustment with type of adjustment and situation as independent variables across three countries

Effects		Canada (n = 50)	Hongkong (n = 45)	People's Republic of China (n = 50)
Type of adjustment (A)	Sum of squares	101.17	106.72	493.67
	F-value	5.96**	5.13**	16.99**
Situation (S)	Sum of squares	335.79	240.98	541.47
	F-value	19.78**	11.58**	18.63**
A × S	Sum of squares	95.82	67.64	62.44
	F-value	1.88*	1.08	0.72
r^2		.11	.08	.13

*$p < .05$.
**$p < .01$.

Implications

One important consideration underlying many international marketing plans is the extent to which traditional cultural values persist in a rapidly changing environment. This question is especially crucial when managers approach the world's most populated and underexplored market, China. One motive of our study was to investigate how much of the traditional Chinese value system persists after 38 years of communist philosophy and more than eight years of modernization.

We hypothesized and found that all four Chinese values investigated not only persist, but influence PRC executives' decisions and their reactions to the environment. The values of saving face, long-term exchange relationships and restricted competition, unquestioned respect for leaders, and pan-ethical views are well reflected in their market entry and product decisions. Their tendencies to hold dichotomous and fatalistic views of their environment are evident in their decision process.

We discovered, contrary to common views held by other authors as well as our own hypothesis, that PRC executives are more decisive than either Hongkong or Canadian executives. Though we assumed that the Chinese acceptance of hierarchy and quest for harmony would reduce their willingness to make a decision, perhaps their inclination for uncertainty absorption leads to increased decisiveness.

Another interesting finding is the effect of culture on risk-adjustment behavior. PRC executives engaged to a lesser degree in adjusting their decision environment than either Hongkong or Canadian executives. They preferred strategies that would reduce their personal exposure to failure. In contrast, both Hongkong and Canadian executives showed marked preference for strategies to control their environment.

Traditional cultural influences are consistently challenged by exposure to different values. Executives from Hongkong were influenced more by their exposure to Western business practices than by their Chinese heritage, though some residual influence of such deep-rooted values as face saving and pan-ethical views is reflected in their choices. We thus find that the process of globalization is uneven in its effect on different cultural norms. The persistence and dynamism in cultural values clearly suggest the need to trace, monitor, and understand cultural factors in international marketing plans.

Conclusion

Our findings suggest that ethnic cultures do matter (at least for Chinese and Canadian executives) in marketing decision making. A general comparative analysis of cultures may help marketing executives to anticipate the responses of their rivals, understand more accurately their customs in business transactions, and deal with colleagues of different nationalities in joint decision making. Culture makes a difference in problem identification and in the objectives motivating choice. Culture also may make a difference in the communication of problems and recommendations, and particularly in the decisiveness of recommendations. Failure to understand these differences may lead to "noisy" communication, misinformation, and misunderstanding. Culture also makes a difference in individual strategies to adjust decision situations to facilitate choice and mitigate undesirable consequences for the organization and the decision maker.

Our investigation also demonstrates, however, that in a marketing world characterized by intensive communications, standardization, and the employment of similar decision technologies, cultural differences tend to diminish. Indeed, the process of globalization (Levitt 1983) on the supply side has already begun.

APPENDIX A

General Products International, Inc.
Memorandum

To: Mr. Chan Wing-Tat   From: Lee Ka-Keung
                                                   Assistant to V.P.
                                                   International Operations
                                   Date: June 4, 1986

We have completed our annual review of the European Division's product line for the upcoming meeting of the Executive Committee. There were no real surprises and in general the European Division has had a good year. One issue that is sure to come up in the Executive Committee meeting, however, is what to do with the Natural Beauty Care product line that has been losing money since it was introduced a year ago.

I don't need to go into the background of this line because you initiated and managed the Natural Beauty Care line when you were Marketing Manager with the European Division. The President of the Division has expressed his concern about this product's losses of $500,000 (U.S.) during its first year of sales in Europe. The feeling seems to be that the use of traditional Asian beauty aids derived from natural ocean vegetation and sea life has a difficult time catching on with Europeans.

It seems that we have two options with this product line. We can scrap it now with no future consequences except incurring our past losses. Alternatively, we can invest another $600,000 (U.S.) in marketing the natural beauty idea. The chances of success do not seem too good and are estimated by the European Division to be maybe one chance in five. However, if successful, we would receive an expected profit of $3 million (U.S.) net of the marketing expenses. If unsuccessful, we would lose another $150,000 in addition to the $600,000. These figures do not include last year's loss of $500,000.

You will likely be called on at the Executive Committee meeting on June 15th to express your views on this product line, so let me know if I should do anything else to help you on this issue before the meeting.

APPENDIX B

Mr. Lee Shing-Tak
Vice-President
International Operations
General Products International, Inc.
2300 Alexandra House
5000 Queen's Road
Hongkong

Dear Mr. Lee:

Last week the president of Tak On's Brazilian Division called me to see whether General Products International might be interested in a joint venture with them in South America. I am not surprised at this suggestion because they must still be hurting from the major losses they incurred in their failed venture in the Middle East. Tak On is General Products International's closest competitor and we haven't had a joint venture with them in quite some time.

However, remember that Tak On helped us out in our European venture in the late 1970s and we have had good relations with their management for many years. So far they have always competed with us fairly.

The proposed joint venture sounds quite promising. We and Tak On would jointly produce our standard water pumping equipment in our respective Hongkong factories and market this equipment under a single new brand name in Brazil. All costs, revenues, and profits would be shared equally and both firms would put up half of the estimated initial investment of $1 million (U.S.). Tak On said they needed our participation in the joint venture to obtain the needed investment capital and to share the risks of a new market entry. They also had heard that we have been considering an independent entry into Brazil's water pump equipment market and believe a cooperative joint venture would make both companies better off than a competitive battle for this new market.

Our analysis shows that a joint venture would yield a 20% return on investment for both firms. Tak On has already acquired strong support from the Brazilian government and this market should continue to expand. We have the necessary production capacity and we would be helping Tak On to get back on its feet after the difficult period it has been facing.

Alternatively, we can enter this market alone as we have been planning. In a competitive venture against Tak On, however, there is uncertainty about how much of the market we could capture. If Tak On doesn't have the resources to make a strong independent entry, we should gain a large market share. In this case we would earn a 25% return on our somewhat higher investment. On the other hand, Tak On might focus its energy on this new market because we had rejected their offer of a joint venture. Under this scenario, we could get only a small share of the market and perhaps only a 10% return on investment. Because of Tak On's situation, we believe the chances are two out of three that we could get a larger market share in a competitive venture and there is a one-third chance of getting a small market share.

Tak On has asked us to decide on their offer of a joint venture by June 12. Please let me know your thinking on this question so a formal reply can be made.

Yours truly,

Cheung Yee-Ching
President
South American Division
General Products International

APPENDIX C

May 30, 1986

Mr. Chan Wing-Tat
Vice-President, International Operations
General Products International
2300 Alexandra House
5000 Queen's Road
Hongkong

Dear Mr. Chan:

Congratulations on your new appointment. I am sorry to greet you with a problem so early in your new position, but we have a pressing situation in the

North American Division that requires your recommendation and you asked to be consulted on all international contracts.

Six months ago the Division began negotiating a contract to supply a robot toy to a New York wholesaler. During this period we have been investigating two alternative designs for the toy. One design is a standard one we have used successfully in several similar toys marketed throughout the world. The technology for producing this standard toy is well-known and we are sure to make a return of about 25% on our investment because the market for this design is large and stable. The vast majority of the engineering and marketing people in the Division recommend going with this standard design.

However, a couple of very knowledgeable people from the research and marketing departments support a new design they have extensively researched; but there is littler experience in marketing the new design though the costs in producing both designs are roughly the same. They argue the market for the standard design is not expanding and the Division needs to produce innovative products. The new design has its problems also. The major uncertainties seem to be whether this design will allow the toy to hold up under hard use and whether the North American market will accept the new design. Advocates of both designs agree that the new design has a much greater potential than the standard design. If it is accepted in the market and stands up to use, the new design could lead to a 40% return on investment. If not, the new design would yield only a 10% return, well below our Division's average return of 20%. Both groups also agree that the chances of success for this new design are 50-50.

The urgency on this issue is caused by the New York wholesaler's requirement that we complete the contract (with the design specified) no later than June 10, 1986. Starting production later than this date would jeopardize Christmas sales in North America. The wholesaler has no preference on the two designs because its fees are fixed as our foreign agent.

Shall we go with the standard design that has the support of the majority of our engineers and marketing people, or with the new design even though it has few advocates? Please let me know your recommendations on this issue as soon as possible.

Yours truly,

Raymond Lee
President
North American Division
General Products International

APPENDIX D

General Products International, Inc.
Memorandum

To: Mr. Chan Wing-Tat   From: Frank Chin
                                          Head, Customer Service

                                   Date: May 31, 1986

We have received three complaint letters within the last week from customers who have had serious problems with our new household electronic control panel. Two letters were from U.S. customers and one was from a Canadian customer. It seems that if the buttons are pushed in one particular sequence all appliances hooked up to the panel are automatically shut down. I checked with the manufacturing group that produces these units and they have confirmed the problem. It seems to be a programming flaw in the design of the control unit.

Although there appears to be no safety problem, the malfunction could seriously inconvenience customers by shutting down refrigerators, freezers, air conditioning units, and the like. We must take some action quickly to correct the problem. Two options have been suggested by the manufacturing group. First, they could recall all the units and replace the programming unit. We have already sold over 100,000 of these units internationally which retail for about $500 (U.S.). The recall and replacement costs would be about $50 for each unit. This adjustment would therefore cost the firm about $5 million (U.S.).

A more cost effective solution would be to mail each customer who sent in his warranty card a notice advising him of this problem and cautioning him against pushing the buttons in this particular sequence. This option would cost only $500,000 U.S. because we have the warranty list on our computerized database. The problem is that not all customers sent in their warranty cards so they would not receive our correction notice and even those who do receive the notice might not read it. If the problem occurs frequently enough, our customers might think our products are of poor quality and our reputation as a high quality producer might be tarnished. Our expected profits of $20 million for this year should not be affected. However, if your image as a quality producer deteriorates our expected profits of $20 million per year for the remaining four year life expectancy of the product will likely drop to only $15 million. I hope this doesn't happen, but the sales people I have contacted here estimate about one chance in four that the sales drop could occur.

The production, marketing, and design people at the headquarters have all put their heads together on this problem but these two options are all that we could come up with. What do you think? We need to come to a decision by June 12.

REFERENCES

Anderson, Erin and Anne T. Coughlan (1987), "International Market Entry and Expansion via Independent or Integrated Channels of Distribution," *Journal of Marketing*, 51 (January), 71–82.

Cascio, Wayne F. (1974), "Functional Specialization, Culture, and Preference for Participative Management," *Personnel Psychology*, 27 (4), 593–603.

Chakravarti, Dipankar, Andrew Mitchell, and Richard Staelin (1981), "Judgement Based Marketing Decision Models: Problems and Possible Solutions," *Journal of Marketing*, 45 (Fall), 13–23.

Chan, Wing-tsit (1967), "The Individual in Chinese Religions," in *The Chinese Mind*, Charles A. Moorehead, ed. Honolulu: University of Hawaii Press.

_____ (1986), *Chu Hsi and Neo-Confucionism*. Honolulu: University of Hawaii Press.

Ch'ien, Mu (1973), "On the Systems of Academic Knowledge," in *Higher Education and University Students*, Philip Shen, ed. Hongkong: University Press, 15–32 (in Chinese).

Erickson, Gary M., Johny K. Johansson, and Paul Chao (1984), "Image Variables in Multi-Attribute Product Evaluations: Country-of-Origin Effects," *Journal of Consumer Research*, 11 (September), 694–700.

Frederiksen, N., D. R. Saunders and B. Wand (1957), "The In-Basket Test," *Psychological Monographs*, 76, 438.

Gill, R.W.T. (1979), "The In-Tray (In Basket) Exercise as a Measure of Management Potential," *Journal of Occupational Psychology*, 52 (June), 185–97.

Han, Xinlan (1983), "Democratic Management in China's State-Owned Industrial Enterprises," in *China's Management Reforms*, K.C. Mun and K.Y. Wong, ed. Hongkong: New Asia College, The Chinese University of Hongkong, 117–32.

Hendry, Steven R. (1986), "The China Trade: Making the Deal Work," *Harvard Business Review*, 64 (July–August), 75–84.

Hofstede, Geert H. (1980), *Culture's Consequences*. Beverly Hills, CA: Sage Publications, Inc.

Johansson, Johny K. (1986), "Japanese Marketing Failures," *International Marketing Review*, 3 (3), 33–46.

Lazer, William, Shoji Murata, and Hiroshi Koska (1985), "Japanese Marketing: Towards a Better Understanding," *Journal of Marketing*, 49 (Spring), 69–81.

Lee, Kam-hon (1982), "Personal Values and Consumption Behavior, a Comparison Between Chinese and Western Managers," in *The Sinicization of Social and Behavioral Science Research in China*, Institute of Ethnology Academic Sinica Monograph Series B, No. 10 (April), 441–67 (in Chinese).

Levitt, Theodore (1983), "The Globalization of Markets," *Harvard Business Review*, 61 (May–June), 92–102.

Little, John D.C. (1970), "Models and Managers: The Concept of a Decision Calculus," *Management Science*, 16 (April), B466–B485.

_____ and Leonard M. Lodish (1981), "Comments on Judgement Based Marketing Decision Models," *Journal of Marketing*, 45 (Fall), 24–9.

MacCrimmon, Kenneth and Donald A. Wehrung (1984), "The Risk In-Basket," *Journal of Business*, 57 (July), 367–87.

_____ and _____ (1986), Taking Risks. New York: The Free Press.

McCullough, James, Chin Tiong Tan and John K. Wong (1986), "Effects of Stereotyping in Cross Cultural Research: Are the Chinese Really Chinese?" in *Advances in Consumer Research*, Vol. 13, Richard J. Lutz ed. Provo, UT: Association for Consumer Research, 576–8.

Meade, Robert D. (1969), "An Experimental Study of Leadership in India," *Journal of Social Psychology*, 79 (December), 283–4.

_____ and William A. Barnard (1973), "Conformity and Anticonformity Among Americans and Chinese," *Journal of Social Psychology*, 89 (February), 15–24.

Montgomery, David B. and Charles B. Weinberg (1979), "Toward Strategic Intelligence Systems," *Journal of Marketing*, 43 (Fall), 41–52.

Moore, Charles A. (1967), *The Chinese Mind*. Honolulu: University of Hawaii Press.

Naor, Jacob (1986), "Toward a Socialist Marketing Concept — The Case of Romania," *Journal of Marketing*, 50 (January) 28–39.

Pye, Lucian (1983), *Chinese Commercial Negotiation Style*. Cambridge, MA: Oelgeschlager, Gunn and Hain.

Redding, S.G. (1982), "Cultural Effects in the Marketing Process in Southeast Asia," *Journal of the Market Research Society*, 24 (2), 98–114.

Tan, Chin Tiong and John U. Farley (1987), "The Impact of Cultural Patterns on Cognition and Intention in Singapore," *Journal of Consumer Research*, 14 (March), 540–4.

Tse, David K., Russell W. Belk and Nan Zhan (1988), "Learning to Consume: A Longitudinal and Cross-Cultural Content Analysis of Print Advertisements from Hongkong, People's Republic of China and Taiwan," *Journal of Consumer Research* (forthcoming).

Tung, Rosaline L. (1981), "Patterns of Motivation in Chinese Industrial Enterprises," *Academy of Management Review*, 6 (July), 481–9.

Wallendorf, Melanie and Michael D. Reilly (1983), "Ethnic Migration, Assimilation and Consumption," *Journal of Consumer Research*, 10 (December), 292–302.

Wehrung, Donald A., Kam-hon Lee, David K. Tse and Han Vertinsky (1988), "Adjusting Risk Situations: Theory and an Empirical Test," working paper, University of British Columbia.

Wu, John C.H. (1967), "Chinese Legal and Political Philosophy," in *The Chinese Mind*, Charles A. Moore, ed. Honolulu: University of Hawaii Press.

Yin, Hai-kuang (1967), *The Future of Chinese Culture*. Hongkong: The Arts Book Store.

DAVID K. TSE is Professor of Marketing at the Department of Business and Management, City University of Hongkong.

KAM-HON LEE is Professor of Marketing and Dean of Business Administration at the Chinese University of Hongkong.

ILAN VERTINSKY is Professor of Policy and Director of the Cneter of International Business Studies, Faculty of Commerce and Business Administration, University of British Columbia.

DONALD A. WEHRUNG is Associate Professor of Policy, Faculty of Commerce and Business Administration, University of British Columbia.

22 The Trading House and the Challenge from the Far East

Norihiko Suzuki

I   Introduction

Researchers in export management have studied the various aspects of export activities of manufacturing firms (Cavusgil, 1976; Bilkey & Tesar, 1977; Bilkey, 1978; Brasch and Lee, 1978; Johnston & Czinkota, 1982). The export entry and expansion processes have been analyzed as a diffusion process (Tesar, 1975) as well as from the decision-making and information-processing perspectives (Reid, 1981). The characteristics commonly observed in these export-behavior models can be summarized as follows:

1.   The focus of research has been limited to the small-sized firms about to engage in export business or to those with a limited experience in the field (Bilkey & Tesar, 1977). Hence, the discussion has been centered on the newcomers and have limited export activity (Wiedersheim-Paul et al., 1978).

2.   The export models found in the literature are geared to analyzing the export behavior of manufacturing firms in the West. Consequently, such models have limited applicability when extended to the export activity of other countries, particularly from the Far East, on which the dynamism of future world-trade expansion is said to be largely dependent.

3.   Furthermore, the export models are geared solely to the exporter, thus underestimating the role and importance of the importer in the "game of trade."

Reproduced with permission from *Advances in International Marketing*, 3 (1989), pp. 249–258.

The trend observed among researchers of the West may be rationalized in light of the realities existing in the West, and in particular in the United States. Given the huge domestic market and unlimited natural resource wealth with which the United States is blessed, it has to be far less dependent on the foreign markets than countries from the Far East. On the other hand, the Asian nations, having a higher dependency on export trade for their survival, are engaged in a more dynamic trading activity and have far greater experience in foreign trade than do the Western nations. Hence, models developed in the Western literature are, in a sense, not always adequate in capturing the complex interactions in the export-import trade of these nations.

The time is ripe to develop more comprehensive models depicting the dynamic relationship of exporter and importer. In addition to developing such a model, this paper will introduce a third party: the trading house, which has remained indispensable to the success of the Asian nations in the world markets.

Hence this paper aims to develop a comprehensive model depicting the triangular relationship between exporter, importer, and the trading house, and to analyze the complex interactions involved in foreign trade. Such a model is assumed to have far-reaching implications for the West in view of the growing involvement of Western firms in the developing countries of the Far East.

II   The Far East model of trade

The players in the simplest trade scene are two: the exporter and the importer in their respective countries. Those trade partners may or may not know each other well. The latter case, that is, unfamiliarity between the trade partners, is not uncommon, and it is in this sort of unfamiliar trade relationship that the trading house is needed as an intermediary. The function of a trading house is basically that of a matchmaker between the potential seller and buyer. The trading house provides both the exporter and importer with a negotiating opportunity and participates in the negotiation as a mediator, sometimes representing the exporter side, and other times, the importer side. This tripartite relationship among exporter, importer, and the trading house as moderator is illustrated in Figure 1.

A unique characteristic of the trading house in this tripartite relationship is that, because it often acts as agent for the exporter and at the same time as agent for the importer, the trading house has to contain organizationally and functionally two diverging interests: In Figure 1, portion A of the trading house organization represents the exporter's interest, aiming at the maximization of the exporter's profit, and portion B depicts the importer's interest with the objective of maximizing the importer's profit. The function of the trading house is therefore to find the point of compromise, an optimal one if not the best one for both clients.

The reward to the trading house is payment for its service of compromising the inherently conflicting interests of the exporter and importer in terms of their profit maximization. The amount of reward for the trading house is assumed to be large when the task of compromising the two parties is very difficult, requiring an intensive involvement of the trading house in the negotiation between exporter and importer.

Figure 1   The Far East trade model

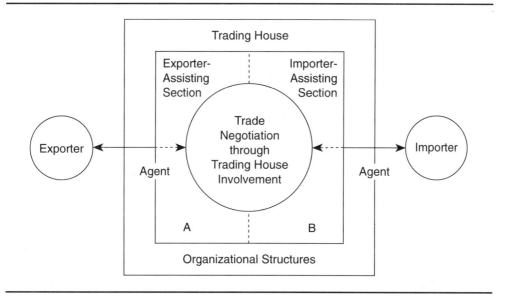

III   Exporter and importer categories

The process involving a manufacturing firm in the export business has been found to be similar to the diffusion process of information/technology (Rogers, 1971; Tesar 1975). The diffusion process applied to marketing also enables us to classify export manufacturing companies according to their degree of motivation, their preparation for the export business, and the timing of their involvement in the export activities. The manufacturing companies which are, or intend to be, involved in the export business can be classified into four categories:

1. *The Innovative Exporter.* This type of manufacturing company is highly motivated to be involved in and initiate export activities. It attempts to exploit any possibility of export business through its own effort, as well as through the assistance of a trading house to some extent. The main

characteristic of this kind of company is that it tries to differentiate itself from others by initiating the export business of unique and/or new items to the foreign markets (Cateora, 1983).

2.   *The Early Exporter.* Seeing the success of export by the innovative exporter, this type of manufacturing company quickly follows its leader. The early exporter is also motivated to export its items, but less so than the innovative exporter in the risky development of the unfamiliar foreign market. This sort of company makes export personnel available for catching up with the innovative exporter. The risk and uncertainty inherent in the foreign markets are reduced by the time of market involvement by this early exporter compared to the innovative exporter's initial exploitation of foreign markets.

3.   *The Late Exporter.* The third type of manufacturing company is the late exporter who holds a conservative and risk-aversive stance toward export opportunities. Only when the company feels that the profit will be secured without any unexpected risk, would it go into the export business. Its involvement in export would not be on a regular basis.

4.   *The Timid Exporter.* Unless the company is forced to go into the export market, probably as a result of losing domestic trade to competition and/or the stagnation of the domestic economy, the timid exporter would not go into the export market. The shortage of available export personnel and accordingly, the lack of export experience are the major causes of this timidity.

   On the importer side, we are also able to follow classification procedures similar to those for the export manufacturing company, which also fall into four categories of importing companies and/or agencies.

1.   *The Innovative Importer.* In the foreign market this type of buyer, usually small in number, shows a keen interest in a new product brought in from abroad. By importing the new product first, the company tries to take the lead in dominating the market. The innovative buyer-importer is also a risk-taker in that it has to introduce a new product to an undeveloped market. The product is, in that sense, highly differentiated in the foreign market. The reward and/or penalty of taking the risk will be enormous. If the new product is well accepted and therefore able to establish its brand in the foreign market, then the reward for the risk of importing the item will be large enough to compensate the effort and expenditure that were required to initiate the purchase of the item and enable the company to dominate the market.

2.   *The Early Importer.* Witnessing the successful penetration of a new product introduced by the innovative buyer, this group of importing companies will quickly follow the leader to import the same items from abroad. The market risk and uncertainty inherent in the new product introduction will have been reduced by this time thanks to the trial-and-error by the innovative buyers.

3.   *The Late Importer.* The late importer will join the two preceding groups in the import business only when it becomes clear that no major risk is involved in the business and the profit is secured.

4.   *The Timid Importer.* The last category of importer-buyer is the counterpart of the timid exporter. The timid importer has little motivation to import the item from abroad. This type of buyer is the last to import the item. In that sense, the items to be imported by the timid importer will most likely be less risky and therefore well known in the foreign market; that is, a standardized commodity.

The four types of exporting manufacturing companies can be ordered according to their degree of motivation as well as preparation for and timing of involvement in the export business: (1) the innovative exporter, (2) the early exporter, (3) the later exporter, and (4) the timid exporter. The same array can be developed for the importing companies, also ranking the four different types according to their degree of eagerness, and readiness for involvement and timing of entry in the importing business: (1) the innovative importer, (2) the early importer, (3) the late importer, and (4) the timid importer. By integrating these two arrays of exporter and importer categories, we can illustrate all the possible matches of exporter-importer interaction in a comprehensive way.

The function and contribution of the trading house is, as mentioned earlier, to help match the exporter and importer with varying degrees of motivation and readiness for trade so that both parties can reach a trade agreement. Figure 2 illustrates the comprehensive matrix of exporter-importer interaction through the trading house's matchmaking effort.

IV   Analysis of exporter-importer interaction

Each cell in Figure 2 describes the summary of the exporter-importer interactions through the assistance of the trading house. In general, the exporting manufacturing company is observed to be more aggressive, motivated, and ready for the transaction than the importer in the territory of the upper-right half of the interaction matrix (the triangle above the diagonal from the upper left down to the lower right). In the lower-left-hand triangle, the

Figure 2   Summary of exporter-importer interaction through the trading house

Importer-Assisting Section of Trading House				
Exporter category \ Importer category	Innovative Importer	Early Importer	Late Importer	Timid Importer
Innovative Importer	Trading house assistance seldom needed	Small amount of assistance to importer needed	Considerable amount of assistance and encouragement to importer needed	Significant amount of assistance and encouragement to importer needed; no risk/secured profit assured
Early Importer	Small amount of assistance to exporter needed	Small amount of assistance to both parties needed	Small amount of assistance to exporter; considerable amount of assistance to importer needed	Small amount of assistance to importer; significant amount of assistance to importer needed; no risk and secured profit assured
Late Importer	Large amount of assistance and encouragement to exporter needed	Small amount of assistance to importer; large amount of assistance to exporter needed	Considerable amount of assistance and encouragement to both parties needed	Significant amount of assistance to importer; considerable amount of assistance to exporter needed
Timid Importer	Significant amount of assistance and encouragement to exporter needed; no risk/secured profit	Small amount of assistance to importer; significant amount of assistance to exporter needed	Significant amount of assistance to exporter; considerable amount of assistance to importer needed	Significant amount of assistance and encouragement to both parties needed; no risk/secured profit assured

(Left axis: Exporter-Assisting Section of Trading House)

importing company exhibiting an active intent to buy the commodities from the foreign buyer is more aggressive than the exporter in seeking the trade partner.

The major function and contribution of the trading house to the exporter-importer interactions in the upper-right-hand triangle (where the exporter is more aggressive than the importer in an attempt to reach agreement in their negotiation) is to watch and check the aggressive exporter's behavior so that it will not hurt a disadvantaged importer (late and/or the timid ones), while encouraging the importer to initiate the steps to foreign trade activities with the aggressive exporter.

In the lower-left-hand triangle of the exporter-importer matrix, however, the situation is totally different: The exporting manufacturing company is less motivated, and may be reluctant to engage in the export business due to various reasons, while the importer is very eager to seek foreign sellers to buy its commodities. In this kind of situation, the function of the trading house is to encourage the exporter to sit down at the table and negotiate with the importer in order to conclude the contract.

The four cells composing the diagonal indicate that both exporting as well as importing companies are at the same level of motivation and readiness for trade, which, in a sense, results in a transacting stability between them. The first two cells in the diagonal (those in the upper-left) illustrate the situation in which both exporter and importer are very positive toward the trade between them: They are likely to reach the trade contract with little input assistance from the trading house. In the first cell of the diagonal, particularly the interaction between the innovative exporter and innovative importer, involvement of the trading house as moderator would be unnecessary or, if necessary, minimal. In the third and fourth cells in the diagonal, however, the assistance of the trading house is greatly required for the achievement of trade contact because both the exporter and importer are either late or timid in their motivation and readiness for foreign trade. Without the strong encouragement and assistance of the trading house, neither would be motivated to commence foreign trade.

In Figure 2, therefore, the negotiations between the exporter and importer depicted in the cells enclosed by the double lines are assumed to require less involvement and assistance from the trading house because both exporter and importer are well motivated. The reward to the trading house for its service as a mediator, therefore, is assumed to be small. On the other hand, the negotiations between the exporter and importer outside the double lines need a considerable amount of assistance from the trading house in order to be concluded successfully because either or both exporter and importer are less motivated for trade. The reward to the trading house for its service in the negotiations outside the double lines is therefore assumed to be substantial.

V   The alternative role of the trading house

The trading house is assumed, by definition, to function as the mediator between exporter and importer. It attempts to exploit all possible opportunities and deals between exporter and importer with expectation of payoff for its service.

There seem to exist, however, two basic patterns of trading house involvement in exporter-importer interactions: (1) balanced mediation, and (2) unbalanced mediation.

1. *The Balanced Mediation.* When the trading house mediates both exporter and importer in the same (or at least the similar) categories, that is, the early exporter-early importer combination (same category) or the innovative exporter-early importer combination (similar category), the amount of mediating input by the trading house may be equally allocated to exporter and importer because both are assumed to have the same and/ or similar level of motivation, readiness, and timidness (if any) for the trade. This type of mediator involvement, which allocates its mediating input rather equally to both exporter and importer, can be called balanced mediation by the trading house. In Figure 3, the truly balanced mediation cases of the trading house can only be traced along the diagonal where both exporter and importer possess the same attitudes toward trading, and are therefore classified in the same categories: the innovative, early, late and/or the timid exporter-importer combinations respectively. Including the cases of semibalanced mediation such as the innovative exporter-early importer combination in Figure 3, for example, (also see the other cells near the diagonal), we can draw the balanced mediation area enclosed by the dotted line in Figure 3.

2. *The Unbalanced Mediation.* In the cells where the urgency and motivation for the trade are very different for exporter and importer, for example, the early exporter-timid importer combination, the amount and direction of the mediating input by the trading house will be one-sided; that is, mainly directed toward the timid importer. Therefore, the involvement of the trading house in this case is unbalanced, learning more to the timid importer than the well-motivated exporter.

We can observe two unbalanced patterns of mediation in Figure 3: (1) the unbalanced mediation concentrating on the exporter side (the late and timid exporters), which is illustrated in the lower-left-hand area, and (2) the unbalanced mediation concentrating on the importer (the late and timid ones) located in the upper-right-hand area.

For sound development of function and organization of trading house, it is very important not to be excessively involved in unbalanced mediation only for one type of trading partner (either the exporter or the importer). Unbalanced mediation by the trading house in an excessive and continuous pace might cause, in the long run, a functional as well as organizational imbalance in the trading house. Even in the difficult case where the trading house has to deal with

Figure 3 Two types of trading house mediation

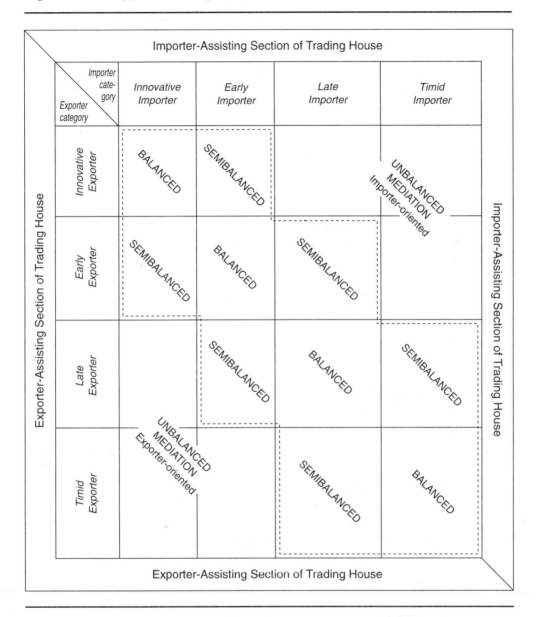

unbalanced mediation, an effort should be made to help the disadvantaged trade partner (the late/timid one, *vis-à-vis* the innovative/early categories) reach the level of the advantaged partner in its positive attitude toward the foreign trade. The trading house can then resume its functional and organizational balance as mediator through assisting the disadvantaged party.

Conclusion

In the Far Eastern nations, there have been arguments suggesting the possibility of a diminishing role of the trading house in the face of the growing powers of manufacturing companies with their own export/import divisions (Shosha-Shayo Ron — the declining trading house arguments). In reality, however, the size of the trading house and its relative importance at large in the trade context of the nation's export performance has been on the increase (Shosha Kino Kenkyu Kai, 1975), suggesting that the trading house has been and will remain indispensable to trade in the Far East. Nonetheless, researchers in the West have shown little interest in the activities of the trading house in their attempts at export model building.

More conceptual as well as empirical research is needed in understanding the behavior and activities of the trading houses, which have made and continue to make significant contributions to the export performance and development of nations in the Far East. A thorough understanding of their activities may have far-reaching implications in the revival of American trade in international markets.

REFERENCES

Bilkey, W.J. (1978). "An attempted integration of the literature on the export behavior of the firm." *Journal of International Business Studies*, 9(1), 33–46.

Bilkey, W.J., & Tesar, G. (1977). "The export behavior of small sized Wisconsin firms." *Journal of International Business Studies*, 8(1), 93–98.

Brasch, J.J., & Lee, W.Y. (1978). "The adoption of export as an innovative strategy." *Journal of International Business Studies*, 9(1), 85-93.

Cateora, P.R. (1983). *International marketing* (p. 505, 5th ed.). Homewood, IL: Richard D. Irwin.

Cavusgil, T.S. (1976). *Organizational determinants of firm's export behavior: An empirical analysis.* Ph.D. dissertation, University of Wisconsin at Madison.

Johnston, W.J., & Czinkota, M.R. (1982). "Managerial motivation as determinants of industrial export behavior." In M.R. Czinkota & G. Tesar (Eds.), *Export management: An international context.* New York: Praeger.

Reid, S.D. (1981). "The decision maker and export entry and expansion." *Journal of International Business Studies*, 12(2), 101–112.

Rogers, E.M. (1971). *Diffusion of innovation.* New York: Free Press.

Shosha Kino Kenkyu Kai [The Study Group of Trading House Function]. (1975). *Gendai Sogo Shosha Ron* [The Modern General Trading House]. Tokyo: Tokyo Keizai Shimposha.

Tesar, G. (1975). *Empirical study of export operations among small and medium-size manufacturing firms.* Ph.D. dissertation, University of Wisconsin, Madison.

Wiedersheim-Paul, F. et al. (1978). "Pre-export activities: The first step in internationalization." *Journal of International Business Studies*, 9(1), 47–58.

NORIHIKO SUZUKI is Professor of International Business at the International Christian University.

23 Global Asia in the 21st Century

Barry Wain

Barry Wain dissects the Asian economic miracle, offers explanations for its success and charts the region's future.

It is misguided to believe that forecasts can be made with any accuracy over 25 or 30 years. Twenty-five years ago, China was convulsed by the Great Proletariat Cultural Revolution and the war in Vietnam was escalating dangerously, establishing a pattern of violence, revolt and mayhem for the entire region. Apart from the social and economic damage that China did to itself in the Cultural Revolution, the officially inspired campaign spilled over into the neighboring countries: Burma, Nepal, Mongolia, Cambodia, Indonesia, Hongkong, Macao, Japan, Ceylon, Malaysia and Singapore. As efforts by those countries to meet the challenges were denounced by Beijing, vicious anti-Chinese riots broke out in Delhi, Kuala Lumpur, Penang, Jakarta and Rangoon.

In Vietnam, the United States was stepping up the bombing of the North, whittling down the number of targets that were off limits to their aircraft. They systematically took out bridges, roads, railways, power stations, factories and airfields, getting nearer and nearer the center of cities and towns — and closer to the Chinese frontier, raising the possibility of Beijing's intervention in the war.

Although the threat of famine had eased, Asia still faced the daunting task of trying to feed its teeming millions. That was the major problem. By one authoritative estimate, 700 million Asians were undernourished and 200 million were starving. At the core of the problem was a critical shortage of rice. Many countries were forced to take drastic action to avoid a crisis or catastrophe. Singapore, for example, began a full scale campaign to persuade its people to eat wheat instead.

Reproduced with permission from *The Asian Manager*, 6 (May–June 1993), pp. 20–26.

A new attempt at sub-regional cooperation, the Association of Southeast Asian Nations had just started. ASEAN replaced the moribund Association of Southeast Asia, or ASA, and although the aims and objectives were similar, ASEAN, with a hint of what the future held, gave its highest priority to the need to speed up economic development.

An economic miracle

Who could have predicted 25 or 30 years ago that Asia held such promise? The grim outlook that I have described held few clues to the economic miracle that was to come. And yet, in the past three decades, the major countries of Asia have developed rapidly, transforming the region into the most dynamic in the world. Asia has grown not only faster than other regions such as Latin America or Africa, it has also been able to sustain growth where others could achieve at best intermittent progress.

Interestingly, the powerful initial surge, or takeoff, seems to occur in waves: It started in Japan in the 1950s and continued there into the first part of the 1970s. The focus then shifted in the 1960s, 1970s and '80s to the four Tigers, or Little Dragons, which are also called the four NIEs, for newly industrialized economies — Hongkong, Singapore, South Korea and Taiwan. Then followed the 1970s and '80s boom in Southeast Asia, particularly Thailand, Malaysia and Indonesia. The spotlight is now playing in new areas — Southern China, Vietnam and India.

Japan grew out of poverty and into the world's second-largest economy by aggressively exporting, mainly to the United States, and to a lesser extent, Europe. The other Asian states have followed the Japanese experience and traded to prosperity. Moreover, the speed of industrialization has accelerated with each successive wave: Japan took nearly a century to build a modern economy. The NIEs achieved that in about 30 years. And it is most likely that the Southeast Asian and Southern China players will achieve the process even faster. Of the world's fastest growing economies in the past three decades, seven belonged to Asia. While world-wide living standards doubled on average in that period, average incomes in several East Asian countries quintupled.

Global share

An outcome of this powerful export-led growth has been an increasing role for Asia in the international economic order. For instance, Asia's share of world trade approached 25% by value in 1991 compared with just 10% 30 years ago. If we widen the definition of the region to include the entire Asia-Pacific, which of course encompasses the United States, the area produces nearly half of the world's output of goods and services and accounts for more than one-third of global trade.

Indeed, the world has come to depend on the economic dynamism of the region. Asia has emerged as a powerful engine of global growth. Economic prosperity in this region now means economic prosperity for everybody.

Success speculation

The reasons for this unparalleled and unprecedented success have been the subject of endless study, speculation and conjecture. The irony is that while just four decades ago, social scientists sought a hypothesis to explain why Asian economies remained stagnant, now they are seeking a ready explanation for their dynamism and vibrancy.

The truth is that there is no single model or recipe for this success. One has only to look at the wildly different ways Taiwan and Korea have gone about industrializing. Seoul poured credit into a handful of very large companies called *chaebol*, modelled on the *zaibatsu* that built Japan, while Taipei relied on tens of thousands of small factories. In the absence of a neat answer, we've been treated to all sorts of theorizing about Confucianism and Eastern values. Lee Kuan Yew, the former prime minister of Singapore, pinpoints what he calls "the intangibles" — among them "a belief in hard work, thrift, filial piety, national pride." Others maintain plain, simple greed. Certainly no one can deny self interest. You may have heard that in Hongkong we define sexual pervert as a man who loves women more than money!

Success explained

Still, I do think it is possible to identify some common features in the successful Asia-Pacific economies, features that often contradict the prevailing views and orthodoxy of the West:

- *First, strong government and political stability.* A form of government has developed in the region that political scientists call "soft authoritarianism." Its characteristics include a willingness to do whatever is necessary to achieve national development, with little need or opportunity for opposition groups to function. Indeed, the legitimacy of these governments rests primarily on their ability to achieve and sustain economic growth.
- *Second, a deep commitment to markets and the creation of a flourishing commercial and business environment.* This doesn't always mean completely free markets. Those strong governments, served by elite bureaucracies, intervene in their economies as often as deemed necessary with the exception of Hongkong's *laissez faire* administration, and even get involved in public housing and other areas. While they make mistakes, these governments are economically enlightened and always seem to get right crucial elements — for example, prices, so that there is no doubt goods are internationally competitive.

- *Third, a close and cooperative arrangement between the public and private sectors, epitomized by the expression, "Japan, Inc".* Despite authoritarian rulers, powerful bureaucrats and sometimes overbearing militaries, the climate for the private sector remains friendlier than it is elsewhere.
- *Fourth, a warm welcome for foreign direct investment.* These countries have promoted growth through exporting after realizing much earlier than most other developing nations the limitations of an import substitution strategy. They haven't feared loss of identity or exploitation by multinational corporations, but rather have used them to create jobs, transfer technology and gain access to overseas markets. Thus have they turned a once heretical approach into conventional wisdom.
- *Fifth, the cooperative, special role of workers.* Here is where Confucianism comes in. The state has taken the lead, investing heavily in education and training. For their part, workers have been prepared to go along or have been persuaded to go along, learning new skills, adapting to changing environments and often having to sacrifice immediate personal reward for the collective good. By ensuring that as many people as possible share the benefits of prosperity, however, governments have effectively conveyed the message: "We are all in the same boat."
- *Sixth, and finally, I would have to include the rather unique role that the United States has played since World War II.* Pax Americana provided not only the security umbrella for this development but set the example for Asia-Pacific nations. The United States encouraged a sense of free enterprise and capitalist development, and in addition opened its huge market to the region's products, notably commodities and manufactured goods.

Plaza Accord

A key turning point in the whole process of economic development in Asia was the realignment of exchange rates in 1985–86 especially the strengthening of the yen that followed the Plaza Accord. That realignment sharpened contrasts in comparative advantages within the region. It set in motion, or accelerated, a series of changes that created dazzling new investment flows and trading networks among these countries.

Again, Japan led the way to remain competitive, Japan started to move its manufacturing operations offshore. It took them first to the NIEs and then increasingly to South-east Asia. The NIEs, in turn, followed the Japanese, taking their manufacturing operations to locations with cheaper land and labor to Thailand, Malaysia, Indonesia and China.

The three Southeast Asian commodity producers — Thailand, Malaysia and Indonesia — were able to take advantage of this influx of investment to lessen their dependence on agriculture and, in the case of Indonesia, oil. Like the

NIEs, they are well on the way to developing strong manufacturing bases that are fuelling export-led growth.

So prosperity has proved contagious and has rolled southward in waves — accelerating all the while, as I noted earlier.

Asian integration

The processes I have been describing are tending to integrate Asia, adding an extensive network of regional economic and financial linkages to traditional international connections. It is worth noting that links in Asia are being forged almost exclusively by private sector initiatives, in contrast with the European Community, for example, which is based on government arrangements. These ties are created by geographic and economic complementarities — sheer market forces — not on formal decisions to exchange preferences and directly or indirectly discriminate against others.

Intra-Asian trade is booming. In earlier decades, Japan and the NIEs owed much of their enviable economic growth to their ability to sell more and more manufactured goods to markets outside the Asia-Pacific. But it has been apparent for some years that the United States and Europe could not — and would not — accept further large increases in Asian exports. Therefore, the countries of the region have learned to depend to a greater extent on trade within the region.

Between 1987 and 1990, intra-Asian trade rose by an average of 21% a year which was almost twice the growth rate of trade between Asia and North America. Significantly, Asia has emerged since the 1980s as the single largest export market for both the NIEs and the Southeast Asian group — Thailand, Malaysia, Indonesia plus the Philippines this time. Altogether, intra-regional trade increased from 34% of Asia's total trade in 1980 to 43% in 1990.

There is also a growing realization of foreign direct investment in Asia. American and a few major European companies continue to build and operate production facilities, but their role has been overshadowed by the new foreign direct investment coming from within the region itself. And it is coming not only from Japan and the NIEs, though the growth in the investments of Hongkong, Singapore, South Korea and Taiwan has been extremely dramatic.

Indeed, the four NIEs, taken together, are investing as much as Japan. But, in addition, almost every developing country in Asia is investing overseas — and increasingly in other Asian countries.

Growth areas

Behind this move offshore — begun seriously by Japan in the wake of the 1985 Plaza Accord that helped strengthen the yen by 50% — is the search for cheaper land and labor. The movement has become something of a stampede, giving rise to the concept of growth areas, often consisting of a combination of parts of countries as well as states themselves.

The most outstanding is Southern China, sometimes called Greater China, because it connects Taiwan to mainland China through and with Hongkong. Since the opening of China in 1978, Guangdong province, with three of the country's four Special Economic Zones, has become inextricably linked with neighboring Hongkong. With a population of 60 million, bigger than that of either Thailand or Britain, Guangdong is the fastest growing region in all China, with the highest level of both consumption and production of goods. For all practical purposes, Guangdong is a separate country, with Hongkong its engine and capital — and if it really were separate, it would be the fastest growing country in the world.

The joke is that Guangdong is more like a colony of freewheeling Hongkong than a province of communist China. One example: Hongkong manufacturing companies today employ more than three million workers across the border in China and fewer than 600,000 in Hongkong. Cumulatively, Hongkong companies have invested about US$20 billion in Guangdong. The entire Pearl River Delta really has become an extension of Hongkong — following Hongkong time, watching Hongkong television, sharing the same impatient desire to get ahead.

While political tensions prevail, Taiwan companies invest in China and trade with it mostly through Hongkong. Driven by the same commercial considerations as their Hongkong brethren, Taiwan businessmen channel investment into Fujian, a coastal province across the narrow Taiwan Strait that shares a border with Guangdong, and to Guangdong itself. Today, investment is estimated at around $10 billion, spread among more than 3,000 factories.

China's paramount leader, Deng Xiaoping, gave the area his blessing on a visit early last year when he called Guangdong Asia's "fifth tiger," and urged the creation of "little Hongkongs" all along the southern coast. The pace of development, already frenetic, has become positively frenzied. Thus is Southern China roaring ahead, fuelled by overseas-Chinese money and business acumen, as well as linguistic, social and religious affinities.

Vietnam, too, is ready to catch fire and will possibly lead all of Indo-China into a more prosperous future. Although temporarily overshadowed by the conversion of Eastern Europe and the old Soviet Union to capitalism, Vietnam has gone as far as most communist and former communist countries along the road to a market economy. While retaining its commitment to a one party-state — like China — it is eager to participate in the international division at labor, seeking foreign investment that might be attracted by abundant natural resources and, again, low costs. Vietnam's opening just over six years ago, has excited strong regional interest, with Taiwan and Hongkong leading the foreign investment push.

For the time being, Hanoi is hampered by an American economic embargo that blocks substantial Japanese investment and multi-lateral assistance by such organizations as the IMF and World Bank, which is essential to rebuild the country's infrastructure. But the embargo will be lifted before long, probably this year, and the gold rush will be on — led by Japan.

Worthy of note also is that India, too, has joined the ranks of believers, weighing in with sweeping industrial, trade and investment reforms intended to deregulate its economy. Most multinationals had written India off over the years, finding it too wedded to self-sufficiency and other outmoded socialist notions to make investment worthwhile. When the government of Prime Minister P.V. Narashima Rao produced the first flurry of policy reversals in July 1991, they were greeted skeptically. Mr. Rao has continued to progressively dismantle what is known as "the license Raj," despite domestic political opposition and his party's shaky hold on power.

Even the successful Southeast Asian countries are continuing to open their markets. Malaysia is liberalizing as it industrializes. Thailand started to reduce tariffs seriously under the year-long temporary premiership of Anand Panyarachun. And Indonesia is getting results as it works steadily on a program of deregulation.

Clouds of concern

Of course it is not all plain sailing. Some countries are being left by the way side — among them the Philippines — and even the successful ones are encountering major environmental and infrastructure problems. Politics, too, can inject a note of uncertainty — witness the current squabble between Britain and China over Hongkong's future.

While the end of the Cold War and the disappearance of what was regarded as the Soviet threat should portend a period of peace that can only be favorable for economic advancement, the Korean peninsula remains dangerously divided and Cambodia has yet to convert its ceasefire into genuine reconciliation. Asian political leaders worry that a hasty withdrawal of American forces may leave a power vacuum. They are also wary about domestic political instability, exemplified by last year's upheaval in Thailand, and the possible outbreak of localized disputes between neighbors.

The most real and immediate concern, however, is in the economics sphere: The possible collapse of the global trading system represented by GATT — the General Agreement on Tariffs and Trade. This is the system that is directly responsible for much of Asia's success. Although free markets have prevailed in spectacular fashion over central planning, the international commitment to the Uruguay Round of GATT negotiations, begun in 1986, have failed to conclude their discussions on an already-extended schedule. Further undue delay in concluding the Round could seriously erode confidence in the GATT system.

While these talks drag on, world trade continues to expand, though not as fast as in earlier decades. One reason is that protectionism, in all its new guises and forms, is also growing. At the same time, regionalism has begun to emerge as a potent — and potentially unsettling — trend in international economic and political life.

The nations and companies of Asia view growing regionalism in Europe and North America with varying degrees of apprehension. They don't really know yet what EC integration, with the unified market that was ushered in this year, perhaps eventually extending to cover all of Western Europe, will mean for the rest of the world, particularly for Asia. Similar uncertainties hang over the United States, which has negotiated with Canada and Mexico the North American Free Trade Agreement, known as NAFTA.

What is clear to Asia, however, is that Western Europe and North America both constitute major portions of the global economy, and that coalescing regionalism will have an enormous effect on outsiders. The real issue for Asia is whether an economic bloc is beneficial or pernicious — whether it reduces external as well as internal barriers and expands trade, or instead raises external barriers. Even if the EC and NAFTA have been initiated to derive greater efficiency and vitality from economies of scale and increased competition, they will trigger the formation of protectionist regional blocs if they adopt closed policies.

More to come

Still, Asia is likely to increase the global stake while continuing to outpace its rivals for the foreseeable future. While the world economy stagnated last year — and even Japan faltered — many of the developing countires of Asia shrugged off the recession in the West to record growth rates of the order of 5% to 12%.

So while I said at the outset that it is impossible to predict 25 or 30 years ahead with certainty, I am fairly confident of the direction. It seems likely that the successful East Asia economies, excluding Japan, will grow by 6% to 8% a year for the next decade — two and a half times faster than Europe and much faster than Latin America.

There is a momentum at work that is certain to carry large parts of the region to new levels of economic development. These countries have somehow acquired the ability, as one report has put it, to "adopt new approaches that emphasize the freeing of market forces through deregulation, privatization and the elimination of constraints on trade and investment." And consider this: More than half the increase in the world's labor force over the next 25 years will take place in this region.

One economic guru, Gus Hooke, who previously worked for the IMF, calculated the industrialized countries now account for 74% of the world economy and Asia, excluding Japan, just 9%. He believes that by the year 2050 the OECD share will fall from 74% to 12% and developing Asia's share will rise from 9% to 57%. According to his scenario, the top three economic powerhouses then will be China with 15% of world income, India, with almost 10% and the US with 5%.

This inexorable shift in economic power away from Europe and North America has led to the notion of a Pacific Century. Although that notion may seem challenged at times by the dramatic events taking place in Europe and elsewhere, I have no doubt that Asia-Pacific will become increasingly important in world affairs, even if Gus Hooke is a bit off mark with his long range forecasts. Asia is where the action will be, at least until the dawn of the 21st Century — and quite possibly for decades beyond.

DEVELOPING WORLD MARKETS

Regionalism vs. multilateralism

The big debate continues. Is the world going to continue to become an ever-more integrated economy — or are we going to see it split into regional trading blocs?

Internationalists see regional groupings as stepping stones to greater international trade and investment. Tackling the hard issues of dismantling tariff and investment business on a regional basis makes it a manageable process.

As each region frees up trade between countries within them, they become richer and better importers from outside their region. Their companies become more efficient and confident and seek to expand outside their regions. The global nature of companies makes them exert political influence in favor of an open trading system. Some 20% of trade in both the US and Japan is between domestic firms and their foreign affiliates.

The North American Free Trade Area (NAFTA) has been at pains to stay with GATT. Trade will be created as a result of regional GNP being higher than it would have been otherwise. Protectionist pressure will be concentrated on politically sensitive areas such as agriculture. That is the case for the optimists. Trade between EC members went up from 50% of the total in 1980 to 60% 10 years later. But EC total trade has gone up by half. And trade with East Asia has gone up tow-and-a-half fold.

Regionalists say that a political dynamic builds up which favors those inside the fortress — and this creates antagonism with other fortresses.

Regional grouping allows the bad guys — e.g., agricultural lobbies — to get together. The EC is spending more on agricultural support than if each country had been left to its own devices.

The EC or NAFTA will create the opportunities for lobbies to moan and groan about the fairness of trade — the playing field's not being level. Japan first and now Asia as a whole is increasingly regarded as more of a threat to North America and Europe than an opportunity. Expect more Asia-bashing — unless the North American and European economies are more successful.

An open tripolar world

Can we assume that economic forces left to themselves will be on the side of the internationalists and will lead to a benign, tripolar world, in which each region increases intra-regional trade and investment?

Idealism and increasing interdependence are not sufficient by themselves to maintain the pace of integration. It is vitally important for the world that the GATT talks succeed. The vision of an Asia standing alone is exciting — but in the meantime, we are talking about $500 billion of trade between East Asia and the other two regional blocs.

If that trade is politicized and diverted while Asia is still in its early stages of emergency, then that state of emergence will be delayed and could well be turned into a state of emergency.

So far, Asia has been too muted over the GATT talks. It needs an APEC to speak more loudly for its interests. Japan is inhibited about speaking up because of its massive guilt complex over its $100 billion trade surplus. American companies that are moving their manufacture to cheaper Asian locations are similarly gagged in speaking up publicly for free trade — since it leads to job losses.

An even more integrated world economy cannot be counted on as a fact of life. It is one of those facts that has to be created. The price of free trade is eternal vigilance.

Asian managers and the world economy

The forces leading to globalization of business continue unabated: I, for one, am an unreconstructed globalist. My observations:

• Even more market niches have to be exploited globally to get competitive advantage.

- Corporations are now IT networks organized to source supplies globally.
- Market presence requires, of course, local marketing, but so much of the thoughtware applies around the world.

Build global companies

If I am right, then the first implication for Asian managers is the need to create global corporations. But apart from Japan, Asia is deficient in creating the sophisticated structure combining entrepreneurial talent with analytical ability known as the transnational corporation.

They are difficult to create and have a tendency to fossilize as soon as they are built — look at the recent problems at IBM, General Motors and American Express to name but three fallen stars of the business school case studies.

Perhaps, Asia has viable alternatives in the Chinese family firm, or the Korean *chaebol* but so far the structures in existence have not truly been tested internationally.

With fast-growing domestic markets, and a preponderance of trade rather than investment, there has not been the need to create the learning, transmitting, professionally managed company.

That will change as Asia's economies move up the value-added chain, and lose the advantage of cheapness as labor costs converge. The most prominent model is the Japanese one — but the problem of lifetime employment and company loyalty does not necessarily fit the more individualistic age into which we are moving. Many young Japanese salarymen were getting bored and impatient — until the last few months when they saw cracks in the habits of a lifetime employment.

What the Asian Institute of Management is doing here is of vital importance, because the business cultures of Asia Pacific, to quote Gordon Redding, "do not automatically gravitate towards building complex organizations."

Maybe Asian business enterprises can be internationally competitive and remain simple, family-run and entrepreneurial.

The second imperative for Asian business is to do its bit for making the economic world more interdependent.

In the 1980s, foreign direct investment has been rising faster than world trade for several reasons:

- to reduce the costs of worldwide manufacture;
- to get plugged into the local economy

- to get behind fortress Europe and fortress America and being seen to be good employers and job creators in the process.

Does this seem an unlikely strategy to recommend in the Philippines in 1993? While appropriate for Japan, can it be appropriate for the rest of Asia?

Yes. The way to start as a global investor is by becoming a regional investor. Note that recently the Philippine-based San Miguel Corporation has invested successfully in Hongkong and is now moving into Indonesia.

Foreign direct investment is politically necessary to ensure interdependence and is necessary from a business point of view to learn to manage the process. In the future it will be necessary from an economic perspective because Asia is blessed with a high savings ratio and the Western world and Japan are ageing and will be running down on savings.

My main prescription is that Asia must look beyond Asia. It must build corporations and then use them to become world investing machines.

Excerpted from a speech by David Gordon, CEO of the Economist Group, U.K. at the conference "The Asian Manager: Shaping the Future".

BARRY WAIN is Editor at Large, *The Asian Wall Street Journal.*

24 Asia in the Year 2020: A Regional Scenario

Ibarra C. Gutierrez

What will East Asia be like in the year 2020? Can this booming region, home to the fastest growing economies in the world today, sustain its forward momentum? Will it be able to resolve the many cultural, social, political and economic tensions that even now are threatening to divide its teeming population? More important, what kind of managers will East Asia need by the year 2020 so the region can live up to its rich promise?

To answer these and other questions, the Asian Institute of Management conducted a 12-month survey in eight East Asian countries. (For purposes of the survey, the AIM defined East Asia as the region from Myanmar, around the southern and eastern coast of China, to Korea but excluding China and Japan.) The survey, whose main objective was to come up with a regional scenario for the year 2020 and, thus, guide the Institute in designing its management programs for the next 25 years, involved the AIM's governors, faculty and alumni, as well as noted experts in areas that are of prime interest to East Asians. Researchers in a number of organizations in the region, notably the Center for Southeast Asian Studies of the University of Hongkong, Export Credit Insurance Corporation of Singapore Ltd., Acer Incorporated of Taiwan and Bangkok Bank Ltd., also contributed substantially to the project.

The country surveys — covering Hongkong, Indonesia, Korea, Malaysia, the Philippines, Singapore, Taiwan and Thailand — were spearheaded by the AIM governors and alumni associations concerned and made use of various visioning techniques. For instance, the Singapore survey was based primarily on the government publication *Singapore: The Next Lap*. In like manner, the Malaysian scenario adopted the expectations and plans laid down by Prime Minister Mahathir Mohamad in *Malaysia: The Way Forward*. For Korea, David L. Balangue, a partner at SyCip, Gorres, Velayo & Co. and the auditing firm's

Reproduced with permission from *The Asian Manager*, 5 (April–June 1992), pp. 22–27.

Korean expert who was commissioned to draft the scenario, used *Korea Year 2020: Prospects and Issues for Long-Term Development*, a 1985 study made by the Korea Development Institute, as the jump-off point for his own projections.

The scenarios for the other countries, on the other hand, drew heavily from consultations with various experts. In the Philippines, for example, a modified Delphi method was used which called for a three-stage consultation with 18 experts in the fields of business and industry; agriculture; labor; education, culture and religion; economy and literature/journalism; politics; and non-government organizations (NGOs).

Meanwhile, due to the difficulty of coming up with accurate projections beyond 1997 — the year Beijing regains control over Hongkong — drawing up the scenario for the Crown Colony was delayed. As of press time, the Center for Southeast Asian Studies of the University of Hongkong was still working on the project. (*The Asian Manager* has published the paper in its next issue.)

The country scenarios were incorporated in a paper, *Asia 2020: A Scenario of East Asia in the Year 2020*, which was presented by Dr. Victor A. Lim, Far East Bank & Trust Co. professor of business management at AIM, during the conference "In Search of the Asian Manager for the Year 2020." The conference, held on Feb. 12–13 at the Philippine International Convention Center, was sponsored by the AIM jointly with the Asia Pacific Economic Cooperation's Human Resource Development-Business Management Network.

The world's biggest market

East Asia, already one of the world's biggest markets, will be the largest economic region by the year 2020 with a population of about 650 million and a combined gross domestic product of US$15,000 billion. By this time, some key political changes would have also taken place: the Association of Southeast Asian Nations (ASEAN) which now has as members Brunei, Indonesia, Malaysia, the Philippines, Singapore and Thailand, would have expanded to include Vietnam, Cambodia, Laos and Myanmar; the two Koreas would have reunited; and Taiwan and Hongkong would have reunified with China as autonomous provinces.

According to the AIM survey, the regional business scene will be dominated by Asian multinationals that are owned by East Asian, Japanese and Chinese stockholders. While American and European capital will still be present, their equity shares will be significantly smaller. Capital formation streams will be spearheaded by the overseas Chinese network made up of ASEAN citizens of Chinese heritage who are emphatically nationalistic.

These Asian multinationals will employ host country nations as executives at the highest management levels of their branches and subsidiaries. Branch and country managers will be delegated wider powers over more varied operations.

In the home office, meanwhile, management teams will replace the individual chief executive officer. The "superstar" manager will be a thing of the past.

The use of faster and more efficient information handling and communication systems will eliminate several steps in the decision-making ladder and result in flatter organization charts. This trend will likewise be seen in the public sector following the granting of political autonomy to local government units.

By the year 2020, business ideas and techniques would have become more Asian and less Western. Management methods will be based on adaptations of and improvements on the Japanese kaizen techniques. There will also be a revival of Confucian and related work ethics.

Notwithstanding the move toward more Asian management styles, however, communication within the region will be conducted in a Western language. English will be widely used in East Asia as the language of business.

In the East Asian countries, there will be a major shift in the peoples' source of livelihood away from agriculture to the services sector. Based on the AIM survey, by the year 2020, only about 10% of the region's population will depend on agriculture for their living, while over 50% will be employed in the various service industries.

Industry will continue to play an important role in the economy. According to the country scenarios, key industries will locate in the countryside, prompting the emergence of small- and medium-scale support enterprises that will provide labor-intensive parts manufacture and assembly, minor repair and construction contractors, as well as certain professional and business services.

The location of "pole growth" industries in the countryside will not only attract support and linked enterprises but will also help ease one of the major problems of the region: the over-population and over-crowding of cities. With the economic improvement these industries will generate, farmers will stay in the countryside and the unemployed will be attracted away from the urban areas.

Over-population and other "people problems," however, will continue to be the basic agents of change in East Asia. These include such issues as the unequal incomes between cities and rural areas, between industrialized and developing districts in the same country or among neighboring countries; the aging population on one hand and the rising cost of social services on the other; the realignment of cultures among reunited peoples; and the people's growing awareness of ecology problems.

Meanwhile, the agents of change identified in the survey include longer compulsory education and the shift of concentration toward technical-vocational training, students and workers returning from abroad, and the decentralization of political decisions from the national to local government units.

Following are the highlights of the different country scenarios for the year 2020:

Indonesia: stronger conglomerates

By the year 2020, Indonesia will have an increasing number of stable and financially strong business conglomerates. These conglomerates will result from the economic boom years of the late 1980s through the 1990s, as well as the mergers and acquisitions initiated by both large and small-scale enterprises. These conglomerates will be predominantly owned by Indonesians, a situation which will compel an integration of pribumi and Chinese cultures.

The businesses of these conglomerates will chiefly be in support of a full-blown industrial economy. This is in line with the government's thrust of decreasing the country's dependence on agricultural and oil-based exports and increasing its capacity to manufacture high quality finished products. Indonesia's industrialized economy will be adequately supported by medium-scale industries and a strong agricultural sector that will continue to provide the needed raw materials.

To supply the manpower needs of a growing industrial economy, Indonesia will invest heavily in skills development. People will remain the country's richest resource. By the year 2020, Indonesia's population will reach 253.7 million despite a projected drop in the growth rate from the present 2.1% to 0.66%. Fifty two per cent of the population is expected to live in urban areas, with the bulk concentrated in Java and Sumatra notwithstanding the government's campaign to develop the country's eastern regions.

In support of Indonesia's economic program, specifically, its long-term industrialization plan, education and human resource development will focus on producing competent and professional managers, a highly skilled labor force and self-sufficient entrepreneurs. These will be achieved through the following:

- The government will concentrate on providing technological and vocational courses at the secondary level. Emphasis will also be given to the teaching of English at this level.
- On the tertiary level (universities and colleges, both private and public), the focus will be on the development of entrepreneurial skills needed to run businesses in the manufacturing and agricultural sectors.
- The private sector will provide management development programs to their employees. Programs commonly offered in top business schools in the West will be offered as part of career path programs. These courses should prepare employees to take on higher responsibilities within their respective organizations.

With its heavy investment in human resource development as well as in top-of-the-line technology and processes, Indonesia will produce more sophisticated, functional and independent businesses. Most of these ventures will be fully automated and run by Indonesians, reducing the country's dependence on expensive foreign experts.

Indonesia is also expected to greatly benefit from its membership in the ASEAN, particularly the "growth triangle" it forms with Malaysia and Singapore. While Malaysia and Singapore strengthen their capital base and "export" their capital together with their management and marketing expertise throughout the region, Indonesia will continue to provide a relatively cheap source of skilled labor.

With Indonesia's huge land mass and abundant human resource, it can provide alternative sites for industries in Malaysia and Singapore. This will enhance the transfer of technology to Indonesia which is currently on a 25-year program to industrialize itself. An "open market" policy shall likewise attract the foreign investment required to hasten the country's economic development.

In a nutshell, Indonesia will industrialize to enable it to build a more modern society which, however, will retain its native culture and traditions. This will be achieved within the parameters of Indonesia's brand of democracy, *pancasila*.

Korea: coming to grips with unification

The unification of North and South Korea, expected to occur in the middle to late 1990s, will considerably change Korean demographics and standard of living in the first two decades of the 21st century. By the year 2020, however, significant strides would have been achieved toward the integration of the two economies with only minor issues remaining unresolved, involving mainly regional differences.

The unification, to be bankrolled by the South, will create some dislocation in the South Korean economy in the first decade of the next century. Funds that otherwise would go to housing, social infrastructure and defense in the South will be spent instead in rehabilitating the economy of the North. The benefits of the unification and the integration of the two economies will be felt only starting in the 2010s.

The unification, for instance, will help ease the tight labor situation in the South. The substantial addition to the workforce will reverse the trend and initially result in lower overall labor cost in the peninsula. For the first five years after integration though, there will be discontent among the South Korean workforce because of the movement of labor-intensive industries northward. The resulting stabilization of labor cost in the next five years, however, will increase Korea's competitiveness in the global market.

Two social issues will confront the unified Korea in the year 2020. First, the aging population will become a heavy burden to the government in terms of social welfare, pension and medicare. The government's success in bringing down population growth to 1% since the 1980s and the Korean family's preference to have only one or two children will result in a slightly decreasing labor force. Hence, while the economically active population dwindles, or, at best, remains unchanged, the greying population it supports continues to increase with the aging of the "baby boomers" of the 1950s and 1960s. (Korea's population is projected to reach 75 million in the year 2020, with life expectancy over 75 years.)

By the year 2020, the national welfare pension system started by the government in the mid-1980s will be facing severe funding problems since the initial plan did not factor in the social welfare needs of the North Koreans. As a result, social services, in general, will lag behind demand.

Second, the unification and the wide disparity in income between the North and South will give rise to regional distrust and animosity that are expected to be carried over to the 2020s. The industries in the North will be predominantly controlled by southerners by virtue of their better business skills, bigger capital and superior technology. The northerners, to a great extent, will remain providers of labor to the rich investors from the South. The South will also remain more progressive than the North. Government programs to correct the disparity will be in place by the year 2020, but will likely take another generation to eliminate the problem.

In the business scene, the *chaebols* (conglomerates) that spearheaded Korea's growth in the 1970s–1980s will continue to dominate trade and industry. The increasing globalization of the world economy will show that size and integration are the key competitive factors, prompting Korea to tone down its efforts, started in the 1990s, to reduce the economic power and influence of the conglomerates.

By the year 2020, however, there will be more rationalization in the sense that these conglomerates' industrial concentration will be limited. In addition, there will be less government participation in business and the bulk of trade initiatives will come from the private sector.

The country will be Japan's main rival in terms of technological advances. Korea, Japan and Taiwan/China will be the primary driving forces of the Asian economy, which, by the year 2020, will be the largest trading bloc in the world. The need to compete with a unified Europe and a unified America will increase the need for joint research and development efforts and trade initiatives within the East Asian region. Cross-border investments in the region will be strong, with Korea and Japan as the largest sources of capital and technology.

Malaysia: an affluent domestic market

Malaysia is expected to have a population of 31 million by the year 2020. People will be richer and the standard of living higher, with the country posting a per capital income of M$28,000 (US$10,000). With such a large and affluent domestic market, the Malaysian economy though linked to international markets, is relatively independent and self-sufficient.

The economy is also broad-based and diversified. By the year 2020, the services sector will account for around 55% of GDP. This sector will grow at a much faster rate (10% annually) than the overall GDP growth of 7% per annum from 1990 through 2019. Its major sub-sectors will be electricity, gas and water, as well as transportation, storage and communication. The impetus for the rise of these sub-sectors will come from the privatization of utilities initiated in the 1990s. Other key sub-sectors are finance, education, insurance, real estate and business services, plus the wholesale, retail, tourism and entertainment businesses.

Malaysia's financial industry is seen to provide strong competition to both foreign and East Asian banking and non-banking financial institutions offering various financial products and services in the region. By the year 2020, the country's financial outpost in Labuan would have become one of Southeast Asia's international business centers. Malaysia's securities market, on the other hand, is expected to become the regional market for Southeast Asia with estimated total capitalization in excess of US$300 billion.

The manufacturing sector, meanwhile, is expected to contribute approximately 30% of GDP. The sector will be dominated by a number of large-scale, high-technology plants — belonging primarily to the electrical and electronics industry — producing upscale consumer goods and sophisticated intermediate and final capital goods. These large plants will be supported by small- and medium-scale industries in sub-contract manufacturing of components and precision instruments.

Agriculture will remain an important sector, contributing roughly 6.5% of GDP. The hectarage of agricultural land will be smaller by the year 2020 but yields will be higher. A relatively large migrant labor force and R&D in biotechnology applications will help sustain this sector.

Investments in the services and manufacturing sectors will boost construction, whose share in GDP is projected to reach around 5%. The programmed built-up infrastructure will provide the main impetus for growth to this sector.

In general, the country's business scene will be dominated by joint-venture corporations and by small- and medium-scale enterprises. The business climate will be very competitive, with business firms being very much customer-driven. Efficiency and competitive costs will be the key considerations.

Malaysia's external trade sector, meanwhile, is expected to remain robust, particularly with the establishment of the ASEAN Free Trade Area and the implementation of the market liberalization policies of the General Agreement on Tariffs and Trade (GATT). In this regard, Malaysia will continue its export-led development strategies. It will also continue to attract substantial foreign investment while increasing its outgoing investments in some neighboring countries.

In order to push Malaysia's economic development, more power and control will be given to the central government, although the federal system will still remain in place. Government policies will emphasize economics more than anything else. Within the country, policies will be geared toward further economic development and further enhancing Malaysia's competitiveness in the international market. In its relations with the outside world, Malaysia's policies will be geared toward greater liberalization of trade.

The Philippines: catching up with its neighbors

The image of stability and progress that made the East Asian region so attractive in the last two decades of the 20th century will finally settle on the Philippines by the year 2020. By this time, the intrinsic viability of the country and its people would have emerged from the cloud of man-made and natural disasters that has darkened its future since the restoration of democracy in 1986.

By the year 2020, the Philippine economy will be growing at a healthy clip, still behind its ASEAN colleagues but no longer limping behind everyone. In fact, it will begin to reassert its leadership in the region. The private sector will accept larger responsibilities in basic investments, while the government — both national and local — will give more serious consideration to economic realities in economic planning, monetary policies and fiscal management.

With Filipinos expected to number about 120 million, excluding some eight to 10 million overseas workers and their families living abroad, in 2020, over-population will continue to be a major concern and an important determinant of change. By this year, in fact, the country's swelling population would have forced the government to implement a number of key changes in national policy direction. Beginning at the turn of the century, the government would concentrate its programs on people. In so doing, it would usher in a period of personal prosperity and a higher standard of living affecting even the smaller barrios and the urban poor. Government efforts to equalize income opportunities would relieve inner city congestion while upgrading the quality of life in the rural centers.

The population explosion would have also triggered changes in the educational system. The national government, by the turn of the millennium, would reintroduce the national testing system, but this time it would be implemented through extensive counselling and adapted to community circumstances and priorities. Employment opportunities and attractive salaries would have overcome the bias of the 20th century for white collar jobs. Students readily heed the suggestions of educational counsellors to pursue careers in technology, science and engineering.

By the year 2020, the availability of skilled manpower will lead to the emergence of a large number of small- and medium-scale support industries. The government's concentration on primary and secondary industries that characterized its past incentive programs will shift to the smaller enterprises that support these large concerns by providing industrial, commercial and professional services.

In such a situation, large manufacturing complexes will concentrate on their areas of expertise, leaving services and minor component inputs to small suppliers. Thus, growth centers will attract pole industries surrounded by small, independent ancillaries. This combination will make provincial locations for industrial plants less of a problem.

These countryside developments, though still concentrated in selected areas, will redirect the historical economic trend in the Philippines. The rural areas will experience much faster growth than the larger cities, bringing about a corresponding rise in the standards, tastes and sophistication of the market for manufactured products.

In the cities, the stock market will reach out to both the business community and the housewife-investors. There will be a larger number and a wider variety of listed companies. CEOs will pay more attention to stock price management, including stock and cash dividends, public relations and high-profile growth projects. The stock market, the result of the merger of the two exchanges in the mid-1990s, will become a true capital market.

With the country finally attaining political stability, sizable volumes of foreign investments will come in. (Multinationals, in fact, would have started to return after the 1992 elections.) This time, however, multinationals will look for suitable and responsible Filipino partners. More cautious foreign investors with better funded and more sophisticated partners will replace the unequal partnerships of the Marcos era.

These new multinationals will have two distinct features. First, they will be predominantly ASEAN companies. Several conglomerates similar to Sime Darby will come from Indonesia, Malaysia and Thailand. The Japanese and Koreans will maintain a strong presence, but more funding will originate from Singapore.

Second, these multinationals will pay greater attention to ecology and the environment. The adoption of globalization concepts and concerns in the mid-1990s would fix a sharp focus on the protection of planet Earth.

Singapore: the region's business center

Singapore, which, by the year 2020, would have already attained a developed country status, will be at the forefront of the ASEAN economies, boasting of the highest per capita income in the region. The standard of living will remain high despite the expected increase in the population to four million, a huge jump from the 2.7 million at the end of the 1990s.

Singapore is envisioned to become a "global village," a hub for business and a center for overseas purchasing offices, bunkering and financial services, among others. By this time, the country will effectively be into high value added forms of production and will be promoted and developed in terms of its capabilities in specific niches rather than individual projects.

The "Growth Triangle" involving Singapore, Indonesia and Malaysia will be in an advanced phase with Singaporean companies putting in considerably more investments in Indonesia and Malaysia in particular.

Complementing the development of the country as a major business hub is the concept of R&D business parks to enhance and ensure that Singapore will remain at the cutting edge of specific industrial activities. The industrial parks already existing by the late 1990s will be supplemented by major industrial estates in Ayer Rajah and Rochester Park, an aviation business park near Seletar Airbase and a medical business park near the Singapore General Hospital.

Local enterprises will play an important role in contrast to the reliance on multinationals at the start of Singapore's economic development. They will account for more than 50% of the value added and 70% of the employment evident in the 1990s. Singaporean companies would have grown in size and stature, reaching international standards of production, quality and innovation. They will also be bigger investors outside of Singapore. In their activities, however, these companies will put greater emphasis on ecology and the environment.

Telecommunications and sea and air facilities will be considerably advanced and expanded to meet the anticipated growth in demand. In the area of telecommunications, it is possible that by the year 2020, Singapore will have its own communication satellite. International traffic expansion will be met via the installation of high-capacity optic fibers, satellite-linked submarine cables and new telephone switches. New information technology would also have ensured that a major regional data processing and information center is in place in Singapore.

Airport and harbor facilities will be enhanced and upgraded to enable Singapore to stay ahead as a major "airtropolis" and the busiest container port in the world. In addition, a new port will be opened to meet the expansion in the volume of cargo handled.

As Singapore becomes more global in outlook, emphasis will be given to the fact that Singaporeans should remain "Singaporean" in heart and mind. To help organize the Singaporeans residing abroad, an NGO established in 1991, the Singapore International Foundation, will bring Singapore closer to Singaporeans overseas as well as to ex-Singaporeans and friends of Singapore around the world. It will nurture a Singaporean consciousness among overseas Singaporeans mainly through the Singapore clubs which will continue to expand in size and number throughout the world.

Taiwan: toward greater internationalization

Taiwan, boasting of the biggest cash reserves in the world today, will increasingly look outward. By the year 2020, the Taiwanese economy will be more international, characterized by a bigger number of multinationals with more substantial investments abroad. While trade with America will decrease, trade with Southeast Asian countries, including the People's Republic of China, will increase.

Overall, the economy will grow at a moderate pace of 5%. Prices will remain stable and the unemployment rate will stay low. Due to the shortage of local labor, despite the high wage rates, there will be an increase in the hirings of foreign workers. Capital and labor relationship will become more harmonious. Capital-intensive industries will replace labor-intensive ones.

The services sector will dominate the economy, accounting for 60% of GDP. Financial services will play a central role in the economy. Meanwhile, capital- and technology-intensive manufacturing industries will remain important. The top industries by the year 2020 will be machinery, information, chemicals, precision instruments and equipment.

In contrast, the growth of the agricultural sector will slow down. Agriculture's role in the economy will gradually diminish and there will be a shift toward high value added farm products.

The social welfare system will improve but the increase in benefits plus the rise in the population to 24 million — with people 60 years old and above accounting for 20.7% — could reduce the overall savings rate. This could lead to deficit spending by the government as tax revenues will not be enough to meet expenditures.

In the area of politics, the drive toward democracy will go on, with pluralism continuing to provide the main impetus. This drive will culminate with the holding of direct presidential elections in 2020.

While the idea of an independent Taiwan remains unlikely, the issues dividing Taiwanese and Chinese Mainlanders will diminish. The possible unification with PRC is difficult to predict as it involves too many still unresolved questions. Such a unification, however, could alter everything.

Thailand: private sector-led growth

In the year 2020, Thailand will become a market economy more fully. This will be brought about mainly by the government's liberial economic policy which aims to create competition both domestically and *vis-à-vis* the outside world. In this matter, the private sector will take the lead in deciding the direction the Thai should take. The government's role as controller will weaken considerably, to be replaced by guidance and facilitation. Government intervention will occur only in the face of unanticipated shock in order to maintain overall stability.

Thailand's economic growth will not be very high but will be healthy enough to provide stability in the system. In a comparative sense, Thailand will be one of the leading countries in Asia in terms of economic growth and stability. Price stability will be the top priority of policy-makers to ensure that inflation does not undermine the country's prosperity.

Industries will be relocated to the regions and labor will be able to find employment without moving to Bangkok. Jobs will be more readily available and the standard of living will rise. By the year 2020, Thailand's population would have grown to about 80 million, but per capita income will have risen to US$12,000–$14,000.

Changes in the value of the baht will play an important role in the Thai economy in the face of the internationalization and globalization of business. The Thai exchange rate will probably be more flexible following the forces of supply and demand.

On the trade front, capital goods imported earlier will increase industrial capacity and bolster exports, while the diversification of export markets will stabilize export earnings. Income from tourism will continue to grow at a rapid pace. However, Thai tourists going abroad will also increase due to the improvement in the standard of living. Remittances from Thai workers abroad will drop as Thailand will become a net importer of labor. Meanwhile, international movements of capital, both direct and portfolio investments, will grow as Thailand is envisioned to become a financial center in the region.

Production in the manufacturing sector will outpace that of all other sectors so that the share of manufacturing in GDP will rise to around 35%. Industries are likely to become capital- and technology-intensive. Thus, there will be an increase in the demand for more capital and skilled labor, particularly, well-trained executives and technicians.

Multinationals will have a large role in Thailand. Competition will be fierce. Large core industries will sub-contract parts and accessory production to small- and medium-sized companies. This will be the primary incentive for smaller companies to organize and grow.

Pollution will become a major problem but this will be eased by the adoption of preventive measures and the spread of industries to remoter areas. The electronics and jewelry industries will become even more prominent.

In 2020, Thailand should still be a food-surplus country. Production of basic crops such as rice will remain sufficient for domestic consumption and export. However, Thailand's competitiveness in the production of crops will go down as wages rise, land becomes more expensive and the country becomes more industrialized. Thus, Thailand's role as a major food exporter in Asia will gradually diminish. One important development in the agricultural sector, however, will be the import of agricultural products for processing into high value added products for re-export.

With regard to the movement of capital, direct foreign investment in Thailand should continue to grow and continue to play an important role. Industries which will invest in Thailand will be of the high-end product type because they need modern production systems and quality labor. Meanwhile, Thai resident investment overseas will increase, particularly in Indochinese countries.

Capital movements in the form of borrowings and investment in financial assets will become more flexible due to the relaxation of foreign exchange controls and it is possible that Thailand may become a net lender.

25 The Global Economy
War of the Worlds

Pam Woodall

Over the next 25 years, the world will see the biggest shift in economic strength for more than a century. Today the so-called industrial economies dominate the globe, as they have for the past 150 years or so. Yet within a generation several are likely to be dwarfed by newly emerging economic giants. History suggests, alas, that such shifts in economic power are rarely smooth. A growing number of people in the rich industrial world are already urging their governments to prepare for battle against the upstarts.

The upstarts are heartwarmingly many. Scores of countries in the third world and the former Soviet block have embraced market-friendly economic reforms and opened their borders to trade and investment. These policies promise rapid growth in more economies than ever before. The four Asian tigers (Hongkong, Singapore, South Korea and Taiwan) that have pushed aggressively into western markets in the past three decades have a combined population of only 73m; even adding in Japan, the original Asian tiger, the total is less than 200m. Now, however, more than 3 billion people in Asia, Latin America and Eastern Europe are joining the rich world's 1 billion or so in the market-economy club.

This survey examines the implications for today's rich countries of this extraordinary prospect. It asks what the pressures on the West may be, and how they can best be coped with. It argues, despite the scale of the coming changes and despite the difficulties they will cause, that there is little reason for alarm. For the rich world, almost as much as for today's poor countries, the next 25 years will be a time of unprecedented opportunity.

Southern discomfort

How big will the change be? Some developing countries are bound to stumble on the road to reform. The economic prospects of Brazil and Russia, for

Reproduced with permission from *The Economist*, 1 October 1994, pp. 3–6.

example, are fragile; and the outlook for most of Africa remains grim. But so long as most developing countries stick to their reforms and avoid political upheavals, much of the third world stands its best chance for decades of achieving sustained expansion. The World Bank forecasts in chart 1 suggest that over the next ten years, developing countries (including the former Soviet block) will grow by nearly 5% a year, compared with a rate of 2.7% in the rich industrial world. A gap as big as that, the biggest since before the second world war, will perceptibly alter the world economy.

Chart 1 The coming boom
Real GDP growth, annual average %

	1974–1993	1994–2003
Rich industrial countries	2.9	2.7
Developing countries	3.0	4.8
of which:		
East Asia	7.5	7.6
South Asia	4.8	5.3
Latin America	2.6	3.4
Eastern Europe and former Soviet Union	1.0	2.7
Sub-Saharan Africa	2.0	3.9
Middle East and North Africa	1.2	3.8

Source: World Bank

The rich industrial economies' dominance over the world economy is already smaller than is generally recognised. If output is measured on the basis of purchasing-power parities (see box on page 330), then the developing countries and former Soviet block already account for 44% of world output. At current growth rates, the industrial economies with account for less than half of world output by the end of the decade. And if developed and developing countries continue to grow at the pace forecast by the World Bank for this next decade, by 2020 the rich world's share of global output could shrink to less than two-fifths.

Applying the World Bank's regional forecasts to individual countries changes the world GDP league table radically too (see chart 2). Big economies are not necessarily rich economies: compare India and Italy today. Nonetheless, it is striking that, if those forecasts are right, within a generation China will overtake America as the world's biggest economy; and that by 2020 as many as nine of the top 15 economies will be from today's third world. Britain might scrape in at only 14th place, compared with eighth today, having been overtaken by such countries as Taiwan and Thailand.

Chart 2   2020 vision

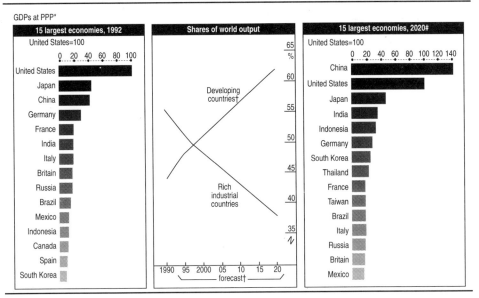

Source: World Bank
*Purchasing-power parity   †Including Eastern Europe and former Soviet Union   #Forecast assume
countries continue to grow at regional rates projected in the World Bank's *Global Economic Prospect*

Crude extrapolation is, of course, bad forecasting; Asian economies' growth rates will surely slow as they become richer and come to resemble today's rich economies; trend-busting events may well occur. It is, for example, extremely unlikely that Taiwan's income per head in 2020 would be almost double America's — as these projections imply. Yet history is full of episodes of economic leap-frogging, some of which took place surprisingly fast.

The West's anxieties about all this are as much to do with changes in the structure of the developing economies as with mere size. The old notion of developing countries as exporters of raw materials from which they earned the revenue to pay for imports of manufactured goods from the West has long been out of date. So, indeed, has the old nomenclature. In this survey third world, developing, poor and emerging economies will be used interchangeably to refer to developing countries, even though many may soon belong to the "developed" world. Manufactured goods now account for almost 60% of their exports, up from 5% in 1955. The third world's share of world exports of manufactures jumped from 5% in 1970 to 22% in 1993 (see chart 3).

As emerging economies' exports, boosted by the lowering of trade barriers agreed under the GATT's Uruguay round, continue to grow, so will the resentment of many people in today's rich nations. Many politicians,

Chart 3 Young pretenders
% of world exports of manufacturers

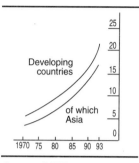

Source: GATT

businessmen and even economists in America and Europe fear that the success of these new competitors will come at the expense of the first world.

They allege, for instance, that the rich world's workers will be ruthlessly undercut if its markets remain open to goods from developing countries. Chinese and Indian workers are willing to accept an average wage of little more than 50 cents an hour, compared with average hourly labour costs of around $18 in developed countries. Fierce competition from low-wage countries, it is claimed, will steal "our" jobs, thanks to their "unfair" advantage of cheap labour, poor working conditions and lax environmental controls.

Worries about competition from low-wage countries are as old as trade itself. What is different this time is the sheer weight of new competition; the new mobility of capital and technology; and the fact that more third-world workers are educated and so capable of operating even complex machinery. The emergence of a pool of cheap, educated labour in the third world with access to first-world technology, it is argued, means that workers in rich countries will be forced to settle for third-world wages and labour standards. Such claims were paraded by American opponents of the North American Free-Trade Agreement (NAFTA) — remember Ross Perot's "giant sucking sound" as jobs crossed the border from the United States to Mexico — and more recently by critics of the GATT.

Europe, especially France, is even more awash with pessimists. One of the most vocal is Sir James Goldsmith, an Anglo-French tycoon turned politician who has frequently argued that free trade is acceptable only between countries at similar levels of economic development. Another is Maurice Allais, the French Nobel prize-winner for economics in 1988, who has published a series of articles in *Le Figaro* over the past year on the "insidious" effects of free trade. He claims that free trade with developing countries will lead to mass unemployment and huge wage inequalities, as production and jobs shift to low-wage countries, thanks either to a surge in imports or to a massive migration of firms to low-wage countries. The result, he says, will be a social explosion in Europe. And the way to avoid it, he suggests, is to erect import controls to keep out third-world competition.

Role reversal

One irony in all these worries about the "threat from the third world" is that in the 1950s and 1960s developing countries regarded trade with the West as a threat to their own industrial development. Western socialists similarly argued that the third world was being exploited by multinational companies. Now the third world is perceived as villain, not victim. The fact that people in rich countries now fret about developing countries' success, not their poverty, is itself a remarkable tribute to those countries' economic reforms.

For faster growth in the third world ought to be welcomed by everyone. Not only will it relieve poverty in developing countries; it will also provide outside traders with marvellous new business opportunities. True, rich-country producers will face a vast number of new competitors; but as these competitors become richer, they will also provide the West with a vast number of new customers. Developing countries are likely to account for around two-thirds of the increase in world imports over the next 25 years.

Fears that the third world will steal output and jobs are based on the mistaken belief that any increase in one country's output must be at the expense of another's. A second's thought should show that this is a fallacy. Increased exports give developing countries more money to spend on imports. Most developing countries spend all the foreign exchange they can lay their hands on, to buy imports of capital equipment and branded consumer goods — mainly from developed economies. An increase in output in a poor country is more likely to increase than to reduce output in rich countries.

Trade is never a zero-sum game. A bond dealer, for example, is quite happy to pay a low-wage laundry worker rather than wash his own clothes; he can earn more money trading bonds than being elbow-deep in soap-suds. Specialisation increases the living standards of both parties to the transaction. The case for free trade with China is no different. If China makes shoes more cheaply, then it makes sense for America to buy them with the money it earns selling sophisticated consumer goods to the Chinese. American consumers will benefit from cheaper shoes.

A common objection to this is: what if, because of its low wages and access to first-world technology, China can make almost everything more cheaply than America; does that not mean America could end up importing everything from China, putting all its jobs at risk? No. Because of the skill composition of its labour force, China will enjoy a bigger cost advantage in low-skill labour-intensive industries than in others. In the economic jargon, this is its "comparative advantage", a concept put forward by David Ricardo in the early 19th century. It is a basic principle of economics that all countries are better off if they specialise in industries in which they possess a comparative advantage. America and other rich economies must, by definition, always have a comparative advantage too.

Overall, the rich industrial economies will gain from the enrichment of poor countries. Faster growth in emerging economies is already providing a powerful stimulus to growth in the rich world. That is convenient, for it comes just when it seemed likely (mainly for demographic reasons) that rich countries would be entering a period of slower growth. Indeed, thanks to the boom in the third world, the world economy could in the second half of the 1990s experience its fastest growth since before the 1973 oil price shock. Global growth might nudge 4% a year.

That does not mean that everybody will be a winner. Today's rich economies face some painful adjustments in the years ahead. This survey will focus on four particular concerns: the likely decline in the jobs and real wages of low-skilled manufacturing workers; the risk that heavy investment demands of developing countries will drive up real interest rates; the risk that a worldwide boom will push up the price of oil and other commodities, reigniting inflation; and the pressure on the environment arising from high-speed growth in energy-thirsty third-world economies.

Within countries there will be losers, even if these are outweighed by the winners. Low-skilled workers, in particular, are right to be worried. There is a risk, as Mr Allais has argued, that widening inequalities between winners and losers could create social and political tensions. And this is likely to put pressure on governments to protect industries and jobs that come under attack. It would be a bitter irony indeed if the success of market economics in the third world proved to be the biggest threat to its survival in the rich industrial world.

ECONOMIC WEIGHT-WATCHING

The International Monetary Fund caused a stir in 1993 when it radically revised the weights that it uses to add together growth rates and other economic indicators in different parts of the world. Overnight the relative importance of the third world doubled.

The IMF's old weights were based on countries' GDPs converted into dollars at market exchange rates. The snag with this is that exchange rates rarely reflect relative price levels in different countries. Developing countries' exchange rates are usually undervalued. And even if it were true (as some economists argue) that exchange rates tend, over time, to equalise the prices of internationally traded goods, big differences would remain in the prices of non-traded goods and services. In developing countries, labour-intensive services such as domestic help and haircuts are cheaper than in rich countries. So using exchange rates to convert local currency GDPs into dollars understates the value of their output relative to rich countries.

The strongest sign that the IMF's previous GDP weights were badly flawed was that they suggested that the weight of Asia (excluding Japan) in global output had fallen from 8.3% in 1985 to 7.3% in 1990, even though it was the world's fastest growing region. Sensibly, the IMF has now switched to purchasing-power parities (PPP), which take account of differences in price levels, to convert GDPs into dollars. Suddenly, the world takes on a very different shape. Using PPPs, Asia's share of world output in 1990 jumps from 7% to 17%. The revised weight for all developing countries leaps from 18% to 33%. Adding in Eastern Europe and the former Soviet Union takes the total for the "third world" to 44% (see chart 4). In other words, the rich industrial economies now account for just 56% of global production, considerably less impressive than their weight of 73% under the IMF's old figures.

Chart 4   Larger than life
             World output: % shares, 1990

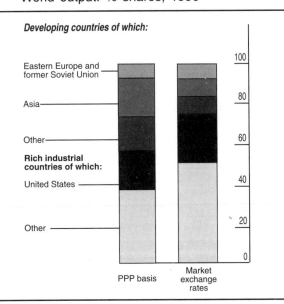

Source: IMF

Not everybody agrees with the new weights, but most economists accept that the new figures are closer to the truth than the old ones. China's PPP estimate is particularly uncertain. The IMF puts China's GDP at $1.4 trillion in 1991, making it the world's third-biggest economy (behind America and Japan). But alternative estimates range up to $3.4 trillion, which could make it the second biggest. It is only a matter of time before it will be the biggest.